*Comparative Perspectives
on Judaisms
and Jewish Identities*

Comparative Perspectives on Judaisms and Jewish Identities

STEPHEN SHAROT

Wayne State University Press
Detroit

© 2011 by Wayne State University Press, Detroit, Michigan 48201. All rights reserved. No part of this book may be reproduced without formal permission.

15 14 13 12 11   5 4 3 2 1

Library of Congress Cataloging-in-Publication Data

Sharot, Stephen.
Comparative perspectives on Judaisms and Jewish identities / Stephen Sharot.
p. cm.
Includes bibliographical references and index.
ISBN 978-0-8143-3401-0 (pbk. : alk. paper)
1. Judaism—History. 2. Judaism—Comparative studies. 3. Jews—Identity. 4. Ethnicity. 5. Ethnic relations. 6. Judaism—Relations. 7. Messianic Judaism. 8. Antinomianism—History of doctrines. I. Title.
BM155.3.S53 2011
296.089—dc22
2010013497

Typeset by Maya Rhodes
Composed in Dante MT and Fairfield LH

For Tami

Contents

Preface ix

Part 1: Wide Comparisons, Within and Without

Introduction to Part 1   3

1. Religious Syncretism and Religious Distinctiveness   10

2. The Kaifeng Jews: A Reconsideration of Their Acculturation and Assimilation in a Comparative Perspective   42

3. Elite Religion and Popular Religion: The Example of Saints   58

Afterword to Part 1   80

Part 2: Religious Movements

Introduction to Part 2   85

4. Jewish Millenarian-Messianic Movements: Comparisons of Ashkenazim, Sephardim, and Italian Jews   91

5. Millenarianism Among Conversos (New Christians) and Former Conversos (Returnees to Judaism)   105

6. The Sacredness of Sin: Antinomianism and Models of Man   123

Afterword to Part 2   139

Part 3: Jewish Identities

Introduction to Part 3   145

7. Formulations of Ethnicity and Religion Regarding American Jews in the Writings of American Sociologists   151

CONTENTS

8. Judaism and Jewish Ethnicity: Changing Interrelationships and Differentiations in the Diaspora and Israel   167

9. Jewish and Other National and Ethnic Identities of Israeli Jews   183

   Afterword to Part 3   197

   Part 4: Judaism in the Sociology of Religion

   Introduction to Part 4   201

10. Secularization, Neotraditionalism, Polarization   206

11. Public Religion, Privatization, and Deprivatization in Israel   232

    Afterword to Part 4   253

    A Final Afterword—Boundaries: Comparisons and Shifts   257

Notes   263

Index   313

Preface

The Jewish communities included in this book range widely over space and time, from Imperial China and Renaissance Italy to contemporary Israel and the United States. The plural *Judaisms* in the title denotes the extensive differences in the religious characteristics of the various communities that are considered. In some chapters other religions, apart from Judaism, are included in the analysis. The common factor in this wide range of communities, periods, and religions is the comparative perspective. The comparisons of religious developments in Jewish communities are a major focus, but "other religions" enter into the comparisons, not only as major elements in the environments of Jewish communities but also as comparisons with respect to certain religious phenomena (saints, antinomianism) that have been present in Judaism.

The emphasis on comparison in my work began at an early stage. As an undergraduate at Leicester University, I was thinking of possible topics for a graduate thesis, and I read Marshall Sklare's *Conservative Judaism.* The type of American synagogue Judaism that Sklare described appeared to be quite different from the Judaism of the English Orthodox synagogue with which I was somewhat familiar. My knowledge of Judaism was mostly limited to the context of the synagogue to which my parents had sent me for Sunday school and in which I had had my bar mitzvah. Although my parents were highly acculturated English Jews and my father was an atheist, I was sent to the local synagogue to imbibe some Jewish identity. We lived in an outer London suburb with relatively few Jews, and the Orthodox synagogue was the only one in the area. If there had been a Reform or Liberal synagogue closer to home, I might have been sent there, although my father, whose own Polish-born father was a practicing Orthodox Jew, was familiar only with Orthodoxy. Non-Orthodox synagogues were few and far between in England, and my parents certainly had no objection to the local synagogue as an Orthodox one. This seemed quite different from the American scene, and reading Sklare's work prompted me to ask why developments in Judaism in England and the United States appeared to be so different.

PREFACE

The patterns of Jewish immigration in the nineteenth and twentieth centuries to England and the United States were similar: in the earlier and middle decades of the nineteenth century from the German states and principally from eastern Europe since the 1880s. The Reform synagogues established by the American Jews from Germany and the Conservative synagogues, which attracted a large proportion of the second generation of American Jews from eastern Europe, appeared to be different from the dominant Orthodox-type synagogue in England. The detailed analysis in my doctoral thesis, taken at Oxford University, focused on the United Synagogue, the largest organization of Orthodox synagogues in the greater London area, but I included comparisons with other European countries and the United States. I attempted to explain the different religious developments in the various communities by relating them to the non-Jewish religious and cultural environments and the position of the Jews within the social structures of the "host" societies. These comparisons were the focus of my first book, *Judaism: A Sociology*.

I was able to expand my knowledge of American Jewry when I won a postdoctorate Harkness Fellowship, which I took in New York and Berkeley. After four years as a lecturer at Leicester University, I moved to an academic position in Israel, first at the Hebrew University and then at Ben-Gurion University of the Negev. Judaism in Israel became an important topic of my research, and from a comparative point of view, it is instructive to compare Judaism where Jews are in the dominant majority with Judaism where Jews are the minority.

My perspective on Judaism has always been that of the sociology of religion, and it has differed from most sociologists of the Jews who have tended to relate to religion as one dimension of Jewishness and have rarely drawn on concepts from the sociology of religion. It was also rare for sociologists of the Jews to compare Judaism with other religions, although this has changed somewhat in recent years. I extended my comparisons of religious developments in Jewish communities to include the communities of Imperial China, India, and the Middle East, and perhaps these comparisons contributed to my decision, later in my academic career, to turn to a wide-ranging comparison of the interactions between elite and popular forms of religion in the world religions. The knowledge that I gained from my investigation of the world religions helped, in turn, to deepen my understanding of the differences among the Jewish communities located in those different religious environments.

This book represents a late career review of my comparative interests in religious developments, both among Jewish communities and between Judaism and other religions. The book is divided into four parts. In the first part I compare religious developments in premodern and early modern Jewish communities; in the second part I focus on Jewish religious movements, especially messianic-millennial and antinomian ones, in the premodern and early modern period; in the third part I deal with the relationships of Jewish religious and ethnic identities in the modern period; and in the fourth part I relate developments in Judaism in the modern period to theoretical debates on secularization, fundamentalism, and public religion in the sociology of religion. Most chapters began as published articles, but my revisions have been extensive and I have incorporated a lot of new material and included the most recent scholarship and developments since the publication of the articles. The following is the list of my published material on which I have drawn.

> Chapter 1: The first formulation appeared as "Minority Situation and Religious Acculturation: A Comparative Analysis of Jewish Communities," *Comparative Studies in Society and History* 16 (June 1974): 329–54. A revised version appeared in *Comparing Jewish Societies*, ed. Todd M. Endelman (Ann Arbor: University of Michigan Press, 1997), 23–60.
>
> Chapter 2: "The Kaifeng Jews: A Reconsideration of Acculturation and Assimilation in a Comparative Perspective," *Jewish Social Studies* 13 (winter 2007): 179–203.
>
> Chapter 3: This chapter does not draw on a published article, but some of the material was incorporated into my *Comparative Sociology of World Religions: Virtuosos, Priests, and Popular Religion* (New York: New York University Press, 2001).
>
> Chapter 4: The first formulation appeared as "Jewish Millenarianism: A Comparison of Medieval Communities," *Comparative Studies in Society and History* 22 (July 1980): 394–415. A revised version appeared in Endelman's *Comparing Jewish Societies*, 61–87.
>
> Chapter 5: Some of the material is drawn from Chapters 6 and 7 of my book *Messianism, Mysticism, and Magic: A Sociological Analysis of Jewish Religious Movements* (Chapel Hill: University of North Carolina Press, 1982).
>
> Chapter 6: "The Sacredness of Sin: Antinomianism and Models of Man," *Religion* 13 (1983): 37–54.
>
> Chapter 7: "A Critical Comment on Gans' 'Symbolic Ethnicity' and 'Symbolic Religiosity' and Other Formulations of Ethnicity and Religion Regarding American Jews," *Contemporary Jewry* 18 (1997): 25–43.
>
> Chapter 8: "Judaism and Jewish Ethnicity: Changing Interrelationships and Differentiations in the Diaspora and Israel," in *Jewish Survival: The Identity Problem at the Close of the Twentieth Century*, ed. Ernest Krausz and Gitta Tulea (New Brunswick, NJ: Transaction, 1998), 87–105.
>
> Chapter 9: "Jewish and Other National and Ethnic Identities of Israeli Jews," in *National Variations in Jewish Identity*, ed. by Steven M. Cohen and Gabriel Horencyzk (Albany: State University of New York Press, 1999), 299–316.
>
> Chapter 10: "Judaism and the Secularization Debate," *Sociological Analysis* 52 (fall 1991): 277–91.
>
> Chapters 10 and 11: "Judaism in Israel: Public Religion, Neo-Traditionalism, Messianism, and Ethno-Religious Conflict," in *The SAGE Handbook of the Sociology of Religion*, ed. James A. Beckford and N. J. Demerath (Los Angeles: Sage, 2007), 670–96.

PART I

Wide Comparisons, Within and Without

INTRODUCTION TO PART I

The absence of a strong comparative dimension in Jewish studies has been noted by both historians and sociologists. When Jewish historians make comparisons, they generally highlight the uniqueness of a particular community on which their studies are based rather than demonstrate and explain similarities and differences among a number of communities. Comparative studies of Jewish communities by sociologists tend to be of two types: (1) comparisons of the pre-emancipation European communities with communities of the modern era (these comparisons often take the United States as the model of modernity and emphasize that "America is different")[1] and (2) comparisons of the Judaism and the Jewishness of the communities in the United States and Israel.[2] Sociological comparisons of traditional, or premodern, Jewish communities are one of the lacunae in the narrow span of comparative Jewish studies.

The infrequency of the explicit application of the comparative perspective in Jewish studies might at first appear surprising because the fact that Jews have lived in many different societies would seem to invite the comparative approach. Yet Jewish historians and social scientists of traditional Jewish communities tend to assume a basic Jewish pattern and to characterize the different communities as variations of that pattern. Unlike other nations, Jews are held to have remained essentially unchanged, and the notion of continuity is upheld by distinctions between a stable "essence" and changing "appearances" derived from non-Jewish environments.[3]

The belief that a Jewish autochthonous form can be separated from external influences is linked to the presupposition that the survival of the Jews as a distinctive people in premodern contexts can be explained by their religious separatism. The commitment and devotion of traditionalist Jews to their religion and the nature of that religion—its ritualism and halachic regulation—is frequently put forward to account for Jewish continuity and the singleness of Jewry wherever Jews are found. The Jewish religion is said to account for the survival of the Jews, "despite persecution," as in Europe, and "despite tolerance," as in traditional China and precolonial India.[4] One implication of this argument is that secularization, the decline in the social significance of religion, is seen as a threat to the continuation of Diaspora Jewish communities in the modern era.

In his introduction to *Comparing Jewish Societies*, Todd Endelman sought to explain the lack of comparisons by Jewish historians in terms of the political ends and institutional structure of Jewish historical writing and training. Endelman empha-

3

sized the contribution that comparisons could make to the development of Jewish studies and noted that the diasporic character of Jewish history, with its lack of territorial focus, is especially suited to comparative treatment. He made a useful distinction between internal comparisons (the comparison of Jewish communities across time and/or space) and external comparisons (the comparison of Jews with non-Jews, either in the same place or in different national contexts).[5]

Internal comparisons have advanced in the past few years and include Jewish-Gentile relations in medieval Europe and Islamic countries,[6] the German and English Jewish communities in the nineteenth and early twentieth centuries,[7] and the postemancipation French and American communities with an emphasis on the political contexts of the "host" nations.[8] Few additions have been made in recent years to the external comparisons that were included in Endelman's book: Dean Phillip Bell compared Jewish and Christian identities in the fifteenth century,[9] and Elisheva Baumgarden compared Jewish and Christian family life in medieval Europe.[10] For more than a decade the term *diaspora* has been applied extensively to a wide range of ethnic and religious groups. However, most writers in the field of diaspora studies treat the Jewish Diaspora as the paradigmatic case or ideal type,[11] and they have rarely attempted to compare Jewish and non-Jewish diasporic communities in particular nations or civilizations. External comparisons by sociologists have been limited mainly to studies of the adaptation and mobility of Jewish and other immigrant groups, particularly Italians, in the United States.[12]

With respect to internal comparisons, an emphasis on the universal, unifying functions of the Jewish religion for Jewish communities has inhibited the application of a comparative approach that seeks to relate variant cultural and religious developments among Jewish communities to the non-Jewish social and cultural environments. Such a comparative approach was advanced more than thirty years ago by the sociologist S. M. Lipset, who wrote that "the comparative study of the Jew must be linked inseparably with the comparative study of the Gentile."[13] If we are interested in comparing religious developments among Jewish communities, such a comparison cannot be separated from the religious syncretism with and distinctiveness from coterritorial religions.

Some writers have objected to the use of the term *syncretism* because of its evaluative connotations. The Oxford English Dictionary defines syncretism as an "attempted union or reconciliation of diverse or opposite tenets or practices." In many cases this might be evaluated as a positive endeavor, but, as applied to religion, the term has long been one of disapprobation, denoting a confused mixing of religions or religious inauthenticity. Anthropologists, in particular, have objected to the term on the grounds that it assumes a "pure" or "authentic" tradition against which syncretic developments are held to deviate. Syncretism is problematic because the notion of tradition is problematic. What are perceived as traditions are often invented and are themselves the outcome of diverse cultural sources.[14] However, from a social-scientific point of view, syncretism can be divorced from associative evaluations, either positive or negative.

Syncretism is understood here to denote a process in which one group or social category, such as a tribe, an ethnic or religious minority or majority, or a nation, adopts one or more cultural items, such as symbols, rituals, and beliefs, from another group or social category. This process need not necessarily reduce the group's cultural or religious distinctiveness, and it may even reinforce it. The effect on the group's distinctiveness will depend on whether and to what extent the adopted cultural item is transformed by the features of the absorbing culture. A group is unlikely to adopt practices and beliefs from other groups in a wholesale fashion. The process of adoption involves some kind of transformation, a deconstruction and reconstruction, that may convert the cultural items into the group's own symbols and meanings. Syncretic strategies vary; they may reduce cultural differences, which we call an outward or centrifugal tendency, or they may serve to strengthen cultural differences and group boundaries, which we call an inward or centripetal tendency.

Examples of centripetal syncretism are provided by Harvey E. Goldberg, an anthropologist who studied the customs of Jews in Muslim Libya. Goldberg emphasized the centrality of religious texts and the availability of religious elites to interpret them in the transformation of beliefs and practices from the Gentile environment into distinctive Jewish forms. Popular rites that were shared with Gentiles, such as the bride-price paid to the father of the bride in both Muslim and Jewish marriages, could be refashioned and made more distinctively Jewish by interpreting them through the mediation of authoritative texts. Common customs could also take on separate or additional meanings specific to one group. For example, a common custom of Muslims and Jews was for a bride to throw an egg against the wall of her groom's house before entering it. In addition to the symbolism of the loss of virginity, which was common to both groups, the act was understood by Jews to refer to the destruction of the Temple.[15]

Similar issues to those posed by the use of the term *syncretism* have arisen with respect to the use of the term *acculturation*, which has commonly been applied to cases in which the cultural distinctiveness of a group, particularly an ethnic or religious minority, diminished as it adopted beliefs and practices from the majority or "host" society. Historians of medieval and early modern European Jewry modified the usage of the term *acculturation* by emphasizing that Jewish acculturation did not necessarily involve a weakening or dilution of Jewish religious and cultural distinctiveness. Robert Bonfil criticized Jewish historians' application of acculturation to the history of Jews in Italy during the Renaissance of the fifteenth and sixteenth centuries. He questioned the portrayal of Italian Jews as responding to a more tolerant society by giving way to centrifugal forces and forsaking their Jewish distinctiveness. According to Bonfil, the situation of Italian Jews did not fundamentally change; they lived under the same conditions of social inferiority as Jews in other European countries, and attitudes of "religious otherness" remained basic to the interaction of Jews and Gentiles.

Bonfil acknowledges that it is possible to find numerous cases of Jewish adoption of attitudes, aesthetic tendencies, tastes, and cultural behaviors similar to their

Gentile neighbors, but he refers to these as simple cases of cultural conformity. It is inappropriate to classify them as acculturation because they do not reflect a desire among Jews to be more like Christians or to redefine their identity. Bonfil claims that cultural conformity, a generally unconscious process, has no relation to widespread conversion, a personal choice to adopt the identity of the Other motivated by utilitarian considerations, often by the poor who sought to escape their poverty, or by personal convictions.

Bonfil questions the interpretation of evidence that some historians have used to make a case for acculturation among Renaissance Jews. One example is the Jewish sumptuary laws, particularly those that regulated clothing, which some historians take as evidence that wealthy Jews were imitating the fashions of the Christian upper class. One reason for the regulations, according to Bonfil, was to avoid Christian envy and higher taxes. A more important reason was the desire to mitigate the Jewish condition of inferiority by adopting more rigorous norms of austerity than those of Christians. Thus the regulations served to reinforce Jewish distinctiveness, as did cases of acculturation, such as the incorporation of Italian poetry forms into the forms and contexts of Jewish traditions. Texts of non-Jewish philosophers, from the classical Greco-Roman age on, were read through a prism that filtered those elements that reinforced Jewish cultural identity; every cultural item and social arrangement that was considered worthwhile was claimed to have a Jewish origin.[16]

In contrast to Bonfil, who focused on the situation of Italian Jews before their segregation in ghettos, Kenneth Snow wrote on the Jewish ghetto in Rome in the sixteenth century. Snow showed that the process of Jewish acculturation was not substantially changed by their confinement to the ghetto. He states that Jewish acculturation—the adoption, adaptation, and modification of cultural items from non-Jews—served to strengthen Jewish identity as well as their identity as Romans. Jews continued to selectively adopt practices, such as matrimonial customs, from Christian Romans, and with subtle modification they inserted the customs into the rubrics of Jewish law and custom. With respect to the timetable of engagement, betrothal, and the wedding ceremony, Jews followed, with minor differences, the practices of Roman Christians, but Jewish women were accorded more rights and privileges than Christian women were. Unlike the Christians, who had before them the model of the Holy Virgin, Jews did not idealize women's bodies as inviolable sanctums and they did not make a cult of a daughter's virginity at marriage.[17]

If particular processes of acculturation could serve to reinforce Jewish distinctiveness, they could also function as a Jewish critique of the Gentile religion. Amos Funkenstein gives an example from the writings of the famed eleventh-century commentator of the Talmud, Rashi (acronym of Rabbi Shlomo Yitzhaqi), who adopted one of the cardinal tenets of Christianity, the dogma of vicarious suffering as a means of salvation, to deny the notion that Christ was the suffering servant of God. Rashi argued that the "Servant of God" in Isaiah 53 does not refer to an individual but to the Jewish people, who, through their suffering and humiliation in dispersion, atone vicariously for the sins of all nations.[18] Ivan G. Marcus extended such arguments to the study of popular religious practices in his study of Jewish acculturation in medieval Europe. He showed how Jews in medieval Christendom adopted Christian themes and iconography and fused them with Jewish customs and traditions in ways that often inverted the Christian meanings. Marcus wrote that, in contrast to "outward" acculturation, which he identified as a modern phenomenon that weakens Jewish identity, the "inward" acculturation of medieval Jews strengthened their Jewish identities.

Marcus questioned a common assumption that the Jews of medieval northern and central Europe, and in particular the rabbinic elite, lived in cultural isolation from the Christian environment. Daily interaction between Jews and Christians was common, and Jews were certainly cognizant of and influenced by Christian culture. The influence of that culture is evident in the emergence of a school initiation ceremony for Jewish children in the late twelfth and early thirteenth centuries. The ritual was prompted by changes in Christian rites of passage for children and, in particular, by a new emphasis on children taking their first communion at school age. The Jewish ritual included the child licking honey from an alphabet tablet and reading and eating inscribed honey cakes and hard boiled eggs. In accord with the Jewish mystical tradition, which held that the Hebrew alphabet was a formulation of the divine name, the child's licking of the honey off the Hebrew alphabet represented the eating of God's name. The honey cake was a Jewish equivalent to the Eucharist, and the Jewish child who was brought by his father to school to learn the Torah replaced the contemporary Christian usage of the Christ Child as a sacrifice in the Eucharist.

The Jewish ritual proclaimed that it was the study of the Torah and not the belief in Jesus that would bring salvation. Medieval Jews were aware of the major Christian symbols, and they adopted them in a selective fashion in order to negate them. The transformed Christian symbols were used to affirm that it was the Torah and not Jesus that was the true bread or manna. Thus the adoption of Christian cultural motifs, genres, and rituals did not result in the Jews becoming less Jewish or more like the Christian majority. Rather, the Jewish reworking of aspects of Christian culture constituted a denial or parody of Christianity and a further confirmation of the truth of Judaism.[19]

Marcus's distinction between outward and inward acculturation is useful, but we should not assume that acculturation in the premodern period was always inward. Premodern Jewish communities varied considerably with respect to their forms of acculturation. Goldberg's point about the importance of sacred books suggests one reason why the forms of acculturation might vary. Jewish religious distinctiveness was more likely to be attenuated where the religious texts were absent or lost and where no scholarly elite was available to shape syncretism into separatism. However, Jewish communities with sacred books and religious specialists have varied considerably in their levels of acculturation to the non-Jewish environment. The relative emphases that Jewish communities have put on the value and status of religious scholarship is itself a consequence of levels and forms of acculturation.

INTRODUCTION TO PART 1

Even though acculturation in premodern Jewish communities was not necessarily inward, acculturation in modern Jewish communities is not necessarily or unambiguously outward. Modern communities are unlikely to forge non-Jewish customs into polemical statements against non-Jews, but this does not mean that non-Jewish customs are adopted passively or without some form of Judaizing. Marcus tends to assume that outward acculturation involves assimilation, but this is not necessarily the case. Assimilation refers to the extent to which minority members interact socially with the majority, ranging from social isolation to social absorption, from a few restricted contacts to many highly formal secondary relationships to contacts that include relationships of a primary type, such as friendship and marriage. Acculturation and assimilation are generally interrelated; either one can be studied as a dependent or an independent variation in relation to the other. The degree of interrelationship between acculturation and assimilation varies enormously empirically, but certain limited generalizations can be made. For example, although substantial assimilation will nearly always involve substantial acculturation, substantial or even total (outward) acculturation will not necessarily involve assimilation. An ethnic group can retain its cohesiveness and social boundaries despite its adoption of the cultural patterns of the majority or core group.

Religious syncretism, acculturation, and distinctiveness and their sociocultural determinants are the foci of the first two chapters in this part. In the first chapter I provide an internal comparison of premodern Jewish communities in China, India, the Middle East, and Europe. In chapter 2 I discuss both acculturation and assimilation and provide an external comparison between the Jewish community and the Islamic and Christian minorities in premodern China. In chapter 3 I move away from the issue of religious syncretism and distinctiveness by comparing Judaism and other world religions with respect to a particular religious phenomenon—saints. A comparison of saints points both to universality in world religions and to the particular manifestations of that universality.

The problems involved in an attempt to explain variations in Jewish religious separatism and syncretism among widely different societies have to be acknowledged. A comparative analysis of Jewish communities within societies that share important characteristics is likely to be more fruitful than a comparison within societies that differ in fundamental ways. Within a narrower range of comparison, it would be possible to control for common factors, treating them as parameters, and then to proceed to examine the influence of the factor or factors that are not held in common. A comparison of Jewish communities in traditionalist settings restricts the comparison to societies where religion, which may be insular or permeable, is socially significant throughout the society. However, premodern Jewish communities were situated in societies (Middle East, India, China, and Europe) that differed greatly in the characteristics of their religions and social structures. The cultural and social environments are different in so many respects that it is impossible to control each of the possible influences in order to show their relative importance. My approach has been to begin by comparing communities that differ widely with respect to their non-Jewish sociocultural environments and then to go on to compare communities in sociocultural environments that are similar in a number of significant respects. As the range of comparisons becomes more restricted, as in a comparison of Western Jewish communities, certain factors relevant to the wider range, such as different world religions, can be treated as parameters. It is hoped that a comparison of communities in vastly different environments will at least point to the most significant factors that account for the gross differences in religious distinctiveness and syncretism.

I. RELIGIOUS SYNCRETISM AND RELIGIOUS DISTINCTIVENESS

Judaism became identified with a particular people who sought to uphold their religion's boundaries from other religions, but Jews migrated to societies with religions that differed considerably in their permeability or insularity and in their tolerance or intolerance toward other religions. These religious differences were likely to affect the extent to which Jews maintained or strengthened their religious distinctiveness or, alternatively, developed in a more syncretistic direction. In addition to their religious differences, the societies to which Jews migrated differed in their social, economic, and political structures. It has been argued that the Jews' religion produced their social separation, even though they lived with non-Jews in common socioeconomic and political structures, but it can also be argued that the extent to which Jews emphasized their religious separation depended on the characteristics of the social structures of the host societies and the positions that the Jews held within those structures.

The social structures and the structural locations of the Jews determined the types and possibilities of social interaction between Jews and Gentiles. The dependence of Jews on the products and economic services of non-Jews made total social isolation impossible, but this left a wide range of possibilities, from minimal contacts, restricted to highly formal secondary relationships, to an extensive and wide variety of contacts, including friendship and intermarriage. The range and nature of social contacts with Gentiles in turn affected Jewish religious orientations. The central argument of this chapter is that an explanation of variations in Jewish religious distinctiveness and syncretism can be found by comparing the non-Jewish religions and the social structures of the societies in which Jews lived.

Dispersal

The diaspora of the people who came to be known as Jews began in the eighth to sixth centuries B.C.E. with the conquests of the ancient kingdoms of Israel and

Judea. After the northern kingdom of Israel was conquered by the Assyrians in 722 B.C.E., its exiled population assimilated into the Assyrian world; known as the "ten lost tribes," they have frequently been the subject of mythmaking and have been linked to millenarian scenarios. The Diaspora takes on importance after the Babylonian conquest of the kingdom of Judea and the destruction of the First Temple in 586 B.C.E. Part of the Judean population, including the elite, was exiled to Babylonia (present-day Iraq), where they integrated into the society but retained their religious identity. The conquest of Babylon in 538 B.C.E. by the Persians made the return of Jews (Judeans)[1] to Judea possible. There they reestablished the Temple, completed in 516 B.C.E., under Persian rule. Most Jews in Babylonia chose to remain there, and the Diaspora became more extensive as Jews participated in the long-range Babylonian trade routes.[2] The Jewish Diaspora widened following the conquests of Alexander the Great and the collapse of the Persian Empire in the fourth century B.C.E., and migration from Judea, most of it voluntary, continued during the Second Temple period. The Greek diaspora encouraged the Jewish one, and in the late second century B.C.E., there is evidence of Jews in Egypt, Syria, Mesopotamia and the Iranian plateau, the cities and principalities of Asia Minor, Greece, Crete, Cyprus, and the Aegean islands. Jews of the Diaspora far outnumbered those in Judea during the Second Temple period.[3]

With the destruction of the Second Temple by the Romans in 70 C.E. and the crushing of the Jewish revolt in 132–135 C.E., the Jews became a truly diasporic people. Their further dispersion followed the political expansion and long-range trading routes of the Roman and Arabic empires, and their numbers were augmented in a number of cases by conversions of the indigenous populations. Conversions of rulers to Judaism, which appear to have been assertions of their kingdoms' political independence, were recorded in Adiabene (Parthia, now Iraq) in the early first century C.E., Yemen in the sixth century, and the Khazar Kingdom, ruled by predominantly Turkic tribes, in the eighth century. The extent of conversion to Judaism of the populations in these and other areas is an issue of some controversy. Paul Wexler has argued that conversion played a major role in the development of all Jewish Diaspora communities after the Roman destruction of Judea. He writes that conversions to Judaism were extensive in the pre-Islamic period in North Africa, especially of Berbers, and that converted Slavs and Turks constituted the major element of the Jewish population of eastern Europe.[4]

The Arabic conquests brought about 90 percent of the Jewish population under Islam, and this remained the case until the late eleventh century.[5] At the time of the Muslim invasions, there were probably fewer than 200,000 Jews in the Arab East and about 20,000 in the Maghreb.[6] Although many Jews converted to Islam, the number of Jews increased in the centuries after the conquests, and Jewish communities spread from the Middle East into North Africa and the Iberian Peninsula.[7] From the area of the first Diaspora, the Middle Eastern and Mediterranean territories, the Jews dispersed farther north and west into Europe. One migration stream extended from Italy to the cities of Germany and northern France. Another was from Spain to Provence and from there to northern France and Germany. There is evidence of a Jewish community in Cologne in the first half of the fourth century C.E., and it is likely that Jews settled in several other localities in the Rhineland in Roman times. However, evidence of the uninterrupted settlement of Jews who came to be known as Ashkenaz begins only in the ninth century. A smaller number of Jews settled farther south in the Sahara and farther east in the Caucasus, Turkistan, Afghanistan, India, and China. Jews remained concentrated on the Mediterranean coast in the early Middle Ages, and it is between the eleventh and thirteenth centuries that new Jewish settlements were established in the heartlands of Germany, France, and England. Expulsions beginning at the end of the thirteenth century resulted in the migration of the Ashkenazim eastward, and in the seventeenth century eastern Europe became the major center of Ashkenazic Jewry.[8]

The existence of the Cochin Jews on the Malabar coast of southwest India in the tenth century is firmly established, but the origins and date of settlement of the more numerous Bene Israel in the Konkan region, close to Bombay, are obscure; a reference by Maimonides suggests that a Jewish community other than the Cochinis existed in India in the twelfth century, but the earliest written mention of Jews permanently settled in the Konkan region appears only in 1738. The Indian communities retained their demographic viability, and the majority migrated to Israel after the foundation of the state.[9]

The presence of Jews in China is documented for the eighth century C.E., and there are indications of settled Jewish communities in China in the ninth century. Various sources—Chinese, Christian, and Arab—refer to Jews living in a number of Chinese towns in the thirteenth and fourteenth centuries, but after 1342 there are no further mentions until the middle of the sixteenth century, when Jesuit missionaries began to report on their meetings with Chinese Jews in the city of Kaifeng. At the beginning of the seventeenth century, the Jews in Kaifeng made up the sole remaining Jewish Chinese community, and when the last synagogue was demolished, around 1860, only a few impoverished individuals who identified themselves as Jews remained.[10]

Initial Dispositions and Minority Situations

The Jews who lived outside Judea in the Hellenistic and pagan Roman periods, before the destruction of the Second Temple and the suppression of the revolts, did not think of themselves as living in a diaspora. Like other peoples, they had settled voluntarily outside their place of origin without abandoning their identity.[11] Their belief in a God whose temple was in Jerusalem disposed them to distinguish themselves from other peoples, but they did not seek to segregate themselves and they did not differ from others in their names, appearance, clothing, language, or occupations. They tended to live together, but in most cities their neighborhoods were not exclusively Jewish. In many places Jews had legal privileges and were economically and socially prominent, and for these reasons some Gentiles converted to Judaism or simply declared themselves Jews.

The special cultural or religious practices of the Jews in antiquity resulted in only moderate levels of separation. From the early Hellenistic period they had a corpus of scripture that was translated into Greek and provided a frame of reference for their behavior. Some Jewish writers attempted to distinguish between those parts of the dominant culture that they adopted, such as the Greek language and literary forms, and other parts that they rejected, primarily religious forms. However, the canon had not yet been fixed and the components of a Jewish culture and religion had not yet been clearly formulated. The boundary line between Jews and others was soft and permeable. Observance of Jewish laws was not an infallible indicator of Jewishness because some, perhaps many, non-Jews attended their religious services and festivals, abstained from work on the Sabbath, and possibly observed other Jewish customs.[12] This situation changed as the pagan world gave way to the Christianized Roman Empire and the Islamic conquests. The ambiguity that characterized Jewish-Gentile relationships in antiquity ended with the regulations governing relationships between religious populations, imposed by the Christian and Muslim regimes, and the systematic rules and procedures formulated by the rabbis.

Precepts and prohibitions that contributed to the separation of Jews from Gentiles were multiplied in what came to be known as the Talmud, a huge corpus of religious literature produced by the scholarship of the sages of the religious academies of Palestine and Babylonia over the first six centuries of the Common Era. Oral traditions were eventually edited around the year 200 C.E. into a large corpus known as the Mishnah, and the subsequent voluminous commentaries on this literature came to be known as the Gemara. The sages determined that there were 613 basic religious obligations (mitzvot, singular mitzvah), and from each of these further precepts were derived, resulting in an ever-expanding corpus of Jewish law known as the Halacha (literally, path or way). The Palestinian Gemara was completed in about 450 C.E., but it was the Babylonian Talmud (Mishnah plus Babylonian Gemara), completed in about 600 C.E., that came to be accepted by most Jewish communities as authoritative.

The Judaism that was developed by the religious academies in Babylonia was more appropriate to life in the Diaspora than that developed in Palestine. The aspects of the religious law that were relevant to the Land of Israel, such as issues that related to agriculture and special laws of ritual purity, were largely omitted, and greater attention was given to the adjustment of the law and religious practice in a Gentile environment by focusing on such activities as prayer, religious holidays, business conduct, and family life.

The diffusion and acceptance of the Babylonian Talmud was assisted by the Islamic conquests and the establishment of the Caliphate, political units that ruled over extensive areas. Arabic rule created the conditions for communication networks and cooperation among Jewish communities of the Middle East, and the involvement of Jews in trade between Muslim lands and Christendom extended the communication networks into Europe. The Abbasid Caliphate supported the authority of the *geonim* (singular, *gaon*), the heads of the Talmudic academies in Babylonia. It was from the seventh to the eleventh century, known as the geonic period, when the Hebrew text of the Bible was authoritatively fixed, the prayer book compiled by the *geonim* became standard, and the Babylonian Talmud became the authoritative religious guide and the major object of study. Most Jewish communities under Islam came to accept the authority of the Babylonian Talmud, as did the growing European Jewish communities in the last centuries of the first millennium. The Jews who founded communities as far east as India and China were most likely to have come from Persia or from other Talmudic communities of the Near East.[13] Thus, around the turn of the millennium, a common religious base existed among most Jewish communities.

Religious Syncretism and Distinctiveness

An obvious place to begin a comparison of religious syncretism and distinctiveness among Jewish communities is the Middle East. In contrast to the Far East and Europe, the Jews had not transplanted their culture to an alien environment but were from the outset very much part of the indigenous culture. The expansion of the Arabic Empire facilitated the widespread dispersion of Jews throughout the Middle East, but in many areas Jews were established long before the advent of Islam. In its formative stages Islam incorporated many religious, legal, and moral conceptions from the Jews, and although the boundaries between Islam and Judaism were clearly drawn by both religions, Jews and Muslims continued to share many beliefs and practices. It is often difficult to know the direction of the influence of the two religions on each other, but the general tendency is for a dominant majority to influence a subordinate minority.

Outwardly, there was little to distinguish Jews from Muslims. Jews developed variants of the local forms of Arabic, but basically they spoke the same language, and despite occasional regulations seeking to differentiate Muslim and Jewish dress, their clothing styles were similar or identical. It has been said that the Middle Eastern Jews were "Arab in all but religion," but this phrase assumes that a clear distinction between religious and secular areas of culture can be made in premodern societies. In fact, a minority's adoption of the dominant language is bound to have implications for its religion. By about 1000 C.E. most Middle Eastern Jews had, like the rest of the population, adopted Arabic, and this involved the adoption of religious concepts and ways of thinking that were expressed in Arabic. The Jews used Arabic for translating and teaching the Bible and for discussing Jewish law and ritual. In most areas, including the non-Arabic-speaking areas such as Persia, Anatolia, Kurdistan, and the Berber highlands of North Africa, the Jews developed their own dialects of the major language, incorporating Hebrew and sometimes

Aramaic words. Jewish dialects varied in their relative distinctiveness, but they were never so great as to impede communication between Jews and Muslims.[14]

The religious little traditions of Jews and Muslims overlapped considerably. The belief in spirits (*jinn*) and the forms of protection against them were common to Muslims and Jews. Also common were many folk remedies for overcoming illnesses and barrenness. Jews were recognized by Muslims in Morocco as having a particular expertise in rainmaking. One central practice, especially important in North Africa, that had many pre-Islamic elements but was brought into the framework of both Islam and Judaism in the Middle East was pilgrimage to the tombs of saints. Both Muslims and Jews sought the intercession and protection of the saints (sometimes the same saints), placing candles and oil lamps on the shrines and performing rituals by the tombs. Family pilgrimages were made when important family events occurred, and collective pilgrimages were made on the anniversary of the death of the saint. Other shared beliefs and practices were associated with sorcery, divination, ecstatic prophecy, the evil eye, the magical significance of numbers, and the protective power of amulets.

Jews were also influenced by more "orthodox" Islamic practices. The short, intense features of Muslim prayer impressed the Jews, whose own religious services displayed far more decorum than the services of European Jews. Adaptations of Muslim models were evident where Jews made extensive preliminary preparations for prayer, performed ritual ablution of both hands and feet, and arranged worshipers in rows continuously facing Jerusalem. Islamic religious movements also made an impression on Jewish religious circles. A group of Jewish pietists in thirteenth-century Egypt adopted the Sufi practice of contemplation in a solitary retreat where they would ritually repeat divine names. The pietists stated, however, that such practices were of Jewish origin.[15]

The *mimuna*, a festival particular to Moroccan Jews that celebrates the end of Passover, demonstrates a complex dynamic between the cultural influence of the environment and the cultural expressions of Jewish particularity. The themes and symbols of the festival, expressing fertility and renewal, had their counterparts in a Muslim festival, and Muslims contributed to the Jewish festival by selling or providing as gifts bread and greenery. Passover, which celebrates the Exodus from Egypt, involves practices, such as the eating of unleavened bread, that represent a withdrawal of Jews from non-Jews; the *mimuna* represented a reintegration into the wider milieu when the Jews indicated their commonality with the wider population by wearing the costumes of Muslims. The concentration of Jews in urban occupations meant that they were dependent on Muslim peasants for agricultural produce. The Muslims, in turn, would approve those Jewish rituals involving fertility. The various Jewish interpretations of the festival that sought to find its origins in Jewish tradition may have served to camouflage its obvious links with the Muslim cultural environment.[16]

The distinctiveness of Middle Eastern Jewish communities as religious minorities varied greatly. As noted, most communities adopted the Babylonian Talmud, but with the fragmentation of the Abbasid empire into regional powers, the influence of the Babylonian center began to decline, and during the late Middle Ages Jewish populations under Islam developed predominantly regional, local, and communal identities. A number of subcultural areas of Middle Eastern Jewry have been distinguished: Morocco, the Fertile Crescent (including Egypt, Palestine, Syria, and Iraq), Turkey, Yemen, Kurdistan, and Persia. Many communities developed relatively independently and evolved their own religious customs, often influenced by the local Muslims.[17]

Few anthropological studies have been conducted on traditionalist Middle Eastern Jewish communities outside Israel before their disintegration after 1948, but two studies, one of Jews in northeastern Iraq and the other of Jews in the northwestern Sahara of Algeria, provide interesting cases for comparison, especially because both communities had no significant contact with other Jewish communities. In northeastern Iraq the Jewish culture demonstrated many similarities with the Kurdish Muslim culture. In addition to sharing values with respect to such areas as marriage, family, and honor, they also held common magical beliefs and worshipped at the same holy graves. The Jews observed the Sabbath, dietary regulations, and the purity laws, but their religion was maintained mostly by oral tradition; they had virtually no knowledge of the Talmud, and religious learning was not important.[18] In contrast, the Jewish community in Ghardaia in the northwestern Sahara shared few religious practices with the neighboring Muslims. They adhered rigidly to traditional Jewish values and practices, prayed in the synagogue three times a day, and highly valued religious learning. Integrated with the great tradition were local magicoreligious practices whose historical origins were often lost, but only a few of them were held in common with Muslims. The customs peculiar to the Ghardaia Jews sometimes functioned to uphold great tradition values; for example, at the age of 5 every boy had to undergo an elaborate ceremonial initiation that served to dramatize the importance of religious learning for Jewish males.[19]

Although the Middle Eastern communities varied greatly in their religious distinctiveness and syncretism, most of them were neither as highly syncretistic as the communities of China and India nor as highly distinctive as the pre-emancipation European communities. The first Jews to settle in Kaifeng had probably been merchants from Persia,[20] and there is little doubt that they were familiar with Talmudic Judaism. Many of the community's texts, possibly including Talmudic tractates, were destroyed by a flood in 1642, but salvaged texts, including Torah scrolls, were transcribed, and the prayer books that survived into the nineteenth century included liturgies for the Sabbath and festivals.[21] It appears, however, that Chinese influences entered the Jews' beliefs and practices at an early stage, and visitors from the West in the seventeenth and eighteenth centuries found highly acculturated Jews who dressed like other Chinese, spoke the same language, ate the same food, worked in the same occupations, and married non-Jewish Chinese, absorbing the non-Jewish women into the community. The religion of the Chinese Jews combined certain distinctively Jewish beliefs and practices with beliefs and practices from the Confucian, Buddhist, and Taoist religions. The influence of the religious environment was clearly visible in the architecture of the Jewish temple, the use of non-Jewish ritual objects, the observance of Chinese seasonal festivals, ancestor worship, the absorption of Chinese rituals into the rites of passage, and the use of inscriptions written on stone tablets for the transmission of religious beliefs.[22]

Unlike the Chinese Jews, who were finally totally assimilated into the non-Jewish population, the Cochin and Bene Israel communities in India remained demographically viable, but during their periods of isolation from other Jewish communities, their Judaism lost much of its distinctiveness. They adopted many Hindu customs and were assimilated into the caste system. The isolation of the Cochin Jews was much less complete than that of the Bene Israel, but it is evident from thirteenth-century tombstones that the Cochin Jews had at that time an imperfect knowledge of Hebrew and the Bible, and evidence from more recent times shows that they shared folk symbols, heroes, and folk songs with neighboring Hindus, Muslims, and Christians.[23] The Cochin Jews were divided into subcastes of "white" and the more numerous "black" Jews; the black Jews were probably descendants of converts from and intermarriages with the indigenous population. Taboos on intermarriage and free social contacts, as well as outbursts of antagonism, characterized the relationships between the two subcastes.[24] The white Cochinis had more contacts with and were consequently more influenced by the European, mainly Sephardic, Jews who arrived with the European colonial powers. At the end of the seventeenth century a Sephardic Jew from Amsterdam recorded that Cochini rites were similar to those of his own community, but he noted certain unusual features, such as the congregation going barefoot in the synagogue.[25]

The Bene Israel in the Konkan occupied a low-caste position of oil pressers, and they were known as Saturday Oilmen because they rested their oxen on Saturday, as opposed to the Hindu Monday Oilmen, who rested their oxen on Monday.[26] Little is known of the religion of the Bene Israel before their "discovery" by Christian missionaries and Cochin Jews. The missionaries taught them to read and understand Hebrew and provided them with the Jewish Bible in Marathi, and the Cochinis introduced them to the liturgy and laws of Talmudic Judaism. Before these influences the Bene Israel did not have the Bible, the Talmud, or Hebrew prayer books. Their only Hebrew prayer was the Shema, which was repeated on many ritual occasions, including circumcision, marriage, and death. What appeared to outsiders to be the remnants of Judaism included the observance of Saturday as a day of rest, circumcision on the eighth day after birth, some dietary restrictions, and the observance of certain festivals that were similar in content and time of observance to familiar Jewish festivals.

If the forebears of the Saturday Oilmen had been Talmudic Jews, their Judaism had clearly undergone extreme attenuation over time and they had undergone massive acculturation to the religious beliefs and practices of their Hindu and Muslim neighbors. Shared customs included ceremonial food offerings, certain marriage and funereal customs, and prohibitions on the remarriage of widows and eating beef. In those places where they did not have their own cemeteries, the Bene Israel buried their dead in Muslim cemeteries. The relative influence of Muslims and Hindus on the Bene Israel cannot be estimated because the Muslims were themselves heavily influenced by Hinduism, and all religious groups in India were incorporated into the caste system.[27] The Bene Israel were divided into two subcastes: the Gora (white) and the Kala (black). The Gora, who claimed that they were the pure descendants of the original Jewish settlers, were considered higher in caste than the Kala, but in contrast to the subcastes of the Cochin Jews, the Bene Israel subcastes did not differ in skin color; the Gora were more numerous than the Kala, and the Kala were permitted to worship in the Gora places of worship.[28]

The fasts and festivals of the Bene Israel had Marathi names, and their observance pointed to considerable syncretism: The Feast of the New (Year) and the Holiday of the Closing of the Doors corresponded to Rosh Hashanah and Yom Kippur; the Feast of (partaking of) Khir corresponded to Sukkot; the Feast of Holi, a Hindu festival of a carnival nature, synchronized with Purim; the Festival of Jar Closing, in which a jar containing a sour sauce mixture was covered up and opened after eight days, corresponded to Passover (but with no reference to the deliverance from Egypt); and the Fast of Birda, which was broken at the end of the day by the partaking of Birda curry, corresponded to Tisha b'Av.[29] A complex of beliefs and rituals unique to the Bene Israel was centered on Eliyohu (Elijah), and an annual pilgrimage was made to a village where Elijah was said to have appeared and then ascended to heaven.

A ceremony that paralleled similar ceremonies among both Hindus and Muslims was the ceremony of Malida, the Feast of Eliyohu, which was undertaken to show thanks and fulfill obligations to the divine on such occasions as recovery from an illness or completing a journey.[30] The origins of the Malida ceremony are unknown, but it appears to have involved some Judaization of Hindu ceremonies in which offerings were made to gods or divine patrons. In comparison, the Holiday of the Closing of the Doors involved the adaptation of a Jewish holiday, Yom Kippur, to the ritual framework of the caste system and the expansion of Jewish motifs through the incorporation of Hindu modes. On the day of the holiday the Bene Israel atoned for their sins by living like Hindu ascetic-renouncers and secluding themselves behind locked doors, thereby avoiding all contact with and pollution from non–Bene Israel. They expressed their purity by dressing in white, fasting, and bathing. The holiday reaffirmed their exclusivity as a community, uniting all its members, including their dead ancestors, who were believed to have returned and become reunited with the living on the day. After the termination of the fast, the ancestors were believed to depart from the world, and the Bene Israel resumed contact with their Hindu and Muslim neighbors, giving alms to low-caste Hindus. By becoming pure ascetics and Brahmin for a day, the Bene Israel were affirming both the distinctiveness of their group and the legitimacy of the hierarchical caste system.[31]

Although most Jewish communities under Islam displayed a greater religiocultural distinctiveness than the Jews of China and India, it is the Jewish communities in the Christian societies of medieval and early modern Europe that provide the strongest contrast with the Jewish communities of the East. The medieval Jewish communities under Christendom can be divided into the cultural units of Christian Spain, Mediterranean France (the Midi), Italy, and the northern European communities, especially central France and Germany, usually called Ashkenaz. The Ashkenazim, who in the early modern period came to be demographically concentrated in eastern Europe, provide us with the clearest example of the reinforcement of religious distinctiveness.[32]

The Ashkenazim came to put a great emphasis on the strict interpretation of the religious law and the stringent observance of religious ritual. Unlike the Talmudic-era Babylonian communities, whose size and occupational differentiation made economic self-sufficiency possible, most European Jewish communities in the Middle Ages were small; their dependence on non-Jews for produce and services required lenient interpretations of some of the religious laws. For example, the eating of bread made by Gentiles was permitted because Jews were not able to produce sufficient quantities. The drinking of wine made by non-Jews remained forbidden, but because Jews were not able to grow their own grapes, a solution was formulated through a division of labor: Gentiles were engaged in the preparatory stages, and Jews prepared the wine for Jewish use. These necessary compromises were accompanied by a multiplication and hardening of halachic rules in those areas in which economic dependence was not the issue. This elaboration of the Halacha reinforced religious distinctiveness and set Jews apart from Christians and from Christianity, which Jews passionately repudiated.[33]

Religious practices, such as the donning of tefillin and the wearing of *tsitsit*, which in the early Middle Ages were neglected in some communities, were revived in the twelfth century and came to be strictly observed.[34] The extension of halachic regulations by religious elites, such as the Franco-German Tosafists in the twelfth and thirteenth centuries, were gradually accepted by most Jews. For example, a few lines in the Talmud about salting meat were transformed into a comprehensive set of regulations that, together with other extended rules of kashrut, came to minutely govern the preparation and cooking of food in Jewish kitchens.[35]

Stricter precepts concerning contacts with non-Jews were extolled by the Hasidei Ashkenaz, a small elitist group in thirteenth-century Germany who combined strenuous halachic standards with pietistic mysticism. It has been argued that their forms of penitence were influenced by Christian pietistic movements, including those of mendicant friars, but if this was the case, they succeeded in transforming these influences into distinctive Jewish forms. These Jewish pietists permitted contact with Christians only when Jews were in the hierarchically superior position, as they were when they employed Christian servants. Otherwise, contacts with non-Jews were to be avoided. Resistance to their religious revisions by other Jews led the pietists into a somewhat sectarian stance even within the Jewish community, but features of the movement were eventually incorporated in somewhat less radical forms into the religion of Ashkenazic Jewish communities.[36]

The ever-growing commentaries on the Talmud were codified in the sixteenth century in the *Shulkhan Arukh*, which was adopted by Jewish communities as their guide to ritual observances, the regulation of social, economic, and familial relationships, and personal appearance. The extension of the religious meanings of Jewish cultural distinctiveness to clothes became especially evident in eastern Europe. The long black caftans and large hats, which had been the costume of Polish nobles in the seventeenth century, became distinctively Jewish in the eighteenth century, and after the inroads of secularization in the nineteenth century, they became the outward sign of the religious as opposed to secular Jew.

Like Middle Eastern Jewry, the religious distinctiveness of Ashkenazic Jewry was expressed through a distinctive sacred language, Hebrew, but the Ashkenazim reinforced their distinctiveness through the Yiddish language, which differed far more from the environmental vernaculars of non-Jews than the Jewish variants of Arabic. Yiddish developed as a fusion of the German, Hebrew, Aramaic, Laaz (Jewish Romance), and, at a later stage of its development, Slavic languages to become an indigenous Jewish language. Not only did Yiddish become the major Jewish vernacular, but it also became the vehicle of oral religious studies, from the elementary school to the yeshiva. Most religious scholarship continued to be written in Hebrew, but rabbis conducted their oral discussions in Yiddish, preaching was in Yiddish, many prayer books came to include large portions of text in Yiddish below the Hebrew text, and supplicatory prayers appeared in Yiddish.[37]

The way of life regulated by the Halacha, which made for the all-encompassing distinctiveness of the Ashkenazim, was related to a central religious value that also contributed to it: the study of the Torah. The study of the Torah made comprehensive observance of the mitzvot possible, and its influence was apparent in the patterning of gender relationships, the institutions of education, and the determination of status. Torah study was important primarily for men; the role of women was to assist men in living according to this value. The ideal was that not just the scholarly elite but all Jewish men would study the Torah, perhaps on a certain day of the week or for a fixed time each day. For those who lacked the intellect or education necessary for this study, the rabbis introduced selections from the major religious texts into the synagogue services, so that all could obey the commandment to study, if only symbolically. Status and prestige in the community depended on the level of scholarship. Wealth was not sufficient in itself to achieve the highest status, although wealth and scholarship often went hand in hand. A number of educational institutions provided at least an elementary religious education for most males, but their major aim was to produce scholars who would study at the yeshivas. Marriages were often arranged according to the religious scholarship of the prospective bridegroom, and it was not unusual for a wealthy man to support his son-in-law while the latter devoted his time to study. The wife of a scholar often managed the family business, thereby giving her husband time to study.[38]

The Ashkenazic communities were more culturally insular than other Jewish communities, but no Jewish minority was immune to the influences of the dominant religion and culture. The influence of the architectural styles of cathedrals and churches was evident in many synagogues, illustrations in Hebrew books were similar to those in non-Jewish art, and games with Hanukkah dreidels and excursions on Lag b'Omer were similar to customs among non-Jews.[39] The custom of giving Jewish children a second name in German communities, which was especially prevalent in smaller towns, stemmed from German folk influences.[40] Many magicoreligious beliefs and customs were shared with the non-Jewish population. Beliefs in demons and witches, the invocation of spirits, the interpretation of dreams as portents, the reading of the stars, and the use of amulets, incantations, and all kinds of folk medicines to cure illnesses were shared by Jews and Christians or were similar in many ways. Much of this folk magic was adopted by Jews from Christians, but influences were not always in one direction. The magical property of kabbalistic signs were incorporated into the folkways of German Christians.[41]

Although Jews adopted magical devices from Christians, the symbolic meanings they attributed to those devices often differed from those of Christians. For example, both Jews and Christians in Germany protected children from the assaults of the devil or demons by lighting twelve small candles and one large one, but for Christians the candles symbolized the beneficent presence of the twelve apostles and Jesus, whereas for Jews the candles symbolized the twelve tribes of Israel and the Patriarch.[42] Rabbis tended to take a permissive and pragmatic attitude toward such folk magic, and they sometimes defined magical practices as techniques that entailed no violation of the Halacha. Scholarly Jews who extended their knowledge to astrology and kabbalah were regarded as the most potent prophets and miracle makers. Popular customs did not escape the textual orientations of the Ashkenazim, and exegetical discussions of magical beliefs tended to blur the lines between learned and popular medieval culture and reduce the impression of a shared popular culture among Jews and Christians. The cultural influences of the non-Jewish milieu were always active, but they were little recognized because the rabbis always legitimated their customs by references to the indigenous criteria of Jewish religious texts or the immutability of age-old Jewish customs.

As noted, the demographic centers of the Ashkenazim—central and western Europe in the medieval period and eastern Europe in the early modern period—were the most separatist of the Jewish cultural units under Christendom. Compared with the Ashkenazim, the Sephardim of the Iberian Peninsula adopted a greater part of the dominant culture and observed fewer rituals, interpreted the religious law less strictly, and took less heed of their rabbis. References to the lax religious observance of Spanish Jews were common in the thirteenth century, and rabbis and Jewish communal officials denounced those Jews who assumed features of Christian identity, such as the clothes commonly worn by Christian burghers and nobles. Religious indifference was especially common among rich Sephardim, especially courtiers, who found that Jewish religious requirements were not always compatible with court life.⁴³ Averroism, which stressed the superiority of reason over faith, spread among some wealthy Sephardim, whereas other wealthy Sephardim were engaged in the study of the kabbalah. Some of the kabbalists attacked their peers for their rationalism and accommodation to the non-Jewish world.⁴⁴

Anxieties expressed by Jews in medieval Spain that their compatriots' acculturation would lead to assimilation in the form of conversion were not unfounded. Mass conversions followed the massacres of Jews in 1391, but many Spanish Jews had adopted Christianity before that date in relatively tolerant conditions. Some Jewish intellectuals in the fifteenth century compared unfavorably the religious laxity of Spanish Jews with the piety of Christians. It was, however, the delights of Christian secular culture rather than the religiosity of pious Christian groups that proved attractive to many Spanish Jews.

The secular tendencies among the Sephardim explain, in part, why they often acted differently from the Ashkenazim when faced with the alternatives of conversion or death. Many Ashkenazim, including some entire communities, converted under such pressure, but the majority remained faithful, believing that they ensured their path to heaven by the choice of death. Martyrdom became an ideology and an institutionalized ritual; for the "sanctity of the name," those Jews faced with the threat of forced conversion first recited benedictions and then killed their children and themselves. This phenomenon did not appear among the Sephardim until the end of the fourteenth century, and then only a small minority pursued martyrdom; the great majority, like the Jews under Islam in similar circumstances, preferred to submit to conversion.⁴⁵

Environmental Culture and Social Structure

An explanation of differences among Jewish communities with respect to religious syncretism and distinctiveness must take into consideration the demographic distribution and communication networks of world Jewry. Urban concentration did not guarantee continuing religious distinctiveness, and rural distribution did not necessarily weaken it, but the number of Jews within a geographic-cultural area and the possibilities of contacts with Jews in other cultural areas were significant factors. Small Jewish communities within large, broadly homogeneous cultural areas, with little or no contact with denser Jewish concentrations elsewhere, were more susceptible to non-Jewish influences.

A study of the memorial book of the Kaifeng community suggests a population of between 700 and 750 Jews in the seventeenth century, and this was in a city whose population in the Sung era may have exceeded 1 million. With the possible exception of Hangchow, there had probably been fewer Jews in other Chinese cities.⁴⁶ In the first centuries of its existence, the Kaifeng community no doubt had contacts with other Jewish communities in China and with non-Chinese Jews who traveled to China along the silk route and by sea, but by the beginning of the seventeenth century the Kaifeng community had been cut off for several centuries from contact with and knowledge of other Jewish communities.

Jewish communities in India also had little or no contact with other Jewish communities for a long period. The Cochin Jews, whose existence on the Malabar coast of southwestern India beginning in the tenth century is firmly established, may never have fully lost contact with other Jewish communities, but for many centuries such contacts were sparse and infrequent. Travelers from the West, including Jewish travelers, reported on them in the twelfth century, and the arrival of the Portuguese at the end of the fifteenth century introduced some Jews from the Iberian Peninsula who intermarried with the Cochin Jews. Dutch rule in the second half of the seventeenth century greatly facilitated contact with the Amsterdam Jewish community, and from that time the Judaism of Cochin Jews was heavily influenced by Europe.[47]

The number of Cochin Jews in the 1940s, before the emigration of most Indian Jews to Israel, was no more than 3,000, and they were greatly exceeded by the Bene Israel, who numbered from 15,000 to 30,000 at that time. Before their settlement in Bombay, beginning in the mid-eighteenth century, the Bene Israel had lived scattered in many villages in the Kulaba District of Konkan. The number of Bene Israel in the middle of the eighteenth century has been estimated as no more than 5,000, and the number of families in each village was probably no more than twelve to fifteen. Migration to Bombay, the influence of Christian missionaries, and intensified contacts with other Jews, Cochini and European, brought the Judaism of the Bene Israel more into line with that of other communities.[48]

Geographic mobility was not common in premodern communities, but Jews were more mobile than most, and although often irregular, the network of contacts and ties among the European communities and the Middle Eastern communities supported the knowledge of and identification with a people whose boundaries stretched far beyond the immediate community. The extensive contacts among Jewish communities under Islam in the centuries after the Islamic conquests were made possible by large Islamic political units that encouraged Jewish supercommunal institutions. The Babylonian center was the center of Jewish networks until the eleventh century, and, following its decline, new regional centers arose in several parts of the Islamic world. During the late Middle Ages supercommunal relationships declined and the local community prevailed as the basic cell of Jewish public life.[49]

Probably no Jewish community in the Middle East or Europe was cut off from other Jewish communities for such an extended period as those in China and India, but the Jewish communities under Islam, such as those in the Grand Atlas of southern Morocco, the Algerian desert, Yemen, Kurdistan, the Caucasus, and Afghanistan, were isolated for long periods. The majority of Jewish communities under Islam had little or no contact with those in Christendom up to the nineteenth century. Many of the Jews who were expelled or migrated from Spain and Portugal at the end of the fifteenth century settled in and influenced the cultural developments of Jewish communities in North Africa and the Ottoman Empire, but many communities under Islam remained untouched by Sephardic influence.[50]

The number of Ashkenazim rose slowly in the later medieval period, and at the end of the seventeenth century, when there were about 1 million Ashkenazim in Europe and 1 million Jews in the Middle East, the Ashkenazim began to outstrip the Middle Eastern Jews demographically. The absence of strong political entities in Christendom favored the autonomy of the local Jewish community, but although the Ashkenazim were scattered in many small communities across Europe's many states, they came to forge a dense network of contacts. No medieval state had an Ashkenazi presence of more than 1 percent of the population, and in no medieval city did the Ashkenazim exceed 1,500 people.[51] After many Ashkenazim migrated eastward in the later medieval centuries, they came to be more densely concentrated in parts of Poland-Lithuania. In 1760 the 750,000 Jews in the Polish Commonwealth formed more than 5 percent of the total population, and in a society that was mostly rural, the Jews constituted about half of the urban population. The 1763–64 Polish census found that nearly one-third of the Jews lived in villages and that a larger proportion lived in small towns with fewer than 500 Jews. Only twelve towns had more than 2,000 Jews, but a significant proportion of Jews lived in towns with a Jewish majority.[52]

Although the Jewish communities with the most syncretistic religious systems were found among those isolated for long periods from the denser settlements of Jewry, some isolated communities retained high levels of religiocultural distinctiveness, and the history of Western Jewry since the eighteenth century has shown that large numbers, extensive communication, and a sense of identity with a far-ranging people do not prevent substantial acculturation. An explanation of variations in Jewish religious syncretism and distinctiveness requires, therefore, an analysis of the religious cultures and social structures of the wider Gentile societies that would influence barriers between Jews and non-Jews.

China

The social significance of religion was extensive in traditionalist societies and played an important part in the dominant groups' orientations to religious minorities. The major religions in China were both permeable and pluralistic; they combined and reconciled diverse beliefs and practices, and little or no attempt was made to demand the exclusive allegiance of worshipers. In adopting non-Jewish practices, Chinese Jews followed the general Chinese practice of observing sacraments from a number of religious traditions—Buddhist, Taoist, and so on—side by side.

Confucianism, the official Chinese state doctrine, was neither a state religion nor a church in the Western sense; the literati espoused a doctrinal orthodoxy and emphasized the necessity of performing certain rites, but there was little or no attempt to coerce others. The Chinese political elite permitted and encouraged religious syncretism if it was politically efficacious to the state. Max Weber wrote that "the most important and absolute limit to practical tolerance for the Confucian state consisted in the fundamental importance of the ancestor cult and this-worldly piety for the docility of the patrimonial subject."[53] Like Muslims, with whom they were often confused, the Chinese Jews found that there was little or no formal constraint on them to conform to non-Jewish beliefs and practices so long as they recognized the ancestral cult and the religious status of the Chinese emperor.

The Chinese ruling strata perceived their empire as the universe, composed of concentric circles that became increasingly barbarous the farther they lay from the Chinese core.[54] Their disdain for barbarian foreigners was occasionally expressed in restrictive edicts of a temporary nature against people, mainly Muslims, of recognizable foreign extraction. The Chinese Jews were frequently called blue-capped Muslims because of the color of their headgear during prayer, but their long-term residence, appearance, and behavior made them indistinguishable from other Chinese. Resident in Kaifeng, the cultural and political center of the Sung dynasty, the Jewish community was at the core of the Chinese universe. Therefore there was no cultural basis for subjecting them to any differential legal, political, economic, or social treatment.

The important elements of the Chinese social structure—the extended family, clan, and political rule by a centralized bureaucracy—did not dispose the Jews to enter a peculiar structural niche in the society. The original Jewish settlers in Kaifeng were probably specialists in the manufacture, dyeing, or pattern printing of cotton fabrics, but economic diversity among native Kaifeng Jews is illustrated by a 1512 inscription that mentions degree holders, civil and military officials, farmers, artisans, traders, and shopkeepers. In the fifteenth, sixteenth, and seventeenth centuries, a number of Jews attained high political and military posts, and others were successful as physicians and scholars.[55]

Most Kaifeng Jews were members of the small Chinese merchant-artisan class that occupied a social position between the mass peasant base and the literati, but beginning in the fourteenth century, Kaifeng Jews entered the scholar-official class in increasing numbers, some coming to hold important positions. In contrast to the free towns of Europe, Chinese towns were seats of the mandarinate, and the ambition of most merchant families in the towns was to break into the scholar-official class.[56] The literati was not a completely closed class, and in the large, wealthy imperial city of Kaifeng, Jews as much as others could take advantage of the limited opportunities for mobility.

Song Nai Rhee has argued that the civil service system transformed Jewish intellectuals into Confucian literati, a transformation that affected their total philosophical and religious perspective. Some members of the Jewish community, who were more conscious of their religious distinctiveness, disapproved of the Confucianization of the community's intellectuals, but, as members of the Chinese elite, the Jewish scholar-officials were bound to have an important influence on the whole community. Participation in the civil service also contributed to intermarriage and assimilation; the Jewish literati had to leave Kaifeng because, like all other civil servants, they were prohibited from holding official positions in the place of their birth.[57] It can be hypothesized, therefore, that the substantial religious syncretism of Chinese Jews was related not only to the permeability and pluralism of Chinese religion but also to the Chinese social structure, which permitted the socioeconomic integration of the Jews in Chinese society.

India

Like the Chinese religions, Indian Hinduism was absorptive and pluralistic toward minority religions. The dominant Hindus tolerated religions that did not threaten the caste system and the supremacy of the Brahmins, but although they were pluralistic in the sense that they did not actively attempt to enforce a Hindu monopoly, the assimilative character of the caste system and the permeable boundaries of the Hindu religion resulted in a virtual monopoly of Hinduism over much of India.[58] Although the Bene Israel had acquired the status of a low caste, it had presumably been to their advantage to voluntarily accept certain Hindu rituals and the caste system; it was difficult for an alien and therefore impure group that was not economically self-sufficient to exist outside the Hindu community. Once the Jews had adopted the caste system and some principal practices of Hinduism, their own distinctive beliefs and rituals were tolerated within the Hindu community itself. The Indian Jews constituted small *jatis* (castes) within an ocean of thousands of other *jatis* that varied greatly with respect to their gods, rituals, and customs.

Although the general orientations of Hinduism favored a syncretic Jewish religion, the Indian social structure did not induce substantial assimilation. There were two opposed bases of social solidarity in traditional Indian society: the solidarity of village and the solidarity of caste.[59] Indian villages were largely autonomous units; India did not have any large-scale interregional religious institutions, and the authority of secular leaders rarely extended to the internal affairs of the village. It is clear that the close association between the Bene Israel and Hindus and Muslims in the villages of Konkan occasionally resulted in intermarriage, but the solidarity of caste reinforced their social boundaries and enabled them to survive as a distinctive group. As in China, Jews in India were not singled out for differential treatment as Jews, but, unlike in China, their integration into the Hindu religiosocial system contributed to their social preservation.

Middle East and North Africa

In contrast to the religions of the East, Islam developed out of a monotheistic tradition, inheriting from it strong dispositions to religious boundary maintenance. Islam was flexible in incorporating folk beliefs and practices of nominally Muslim populations, but its permeability was slight compared with Eastern religions, and the dominant Islamic groups were consistent in their rejection of distinctive Judaic beliefs and practices. Again, in contrast to Eastern religions, which were generally content to coexist peacefully with other religions, Islam has often been markedly monopolistic; it has sought, often with success, to establish itself as the only religion in a particular area by converting or eliminating non-Islamic religious groups. Islamic monopolism was mainly directed toward "pagans" or nonmonotheists, however; its disposition toward Jews and other "peoples of the book" was, in general, more pluralistic than monopolistic. Mohammed established the general principle that adherents of non-Islamic monotheistic faiths should be allowed to live under Muslim rule, and, although in its early warrior phase this principle was not consistently upheld, religious pluralism became firmly established once the Arabs conquered vast territories containing large non-Islamic populations.

The broad pluralist disposition of the dominant Arabs toward other monotheists was formulated in a number of decrees that provided for the protection of the persons, property, and religious observances of subordinate minorities and imposed additional taxes to be paid by the communities to the Islamic rulers. References to Judaism in Islamic writings were mostly negative, but hostility toward Jews rarely had a religious basis. In contrast to Christianity, Islam arose in an area peripheral to Judaism; it did not present itself as the divine fulfillment of Judaism and gave no special place to the Jews in its sacred history. Islam presented both Judaism and Christianity as deviations from the pure monotheism that it claimed to be reviving, but it did not propound central religious doctrines that related specifically to the Jews. Muslim polemicists concerned themselves more with Christians than with Jews, who were neither a religious nor a military threat.[60] During the medieval period outbreaks of persecution, usually against Christians as well as Jews, were infrequent and limited. The most serious occurred in Egypt and Palestine-Syria from 1012 to 1019 under the Fatimid caliph al-Hakim, in the 1140s in North Africa and Spain under the Berber Almohads, and in 1172 in Yemen. After the persecutions subsided, the Jews and Christians who had been forced to convert to Islam were allowed to revert to their original faiths.

The treatment of Jews and other non-Muslim minorities by Islamic regimes varied greatly from one region to another and from one period to another. The absence of Christians in Morocco after the Almohad persecutions left the Jews as the only religious minority, and from the late Middle Ages and into modern times Morocco was among the least tolerant of Islamic countries. The two other comparatively intolerant countries during that period were Iran and Yemen. The militant Shiite dynasty in Iran, which was enthroned at the beginning of the sixteenth century, subjected its religious minorities, including the Jews, to persecutions and occasionally forced conversions. Shiite rule in Yemen also made for oppressive conditions, but the Sunni Islamic regimes at the center of the Islamic Near East tended to be more tolerant. The conditions of non-Muslims declined under the rule of the "barbarian" military regimes in the fourteenth and fifteenth centuries, revived under the Ottoman Turks in the sixteenth and seventeenth centuries, and then deteriorated again, but over long periods and up to recent times the Jews under Islam enjoyed a comparatively secure existence, free from persecution.[61]

Within the framework of general religious pluralism, the Jews were subject to a certain amount of differential treatment, although, again, this varied considerably between periods and provinces. Fiscal discrimination was heavy in many cases, but with a few exceptions, such as in Yemen, other forms of discrimination were slight. Some of this differential treatment was motivated by a desire to secure the monopoly of Islam over its nominal adherents and to protect Islam from other religions. To demonstrate the superiority of Islam over other religions, numerous restrictions on non-Muslims were introduced concerning such matters as modes of dress, size of buildings, and the carrying of arms. These measures were introduced not to exclude the Jews and other *dhimmis* (protected non-Muslims) from Islamic society but to establish the "correct" hierarchical distinctions. The hierarchical scheme, based on religious principles, was subject to economic and political exigencies; restrictions on *dhimmis* were seldom enforced consistently, and discrimination was intermittent.[62]

Middle Eastern Jews underwent a transformation from an agricultural people to one of merchants and artisans in the seventh and eighth centuries, and the absence of restrictions in the economic sphere enabled them to enter a great variety of occupations and to remain economically undifferentiated from urban Muslims. The positive attitude of Islam toward urban life and trade contributed to the status and integration of the predominantly urban-dwelling Jews. In contrast to Europe, commercial and craft guilds limited to members of the dominant faith did not exist in the early Islamic period, and the incorporation of Jews into unified economic communities, little affected by religious boundaries, continued into modern times. Although Muslims devised legal means to circumvent the religious prohibition on usury and engaged extensively in credit transactions, Islamic restrictions on handling money and fashioning gold and silver objects for sale provided special occupational niches for Jews in some countries. In many cases positions in the military and the state bureaucracy were not open to Jews, but Jews did serve in some state bureaucracies in middle and lower ranks, and under certain sovereigns a few Jews did reach positions of power and influence. The Jewish poor were mostly small artisans and petty traders, although there were Jewish agricultural settlements in some areas, such as Morocco.

In the Ottoman Empire in the fifteenth and sixteenth centuries the Jews were prominent as traders, manufacturers, tax farmers, and customs officials. The Turkish ruling elites were concentrated in government, religious institutions, and the military, and, with respect to those economic activities that they regarded as beneath them, they preferred Jews over Christians, whose loyalty was suspect. The decline of the Ottoman Empire was accompanied by reduced tolerance, growing segregation, and increased poverty; Jews lost their former privileged position and were replaced by Christian minorities.[63]

Towns were fully integrated into the broader political systems of Islamic societies, and the absence of municipal autonomy meant that no corporate structure or urban law differentiated Jews from others. In most cases the residential concentration of Jews was voluntary; predominantly homogeneous religious quarters were customary in Muslim towns, and there was no degradation associated with living in one. There were, however, exceptions. The *mellah* (Jewish quarter) established in Fez, Morocco, in 1438 was intended to protect the Jewish community following attacks on its members. It became the prototype of the Moroccan "ghetto." Those *mellahs* established since the middle of the sixteenth century were intended to isolate Jews rather than to defend and protect them. The *mellah* was often separated by walls from the Muslim quarters, and there were restrictions on Jews when moving outside the *mellah*. In Iran and Yemen the stigmatization of Jews as ritually unclean was used to justify residential restrictions, and in seventeenth-century Yemen, Jews were forced to live in special areas on the outskirts of towns. Such forced residential segregation had no parallel in the Ottoman Empire, and during its heyday, the behavior and attitudes of the Turkish authorities toward Jews tended to be favorable.[64]

Comparisons of conditions among the Muslim states have to be qualified by noting the range of circumstances that prevailed within a single country. These variations have to be understood in relation to the social structures of the Islamic Middle Eastern societies, which were characterized by a division between the administrative cities and towns of the sultans and the fragmented tribal structures that provided the basis of social and political ties in the countryside and desert areas. In Morocco, in particular, no single pattern of Jewish-Muslim relationships can be discerned, and the differences among the Jewish communities in the imperial cities, where the Jewish population could total many thousands, the smaller trading and administrative centers, and the oasis towns and mountain villages with perhaps just a few isolated Jews were considerable. The sultan did not have effective control over the whole country, and in many inland communities, desert oases, and mountainous areas Jews were dependent for their security on tribal and local patrons, to whom they paid tribute.[65]

The Jewish communities under the sultans had their own semi-autonomous community organizations to which the Islamic rulers delegated substantial political authority, including the task of collecting taxes. One later version of this community organization was the Ottoman Millet system, which was extended from the Greek and Armenian communities to the Jews and allowed each religious community to control matters of religion and personal status.[66] In Morocco the ties between Muslim patrons and Jewish clients could interfere with the loyalty of Jews to their community and obstruct the operation of Jewish autonomy. Attempts were made by the Jewish communities to limit the sphere of influence of non-Jewish institutions and to insist on the exclusive jurisdiction of the Jewish courts of law in matters of litigation between members of their communities. But, even where the Jewish institutions were corporate, elaborate, and pervasive, highly personalistic relations could develop between Jews and Muslims, and close and intimate associations were not uncommon.[67]

The syncretistic Kurdish Jews and the more distinctive Ghardaia Jews of the northwestern Sahara were considerably different in their levels of social interaction with Muslims. Most Kurdish Jews were manual laborers who lived in the villages

CHAPTER 1

and small towns of Islamic Kurds. In the small towns they lived by choice in separate quarters adjacent to the Muslim quarters, but many Muslims lived in the Jewish quarters, some even in Jewish households as lodgers or workers. Jews and Muslims visited one other and ate in one another's houses. In contrast, the Ghardaia Jews were highly segregated both from the neighboring Arabs, who belonged to the Malekite sect, and the neighboring Berbers, who belonged to the puritanical Ibadite sect. The Ghardaia Jews lived in a ghetto-like quarter, performed specialized economic functions, and interacted with Muslims only in impersonal relationships.[68] In general, however, the social boundaries enclosing the Jews under Islam were limited and took mainly voluntary forms.

Europe: Ashkenazim

Like Islam, Christianity was an insular religion; although flexible in incorporating pagan folk beliefs and practices that did not present articulate religious alternatives or challenges, it was consistent in establishing clear boundaries with alternative religious systems, such as Judaism. Church authorities differed from Islamic authorities insofar as they were less disposed to take a pluralistic stance toward other monotheistic faiths.

The fact that Jews were the only deviant religious group whose existence was tolerated by the central organs of the church is important to understanding the situation of the Jews in medieval Europe. Muslims were not tolerated except on a temporary basis in Spanish and Italian areas, and Christian heretics were bloodily suppressed. The Jews were the sole recognized representatives of religious deviance, the only group to fall outside the otherwise complete religious monopoly of the church. Ecclesiastical authorities were willing to tolerate the Jews in a submissive state until the end of days, at which time their conversion would herald the second coming of Jesus. The church taught that the exile and submissive state of the Jews was a divine penalty for their repudiation of Jesus and could thus be regarded as evidence for the truth of Christianity. This doctrine did not mean that Christians should not attempt to evangelize Jews, but forced conversion was officially prohibited.

The policy of limited pluralism with regard to the Jews was held relatively consistently by the papacy and the church hierarchy throughout the medieval period; with a few exceptions, they counseled tolerance and restraint during intolerant periods, and they sought to protect Jews and safeguard their property. The church had little executive power outside the papal states and individual bishoprics, but its attitudes toward Jews influenced the policies of secular rulers, who often found that the existence of a Jewish community was congruent with their economic and fiscal interests. Even if they were aware of it, lower church officials and ordinary Christians were less likely to appreciate the official church policy of limited tolerance; local and regional clerics, particularly parish priests and wandering monks, often led or encouraged anti-Jewish outbreaks. During periods of unrest, such as the Crusades and the Black Death, neither the church nor most secular authorities were able or willing to prevent massacres of Jews.

Outbreaks of persecution were more frequent under Christianity than under Islam, and although the church was rarely directly responsible for such acts, its teachings about Jewish guilt and unworthiness provided the perpetrators with encouragement and justification. The first major massacres of Jews in Europe occurred at the end of the eleventh century, when the lower stratum of the crusaders extended the quest of purifying the Holy Land from the pollution of Muslims to purifying Christian territories from the pollution of Jews. In the thirteenth century the accusation that Jews murdered Christian children for ritual purposes replaced the crusader ideology as a justification for killing Jews. By the fourteenth century the popular image of the Jews had became demonized: As "deliberate unbelievers," the Jews were accused of being Satan's associates on earth, and widespread large-scale massacres followed accusations that Jews had caused the Black Death by polluting wells. The destruction of the depersonalized followers of Satan was seen as part of a cosmic battle that would herald Christian salvation.[69]

The tragic side of European Jewish history should not obscure the fact that there were long periods when a limited tolerance, sanctioned by the church, did prevail. But to safeguard its virtual religious monopoly, the church found it necessary to segregate and restrict that group over which its religious authority did not extend. The segregation and subservience of the Jews began in the early centuries of the current era, when the church was having little success in converting the Jews and when it regarded Judaism as a dangerous proselytizing competitor. Yet the church continued to exclude and restrict Jews long after Judaism had ceased to be a threat. During the early Middle Ages, there appears to have been considerable socializing of Jews and Christians, and as late as the eleventh century, church councils were still complaining of Christians partaking of meals and sharing accommodations with Jews.

The establishment of clear boundaries between Christians and Jews was, for the church, a necessary adjunct to its acceptance of the Jewish presence as a personification of the absence of belief and its punitive effects. The protective policy of the church toward the Jews weakened in the thirteenth century, and in the later Middle Ages church regulations providing for the segregation of the Jews were extended and elaborated in minute detail. With the growth of the Jewish population in Poland, the Polish church enacted detailed rulings in the eighteenth century to prevent contacts between Christians and Jews. Prohibitions forbade Christians to dwell or bathe with Jews, to eat with them or serve them, or to attend Jewish celebrations. Churchmen, including bishops, accused Jews of ritual murder, although others moderated their hostility as they made use of Jewish economic services.

Although voluntary residential separation was common throughout the medieval period, the ghetto did not become a state-enforced institution until the fifteenth century. Jews did not oppose the legal institution of separate quarters and, like other corporations, accepted distinctive dress and markings. They did object to the Jewish badge, which was first instituted by the church in the thirteenth century; intended as a sign of humiliation, it took one and a half centuries to become firmly established. The church's increased emphasis on Jewish segregation in the latter part of the medieval age may have been a response to challenges to church power by heretical movements and secular rulers. Some churchmen expressed the view that Jews encouraged, directly or indirectly, the development of Christian heterodoxies and deviations, and through their segregation and submission the church could pretend that it continued to dominate a Christian order.[70]

As self-proclaimed protectors of the church and guardians of Christian piety, secular rulers were influenced by the church's segregationist policies, but they were not totally determined by them. Political and economic interests could outweigh religious considerations. The existence of an independent secular law allowed for the evasion of church policies, and Jews were sometimes able to play secular authorities against the church and to form strategic alliances with both secular and religious powers. The religious orientations of the dominant group cannot alone account for the clear legal, economic, and social separation of the Jews in medieval European society, and it is appropriate to consider the Jews' social position and economic functions in European feudal societies.

The prohibition on Jews owning serfs prevented them from establishing large estates, but European rulers welcomed Jews in the early Middle Ages as merchants who could provide valuable services in international and wholesale trade. In return for substantial fiscal contributions and economic services, princes protected the Jews and their property, applied the most tolerant features of the available legal traditions, facilitated Jewish economic enterprises, and sometimes authorized certain economic functions, such as money lending, to be performed exclusively by Jews. The Jewish occupational structure was at first diversified in trade, crafts, and credit facilities, and despite early medieval disdain for merchants and church antagonism, many Jewish communities achieved social prestige and political influence by their association with the secular rulers. From the period of the Crusades a class of Gentile wholesale merchants grew, and Jews were increasingly restricted to money lending, which was forbidden to Gentiles by the canonical prohibition of the church. Money lending suited the Jews because it was both profitable and allowed them time for religious study.

Jewish participation in agriculture constantly declined; their lands were expropriated, and their insecure position put a premium on owning property that could be moved. As competitors of Christian merchants, Jews did not gain from the more favorable view of commerce that developed in Europe in the twelfth and thirteenth centuries. They were squeezed out of commercial markets, and the prohibition on joining guilds and other discriminatory practices prevented their participation in many crafts. Rulers encouraged Jewish money lending to ensure a continual source of taxable income, and by the end of the twelfth century the word *Jew* had come to mean moneylender. Christians associated usury with heresy and the devil; their dependence on Jewish moneylenders could only compound already existing antipathy toward Jews.[71]

In addition to their economic specialization, Jews were further separated by the corporate structure of medieval society. The early Jewish settlers in some areas received rights and privileges as individuals or as families, but these arrangements gradually took corporate forms as the societies became increasingly feudal. The legal status of the Jewish estate or corporative entity came to be denoted by the term *serfdom*, and although the popes of the twelfth and thirteenth centuries proclaimed the perpetual serfdom of the Jews to the church, jurisdiction over the Jews passed to the secular rulers. The Jews were, in many respects, chattels of the sovereign power, but in the feudal context they were comparatively free because they lived under the sovereign's protection and enjoyed a considerable measure of corporative autonomy. Their legal status in some regimes was considerably better than that of enserfed peasants; they were free to move, held municipal offices in towns, had the right to bear arms up to the thirteenth century, and contributed to the armed defense of the towns. Yet, although their rights and privileges approached in some places those of Christian nobles and burghers, they were less protected than Christian dependents by set rules governing feudal bonds, and their rights and conditions of residence depended more on the will and interests of rulers.

In addition to the religious factor, which prohibited the Jews from taking the oath of the Christian burghers, the continued dependence of Jews on royal or baronial authorities prevented them from becoming part of the corporate unity of burghers. More generally, their subjection to authorities with divergent interests meant that the corporate status of Jewish communities remained abnormal within medieval European society. The Jews constituted one of many corporations within the European corporate system, but theirs was also perceived to be outside that framework. They were civilly unique, living under a law that applied only to them, and in the later Middle Ages, when other corporations and estates were being amalgamated into the states through common legal bonds, the civil isolation of Jews came to parallel their religious isolation and they were expelled from a number of western and central European states.[72]

England expelled its Jews in 1290. France's final expulsion of its Jews occurred in the late fourteenth century, and an increasing number of expulsions from German towns took place in the fifteenth and sixteenth centuries, although these were often temporary. Jews remained in parts of Germany and in Italy, where in the sixteenth century they were placed in ghettos. In the second half of the sixteenth century Jews were readmitted to many of the localities from which they had been expelled, but it was eastern Europe, where Jews were welcomed by the rulers of Poland and Lithuania, that became the location of the largest concentration of Europe's Jews.[73]

The first Jewish communities in Poland benefited from their special relationship with the Polish monarchy, but from about 1580, with the decline of the monarch as a centralizing force, the Jews came increasingly under the control of feudal lords. The strengthening of feudal structures in Poland and the absence of a native merchant class provided economic opportunities for Jews, many of whom became lease holders who paid fixed sums to noble landowners in return for managing and profiting from the estates. As a result, peasant animosity toward noble landowners was deflected toward Jews and was made worse by their humiliation at being placed under the authority of a religiously despised group.

In the eighteenth century Jewish traders controlled more than half of Poland's domestic trade, large numbers worked as artisans, and they were extensively involved in leasing monopoly rights for the production and sale of alcoholic beverages. Polish Jews lived in closer contact with Gentiles than ghetto Jews in Italy and central Europe did, and it was not uncommon for them to drink together in taverns. There were occasional reports of Jewish-Christian romances, but, if discovered, the couple was lashed in public. Intimate contacts occurred but were made rare by the interpenetration of religious and economic tension.[74] The Jewish population in eastern Europe increased rapidly in the nineteenth century, but, although Jews held a comparatively wide range of occupations, they remained a distinctive economic stratum of traders and artisans, mediating between the nobles and the peasant masses. Until the Holocaust the Jews continued to be regarded as strangers in Polish society.[75]

The corporate status of the Jews in medieval European states and early modern Poland not only contributed to their separation from non-Jews but also provided the framework for a semi-autonomous Jewish community in which Jews organized their lives and exercised social control in accord with their distinctive religion. The Jewish communities' collection of taxes, their appointment of leaders and salaried officials—such as rabbis, cantors, ritual slaughterers, beadles, and scribes—and their control of wide areas of daily life, including education, social welfare, and other religious services, often amounted to more autonomy than the municipalities of the medieval cities in which the communities were located. The development of absolutist monarchies in western and central Europe was accompanied by the dismantling of medieval corporations, including those of the Jews, who, unlike other groups, were often expelled rather than incorporated into the more centralized polities, but in eastern Europe, from 1500 to 1648, the Polish Jews created the largest and most extensive network of communal and educational institutions of any European Jewry. After the partitions of Poland (1772–95), the legal foundations of community autonomy were either weakened or abolished, but under Russian rule most eastern European communities continued to retain a high level of autonomy.[76]

The Jewish leaders could enforce their will by fines or corporal punishment, and they could make use of the *herem* (ban), the severity of which ranged from threatened or temporary excommunication to permanent excommunication. The excommunicated were excluded from all religious facilities and possibly also from economic and social relationships. Because excommunication meant exclusion from all society, the excommunicated were forced into a terribly isolated situation.

It was not possible for a Jew to be unaffiliated with the community and yet remain a Jew; Jewish identity was a corporate identity. This extensive social control within the boundaries of highly autonomous communities inhibited deviation from Jewish religious distinctiveness.

Europe: Sephardim

In contrast to the situation of the Ashkenazim in the medieval period, large-scale persecution of the Sephardim in Spain occurred after a long period of relative peace, prosperity, and status. Apart from a temporary setback as a result of the invasion of the Almoravides in the 1080s, Spanish Jews under Muslim rule enjoyed prosperity and high status. This lasted until the invasion of the Almohads in 1147, when many Jews migrated north to Christian Spain, where, beginning with the Christian reconquest in the second half of the eleventh century, their already favorable position improved further. The reconquered territories were characterized by greater religious and ethnic diversity than other Christian societies in which Jews had settled. Iberia's Christian princes adopted in some measure the Muslim model of protected peoples and provided their Muslim and Jewish minorities with legal safeguards, group autonomy, and access to relatively high-status occupations. The Christian kings referred to themselves as the "kings of the three religions," and a pluralistic structure evolved in which a comparatively high level of tolerance characterized relations among the three religious collectivities.

The Christian princes of the reconquest found the Jews reliable allies, and Jewish familiarity with the newly conquered territories was a useful asset. Kings and nobles appointed Jews to important positions as diplomats, financiers, tax farmers, administrators, scholars, and physicians. In Castile, which was often in a state of political disturbance, kings thought that they could trust their Jewish counselors, who were not subject to the conflicting loyalties of their Christian vassals. Jews occupied a wide variety of professions and occupations, and, unhampered by economic discrimination, they were of great importance in the economy of the country; they constituted a large section of the urban population and bourgeoisie and controlled a significant part of Spanish commerce, industry, mining, and viticulture. The ruling elements saw landownership by Jews as being in the royal interest and put no restrictions on their acquisition of estates. Some wealthy Jews owned castles and villages and even exercised feudal rights in the thirteenth and fourteenth centuries. Secular leaders often ignored or opposed decrees of the church that were intended to segregate and discriminate against Jews. Some popes complained about the important positions given to Jews in Spain, but in Spain itself churchmen employed Jews to lease, administer, and collect taxes from the ecclesiastical properties.

Most Spanish Jews lived in Jewish quarters, but up to the latter part of the fourteenth century this was entirely voluntary, and it was not unusual to find Jews living outside and Christians living inside the Jewish quarters. There were no clear external differences between Jews and Christians: They spoke the same language, took similar names, and wore the same style of clothes. The lifestyle of wealthy

Jews, who carried arms, mixed freely in royal courts and noble mansions, and conspicuously displayed great riches and luxury, had no counterpart among the Ashkenazim. The Jewish community itself was split socially between the rich and powerful minority and the small merchants and artisans who made up the majority, but cordial relations between Jews and non-Jews were not limited to the upper stratum: Jewish and Christian burghers had friendly professional and personal relationships; Jewish advocates represented Gentile clients in secular courts; Jewish artisans had Christian customers or worked for Christian employers; Jewish textile merchants employed Christian workers; and Jews and non-Jews joined in common processions, shared the public baths, exchanged gifts on holidays and family occasions, and ate occasional meals together. Jews performed the roles of godparents at Christian baptisms, and Christians performed similar roles at Jewish circumcisions.[77]

Jewish leaders in Spain were faced with the problems of maintaining a tax base, community cohesion, and religious conformity when Jews were allowed to settle outside their designated quarters and socialize extensively with Gentiles. Rabbis expressed their concerns about what they considered the extensive social interaction, including sexual liaisons, with Gentiles, and Jewish communal officials expressed their concerns that Jews turned to non-Jewish judges if they did not receive the verdict they wanted from a Jewish court. Community leaders, to little avail, ordered their members not to move their homes or businesses outside the Jewish quarter and not to sell the land within it to Christians.[78]

Spanish historians have applied the term *convivencia* (living together with others) to denote the relationships of Jews and Gentiles in Spain, but this did not guarantee Jewish security. Even during times of prosperity and social advancement, Jews remained in a precarious situation. As in other European countries, dependence on the Crown brought sudden reversals of fortune as the kings' positions and policies changed. Indications that *convivencia* was breaking down were already present by the end of the thirteenth century. With the reconquest nearly completed and most of the Iberian Peninsula united into a few large kingdoms, churchmen and secular rulers began to treat the Jews more as they were being treated in the rest of Christian Europe. In Aragon the change in church policy began in the middle of the thirteenth century, but in Castile, where Jewish influence in the state, especially in its financial administration, was greater, the status of the Jews remained high and relations between Jews and Christians remained good until the second half of the fourteenth century, when discriminatory and segregative measures began to be put into effect.[79]

The massacres in 1391 destroyed many of the Jewish communities in Castile and Andalusia. They have been interpreted as part of a socioeconomic crisis and class struggle within the wider society, but Jews were the main target of mobs encouraged by popular preachers. The events were followed, in 1412–15, by discriminatory measures that excluded Jews from certain trades, barred them from service in the royal and urban governments, and reduced their social interaction with Christians. The Spanish kings soon abolished many of the anti-Jewish edicts and tried to restore the Jews to their former status. Although this brought some improvement in their situation, it did not restore them to their pre-1391 situation: Many communities were not reestablished, the Jews' political rank and influence declined, fewer wealthy Jews remained, some discriminatory measures were instituted, and the center of Jewish life moved from the large cities to the small towns, where Jews continued as small merchants, shopkeepers, and artisans.

Mass conversions of Spanish Jews accompanied and followed the massacres, the discriminatory measures, and other forms of intimidation, such as forced attendance before Christian preachers and a "trial" of the Talmud. The mass conversions in turn set the stage for the expulsion, as doubts were cast on the sincerity of the converts and Jews were accused of encouraging the converts to return to Judaism or to practice Judaism in secret. The belief that converts who had reverted to Judaism were undermining the true faith induced the Spanish royals, Ferdinand and Isabella, to request an inquisition, which was granted by the pope in 1478. The first trials and burnings of Judaizers took place in 1480. The edict of expulsion in 1492 followed the surrender of Granada in 1491, putting an end to Muslim rule in the Iberian Peninsula, and was recognition on the part of the Crown and the Inquisition that Jews were behind the Judaizing of the converts.[80]

The expulsion was unexpected by the Spanish Jews, whose situation, despite its deterioration, had remained better than that of the Ashkenazim in western and central Europe. The Sephardim in the fifteenth century were not confined mainly to money lending but were found in a wide range of occupations, including the most prestigious; they were not segregated in ghettos but were allowed to mix freely with non-Jews; and they did not feel an enormous cultural gulf between themselves and the non-Jewish population but identified themselves with many aspects of Spanish culture. During the second half of the fifteenth century, the sermons and writings of Jewish scholars continued to express a high respect for the Spanish Christian culture.[81]

Conclusions

The sparseness of historical data on some Jewish communities means that explanations of the gross differences in levels of Jewish religious syncretism and distinctiveness in premodern societies must necessarily be tentative. It is not possible to trace the religiocultural developments of the Chinese and Indian communities over the centuries because most of our information derives from Europeans who visited and described the communities after they were "discovered." In certain cases we can only compare a number of static portrayals of communities at the end of their periods of isolation, and from these we can attempt to reconstruct their histories. Where the distinctiveness of the Jews' religion had become highly attenuated, it would appear that the process occurred over a long period and cannot be explained by the characteristics and orientations of the first generation of Jewish settlers. If the original Jewish settlers had been predisposed to accept other religions and be socially absorbed by the host society, the communities would not have survived centuries of isolation from other Jewish communities, even in a highly attenuated form.

The size of the Jewish populations and their distance from the major centers of Jewish settlement are important factors but should not be overemphasized. Comparatively small numbers and lack of contact with other Jewish communities would only make a community particularly malleable to its cultural and social environment. One important cultural dimension was the degree of boundary maintenance by the dominant religions. Jewish religious syncretism was more extensive in societies in which the dominant religion was permeable than in societies in which it was insular. Although the differences between Judaism and dominant religious systems were initially much greater in China and India than in the Middle East and Europe, the permeability of the Eastern religions contributed to the much greater loss of Jewish religiocultural distinctiveness in the East.

Religions with permeable boundaries are more disposed to pluralism, to tolerating other religions alongside themselves, whereas insular religions are more disposed to monopolism, to demanding allegiance within a defined territory. The greater the tendency of the dominant group to coerce the Jews into accepting the majority religion, the more the Jews emphasized their religiocultural distinctiveness. The greater the tendency of the dominant group to accept the existence of Judaism, the more likely it was that the Jews would adopt elements of the coterritorial religions into their own.

Both religiocultural and social-structural dimensions influenced the extent to which the Jews were separated socially from non-Jews. Where Jews were separated, they were less likely to adopt elements from the non-Jewish religioculture. Where Jews were not so separated and social contacts with non-Jews were more frequent and intimate, extensive syncretism was more likely. The extent to which the Jews were separated within a society was related to the dominant group's disposition to monopolism or pluralism. A totally monopolistic policy, if successful, would have resulted in the disappearance of Jews, but although there were periods of massacres, forced conversions, and expulsions in Europe, periods of pluralism were generally longer. Variations in social separation, therefore, have to be considered within the framework of pluralism, although it is obvious that Jews were more likely to be separated from non-Jews in those societies whose pluralist stance was of a comparatively limited form. In some cases segregation of the Jews was motivated by the dominant group's desire to impose or reinforce its religious monopoly over the non-Jewish population.

Some spheres of separation of Jews from non-Jews were little related, at least in any direct way, to the religious motives and orientations of the dominant group. Differences in the social structures of host societies were also relevant. The European feudal structure of estates and corporations made for the separation of the Jews in the economic, social, and political spheres, and the special nature of the Jewish corporations resulted in their marginalization within European states. Jews were less segregated in the looser social structures of Middle Eastern societies, but the convergence of religion and state under Islam made for some administrative separation and partial communal autonomy of Jews as well as Christians. In China and India Jews were not politically separate, and corporate Jewish polities did not develop. The Indian caste system made for some social separation, but in contrast to the Middle East and Europe, Jews were separated within the dominant religious system, not outside it. The social separation of Jews as castes in India implied a substantial Jewish syncretism, whereas in the Middle East and Europe the greater the social separation of Jews from non-Jews, the greater the tendency of Jews to retain or reinforce their religiocultural distinctiveness.

A Coda: Conceptions of Jewish History and Comparisons

What Salo W. Baron once called "the lachrymose conception of Jewish history" has undergone considerable revision in recent years. The lachrymose accounts of the premodern Jewish Diaspora have focused on European Jewry: the massacres, the persecutions, the accusations of ritual murder, profaning the Host (Christ's body), and poisoning the wells and streams. In what is perhaps the most trenchant critique of the lachrymose conception, Jonathan Elukin objects to reducing the experience of Ashkenazim in medieval Europe "to a one-dimensional account of persecution and violence."[82] He writes that the incidents and periods of violence against Jews were essentially transitory and contingent and that the connections that historians have made between them have created "a deceptive impression of a linked evolution of anti-Jewish sentiment."[83] Elukin emphasizes that stable relationships prevailed between Christians and Jews over lengthy periods. Although acknowledging that testimonies of personal relations between Jews and Christians are rare, he states that the presence of a few Jews in small German towns and villages testifies to a confidence among Jews that they could live in safety among Gentiles.

Elukin writes that it should not be assumed that whenever Jews were attacked, they would view the particular incident as a demonstration of an unchanging anti-Jewish animus among Gentiles. Violence was a prevalent factor in medieval society for both Christians and Jews, and the invective against Jews has to be understood in the context of the rhetorical violence common throughout society at that time. After the attacks during the First Crusade of 1096, it did not take long for Jews to reestablish their communities and become reintegrated into society. The later accusations of Host desecration and other alleged Jewish crimes were localized and of limited duration, and the increased number of expulsions from fifteenth-century German towns were often temporary.[84]

It is misleading to present medieval European Jewish history as a never-ending series of persecutions, but it is also dangerous to overstate an "antilachrymose conception of Jewish history."[85] Historians of the lachrymose school construct their accounts on the basis of preserved records of massacres and persecutions, and because the lengthier, peaceful, "normal" times were not recorded, historians tend to ignore them. However, from a comparative perspective, it is significant that the persecutions and martyrdom became central themes in the collective memory of Ashkenazim. In their ritualization and commemoration of martyrs, Jews drew on Christian notions and rhetoric of martyrdom and translated them into Jewish images and symbols. With its inclusion of calls for divine revenge against Israel's enemies, Jewish martyrdom was an instance of "inward acculturation," the use or subversion of Christian symbols into an anti-Christian stance. Ivan Marcus has written that the Ashkenazim developed their liturgical remembrance of the Jewish martyrs of the First Crusade into "a nearly universal cult in memory of the dead."[86] Later massacres, such as those at the time of the Black Death, provided further content for the cult.

Among Jewish communities elsewhere, including the Jews under Islam, a ritualized memorization of death and martyrdom did not develop. One reason for this was that there was simply less persecution outside Europe. When persecutions occurred in Islamic lands, they were directed at non-Muslims in general or at Jews as members of a *dhimmi* category. These differences influenced Jewish orientations toward the dominant religions. Shlomo Deshen notes that, whereas Ashkenazim reacted to Christian symbols with fear and horror and tried to avoid them, no such feelings were to be found among Moroccan Jews toward Islam. Moroccan Jews certainly believed that their religion was vastly superior to Islam, which they regarded with some disdain, but they did not register the disgust that was evident among Ashkenazim toward Christianity.[87]

Levels of persecution and tolerance represent only one dimension of a comparison of Jewish communities within Gentile environments. Levels of segregation, occupational differentiation, and the positioning of Jews within the political and status systems are no less important. The factors determining either religious syncretism or religious distinctiveness tend to cluster together. In the East infrequent contact with other Jewish communities, permeable environmental religions, the dominant groups' pluralistic orientations, and lack of structural differentiation between Jews and non-Jews cluster together, resulting in a substantial Jewish syncretism. In the West frequent contact among Jewish communities, insular environmental religions, dominant groups' monopolistic orientations, and substantial structural differentiation from non-Jews clustered together. This cluster resulted in a limited syncretism or in some cases a reinforced distinctiveness. To some extent this clustering is a result of the exigencies of logical compatibility of the dimensions. For example, it is more likely that a dominant group that adheres to an insular religion would segregate members of another religion than a dominant group that adheres to a permeable religion. But, although it is not possible to distinguish entirely the determining dimensions, none of them can be entirely reduced or collapsed into the others. For example, it is not possible to predict on logical grounds the extent to which dominant groups adhering to an insular religion will be disposed to segregate members of a minority religion. In other words, the cluster, or convergence of dimensions accounting for syncretism and distinctiveness, is to some extent empirically fortuitous; the clustering could not be predicted from knowledge of the relevant dimensions alone.

This empirical clustering means, however, that the comparative method does not enable us to determine the relative importance of each dimension affecting the level of syncretism and distinctiveness. I have suggested that the demography of Jewish communities and their level of contact with other Jewish communities were less important than either the religiocultural orientations of the dominant groups or the social structures of the host societies, but I have not attempted to state the relative importance of the cultural and social dimensions. The number of empirically divergent cases is not sufficient to enable us to hold each determining dimension constant. This is a limitation that most broad cross-cultural studies using more than one causal factor or variable have to accept.

2. THE KAIFENG JEWS

*A Reconsideration of Their Acculturation
and Assimilation in a Comparative Perspective*

The premodern Chinese Jewish community in Kaifeng, China, is of particular interest because, although it ceased to function as a viable community in the second half of the nineteenth century, it had survived for centuries in relative isolation from the rest of the Jewish Diaspora. The most likely time of the formation of the Kaifeng community was the early Sung dynasty, the end of the tenth century or beginning of the eleventh. Kaifeng, then called Bialiang, was the dynasty's capital from 1126. As a wealthy metropolis it attracted Jewish merchants, probably mostly from Persia, who had traveled the Silk Road. The Jews received permission to build their first synagogue in 1163; they became part of the merchant class of the city, and they married Chinese women, who, according to the patrilineal Chinese system, converted to Judaism.[1] The original Jewish settlers in Kaifeng were probably specialists in the manufacture, dyeing, or pattern printing of cotton fabrics, but economic diversity among native Kaifeng Jews is illustrated by a 1512 inscription that mentions degree holders, civil and military officials, farmers, artisans, traders, and shopkeepers. In the fifteenth, sixteenth, and seventeenth centuries a number of Jews attained high political and military posts, and others were successful as physicians and scholars.[2]

Xu Xin estimates that the size of the community in its early period was between a few hundred and a thousand, but its size grew from natural growth and some immigration, and estimates based on a memorial book completed after a major flood in 1642 suggest that the preflood population was about 4,000. The postflood population was probably less than 1,000, and although the community recovered and grew to possibly 2,000 or 3,000 in the early eighteenth century, more floods and the destruction during the Taiping Rebellion caused a sharp drop in the population, so that by the nineteenth century there were no more than a few hundred.[3]

Kaifeng Jews and Jewish communities outside China had little contact after the abandonment of the Silk Road in the fourteenth century. Other Jewish communities in China ceased to exist by the beginning of the seventeenth century, and

Kaifeng Jews became effectively isolated from the rest of the Jewish Diaspora. Lack of contact with the centers of the Jewish Diaspora and a relatively small Jewish population were no doubt contributing factors to the disappearance of the Kaifeng community, but it is interesting that the Kaifeng community nevertheless lasted for about 800 years.

I begin with an analysis of the Chinese Jews' acculturation and then consider their assimilation. Of course, the acculturation and assimilation of Chinese Jews are interrelated, as are the religious and social-structural dimensions of Chinese society that influenced the acculturation and assimilation of the Jews and other religious minorities in China.

One limitation of any analysis of Jewish religious acculturation and assimilation in China is that almost all the historical evidence on Jews in traditional China is limited to the Kaifeng community. Moreover, the records and information from that community are mainly confined to the reports of Christian missionaries, beginning in the early seventeenth century, and stone inscriptions from the Kaifeng synagogue that were clearly intended to create a favorable impression among the Chinese, especially the literati and officials. The nature of this evidence has colored the analyses of scholars, who have tended to assume that the Kaifeng Jews related almost exclusively to Confucianism, which in turn is represented as a boundary-maintaining religion rather than as one component of the highly syncretistic Chinese religious milieu.

Acculturation

I have argued that two dimensions of the religious systems of the host societies are relevant in accounting for variations in the religious acculturation of the Jews. One is the degree of the religions' boundary maintenance: whether the religions, after their crystallization into identifiable forms, insulated themselves from or remained open to the influences of other religions. The second relevant dimension is the degree of pluralism: whether the religious authorities were disposed to tolerate other religions in close proximity or whether they demanded exclusive allegiance within a defined territory or over a particular population.

The relatively permeable religious boundaries and high level of religious pluralism in traditional China are evident from the fact that the vast majority of the Chinese population, past and present and from all strata, cannot be identified with or internally distinguished by specific religious traditions. Most Chinese participated in religions that have been portrayed as syncretistic amalgams of Confucianism, Taoism, and Buddhism as well as additional elements that cannot be linked to the three major traditions. Three identifiable elites (Confucian literati, Taoist priests, and Buddhist monks) promoted and interpreted the three traditions, but although distinctions among these traditions were made at self-conscious literate levels, the distinctions were less clear at the level of popular practice.[4]

CHAPTER 2

Little or no formal constraint was put on religious minorities in China to conform to Chinese religious beliefs and practices so long as they recognized the religious status of the emperor and the ancestral cult. As Max Weber noted, a rejection of the ancestral cult was viewed by the Chinese regime as a threat to the piety on which the hierarchy of offices and the obedience of subjects depended.[5] Confucianism was tied to the official religion of the state, but it was not contained within the framework of official religion, and it was neither a state religion nor a church in the Western sense. The literati who filled the states' bureaucracy espoused a doctrinal orthodoxy and emphasized the necessity of performing certain rites, but little or no attempt was made to coerce others. The Chinese political elite tolerated "heterodoxy" so long as it did not take the form of a movement that could threaten the state, and religious syncretism was permitted and even encouraged if it was considered politically efficacious.[6] The Kaifeng Jews observed those religious practices necessary for official recognition. They conducted ancestor worship, and the grounds of their synagogue included an ancestral hall with incense bowls and tablets of prominent ancestors. The synagogue also contained an Imperial tablet, although above it a Hebrew inscription praising God indicated to those who understood the writing that God was above the emperor.[7]

Scholars have differed in their relative emphases on the Kaifeng Jewish community's religious distinctiveness and acculturation, but the community achieved (and for a lengthy period retained) an integral balance between religious distinctiveness and religious sinicization. The stone inscriptions from the Kaifeng synagogue, dated 1489, 1512, 1663, and 1679, are the major resource for the analyses of the Kaifeng Jews' acculturation before the community's decline and its loss of virtually all substantive knowledge of Judaism.[8] The emphasis on Confucianism in the inscriptions might suggest that the tiny community was losing its ancestral culture and becoming absorbed into the wider culture. However, because the inscriptions are similar in content, particularly in the way that they represent Judaism in relation to Confucianism, one does not get the impression that much changed in terms of cultural loss and cultural absorption during the nearly 200 years between the first and the last inscriptions. If the community that the Jesuits "discovered" at the beginning of the seventeenth century was a highly acculturated one, this was already the case in the fifteenth century. The inscriptions were written by literati, possibly including non-Jews, who were commissioned to write them, and they appear to be addressed principally to other literati. They represent, therefore, the official face of the community, and it should not be assumed that they accurately portray the beliefs and orientations of the majority of Kaifeng Jews.

The 1489 inscription communicates the messages that are repeated in the later inscriptions; the commonality of Judaism and Confucianism is emphasized, and the Confucian classics are referenced to describe and justify the community's worship and beliefs. The community's religion and Confucianism are found to "agree on essential points and differ in secondary ones"; the principles of both religions "are nothing more than honoring the Way of Heaven (*T'ien Dao*), venerating ancestors, giving high regard to the relations between the Prince and his ministers, being filial to parents, living in harmony with wife and children, preserving the distinction between superiors and inferiors, and having neighborly relations with friends."[9] In a similar fashion the 1512 inscription asserts that, "although the written characters of the Scriptures of this religion are different from the script of Confucian books, yet on examining their principles (*li*) it is found that their ways (*dao*) of common practice are similar." Both follow the Way in relationships, propriety, wisdom, fasting, purifications, sacrifices to ancestors, and in blessings and praising heaven, "the Author and Preserver of all things."[10] The 1663 inscription also asserts that the community's scriptures, although in a different writing, are "in harmony with the principles (*li*) of the Six Classics (of Confucianism), and in no case is there anything not in harmony with them."[11]

Although scholars acknowledge the overt Confucianism expressed in the inscriptions, they have pointed to sections that they interpret as the authors' care to emphasize the distinctiveness of the community's religion. One problem in interpreting these sections is that, even though they point to differences from popular religion, they conform to views found among the literati. Michael Pollak notes that, given the Chinese predilection for images, the rejection of human and other likenesses in the inscriptions is expressed in "surprisingly unequivocal and impudent terms."[12] However, because many Confucian literati also scorned the type of religious imagery prevalent in popular religion, such sentiments may have been meant to garner the approval of the literati rather than to express distinctiveness. The 1489 inscription's insistence that patriarchs of their religion "made no images, flattered no spirits and ghosts, and placed no credence in superstitious practices" and that "the spirits and ghosts could not help men, idols could afford them no protection, and superstitious practices could avail them nothing"[13] could be interpreted as a literati critique of popular Chinese religion.

The Confucian literati influence continues in the inscriptions' conceptions of divinity and creation. According to the 1489 inscription, the "Way of Heaven (*T'ien Dao*) does not speak" and it supports this principle by quoting from the Confucian Analects. Whereas Donald Daniel Leslie writes that the ideas expressed in the inscriptions are "sometimes Jewish in Confucian garb, but more often Confucian per se,"[14] Andrew Plaks refers to the use of such terms as *T'ien* (heaven) and *Dao* (the Way) as part of the "obligatory decorative touches." Plaks acknowledges that the conception in the 1489 inscription of spontaneous generation and the functioning of the universe appears to clash with the Jewish doctrine of volitional creation ex nihilo, but he defends the inscription's rejection of corporeal divinity and the reification of divine will as idolatry as being in line with both Jewish and Confucian thinking. He quotes Maimonides ("He has no bodily form, for He is incorporeal") and notes the concern with which Jewish medieval thinkers removed the anthropomorphism of divine will and power.[15] However, the depersonalized notion of heaven in the 1489 inscription is remote from the Jewish conceptions of God elsewhere. The 1663 inscription conceives of heaven in a more personified fashion and is able to quote from the Confucian Book of Odes to support this: "The *Book of Odes* says, 'Heaven ascends and descends about our doings; it daily watches whatever we are.'" According to the inscription, this quote expresses the same belief as the Scriptures received by Moses on Mount Sinai.[16]

The authors of the inscriptions were able to find in Chinese religion the meanings of *T'ien* that suited their purposes, because that term was imbued with various meanings that differed with respect to impersonal or personal and passive or active idioms. *T'ien* in many Confucian texts was personified as the supreme emperor, the father of all earthly Chinese emperors, but the dominant Confucian conception was of an impersonal, amorphous, supreme principle or force that expressed and sustained an order that was both divine and natural, cosmic and social. The most sophisticated among the literati believed that *T'ien* acted only in an indirect fashion, without intention and with total impartiality, but it was also seen as having a moral will that judged the behavior and determined the destiny of individuals and dynasties.[17] The Kaifeng Jews appear to have been pulled both by the impersonal conceptions of *T'ien* found among sophisticated literati and by the more personal conceptions that conformed to Jewish tradition and were found in popular forms of Chinese religion.

Scholars have interpreted the inscriptions as apologetics intended to impress non-Jewish literati, but in their attempts to downplay the explicit Confucianism of the inscriptions, they have themselves become involved in apologetics. One defense by scholars on behalf of the Kaifeng Jews is to argue that the community was able to grow more Confucianist because Judaism and Confucianism are similar in basic ways. This argument has encompassed ethics, ancestor worship, and the emphasis on learning.[18] Leslie's comment on the similarity between the ethics of Confucianism and Judaism[19] has been repeated by other scholars,[20] but Leslie acknowledges that sufficient similarity exists between the principles of good and evil "in almost all civilized communities for harmony to be easily achieved."[21] The Christian missionaries who entered China around 1600 and the literati with whom they had contact were also impressed by the moral analogies between their religions.[22]

Finding ethical similarities—such as emphasis on good deeds and "doing unto others what you would have them do to you"—is not difficult, but the bases or justifications for the ethical principles in Confucianism are different from those in Judaism outside China. In most forms of Judaism ethics are God given and Jews conform to them to obey God and because they fear his judgment in this world and the next. Although Confucian literati believe that heaven's imperatives provide ideal moral standards, ethical conformity is part of the cultivation of the self that requires the development of the seeds of goodness inherent in human nature.[23] Aharon Oppenheimer writes that Judaism is an ethical religion and that Confucianism is a system of religious ethics, but he overstates his case when he argues that Confucianism rejects any concept of an external source of moral compunction.[24]

According to the authors of the inscriptions, reverence for ancestors was one of the major commonalities of Judaism and Confucianism. Halls for ancestors were built within the synagogue compound, and worship of (literally "sacrifice to," *-ji*) the ancestors was cited a number of times as the principal expression of the community's religion. Ancestor worship was, of course, a common and central feature of all Chinese religion, and no group could become part of the society without adopting it. Scholars have argued that this did not pose a problem for the Jews because, as Leslie put it, the Jewish memorial services for the dead "are similar to Chinese ancestor worship, even though the Jewish theologians insist that it is only God who is prayed to."[25] Plaks writes that ancestor worship was "not necessarily an alien graft since homage to the forefathers of the Jewish people (i.e., the patriarchs Abraham, Isaac, and Jacob) is a central element in Jewish liturgy."[26]

These interpretations of ancestor worship as a foregrounding of Jewish memorial services ignore the extent to which ancestor worship was an integral part of the Chinese religious perspective (which assumed a continuum between humans and the supramundane). Most gods of Chinese popular religion were deified persons, and although ancestors were considered to have less power than most deities, many Chinese believed that ancestor worship had an efficacy that went beyond remembrance and homage. Ancestor worship expressed beliefs of a continuing reciprocity that had material benefits for both sides, even though, in parallel with the relationship of children and parents, the heaviest obligation fell on descendants rather than on the ancestors. The food offered to ancestors reflected the assumption that the needs and purposes of ancestors were similar to those of living people. Family members regularly bowed before ancestral tablets and burned incense, and a more elaborate ritual was performed on anniversaries of the ancestors' deaths, when the favorite food of the deceased was set before them, and on festival days, births, and weddings. The ritual media, such as incense, libations, and offerings, were much the same as those used in rituals directed toward gods, and in return, aid was solicited from ancestors, although they were generally believed to be less powerful than gods.[27] Such forms of reciprocity between dead and living family members are also common in popular forms of Judaism, especially among Middle Eastern Jews.[28] In contrast to Chinese ancestor worship, however, the living are expected to gain the most.

A "rationalistic" Confucian interpretation of ancestor worship emphasizes the caring for the dead as a filial duty with little or no attention to the ancestors' supramundane status or powers. Some Confucianists argue that ancestor worship benefits the living and not the dead, who lack consciousness.[29] Because the writers of the inscriptions were literati, it is possible that they shared these beliefs, but what we do not know is the extent to which the Kaifeng Jews participated in the more popular beliefs and forms of ancestor worship.

The syncretism of the religion of the Kaifeng Jews with Chinese religion is narrowed down by most scholars to a syncretism with Confucianism, and the significance of acculturation to the religious environment is further reduced by the argument that Confucianism is not a religion but an ethical system. Xu has recently argued that Kaifeng Jews never hesitated to use Confucian sayings and customs in the synagogue because Confucianism was not a religion but a social ethic, a humanistic, rational, and secular worldview. Confucianism, Xu notes, is unconcerned with deities or what happens after death; it focuses on the establishment of a harmonious society through ceremonies and correct behavior.[30] It is true that some passages in the Confucian classics express skepticism toward the existence of gods and spirits and that some Confucianists interpret supramundane notions as instruments for the enforcement of social values and the control of the masses, but only a minority within the literati offered such rationalistic interpretations.

Like many Chinese, most literati believed that the cosmos was populated by a wide variety of supramundane beings, such as gods, ancestral spirits, and ghosts, who could be propitiated and appeased by the appropriate forms of offerings and sacrifices.[31] Even those literati who denied the existence of spirits or took an agnostic position participated in rituals addressed to spirits. For some, the question of the existence of deities was secondary to the correct performance of rituals and conformity to customs that were the means by which men could achieve harmony with the cosmos. Respect for rituals was an expression of the natural and social order.[32]

A common view among the literati was that moral and immoral acts called forth rewards and retribution from supramundanes, although views differed on how this relationship operated. Some argued that retribution occurred "naturalistically," as an automatic process of action and response in accordance with the transcendent moral order of *T'ien*. The alternative view was that retribution was the work of the supramundane bureaucracy of gods and spirits, who kept a close surveillance over human behavior and dealt appropriately with the individual's smallest acts and innermost thoughts.[33] Such beliefs should not be viewed as deviating from a deity-free classical Confucianism; ancestral spirits, nature gods, ghosts, and spirits appear in the Analects.

Confucianism, like all Chinese religion, is polytheistic. It is possible that the authors of the inscriptions shared in the more rationalistic forms of Confucianism, but it cannot be assumed that this was the case among the Kaifeng Jews. The popular religion of all premodern societies, including the so-called monotheistic religions, was an enchanted world populated by numerous supramundane beings, and it is likely that most Kaifeng Jews shared the particular enchanted world of the majority of Chinese.

Chinese Muslims

There can be little doubt that the emphasis of the authors of the synagogue stone inscriptions on the commonality of Judaism and Confucianism was related to the entrance of a significant number of Kaifeng Jews into the state bureaucracy of the Ming dynasty (1368–1644). Xu has referred to the Ming dynasty as "a kind of Golden Age" for the Kaifeng Jews, some of whom took advantage of the opportunities in government service through the civil service examinations and in some cases were appointed to high positions.[34] Similar developments occurred among Chinese Muslims; the high level of acculturation among Muslim communities during the Ming period might also be linked to the appointment of many Muslims to military and civil positions.

A comparison of the Kaifeng Jewish community with Chinese Muslims demonstrates that, although the small size of the Jewish community and its lack of contact with other Jewish communities for a long period made it particularly susceptible to the influence of the Chinese milieu, that milieu was conducive to the acculturation of even a large minority. The most relevant comparison is with the Muslims know as the Hui, who, like the Jews, first came to China as traders, many arriving along the Silk Road, and then intermarried with the Han Chinese. Many Hui are the descendants of these traders and the local Chinese converted by them, but unlike the Jews, the Hui were greatly reinforced by a large migration from Central Asia in the thirteenth century, accompanying and contributing to the Mongol conquests. According to the 1990 census, there are 8.6 million Hui in China; they constitute about half of all Chinese Muslims and differ from the Turkic Muslims of western China with respect to their ethnic homogeneity, absence of a national language, and dispersal over large areas of China.

Until the end of Mongol rule in China (fourteenth century), the Hui remained in contact with their countries of origin. During this period they spoke Arabic, their acculturation to Chinese culture was limited, and, as Raphael Israeli wrote, they remained "Muslims in China" rather than "Chinese Muslims."[35] This changed during the Ming dynasty, when the decline in contacts with Muslims outside China and the openness of the literati to religious minorities resulted in considerable acculturation. The Hui adopted Mandarin and Chinese names, and they no longer wore distinctive Muslim clothing outside the mosques. Muslim writings, including a script written in Chinese characters on a monument in a mosque, asserted that Islam and Confucianism were basically the same. Wang Daiyu, the most significant Islamic writer of the Ming dynasty, presented a system of thought influenced significantly by Confucian concepts and ideas.[36]

The Hui spread throughout China during the early years of the Ming dynasty, and their relationships with the dominant Han population varied from region to region. In the northwest, distinctions were maintained, but in some areas of eastern and southeastern China acculturation and assimilation were considerable.[37] Acculturation was particularly extensive in remote, small communities: Ancestor worship was practiced, local spirits were placated, and Chinese mourning practices were adopted. However, even during the Ming period, when acculturation was at its height, the boundaries of Islam remained mostly intact in the large Muslim communities. Many mosques were built in the pagoda shape of Chinese temples, but within the mosques, apart from the mandatory Emperor's Tablets, distinctiveness was retained: Arabic inscriptions of verses from the Koran on the walls, prayers in Arabic, and white-capped, shoeless worshippers performing ritual ablutions.[38]

. Islamic distinctiveness was reinforced when the Ming dynasty was replaced by the Manchu Qing dynasty (1644–1911). At the end of the seventeenth century the lifting of restrictions on foreign trade increased contact with Muslims outside China and enabled more Chinese Muslims to go to Mecca on the hajj.[39] In the nineteenth century a process of deacculturation began with a renewed emphasis on religious distinctiveness, although a syncretistic tendency was evident in the Islamic "New Sect" that, like the White Lotus sects, incorporated forms of Chinese popular religion. On the more elite level a Chinese Muslim treatise linked Islamic and Chinese mythologies, pointing to the common origins of Islam and Confucianism.[40]

Christians in China

The settlement of Christians in China was far more limited than that of Muslims, and the historical data on the minority Christian communities are insufficient to provide meaningful comparisons with the Jews. An early settlement of Nestorian Christians ended with the fall of the T'ang dynasty in 907. They reappeared in the thirteenth century in the wake of the Mongol invasions, but many were driven out by the Ming dynasty in the fourteenth century, and those who remained appeared to have assimilated by the beginning of the seventeenth century, when the Jesuit missionary Matteo Ricci found no traces of them.[41] Christian missionaries entered China in about 1600, and the Jesuits were the first to stay in China for a long period. The missionary nature of the renewed Christian presence means that only a limited comparison can be made with the Kaifeng Jews, but it provides an example of religious groups that, unlike the Kaifeng Jews, were unwilling to adapt to the syncretistic religious milieu and sought instead to impose their closed religious boundaries and exclusiveness on Chinese converts.

Most Chinese had no problem combining Christianity with Chinese religions, but the missionaries forbade such syncretism and demanded an exclusive commitment from their converts. At first, the missionaries believed that it would be easy to convert the Chinese, who quickly declared their agreement with missionary teaching, but for the Chinese the Christian god was simply another new god to be incorporated into the population of deities that was constantly proliferating and being renewed. At the popular level, Christian saints were identified with Chinese saints and transformed into local deities, and Christian images and objects, such as those of the Eucharist, relics, and holy water, could, like the images and objects of Buddhism, be applied as magical formulas to attain this-worldly goals. Although Christian missionaries often encouraged the magical appeal of their religious paraphernalia, they also demanded an exclusive commitment that most Chinese were unwilling or unable to provide. Moreover, Christianity could not be integrated into the Chinese religious milieu because it placed itself above all temporal power, and when the missionaries tried to set up Christian communities, they were accused of sedition.

Like the Kaifeng Jews, the Jesuits sought the approval of the literati, although, unlike the Jews, this approval was seen as a step toward their conversion. The Jesuits succeeded in converting a few literati who were attracted by their scientific knowledge, and Ricci was especially admired by literati for his approval of Confucius, his knowledge of the Chinese classics, and his condemnation of popular forms of religion. The literati rejected Christianity once they came to understand that the Jesuits were proposing an exclusive adherence to a religion whose "Master of Heaven" did not resemble their conceptions of heaven as a spontaneous and impersonal anonymous power of order and animation in the universe. For their part the missionaries deplored the syncretism of the literati and their failure to appreciate that there could be only one truth and that this truth was transcendental and eternal. After about 1620 the Jesuits made no more conversions among the literati, and they directed their efforts to lower strata.[42]

Chinese converts to and sympathizers of Christianity tried to incorporate the religion into the syncretistic Chinese religious milieu by arguing that missionary teachings were in agreement with traditional Chinese ideas, but the missionaries would not let this be carried too far. The Jesuits, and Ricci in particular, were the most flexible, allowing their converts to incorporate selected Confucian-based traditions and practices without extending this tolerance to Buddhism and Taoism. Ricci justified this policy by arguing that Confucianism was basically a secular philosophy, although he acknowledged that it had been adversely affected by Buddhism and Taoism.

The Jesuits were opposed by the Dominicans and Franciscans, who insisted that Chinese converts be compelled to abandon all Confucian beliefs and rituals. The Dominicans and Franciscans were not impressed by the appeal of the Jesuits to the "heathen" emperor to support their case for the secularity of Confucianism. Nor were they impressed when the Jesuits pointed to the Kaifeng Jews' use of Chinese terms for God and participation in ancestral rituals to support their case for some flexibility. The arguments of the Dominicans and Franciscans that Confucianism was part of Chinese polytheism, that its doctrines were irreconcilable with monotheism, and that ceremonies such as the ancestral rituals had no place in Christian worship were supported by the Vatican, which threatened the Jesuits with excommunication if they disregarded the Vatican's rulings forbidding Confucian rituals and rescinding the Jesuit concessions to Chinese converts. The Chinese emperor took offense at the rulings and responded by expelling those missionaries who abided by them.[43]

Assimilation

When we turn from acculturation to assimilation, the importance of numerical differences between Jews and Muslims in China is clearly evident. With respect to assimilation, important elements of Chinese social structure—the extended family, clan, and political rule by a centralized bureaucracy—did not dispose the Jews to enter a peculiar structural niche in society. Most Kaifeng Jews were members of the merchant-artisan class, but, as many scholars have emphasized, the entrance of a number of Kaifeng Jews into the literati and bureaucracy contributed to the community's assimilation.⁴⁴ Jewish bureaucrats had to leave Kaifeng because, like all other civil servants, they were prohibited from holding official positions in the place of their birth. However, this emphasis on the social-structural features that encouraged both the acculturation and the assimilation of Chinese Jews does not adequately address the question of "the survival of the Chinese Jews," to adopt the title of Leslie's book.

Scholars of the Kaifeng community might be divided between those who ask, "How did it last so long?" and those who ask, "Why did it assimilate?" As Pollak wrote, "The most clear-cut object lesson derived by historians and sociologists from the ultimate absorption of the Chinese Jews . . . has of course been that numerically small peoples transplanted into strange and enormously larger societies that do not grind them down or forcibly segregate them have little or no chance of retaining their own cultures or community integrity over the long run."⁴⁵ One might ask, How long is the long run? As Leslie noted, few cities in the world have a continuous Jewish community and synagogue that extends well over 700 years.⁴⁶ Because Pollak, like Leslie, attributes this lengthy history in part to the tolerance of Chinese society, it would appear that tolerance was the cause of both the community's long-term survival and its final disappearance.

Xu acknowledges that the entrance of an increasing number of Jews into the ranks of Chinese officialdom of the Ming dynasty in the sixteenth and seventeenth centuries contributed to the eventual assimilation of Kaifeng Jews, but he describes the Kaifeng Jews in the early eighteenth century as a small yet flourishing community that still observed festivals and held services on the Sabbath. Xu writes that the absorption of the Kaifeng Jews was a long, slow process, but the overall impression that he gives is not so much of a community that gradually assimilated as a consequence of the tolerant features of traditional Chinese society but of a community whose virtual disappearance in the nineteenth century was the consequence of a combination of events related to the decline of China as a whole: floods, the Taiping Rebellion, and the suppression of Muslims with whom the Kaifeng Jews were commonly identified. This community remained vibrant so long as the Chinese empire was strong and relatively stable, but it was too small to withstand the heightened tensions and the crumbling of the empire in the eighteenth and nineteenth centuries.⁴⁷

It should not be forgotten that other Jewish communities in China, some apparently with substantial populations, had disappeared by the seventeenth century.⁴⁸ We will probably never know the factors that accounted for the longer survival of the Kaifeng community because none of the other communities left any records. Xu concludes that the Kaifeng community survived because of its uniqueness, but the absence of information on other Chinese Jewish communities makes it impossible to formulate the nature of this uniqueness. If, for example, the Kaifeng community was unique in maintaining a synagogue over hundreds of years, what was it about the community that led it each time, after an old synagogue's collapse or destruction, to restore a focus of the community? The answer may be that the economic and social opportunities in Kaifeng were greater than those in other Chinese cities and that some of the Jews from the other communities moved to Kaifeng, which had been the capital of the Song dynasty and a thriving economic metropolis. As Xu writes, the "development, growth and fall of the Kaifeng Jewish community parallels in many ways the rise and decline of Chinese society and of the city of Kaifeng in particular."[49]

If the entrance of Jews into the literati contributed to the community's assimilation, what aspects of the social structure of traditional China contributed to the community's survival? Irene Eber has argued that two factors, each related to the sinicization of the community, contributed to its distinctive identity and community survival. One factor was the Chinese patrilineal lineage organization that was adopted by the Kaifeng Jews together with Chinese family names. Chinese lineages generally trace their origin to one ancestor, go by one surname, are domiciled in one locality, and hold some properties, including burial grounds, in common. As patrilineal lineage groups, non-Jewish women who married into the community would adopt the religion of their husbands, and Jewish women who married out would do likewise.

Eber argues that what bound Kaifeng Jews together was not community but family identity; they met in the synagogue as members of Jewish families and not as members of a Jewish community.[50] It is not, however, self-evident why a lineage-based identity would necessarily remain linked to a particular religion, especially within the syncretistic and pluralistic milieu of Chinese religion. Eber writes that, so long as lineages remained Jewish, individual Jews were unlikely to abandon their Jewish identity, but the question then becomes, Why did lineages remain Jewish? One has to fall back on the overly general explanation of family tradition.

The second feature of the Chinese social structure that, according to Eber, reinforced Jewish identity was the importance of religious sects. Most Chinese participated in popular Chinese religion and were not affiliated with a particular religious organization, but a minority had more distinctive religious identities as members of sects. Eber writes that in the eighteenth century and thereafter Kaifeng Jews were identified—and in turn identified themselves—as a religious sect. By using this form of identification, Kaifeng Jews adopted a common Chinese pattern and eschewed any connection to a foreign religion with universal pretensions. The term *jiao* was applied to the Kaifeng Jews between the seventeenth and twentieth centuries, and Eber writes that *jiao* is probably best translated as "sect" in this particular context.[51] However, *jiao* is commonly translated as "religion" or "teaching," and its translation as "sect," placing it in the same category as the White Lotus movements, may be misleading.

The general use of the term *sect* by scholars of Chinese religion writing in English is likely to trouble sociologists of religion. Sects in the sociology of religion are defined as religious movements that differ from other religious organizations in their combination of two characteristics: their claim to a unique truth providing the only way to salvation, and the relatively high level of tension between the movement and its environment. These criteria are applicable to the White Lotus and other Buddhist-inspired movements as well as to movements that emerged among Muslims in China, but they are inappropriate for the Kaifeng Jewish community.

Eber notes that the religion of the Kaifeng Jews was, like the religion of most sects, highly syncretistic. Syncretism was a feature of most Chinese religion, but sects were more explicitly and radically syncretistic,[52] and the motivations behind their syncretism differed from those of the Kaifeng Jews. Chinese sects set out, in a highly self-conscious way, to create a new religious system out of the various religious traditions; they sought to provide a distinctive religion that they claimed restored the true unity underlying the component traditions of Chinese religion.[53] Unlike the sects, the Kaifeng Jewish community did not reach out to nonmembers by claiming an exclusive truth, and its syncretism was an accommodation rather than a challenge to the religious milieu and establishment.

Eber writes that both lineage and sect were forms of identity for the Kaifeng Jews, but these were unlikely to reinforce each other because the general pattern of sectarian membership was to provide an alternative to group membership based on family and locality, not to reinforce it. In contrast to the group basis of Chinese popular religion, it was the individual who was the unit of consideration in sects.[54] Associated as the Kaifeng Jews were with a specific locality, the benefits for them of identifying as a sect would have been dubious. Eber writes that, although sects were suppressed when they developed political aims and became rebellious, they were generally tolerated when pursuing purely religious goals.[55] It is true that many sects existed over long periods in peaceful obscurity,[56] but beginning in the eighteenth century the increased number of political and rebellious sects led to a decline in the state's tolerance of heterodoxy. In general, popular religious movements were persecuted not for their beliefs but because they were regarded as politically dangerous, and there seems to be little reason for the Kaifeng Jews to identify themselves with a type of religious organization that could result in official suspicion.

One dimension of the Kaifeng Jewish community did associate it with sects: its congregational organization with the commitment of its members to their place of worship and its religious leaders. In common with the Islamic communities in China and in contrast with most Chinese, the Kaifeng Jewish community was organized as a congregation, a form of religious organization rare in Eastern societies. With the exception of a tiny minority of devotees who became associated with Buddhist and Taoist monasteries, the major institutionalized religions in China did not have the benefit of a strong commitment among laypersons, most of whom worshipped at a number of temples according to the occasion and the services that they required. Sects were organized as congregations, and the tendency among scholars of Chinese religion has been to categorize all congregationally organized religious groups in China as sects. However, the Kaifeng Jews had both a community-based religion (anchored by lineage organization and ancestor worship to a particular locale) and a congregation with a more exclusive religious commitment among its members than was usually found among most Chinese. The importance of this form of organization for the lengthy survival of the Kaifeng Jews is supported by a comparison of Buddhism and Islam in China.

Buddhism did not enter China as a congregationally organized religion. It did not develop an organized laity with formal relationships to its monks, and most laypersons who worshipped in its temples attended non-Buddhist temples as well. Many Buddhist temples, like Taoist temples, were organized and governed by laypersons who put little emphasis on the relationship between their principal god and a particular religious tradition. Buddhist priests, like Taoist priests, were hired to perform certain rituals, but laypersons took daily care of the temples and often officiated at annual festivals and rites of passage. The importance of laypersons in temple organization left the Buddhist and Taoist priests and monks little autonomous power to prevent the blurring of Taoist and Buddhist religious boundaries within the amalgam of popular religion. As a consequence, Buddhism became a highly syncretized and integral component of Chinese religion without strong institutions and without a large exclusively committed laity.[57]

In contrast, Islam was organized on the basis of congregations. Lay Muslims were attached to particular mosques that they financially supported through organized taxation in the form of *zahat* (alms) and, in the case of more prosperous members, voluntary donations. In addition to worship, the mosques provided various services, including education and welfare, and each mosque had its own imam who possessed a wide area of authority and interpreted Islamic law for members of the congregation. In contrast to Buddhist and Taoist priests, who depended on donations and remuneration from individual clients as payment for their religious services, imams were employed by their congregations.[58] Although Muslims acculturated to Chinese culture, the organizational basis of Islam reduced the assimilation of Muslims and prevented Islam from becoming a syncretic component of Chinese religion.

Although sects emerged from within Chinese Islam, it would be misleading to categorize the whole of Chinese Islam as a sect. Raphael Israeli has written that Chinese Islam occupied a position somewhere between an institutional recognized religion and a sectarian movement. Chinese Islam was similar to sects in some of its ideological characteristics and functions, but unlike sects, its organizational basis was fragmented; local congregations were independent of each other and recognized no outside authority.[59] The sects' recruitment and organization of members across communities did arouse the suspicion of state agents,[60] but most regimes tolerated most forms of religion so long as their organization did not extend beyond the local level. Thus, although almost all Chinese dynasties suppressed sectarian movements, no official governmental persecution against Muslims was recorded until the Qing dynasty, which faced an upsurge of rebellious sects, including Islamic sects that sought Muslim regional autonomy.[61]

The congregational organization of Kaifeng Jews was similar to that of Chinese

Muslims, albeit on a much smaller scale. Muslims were able to find lodging, help, and protection among fellow believers when they traveled throughout China, but this was not possible for Kaifeng Jews after the disappearance of other Chinese Jewish communities.[62] As noted, many Muslims entered the literati and some rose to positions of high rank, but the size and widespread presence of Muslim communities made it far easier for the Muslim literati to remain in contact with their religion than the Jewish literati could. Although a number of Muslim literati no doubt assimilated into the non-Muslim population, the state bureaucracy did not promote Muslim assimilation on a large scale.[63]

Despite its small size, the Kaifeng community's congregational form of organization enabled it to continue over a long period, but the survival of a small community proved impossible in a period of social and political upheaval. Whereas the Chinese Muslims, who numbered in the millions, responded to the decline of the imperial empire by abandoning Chinese customs, emphasizing their separate identity, and fomenting militant rebellion, the Kaifeng Jews were unable to do the same.

Conclusion

Immanuel Kant explained the survival of the Kaifeng Jews as a consequence of the dissimilarity of Judaism and Confucianism, and he argued that when the minority's religion becomes similar to that of the majority, the minority will disappear.[64] Some scholars of Kaifeng Jews clearly disagree with Kant when they argue that the acculturation of the Kaifeng Jews was made possible by similarities between Judaism and Confucianism. As I have indicated, I take issue with this argument: The acculturation of the Kaifeng Jews was a consequence of a syncretistic religious milieu, not merely the result of similarities between Judaism and Confucianism.

Kant was correct in emphasizing the religious differences; the Judaism that was brought to China, in all likelihood from Persia, differed in its fundamental assumptions from Confucianism. Kant was wrong, however, in assuming that in all societies religious acculturation would soon be followed by assimilation. Kaifeng Jews lasted so long because their religious acculturation made it possible for them to reformulate their distinctiveness in a way that allowed for their acceptance within the flexible and pluralistic Chinese religious milieu. In the premodern European societies, in contrast, substantial religious acculturation would have meant assimilation. Substantial religious acculturation within the context of highly bounded religions could only mean conversion, and conversion generally meant assimilation within a generation or two. In fact, the European Jews, the Ashkenazim in particular, reinforced their religious boundaries, building a wall around the Torah as a protection against the idolatrous practices of the non-Jewish religious environment.

Conversion had little meaning for most Chinese, who did not identify with a single religion and participated with no feelings of contradiction in Confucianist, Taoist, and Buddhist temples and rituals. Such flexible boundaries resulted in the voluntary acculturation of a religious minority, but this religious tolerance and pluralism also enabled religious minorities to form separate niches within the religious milieu, like the many Chinese cults distinguished by their devotion to particular gods. The niche occupied by the relatively small community of Kaifeng Jews, however, depended on the stability of the social structure of Imperial China, and, once that structure began to disintegrate, the days of the community were numbered.

3. ELITE RELIGION AND POPULAR RELIGION

The Example of Saints

Folk Religion and Thaumaturgy

I noted in chapter 1 that Jews and non-Jews shared many magicoreligious beliefs and customs, even in those societies, such as medieval western and central Europe and early modern eastern Europe, where religious and social boundaries between Jews and non-Jews were strongest. Although the major beliefs, values, and ritual of what might be called rabbinic, official, or elite Judaism differed greatly from those of the Christian church, at the level of popular or folk religion there was an overlap and mutual influences between Jews and Gentiles. The focus of Jewish popular religion, like the popular religions of all peoples in traditional settings of the world religions, was this-worldly individual or familial problems, goals, and fears.[1]

The particular religious orientation to the world in folk or popular religion can be called magical or thaumaturgical. It is a demand for supernatural or supramundane assistance that provides relief from sickness, deprivations, and evil powers. Thaumaturgy deals with evil not as an ultimate problem but in highly specific forms, such as demons and witches who wish to do harm to the individual and his family.[2] Thaumaturgy was not an important element in the Judaism of the Talmud and the official prayers that attended to the interpretation of the religious law, praise and thanksgiving, recitation and affirmation of the religious code, repentance, and the commemoration of past events. Official Judaism gave little attention to providing individuals with supramundane assistance to obtain their worldly goals or to protect them from supramundane dangers. Rather, the foci of folk religion were to protect the individual against illness and misfortune, such as miscarriages, fire, and theft; to cure illnesses and infertility; and to fight against the evil forces, such as demons and the evil eye.[3]

The division between official and popular religion was reflected in a division of religious functionaries; whereas rabbis dealt with matters of religious law and ritual, magicians provided help in the vicissitudes of everyday life. This was never a rigid distinction; magical knowledge was conserved within rabbinic circles, and some rabbis gained reputations as miracle makers, but the distance between the rabbinic elite and nonscholarly Jews prompted many to seek help from magicians who were closer to them intellectually and socially. Jews would also on occasion turn to popular healers from the non-Jewish population.

Magicians varied in their degrees of professionalization and closeness to the scholarly elite. An example of a relatively professionalized type were the *ba'alei shem* (masters of the name; singular, *ba'al shem*) in Poland from the sixteenth through the eighteenth century. The increase in the number of *ba'alei shem*, beginning at the end of the seventeenth century and continuing in the eighteenth century, was concomitant with the greater popularity of kabbalah, especially what has come to be known as practical kabbalah. The *ba'alei shem* were acknowledged as authorities of magical knowledge, in particular, knowledge of the names of God and of the angels who were believed to effect cures and prevent the impairment of health and welfare by demonic and natural forces. The *ba'alei shem* vocalized the holy names in rituals and wrote them on amulets and other protective charms. In addition to their cures, they were believed to guarantee success in marriage and procreation, force robbers to return stolen goods, free prisoners, cause harm to peoples' enemies, resurrect the dead, provide for the speedy arrival to a distant place in a supramundane manner, and discover a soul's previous incarnations. Their techniques included written incantations, exorcism, chiromancy, and herbal medicine.

The designation of the *ba'alei shem* as kabbalists contributed to their authority and status. Prominent rabbis were included among the *ba'alei shem*, and some were appointed by Jewish communities in official religious positions. Although some rabbinic scholars distanced themselves from practical kabbalah, most members of the rabbinic elite assumed that it was efficacious and some made use of the services provided by the *ba'alei shem*.[4]

It was Israel ben Eliezer, a *ba'al shem* known as the Ba'al Shem Tov (Master of the Good Name, Besht being the common acronym), who was pronounced, long after his death, to have been the first leader of the Hasidic movement, a movement based on the appeal of saints. The Besht did not seek to found a movement, but a range of traits and an endowment of powers that went beyond those of other *ba'alei shem* were attributed to him and were perceived at a later date to be common to the zaddikim, the saintly leaders of the Hasidic branches.

The Besht was a mystic and redeemer as well as a magician. As a *ba'al shem*, he was an expert in exorcism, amulets, and other techniques of magical defense, but he also saw himself as one of those individuals with rare qualities who was able to attain *devekut*, the adherence of the soul to God. He reported that his soul had ascended to the upper worlds, where he spoke with the messiah, and he regarded himself and was seen by members of his circle as a mediator between those upper worlds and earthly existence. As a mediator, he could carry up the prayers of ordinary men and redeem their souls, and he was also imbued with the powers to protect the Jewish community from religious persecution and the plague. Thus the Besht was seen to combine the quintessential talents of a saintly leader that came to typify the zaddikim of the Hasidic movement.[5] He was both a thaumaturge and an exemplar of religious values and modes of religious behavior, traits that characterize saints in general.

Saints and Judaism

It is with respect to the dual functions of exemplar and thaumaturge that saints have occupied an important place in the interaction of religious elites and lay masses, of official and popular religion. An implicit distinction between official and popular religion was made by Robert L. Cohn when he argued that sainthood comes not from the center of Judaism but from its periphery.[6] The center of Judaism for Cohn is classical rabbinic Judaism, and saints come from the periphery of North African Jewry and Hasidism. Cohn conceives of the saint as a model for imitation and an object of veneration, and he writes that, unlike other world religions, classical rabbinic Judaism never officially designated a category of humans as models of pious behavior or worthy of special deference. Thus Judaism does not have the equivalent of the saints of Catholicism and the Christian Orthodox churches, the *walī* of Sufism, the guru of Hinduism, the *arahant* of Theravada Buddhism, and the bodhisattva of Mahayana Buddhism.

Cohn points to characteristics of Judaism that account for the minor role of saints. First and most important, Judaism subordinates the individual to the collectivity. Saints in other religions are involved in the redemption of individuals, but in Judaism salvation is primarily the achievement of the collectivity. It is the religious observance of all Jews and not the intercession of saints that will bring the messiah. The Jewish messiah is yet to come, and Judaism has no unique founder, messianic or prophetic, who in other world religions (Buddhism, Christianity, Islam) has provided a model for would-be saints.

The collective orientation is evident in Judaism's rituals and religious celebrations. Most of the religious festivals commemorate national events and celebrate national salvation. Supplication to God for forgiveness of sins is in the first-person plural ("We have sinned"), and even on those days when Jews seek atonement for their individual sins, they do so as part of a group. It should be noted that the collectivism that, according to Cohn, moves saints to the periphery in Judaism also accounts in part for the relative absence of thaumaturgy in official Judaism. The prayers of petition, calling for the health, sustenance, and deliverance from persecution, sickness, and famine of the Jewish people as a whole are not directed to the worldly goals of individuals and their protection from supramundane dangers. Thaumaturgy was a focus of folk religion and, as noted, also that of saints. Cohn writes that the emphasis on collective redemption in Judaism minimizes any demand among Jews for the intercession of saints in their this-worldly pursuits, but it is not self-evident that collectivism would make the Jews an exception to the otherwise ubiquitous demand in traditional societies for supramundane assistance in this world.

Another fundamental characteristic of Judaism that Cohn notes is not conducive to the production of saints is the emphasis on religious study as an end in itself. The dominant model of religiosity is the rabbinic sage, who always remains subordinate to the Torah he studies. The interpretation of religious law in classical rabbinic literature is conducted without hagiography or accounts of the biographies and personalities of the sages. The emphasis on religious scholarship as a value for all (male) Jews and the egalitarian principle of the same religious law binding all Jews provides no possibility for a separate, superior path, such as that of monkhood.

With respect to other characteristics of Judaism that are not conducive to sainthood, Cohn's comparison is primarily with Christianity. Cults of saints in Catholicism focus on the dead. Judaism's ban on necromancy and its rules of purity severely limit the possibilities of contact with the dead or their relics. Martyrdom is an important element of many Christian saints. Judaism has its martyrs, but their individuality tends to disappear in the highly stylized narratives that represent them as standing for the Jewish people as a whole.

Despite the characteristics of Judaism that minimize the importance of sainthood, Cohn acknowledges that saints were prevalent among Jews in Muslim countries, that they continue to be important among Israeli Jews from Muslim countries, and that among the Ashkenazim saints are central in Hasidism. More generally, Cohn writes that Jews have a propensity to revere mystical leaders as saints and holy men who "have occasionally achieved a status analogous to that of saints in other religions."[7] If sainthood has been common among Jews, one might ask in what sense it is on the periphery. The meaning of periphery for Cohn would appear to be something that is outside the boundaries of classical rabbinic Judaism or official religion, and with respect to the relationship between sainthood and official religion, the comparison is between Judaism and Christianity. Cohn notes that the church hierarchy created the cult of saints to serve its interests. In Judaism, by contrast, no official hierarchy or organization like the church had authoritative means to canonize saints. In this respect, however, it is Christianity, more specifically Catholicism, that is the exception among the world religions.

Sainthood is part of official Catholicism, but as in other religions, the sainthood as represented by the religious elite and the sainthood found in popular religion are different. The comparisons in this chapter focus on the relationships between official and popular forms of religion with respect to sainthood. These relationships have differed and overlapped to various degrees. The general characteristics of Judaism, like those of other religions, have influenced these relationships.

Saints and Max Weber

Saints have been neglected in the comparative sociology of religion. Perhaps one reason for this neglect is that Max Weber, the most important source of conceptual and analytical frameworks for the comparative sociologist of religion, did not distinguish the saint as a religious type alongside such types as the prophet, priest, and magician.[8] In its most general meaning as holy person, the term *saint* can be used to refer to a number of the religious types distinguished by Weber, but as a specific type within popular forms of religion, perhaps the term *mystagogue* comes closest to the common meanings of *saint*: a type with personal rather than office charisma, magical powers rather than divine revelation, and the support of a community or congregation rather than individual clients.[9]

In the absence of a systematic discussion of the saint, it is Weber's discussion of the religious virtuoso that provides a number of relevant points for a comparative analysis of saints, especially as it attends to the interaction of elite and mass religiosity. Weber contrasts virtuoso religiosity and mass religiosity by pointing to the recognition, evident in all world religious contexts, that humans are differently qualified in religious ways and that few are capable of seeking the sacred values in a perfect form.[10] Weber gives various examples of virtuoso religiosity, but the relevance for an analysis of saints is indicated by his particular attention to monks, who have been the major source of saints in a number of world religions.[11]

Weber wrote that hierocratic organizations, which seek to monopolize the distribution of religious benefits within societies, struggle against the autonomous development of virtuoso religion because it is seen as a challenge to the general accessibility to sacred values provided by the organizations. In the hierocratic organizations called churches, in which charisma is separated from the person, the struggle with virtuoso religion is one between office charisma and personal charisma. Rather than deny the legitimacy of all virtuoso religiosity, hierocratic organizations admit that full adherence to the religion's highest ideals is an extraordinary achievement that can be channeled for the benefit of the majority, who lack the qualifications or ability to achieve such heights. Thus virtuoso religions, particularly as organized in monastic organizations, can be transformed into instruments of hierocratic control, even though tensions often persist between hierocrats and virtuosos.[12] The relevance of Weber's discussion for an analysis of saints becomes evident at this point. All world religions formulate a category of persons, living and dead, who are believed to exemplify the sacred values of the religion and who have achieved or are approaching its ultimate goals. Religious elites seek to monopolize the formulation of the category, the labeling of persons who are judged suitable for inclusion within the category, the specification of the benefits that the masses obtain from the category, and the channeling of the interaction between the category and the masses.

Weber's discussion of hierocratic organizations and virtuoso religion can be read as a distinction between two types of religious elites: (1) the hierocratic elite whose regulation of access to religious benefits requires a considerable involvement with society and power relationships and (2) the virtuosos whose concentration on the highest religious values and goals leads many of them to dissociate themselves from society and its institutions. As Weber noted, to gain and maintain support from the masses, virtuosos make compromises with the religiosity of everyday life,

Elite Religion and Popular Religion

but to remain virtuosos, they are required to maintain a distance between themselves and the masses.[13]

Where there is a clear differentiation between hierocratic and virtuoso elites, there is the possibility of alternative formulations of the characteristics and labeling of saints, but as Weber's discussion of the Buddhist case makes clear, the world religions vary considerably with respect to this differentiation. It was the Catholic Church, which came to make a clear distinction between priest and monk, that provided Weber with the framework for a discussion of hierocracy and virtuosity. Weber acknowledged the absence of a distinction between hierocracy and virtuosity in Buddhism when he wrote that Buddhism found the best solution for tension between the two by being, from its beginnings, a religion created by and for monks.[14] In fact, although there is no hierocratic organization distinct from the virtuosos in Buddhism, a somewhat parallel distinction developed between the village and town monks, who performed various religious services for the laity, and the forest monks, who focused on the path of salvation. It was the forest monks who provided the saints of Buddhism,[15] but in religious contexts with hierocratic organizations the hierocracy selected at least some of the saints from its own ranks or past occupiers of offices. Thus members of the hierocracy who held charisma of office when living became attributed with the personal charisma of saints when dead.

Weber wrote that the Eastern religions' emphasis on meditation as the appropriate religious action of virtuosos limited their influence on the religiosity and lifestyle of the masses. The orientation of the masses toward the virtuosos in the East took the form of worshiping them as saints and seeking the use of their powers to attain salvation and mundane ends.[16] This comment of Weber can be extended to popular representations of a category, which may usefully be termed saints, in the contexts of all world religions: Saints are humans, living and/or dead, whose divine status or nearness to the divine provides devotees with the means of attaining soteriological and mundane goals. In contrast to the representation of saints as exemplars of the highest ideals and virtues of the religion, which is common among all world religion elites, the representation common among all world religion masses is that of intercessors, or divine beings in their own right, who attain valued goals for their devotees or followers.

The importance of saints in almost all traditional popular forms of the world religions can be understood as the attraction of the combination of familiar humanness and other divineness. Living or having lived mortal lives, saints are believed to be able to understand and sympathize with human feelings and requests, and even if they themselves have forsaken worldly pleasures, the human natures of saints means that they can empathize with worldly requests. Unlike the remote and awesome high gods, saints are fathomable and accessible, and compared with lower deities, whose natures are often conceived in ambiguous ways, saints are more dependable. But the appeal to saints is also based on their difference from ordinary humans. Although elites are inclined to emphasize the imitability as well as the otherness of saints, it is the dissimilarity of saints, their efficacy because of their embodiment or nearness to the divine, that is dominant in popular religion.

The Catholic Church

The Catholic Church developed the most institutionalized formulation of sainthood among the world religions. The hierocratic features of the Catholic Church, with its level of organization, hierarchy of office charisma, and transnational power that had no equivalent in other world religions, were major factors in this institutionalization. The development in Christianity of what is commonly called the cult of saints, revolving around shrines, relics, and other paraphernalia, was interpreted in the past as one of the church's concessions to polytheistic populations and to vulgarized Christianity. The cult of saints was seen as a strategy of the church to facilitate the conversion and retain the commitment of the ignorant masses.

It is true that saints often took the place of the pagan gods in the Christianization process, but rather than being a grudging accommodation to popular religion, the development of worship centered on saints' shrines was initiated and patronized by bishops in their building of strong ecclesiastical structures linked to political consolidations and economic growth. Economic and political interests were in affinity with religious dispositions: The elite of the church ardently venerated the saints and believed in their miracles.[17]

In comparison with the Christianity of the eastern Mediterranean, where there was more devotion of living saints as intercessors, the Occidental Church attempted to resolve the tension between the routinized charisma of office with the personalized charisma of living holy people by encouraging the cults of dead saints. Living persons, recognized as saints because of their exemplary asceticism and devotions, were difficult for the church to control, but once dead, the official hagiographies presented them as exemplars of orthodox, official doctrines and practice, and the saints' power was channeled in the church's interests.[18] The saints were commemorated on feast days, typically on the purported anniversaries of their deaths, and their miracles were systematically recorded.[19] The church's regulation of saints' relics, by placing them in churches and cathedrals and directing their use, played an important part in making the saints a central part of official Christian worship. Relics were objects of devotion long before the spread of saints' images, and ecclesiasticals argued that relics were superior to images because they would be part of the resurrection. The demand for relics gave rise to duplications, thefts, and transfers.[20]

Offerings to saints provided a source of income for monasteries and churches, and as protectors and patrons of those institutions, the saints reinforced the prestige of abbots and bishops, who were the representatives of the saints in this world and possible candidates for sainthood themselves after they passed on to the next. The monasteries were the major context of canonization in the early centuries of the church; episcopal canonization became an established practice in the tenth and eleventh centuries, and papal canonization developed gradually with the growth of papal authority. Episcopal and papal canonization coexisted for some time, but beginning in the late twelfth century papal commissions were charged with investigating every formal request, and the number of petitions declined as the procedures became more complicated and expensive.[21] The belief, prevalent in the early medieval period, that noble birth was a precondition of the moral and spiritual perfection of saints continued in northern Europe in later centuries, but in southern Europe the religious values of humility and poverty, promoted by the mendicant orders, reduced the proportion of saints from aristocratic and royal families.[22]

The notion of the saint as intercessor was formulated by the early church, which taught that the martyrs passed immediately into God's presence and that, having accumulated a store of merit, they could protect others and intercede for them. When the notion of sainthood was extended from martyrs to others, such as dead bishops, intercession remained a central belief. Jesus was referred to as the mediator because he shared two natures, divine and human, but his mediation did not rule out the need for the intercessors—Mary, the angels, and the saints. As the mother of Jesus who bound men to God, Mary was the most efficacious intercessor, and in the later Middle Ages the church sought to promote devotion to Mary over that of the saints. Although the church came to be sensitive to criticisms of saints' cults, the Council of Trent in 1563 proclaimed that the saints reigned with Christ and it justified seeking their help. However, the number of papal canonizations was low: eight in the fourteenth century, sixteen in the fifteenth, six in the sixteenth, twenty-four in the seventeenth, and twenty-nine in the eighteenth.[23]

In contrast to the elites of other world religions, the elite of the Catholic Church promoted saints not just as exemplars but also as efficacious intercessors. This difference was related to the fact that only in Christianity was there a church that sought a religious monopoly over the masses by incorporating them into a comprehensive system of magicoreligion. In the official procedures for canonization established in the early seventeenth century, miraculous intercession after death was one of the three general requirements that candidates for sainthood, apart from martyrs, had to satisfy (the other two requirements were doctrinal purity and heroic virtue).[24] The incorporation of the masses was only partly successful, however, and the various transformations of saints in popular Christianity resulted in considerable differences between the meanings and representations of elites and masses.

One dimension of the transformations of saints in popular religion was that saints were given greater prominence in the official pantheon than other supramundanes. The official dogma of the church consistently portrayed God as the ultimate source of power, Christ, often together with Mary, as the appropriate center of devotions, and the saints, somewhat lower in the pantheon, as channels through which God's grace was distributed. In popular religion, God and Christ tended to remain in the background as distant entities, and devotions were directed principally to the saints whose power could be thought of in more accessible, personal terms. Despite the efforts of the church to restrict sainthood to the dead, the popular saints included living persons—"holy men" (or women) whose sacredness enabled them to perform social functions, such as reconciling conflicting groups and restoring peace to communities. Examples of living saints as foci of pilgrimage can be found in most periods, up to and including the twentieth century, although their numbers were always small compared with dead saints.[25]

The number of popular saints multiplied far beyond the number canonized by the church. Between 1185 and 1431 there were seventy petitions for canonization, of which half were successful, but there were hundreds more popular saints. Although there were fewer canonizations from the period of the Counter-Reformation, popular saints continued to be just as numerous. Thus for centuries, alongside the official saints, many of whom aroused little interest among the masses, were the popular, mainly local, saints, who were worshiped with little or no involvement of the higher ranks of the church.[26] Unlike the official saints, many of whom were from aristocratic families, popular saints often came from lower strata,[27] and fiestas in their honor included rituals of inversion and reversal, which expressed opposition to the religious elite and the social hierarchy.[28]

By supplying relics, the church contributed to a hagiocentric popular religion that was hardly consistent with its official dogma of the centrality of God and the Christ. As concrete objects, relics appeared to afford direct and immediate contact with the sources of supramundane power, and the saints, through their relics, were believed to be forever alive and participating in communities.[29] In the later Middle Ages the church made greater efforts, often through the mendicant orders, to direct devotions to Christ and Mary, and the pilgrimage sites associated with these figures increased, especially those of Mary. Saints remained central to popular religion, and the activities and objects associated with the saints, such as relics, became part of the Marian devotions.[30] In recent centuries the saints have declined in importance compared with Mary in popular Catholicism,[31] and Mary's prominence surged at the end of the nineteenth and the beginning of the twentieth centuries when a number of Marian pilgrimages and shrines began to attract large numbers from wide areas.[32] With the decline of systems of patronage, which appear to have provided the model for relationships between saints and devotees, it was the family that became more important as an inductive model for relationships with the divine, and it was the mother who replaced the patron saints as the major intercessor.[33]

In popular Catholicism the saints and Mary are called on principally for their thaumaturgical powers in achieving this-worldly goals. This involved some displacement of the hierarchy of goals associated with the saints in official Christianity. Saints were presented by the elite as models of holiness who, by rejecting this-worldly pleasures and mortifying the flesh, demonstrated to others the appropriate path to salvation. The masses subordinated the soteriological linked motifs of the saints to their own everyday concerns: the healing of humans and their animals, recovery of stolen objects, marriage arrangement, and protection of households from thieves, harmful weather, and evil spirits. Two healing saints, Sebastian and Roche, who provided protection against the plague, were worshiped at one time throughout Catholic Christendom, and many other saints specialized in particular illnesses, such as eye troubles or deafness, or in special protection, such as from insects or fire. Nonspecialized saints, including Mary, were also greatly preoccupied with curing illnesses.[34] Cures and other dispensations were effected by a wide variety of procedures that were seen as providing some contact with the saint: touching the saints' shrines, images, and relics and drinking the water used to wash them.[35]

In exchange for the saints' help or protection, individuals and groups promised the saints devotion, obeisance, and behaviors such as fasting and visiting and contributing to the upkeep of the shrine. Rather than the elite representations of the saints as ideal humans who sublimate their own feelings in order to assist others to salvation, the saints in popular Catholicism were participants in relationships of exchange. They were attributed with the emotional attributes typical of humans and, far from being models of mercy and forgiveness, they exacted cruel punishment if they felt slighted or cheated. Saints were subject to humiliation or punishment through their relics and images if it was believed that they had refused a request or failed in achieving their devotees' goals; for example, relics were placed in the ground covered with thorns, and images were whipped or pelted with mud and water.[36]

The importance of saints for this-worldly rather than soteriological goals was evident when vows were made to saints by collective actors or by villages or other communities. The common interest for protection against epidemics, plagues, and drought were the basis of vows that included not working on the saint's day, fasting on the day before, holding a procession to the saint's shrine, and holding a charity feast. In premodern social structures of communities that had clear social boundaries and constituted social worlds apart from other communities, the saint was a divine patron and protector of the community; the saint's image or relics were the major focus of the community's devotions and the central symbols of the community's identity. Thus most of the popular saints held meaning only for those who resided in the location of the saints' shrines, which was generally the village in rural areas and the neighborhood in towns.[37] From about the middle of the twentieth century, when even the most isolated rural areas of Europe were becoming increasingly cosmopolitan, local shrines declined in importance, but a study of a rural area in Spain in the 1960s showed that local shrines were still the foci of community identity. The shrines were "virtually totem objects," and the sharper a community's boundaries and the greater its cohesion, the more likely it was to have a shrine of a saint or Mary as its patron and symbol.[38]

Popular local religion that focused on saints had its own sacred objects, locations, and calendar with its particular feast and fast days, and these practices differed from and occasionally conflicted with those of the church. The church attempted to eliminate local practices around the saints, but although the church might have succeeded in pressuring people to observe a ritual, it was largely unsuccessful in preventing observances. Conflict could occur between a local community and church agencies if the community arranged a celebration around its saint on a day of obligatory rituals in the church calendar, but in general the two pantheons and sacred geographies coexisted and often fused with each other. The generalized devotions propagated by the nonlocated institutions of the church, such as mendicant and teaching orders, missionaries, and the Vatican, were directed to the individual and family and lacked the component of community solidarity and identity of the local shrines. Local communities thwarted the attempts of the elite to integrate them with greater traditional Christianity by appropriating the generalized devotions and focusing them on the shrine.[39]

Up to recent times the veneration of local unofficial saints was recognized and generally unopposed by the bishops, and parish priests were made part of the local popular religion when they were called on to commute vows, pardon a person or community for nonfulfillment, and lead the communities in processions of the saints, especially during times of epidemics, drought, and floods.[40] The church officially recognized some local saints when, in 1635, it made beatification a category of canon law. Beatification implied the recognition of existing saints' cults that had been approved by local churches and local civil authorities.[41] However, the worship of saints moved beyond practices justified by the church when symbols of saints were set up in the fields and mixed with nature and fire religion.[42]

The attempts by post–Vatican II priests in rural areas to redirect the religious action of their parishioners away from thaumaturgy and toward a greater concern with individual salvation involved centering the religion more on God and Christ and reducing the religious activities around the saints. Throughout Europe saint processions have been targets of reform by progressive priests who have objected to the devotion of images and to "profane" action, such as music and dancing, which are part of the festivities around the saints. However, priests have met with lay opposition when they have attempted to remove saints' images from the churches or changed the arrangement of images, placing Mary or Jesus in the place of the saints. This conflict has led some laypersons to become pious anticlerics and to assert that it is laity and not the priests who are the carriers of the eternally valid religion.[43]

Hinduism and Buddhism

No other world religion had a hierocratic organization like the Christian church that developed an official category of saints who were intercessors as well as exemplars. The elites of the other world religions differed, however, in providing a basis for the development of saints by the extent to which they differentiated humans in terms of religious status and qualifications. Hindu and Buddhist elites made clear divisions between the religiously qualified, who were able to aspire to the ultimate salvation of release from the cycle of births and rebirths, and others within the religion who could aspire to the proximate salvation of a good rebirth in the next life, either on earth or in a heaven. The hierarchy of salvation goals required a differentiation of salvation paths: Ultimate salvation could be attained only by ascetic discipline and meditation, which required detachment from the mundane world, whereas proximate salvation was attained by the accumulation of merits. Progress along the path to ultimate salvation required an accumulation of merits in the present and past lives, but this relationship between the two paths did not distract from the formulation that the religious ideal was not incumbent upon all and that only a few could attain the ultimate goal of self-transcendence.[44] Two categories, each with a different salvation goal and its appropriate path, could produce two representations of exemplars, but the virtuoso could be meaningfully considered only within the path to perfection, and an exemplar of what Weber called "average religiosity" could hardly qualify as a saint.

Weber wrote that hierocratic organizations struggle against virtuosos because the virtuoso claim to personal charisma and superior spirituality contradicts the organization's interests in regulating the religiosity of the masses by making the sacred values accessible to all.[45] However, Weber's point that hierocratic elites oppose virtuosos by emphasizing democracy in sacred values is not applicable to Hinduism and Buddhism because they are built on double standards of religious values related to ascriptive categories of humans. Salvation in both Hinduism and Buddhism has been represented in elite formulations as dependent on the achievement of merit accumulation extending over multiple lifetimes, but for single lifetimes the differentiation of religious qualities has prominent ascriptive elements: Only a person born with the appropriate accumulation of merits can take the ultimate transcendental path. In Hinduism the caste system joins religious ascription with socioeconomic ascription, and the highest caste, the Brahmins, have attempted to restrict accessibility to the higher religious goal and path. With the partial exception of Sri Lanka, accessibility to the higher religious path in Theravada Buddhism is not restricted to a particular caste or socioeconomic category, but Buddhist elites claim that, as a consequence of behaviors in previous lives, humans are born unequal in religious qualifications. Thus, at least in the formulations of elites, saints as exemplars of the highest religious values are found within ascriptively delineated categories.

Not all members of the religious elites in Hinduism and Buddhism take the virtuoso path of renunciation, which is the way of saints. Although by no means clear-cut, there are divisions within the religious elites between the more priestly pattern directed toward good rebirths and this-worldly goals, and the pattern of renunciation directed toward release from the cycle of births and rebirths. In Hinduism, Brahmins are associated with the priesthood, and, having admitted the superiority of the path of renunciation, which has attracted individuals from other castes, they have attempted to restrict it to their own caste or, alternatively, to the three upper *varnas*.[46] In the Buddhist monkhood, distinctions are made between the village (and town) monks, for whom monkhood provides greater opportunities to accumulate merit and who provide various religious and social services for laypersons, and the forest monks, always a minority, whose more radical path of renunciation requires them to be more reclusive.[47]

CHAPTER 3

It is the sadhus, the seekers of *moksha* (ultimate salvation) in Hinduism, and the *arahants*, the seekers of nirvana in Buddhism, who provide the candidates for saints in the common elite sense of exemplariness, but the renouncers' goal and path would appear inappropriate to the development of saints in the common popular sense of efficacious intercessors and divine beings. Because renouncers are expected to reduce their interaction with others to a minimum, they normally would have little opportunity to develop as intercessors when alive, and the characterization of *moksha* in Hinduism as an anonymous, impersonal, and blissful state and of nirvana in Buddhism as absolute extinction leaves little possibility for the dead renouncer to intercede on behalf of others. Compared with Christian beliefs in the continuation of the saints' spirits close to God, the notions of fusion with the impersonal divine and of a "blowing out" of illusionary existence do not appear congenial to calling on dead saints as intercessors. The gods and other supramundanes in Hinduism and Buddhism, who reside in paradises or other-worldly realms, provide humans with the supramundane means to obtain this-worldly goals. In the devotionalist movements of Hinduism, the gods not only help their devotees to achieve worldly aims but also provide a path of salvation to a good rebirth or paradise. Elite formulations in Buddhism have generally confined the efficacy of the gods, who have not yet attained ultimate salvation, to the this-worldly goals of devotees. Unlike the Buddhist gods, the dead *arahants* have attained final salvation, and this makes them unsuitable to play the role of popular saints who accomplish the worldly goals of devotees.

Compared with the emphasis on dead saints in Christianity, live saints have been common in Hinduism and Buddhism. Developments within popular Hinduism and Buddhism have included the transformation of ascetic renouncers into saints who are believed to achieve their devotees' soteriological and this-worldly goals. One type of transformation, which is common in Hinduism, is to make the ascetic renouncer a god-man. Another transformation is to tap the supramundane energies engendered by the renouncer's spiritual progress toward salvation for the achievement of this-worldly goals. Elite formulations acknowledge that the path of renunciation generates extraordinary powers but state that the true renouncer will not use those powers. However, the dependence of renouncers on offerings from others has provided openings for communities or movements of devotees; the combination of devotees' entreaties and the renouncers' understanding of their interests has resulted in many renouncers becoming thaumaturges in Hinduism and Buddhism.

In the fluid polytheism of Hinduism, with its vast variety of divinities, numerous god-men or saints have been conceived of as divine. Hindus normally differentiate between immortal deities and mortal humans, but the fluid boundaries between deities and humans in the Hindu cosmology are congenial to the claims of divine status and extraordinary powers of god-men and goddess-women. Hindu saints are often conceived as incarnations of the major gods of the devotionalist communities and movements: Shiva and Vishnu and his avatars, especially Rama and Krishna. The focus of devotionalist movements on a single god entails conceiving other gods as subordinate forms of the god elevated by devotees, and some devotionalist followings of saints believe that the saint is superior to other manifestations of the divine, such as nonhuman deities, who are displaced or relegated by the saint. Divine saints include the dead, such as the founders of monastic orders, and the living, such as heads of monasteries, who, as perfect devotees, may be seen as continuing to manifest the divinity of the original founders.

It would be misleading to argue that the transformation of the ascetic renouncer into a god-man saint originates solely from popular religion. Founders of religious orders have also been acclaimed as gods by their close disciples, who seek to imitate their asceticism. However, a large following can come only from the laity, who, without following the lifestyle of renunciation, aspire through their devotion to the saint to attain the renouncers' goal of salvation as well as this-worldly goals.[48] It is the more sedentarized renouncers, whose residences are located near their communities of origin, who are more likely to direct their religious action to the goals of their lay devotees. This is the case among the renouncers from the Raika people, a camel-herding caste in Rajasthan. Although some Raika renouncers provide no assistance to householders, they are few and most of the renouncers do provide services, the most important of which are blessings that are believed to provide remedies for illness, infertility, and other problems. In contrast to priests, who are expected to perform rituals in accord with strict formulas, the renouncers are free from the structures of ritual obligations, and it is their austerities that are believed to cause an inner transformation, which endows them with a divine power to alleviate sufferings. Renouncers who impose on themselves the most intense austerities are believed to perform the greatest miracles, such as bringing the dead back to life and curing otherwise incurable diseases.[49]

In Buddhism the centrality of the Buddha as a human who rose above the gods by his discovery of the true path to ultimate salvation has created a greater differentiation between humans and deities than in Hinduism. As the exemplar who discovered and took the true way, the Buddha is the greatest of saints, and although the supramundane powers of deities are believed by many to be derived mythically from the Buddha, the recognition of the Buddha as a human who achieved nirvana has not been conducive to god-man cults. However, some popular shrines center on the images and relics of Buddha, and these have been reconciled in various ways to the doctrine that the Buddha is extinct. The bodily relics of the Buddha and other Buddhist saints—their hair, teeth, ashes, and the objects associated with them, such as their alms bowls—are believed to embody the supernatural powers that the saint achieved through his efforts on the path to salvation.

Thus, although neither the dead nor living renouncers are generally considered gods, their supramundane power, which they achieved from taking the transcendental path, qualifies them as saints in the popular sense. The warning purportedly made by the Buddha that renouncers should not be diverted by the special powers that they can wield has been repeated by other Buddhist teachers. Renouncers who have gained reputations as miracle workers may try to escape the attentions of the laity, but the more they have attempted to demonstrate their indifference to the world, the more they have impressed the laity, who see them not only as exemplary pious renouncers but also as miracle makers who heal the sick, bring prosperity, and foretell the future.

The prominent living saint-monks of the forest attract two circles of followers: (1) an inner circle of ordained disciples who wish to learn and follow the path of the meditation masters and (2) an outer circle of rural lay supporters who venerate the saints for their willingness to transfer their blessings to others. Blessings are received through the amulets, which the saints sacralize by chanting words over them, purifying them with sacred water, and performing other acts of transference. The amulets can carry meanings of ascetic practices for the disciple monks and world-affirming prosperity for the lay supporters.[50]

Islam and Judaism

The elites of Sunni Islam and Judaism, the ulema and rabbis, have recognized holy men (almost never women), often from their own ranks, whose exemplary lives in accordance with the religious values and systems of religious laws are believed to have brought them closer to God. These saints have not, however, been differentiated as a particular category of humans to be venerated in official cults. All Muslims and all Jews are understood to be bound to their respective single systems of religious law: They have not been hierarchized in terms of lower and higher soteriological goals, nor has there been a higher path to salvation, such as the supererogatory piety of monastic Christianity. Shi'a Islam has its imams, who are believed to have been divinely chosen and to be infallible, but according to Twelver Shi'is, the largest Shiite group, the last imam went into occultation in the ninth century and is expected to return in the form of the Mahdi, the future savior of the world. In the absence of imams, religious interpretations and functions were transferred to the jurists, who, since the eighteenth century, have formed a hierarchy with the ayatollahs at the top. Sunni Muslims have not had sanctified imams or authoritative bodies to interpret doctrine, and anyone who is able to recite and knows the ritual can lead the Friday prayer at the mosque.

The tendencies of religious egalitarianism in Islam and Judaism, albeit confined to males, were particularly evident in traditional Jewish communities, in which the vast majority of males received some formal religious education. The emphasis placed on the value of the study of the Torah for all Jewish men prevented a sharp distinction between a literate religious elite and an illiterate lay mass. In Judaism as in Islam, however, the vast development of commentaries and interpretations restricted the elucidation of meaning in the sacred texts to a small elite who had acquired specialized training. The scholarship and debates of the rabbinic elite were often remote from the daily life of the Jewish masses, and on some occasions popular leaders challenged the notion of religious study as the major value of Jewish society. Similarly, the esoteric study of the ulema, many of whom were cut off from the social world of the masses, encouraged popular movements to produce their own men of authority.

As scholars and interpreters of their respective religious laws who were neither priests nor monks, the ulema and rabbis were not predisposed to initiate or support a highly differentiated category of saints. Islam had an official status within Islamic states and Judaism was upheld by semi-autonomous Jewish community organizations, but there were no hierocratic organizations like the Catholic Church that could have constituted a body of official saints. However, doctrines of salvation in Islam and Judaism, like those of Christianity, were amenable to the possibility of calling on the help of dead persons who reside with or are close to God. Visiting saints' tombs was admitted from an early date in Islamic canonical law, and most of the ulema schools accepted the miracles of saints. Writing on Morocco, Vincent Cornell states that a significant minority of Islamic saints were legal scholars and that in the hagiography written by ulema, saints were legitimized by their faithful adherence to the Sunna and by their legal expertise. For the ulema hagiographers, miracles had to conform to juridical ideals, and the ulema regarded the manifestation of extraordinary knowledge in the saints' miracles, such as reading thoughts and uncovering hidden secrets, as more significant than the saints' efficacy in healing the sick and subduing spirits. In contrast, most lay devotees were interested in the saints' thaumaturgical powers, and the saints with the greatest reputations were those who demonstrated such powers.[51]

The importance of saints in popular Islam and Judaism has been uneven over geographic areas and periods. In North Africa, where saints were a focal part of popular Islam and Judaism for many centuries, cults of living saints existed side by side with the veneration of dead saints, but the proportions of living to dead saints differed considerably. Saint veneration among Muslims was organized in religious orders dominated by saintly dynasties, and although the worship of dead saints was widespread, most Muslim saints were venerated during their lifetimes and most cultic activity focused on the living saint. Endowed with *baraka* (spiritual power), the living saint traced his ancestry to the founder of his order and to figures from the beginning of Islam, such as Fatima, Mohammed's daughter. The *baraka* was on occasion transferred to a devotee who had served the saint and tended his grave, and the former devotee might then transfer the *baraka* to his sons.

Among the Jews a few families produced two or more generations of saints, but most Jewish saints were recognized as such only after their death, and cultic activities were focused on their graves or shrines. Jewish saints were recognized as having led lives of prayer, study, and ascetic practices, such as prolonged fasts; although some were recognized during their lifetimes as having supramundane powers, magical deeds were usually attributed to them after death. The attribution of sainthood was occasioned by signs, such as a strong light that shone at the moment of their death or a flaming column that appeared above the grave. Saints often revealed themselves in peoples' dreams.[52]

Ernest Gellner wrote that the living saint was the most characteristic religious institution of rural and tribal Islam in North Africa, and he contrasted the personalized, ecstatic, and unscriptural Islam around the saints with the scripturalist, scholarly, unitarian, puritanical Islam of the urban religious elite and bourgeois. Living saints were the arbitrators or mediators among tribes when tribal segmentation and competition produced many problems and disputes and no strong, centralized authority was present to resolve them. Tribesmen were willing to submit to the saint's rulings on local feuds and other problems because the saints had positions outside tribal alliances and feuds and were believed to be close to God. The saints were central figures in the festivals that marked group boundaries and the changing of the seasons, and they had followings also among the urban poor, whose devotion, like that of the tribal and rural populations, was expressed in ecstatic rituals featuring music, dance, alcohol, and trance.[53] A few saints had a reputation for efficacy over a wide range of activities, whereas others developed a reputation for curing specific illnesses. Certain requests, such as help in attracting a loved one, were made only to minor saints. In exchange for their help, the saints received offerings and sacrifices, and bartering over the obligations was not uncommon.[54]

As the holy men of a minority, subject to the power of Muslim rulers and patrons, Jewish saints were less likely to accrue the political functions of Muslim tribal saints, but almost every Jewish community in Morocco had its dead saint whose legends included tales of their protection of devotees from the dangers of non-Jews. Although it was an important function of Jewish saints to protect Jews from Muslims and although many miracle tales told of punishments inflicted on Muslims who had harmed Jews, a number of Jewish saints were venerated by Muslims. Of the 656 Jewish saints that Ben-Ami found in Morocco in recent times, 126 were venerated by both Jews and Muslims; separate claims by Jews and Muslims were made for 36 saints, but Muslims venerated 90 saints whom they recognized as Jewish. Muslims were more likely than Jews to explicitly acknowledge their veneration of the other's saints, and in some cases such veneration culminated in the saints' Islamization.[55]

Before the French came to Morocco in 1912, most Jewish saints had only local reputations, known only to the inhabitants of the villages near the shrine. The extension of the reputations of certain saints over wide areas began particularly in the 1930s, when, with the use of advertising and the dissemination of tales of the saints' miracles, the physical infrastructures of shrines were developed. Committees were formed to organize the activities around the graves, and the sites generated large sums through donations and the sale of honors and items such as candles.

Pilgrimages to the tombs of the Jewish saints were held on the anniversary of their deaths if the dates were known or on religious holidays and other dates with religious significance. Pilgrims would remain for a week or longer. They prayed, lit candles, danced, and held festive meals. On these occasions and also on private visits to the saints tombs, believers sought assistance or gave thanks for the fulfillment of earlier petitions. Petitions related to many spheres of life, but requests for health and healing were the most common. Sleeping at the saint's graveside was believed to effect a cure, and items such as water or olive oil left at a saint's tomb overnight were applied as cures for illnesses. Many of the customs associated with miraculous cures were common to Jews and Muslims. In addition to healing, the saint's control over the forces of nature enabled them to make the sun stand still, bring rain, create springs, and magically produce food.[56]

Saints in North African Islam and Judaism were products of popular religion, but it should not be assumed that the religious elites opposed them or that middle and upper strata were not involved in the worship of saints. Some members of the religious elite, however, did vehemently oppose sainthood; Ibn Taimiya (1263–1328), a famous scholar, condemned the worship of saints and the veneration of the dead as idolatrous and incompatible with the Koran and the sharia, but after his death, many Muslims visited his tomb to seek his intercession. In the late eighteenth century and in the nineteenth century "purifying" movements attacked the notion of intermediaries, and in the twentieth century both religious modernists and fundamentalist movements opposed the veneration of saints. The modernists perceived the saints as relics of superstition, and the fundamentalists rejected them as deviations from the true path and as distractions from radical activism.[57]

Saints as efficacious intercessors were the major feature of Islamic Sufism and Jewish Hasidism, movements that, although historically unconnected, demonstrated remarkable similarities. In both cases groups of mystics with elitist notions, representing alternative religious paths to those of the legalistic traditions of the ulema and rabbis, were transformed into saints of phenomenally successful popular movements. The name Sufi was derived from *suf*, the rough robe of wool worn by early saintly preachers and ascetics. Talmudic literature referred to the Hasid (meaning "pious") as a person who carried out religious commandments above and beyond what is required and who worshipped in an intense manner. Before the emergence of the Hasidic movement, the term was commonly used to designate ascetic individuals who were part of a kabbalistic elite, and during the early formative period of Hasidism the term was used interchangeable with zaddik (righteous). Gradually, as the leaders became known as rebbes or zaddikim, the term *Hasid* came to designate an ordinary person who was a follower of, or "cleaved" to, a Hasidic leader. The term *zaddik*, which in kabbalistic literature signified one of the divine potencies (*sefirot*) that discharged the flow of divine energy to the lower worlds to sustain them, was appropriated by the third-generation Hasidic elite as the standard Hebrew designation of a Hasidic leader.[58]

Before its popularization, Sufism existed for some time as the mysticism of coteries and groups who sought the goal of union with God through asceticism, meditation, and the "annihilation of the self." It developed primarily in Iraq during the ninth and tenth centuries and became established in Khorasan (northern Iran) during the eleventh and twelfth centuries. Over time, relatively informal associations of masters and disciples became formal organizations of *tariquas* (lodges, literally pathways), which began to proliferate around the twelfth century. A master and his disciples lived within a single residential quarter, and group identity was strengthened by special apparel, initiation ceremonies, and distinct forms of mystical prayer (*dhikr*) and, in some cases, ritual dances.

Distinctions between inner circles of adepts and outer circles of affiliates and supporters developed around the leaders, and Sufism came to be characterized by the veneration of the current leaders—the living saints—and the dead saints, who were often believed to be the founders of the particular *tariquas*, or brotherhoods. Mass followings of the *tariquas* emerged in the thirteenth century together with an emphasis on *ziyarut*, or collective visiting of the tombs of the Sufi saints. Insofar as the mystical goal of union with God was incorporated into popular Sufism, it was believed to be achieved through the mediumship of the saint, but more important was the belief that the saints' nearness to God or their divine nature enabled them to cure the sick, to make the barren fertile, and to protect against evil beings and powers. With its focus on saint veneration, Sufism was the principal form by which Islam spread from the central Muslim lands to North Africa, Central Asia, and India.[59]

Hasidism began in the 1730s, centuries later than Sufism, in Podolia, an area of western Ukraine in what was then part of Poland, and it spread rapidly among eastern European Jews in the last decades of the eighteenth century and first half of the nineteenth century. By the middle of the nineteenth century, Hasidism was the dominant form of Judaism in most Jewish communities in Ukraine, central Poland, and Galicia; it had a large impact in White Russia and northern Hungary, and it attracted a large minority in Lithuania. The mystical goal of *devekut*, of cleaving, in the sense of communion rather than full union with God, was held by some Hasidim to be within the capabilities of all Jews, but the more prevalent notion, from the beginnings of the movement, was that direct accessibility to the divine was possible for only a small number of the spiritually endowed and that the only path for the masses was through cleaving to the spiritual few, the zaddikim or saints. Devotion and submission to the zaddik, like devotion and submission to the *shaikh* or *pir* in Sufism, was the means to achieving both this-worldly and other-worldly goals.[60]

As I noted, Israel ben Eliezer, the Ba'al Shem Tov (c. 1700–1760), did not set out to establish a movement, although he is regarded as the founder of Hasidism. The man who came to be recognized as Eliezer's "successor," Dov Baer, the "Great Maggid (Preacher)" of Mezhirech, acted to promote the spread of his teachings, but the "movement" at that stage was confined mainly to elite circles. It was the third-generation leadership, which included many of Dov Baer's disciples, that orchestrated the emergence of a mass movement. It was after the death of Dov Baer in 1772 that the movement quickly became one of hundreds of thousands, and in the nineteenth century it became one of millions.

Like Sufism, the spread of Hasidism was facilitated by its highly fragmented organizational structure. Many zaddikim established their separate courts, and each zaddik had his own disciples and followers, who were often drawn from a wide area. The primary loyalty of many eastern European Jews was no longer to the *kahal*, the geographically defined corporate body, but rather to a particular zaddik and his translocal Hasidic group. Each zaddik's court became a social center for his followers, who would visit it on religious holidays and when they sought the zaddik's intervention, for which they compensated him with a "redemption fee" (*pidyon*). The zaddikim crystallized into a network of dynasties, and most became based on the hereditary principle that the charisma of the zaddik was transferred to his son or sons. The transfer of charisma from zaddik to disciple, important in the early stages of the movement, was largely overtaken in most areas by hereditary succession.[61]

It was the institutionalization of the leadership role of zaddikim that accounts for the growth of Hasidism into a mass movement. The doctrine of the zaddik, as formulated by the third and subsequent generations of Hasidic leaders, linked the Jewish masses to a spiritual elite. Ordinary Jews were called on to adhere to a zaddik, a spiritual leader, who was their connection to the divine realm. It was the zaddik who was able to achieve *devekut*, adhesion to or union with the divine, and this enabled him to draw on the divine powers for the benefit of his community and followers. The zaddik combined the typical roles of the saint—mystic and magician. As a mystic, the zaddik's entrance into the upper realm required his self-abnegation, self-effacement, or annihilation. His success in reaching the divine sphere and his *devekut* was not, however, his final goal, which was to draw on the divine bounty. It was because the zaddik was able to divest himself of materiality that he was able to capture divine power and provide a channel of that power down to his earthly dependents.[62]

Before Hasidism, those who occupied specifically religious roles among eastern European Jewry were divided between the official, such as the rabbis of the communities and rabbinic judges, and the popular, such as the *maggidim* (preachers) and *ba'alei shem*. The zaddikim collapsed the distinction between normative and popular Judaism and blurred the boundaries between official and popular religious leadership. Before they became zaddikim, some had occupied formal positions as rabbis, and others had been engaged in popular religion. Once the zaddikim became prominent leaders, the duties of the local community rabbis became more confined to the interpretation of the minutia of religious law, and the magicians or *ba'alei shem* experienced deprofessionalization and a decline of status. Part of the appeal of the zaddikim was that they combined the high status of the mystic with engagement in popular religion.[63]

Unlike Sufism, which incorporated and adapted already existing saints' cults in such areas as North Africa and India, Hasidism spread among Ashkenazic Jews, whose religion had not been characterized by the veneration of human intermediaries. In Hasidism, as in Sufism, however, notions of the cosmic importance of saints developed. Sufis believed that a hierarchy of saints upheld the order of the universe and that in every epoch there was a saint who was the *qutb* (axis), the perfect human around whom the whole universe revolved. The cosmic role was shared to some degree by the higher saints in the hierarchy, and for some believers, who were especially numerous in India, the saints were an integral part of the divine.[64] In Hasidism the zaddikim were understood to be the "foundation of the world"; God had created the world because of his love for them and expected pleasure from them. The zaddikim contributed to the redemption of the Jewish people and the cosmos by rescuing the divine sparks of God from their captivity within the material and evil world. By their "worship through corporeality," the zaddikim were able to recover and elevate the divine sparks from their profane acts, such as eating, drinking alcohol, coitus, telling folk stories, and dancing.[65]

The cosmic status and roles of the Sufi and Hasidic saints together with their immanence and accessibility made believers confident that a saint's intervention on their behalf would bring miracles in this world. The combination of the roles of cosmic upholder and redeemer, savior of individual souls, and thaumaturge was powerful and attracted believers even in those contexts where saints' cults had previously been absent, as was the case among eastern European Jews. Notions that the charisma of the saints was transferred through discipleship or inherited genealogically facilitated the spread of the movements, as did the religious and social services provided by the centers of the living saints or the shrines of the dead saints. The movements were opposed by the established elites, the ulema and rabbis, who objected to their antischolarly tendencies, ecstatic practices, and focus on intermediaries, but as the movements became more moderate and adopted more legalistic traditions, at least in some branches, the elites came to accept them.[66]

Conclusion

The analysis here has turned on a contrast between the notion of the saint as exemplar, common to all world religion elites, and the notion of the saint as efficacious intercessor or divine being, common to all world religion masses in traditional societies. Saints as virtuosos are a potential challenge to hierocratic elites, who attempt to incorporate them into their institutions and to channel their appeal to the masses in ways that support the hierocracies. These attempts were especially evident in Catholicism, where the church elite constructed dead saints as both exemplars and efficacious intercessors. The popular transformation of the sacred in Catholicism included making the saints the most prominent supramundanes in the pantheon and displacing the elite representations of benevolent beings who worked selflessly for the salvation of others by thaumaturges who entered into relationships of exchange with individuals and communities.

Unlike the Catholic elite, the elites of other world religions did not develop institutionalized patterns of saintly exemplars as efficacious intercessors. The two-tier soteriologies and double religious standards formulated by the elites of Hinduism and Buddhism contributed to a clearly differentiated category of exemplars, but their representations of ultimate salvation (*moksha*, nirvana) were not conducive to notions of efficacious intercessors. The elites admit, however, that spiritual progress on the path to ultimate salvation is accompanied by the capability of extraordinary miracle-making powers, and it is through the operation of such powers, demanded by the masses, that saintly renouncers are transformed into saintly thaumaturges, such as the god-men in Hinduism and the forest monks in Buddhism.

Islam and Judaism have not had either a church to institutionalize sainthood or double religious standards as a basis for a religiously superior category of humans, and saints' cults in popular Islam and Judaism developed relatively independently of the established elites of those religions. Saints, alive and dead, were the foci of popular religion of Muslims and Jews in North Africa, and the phenomenal growth and spread of Sufism and Hasidism can be explained by the attraction of those movements' saints who were thaumaturges and, in some cases, redeemers with cosmic status. Thus popular religious movements that focus on saints have been especially important as forces of religious change and influence in those religions where beliefs and rituals around saints developed relatively independently of the established elites.

AFTERWORD TO PART I

The analyses in the chapters of part 1 can be situated within the subdisciplines of comparative-historical sociology and the sociology of religion. Comparative-historical sociology is distinguished by its concerns with causal analysis, processes over time, and systematic and contextualized comparisons. An interest in causal explanations might be considered part of any social-scientific endeavor, but interpretative perspectives, which deal with the explication of meanings rather than the identification of causes, have become prominent in anthropology and sociology over the last decades. The focus of interpretative perspectives on particular meanings within specific contexts has directed attention away from comparisons, and these tendencies away from causes and comparisons have been reinforced by postmodern approaches.[1]

Max Weber emphasized that the interpretation of meanings and a search for causes are not necessarily contradictory, and of all the classical sociologists, it is Weber who has had the most influence on my work. One important focus of Weber's work was the comparative analysis of religious developments. However, the postclassical revival of comparative-historical sociology in the 1960s and 1970s tended to ignore religion, either as an object of analysis or as an explanation of historical change. The prominent comparative-historical sociologists, such as Moore, Skocpol, Wallerstein, and Tilly, dealt with the causes and outcomes of rebellions and revolutions, democratic and authoritarian regimes, economic reforms, and welfare developments. Explanations were found in modes of production, class relationships, and political struggles, which were understood as material rather than ideal or cultural factors. The core questions were still inspired by Marxism, and when Weber was drawn on, it was for his sociology of classes, status groups, and political regimes rather than for his sociology of religion.[2] The integral relationship in Weber's work of his sociology of religion and his analysis of the "material" elements of economics and politics went unacknowledged.

Sociology of religion remained apart from the second wave of comparative-historical sociology. The few sociologists of religion who produced historical and comparative works, such as Robert Bellah and David Martin, were not included in the discourse of comparative-historical sociology.[3] It has been argued that a more recent third wave of comparative-historical sociology has extended its compass from classes to include races, ethnic groups, gender, and religion,[4] but the subdisciplines of comparative-historical sociology and the sociology of religion still appear to have little interaction. Most comparative-historical sociologists have little sympathy with rational choice theory, which has been prominent in the sociology of religion in recent years. The leading exponent of rational choice theory in religion, Rodney Stark, has written works that draw on historical data, but I have argued that his approach encounters problems when it is applied outside Christianity.[5]

Unlike the works of most comparative-historical sociologists, the major object of analysis of my work is religion. In chapter 1 I attempted to account for the variations in religious syncretism among Jewish communities in the premodern period. In chapter 2 I explained the similarities and differences between the Jewish minority and other religious minorities, particularly the Muslims, in Imperial China. And in chapter 3 I compared the different forms of sainthood in Judaism and other world religions. Religion was also one of the causal factors in the explanations of variations and differences. Explanations were sought not only in large social-structural properties (feudal corporations, tribal structures, caste structures, imperial regimes) but also in the larger cultural properties (religious boundaries, forms of religious pluralism). The importance of religious explanations is particularly obvious in chapter 3: The causes of the variations in sainthood among the world religions were discerned in those religions' soteriologies and organizations, particularly as they impinged on the relationships between religious elites and the masses. The comparisons in chapter 3, which is perhaps more an exercise in comparative religion than in comparative religious sociology, are the most wide-ranging and the least contextualized of the three chapters, although I included a comparison of Jewish and Muslim saints within a particular region (North Africa).

The comparisons in chapters 1 and 2 are both wide-ranging and limited in scope. In the first chapter the societal contexts are wide-ranging and the comparisons are limited by focusing on a particular religious minority, the Jews, in the postantiquity, premodern period. In the second chapter the religious minorities are wide-ranging and the comparisons are limited to a single civilization, Imperial Chinese. The explanations in one chapter serve to reinforce the explanations in the other. The comparative method, delineated by John Stuart Mill as the method of difference, is used to eliminate plausible causal factors.[6] In the comparison of Jewish communities, I discarded the size of the Jewish populations as a plausible cause for the variations in Jewish religious syncretism because I found that, although small Jewish populations in some civilizations were highly acculturated, in other civilizations small Jewish communities demonstrated relatively low levels of acculturation. In the comparison of religious minorities in China, not only the small Jewish community but also the much larger Muslim community was highly acculturated. However, the difference in size did made a difference when Imperial China disintegrated and the niche that had previously existed for a small religious minority was no longer available.

The method of difference has its limitations in eliminating plausible causal factors. Problems in the comparative analysis arise from the interaction effects of causal or contextual factors.[7] The religious variables—strong or permeable boundaries and the disposition to monopolism or pluralism—are themselves related. It is also impossible to measure the relative influence of the religious environments and the social-structural contexts on the levels of Jewish syncretism and acculturation. Comparative analysis of this type falls short of being able to clearly specify causal relationships that hold under particular conditions of time and place. However, other methods have their limitations. Hopefully, it will be deemed sufficient if the analysis has yielded plausible explanations of interesting differences in historical developments.

PART 2

Religious Movements

INTRODUCTION TO PART 2

In part 2 I revisit and revise my analysis of the Jewish religious movements that were the subject of my book *Messianism, Mysticism, and Magic* (1982). The revision incorporates the conceptual framework of religious action that I formulated in my *Comparative Sociology of World Religions* (2001). I focus on two broad categories of religious action (thaumaturgical and transformative), which I adopted from the writings of Max Weber. Thaumaturgy was introduced in chapter 3, on saints. It refers to special dispensation and release sought from specific ills within a nature and society whose basic features are not expected to change. In this type of religious action, supramundane assistance is sought either for protection from evil supramundanes, who wish to do harm to specific persons, or for relief from sickness and other woeful conditions affecting particular individuals and families. In the transformative type of religious action, the goal is to produce a pervasive or fundamental change in nature, society, or the individual. Such a change may involve a change in the supramundane (the divine, the Godhead) itself.

In addition to goals, the components of religious action include the actor (an individual or a collectivity), conditions, and means. The means are those objects, persons, groups, or processes that actors understand can be used or manipulated in the realization of their ends. The conditions are those objects, persons, groups, or processes that actors understand cannot be used or manipulated but that must be taken into account or addressed. The conditions and means in religious action include such elements as the pantheons of supramundanes (gods, devils, spirits, ghosts, etc.), the types of communication with supramundanes (coercion, supplication, etc.), and behaviors in accord with ritual formulas or ethical imperatives.

Two often interrelated subtypes of the transformative type of action can be distinguished. The first is sacralization, in which the goal is to infuse worldly activities with sacredness so that the world conforms to divine directives or ethical imperatives. The second subtype is soteriology, which can take both other-worldly and this-worldly forms. In this-worldly salvation, people believe they will be redeemed from economic and political oppression and suffering, and they expect to become politically dominant or attain social or religious prestige. Examples include messianic kingdoms and rebirth into a higher state on this earth. In other-worldly forms of salvation, people believe that they will be freed from the physical, psychological, and social sufferings of terrestrial life, liberated from the transitoriness of life as such, or redeemed from individual imperfections such as sin and earthly ignorance.

Examples include a state of nonbeing, union with a divinity, and permanent bliss in a heaven. The belief in a transcendental god in the religions commonly called monotheistic has generally ruled out the goal of self-deification, or absolute unity with the divine, but mystics in these religions have sought to approach, cleave to, or reside with the divine.

A strong case can be made that the most prominent transformative goal in Judaism is sacralization of the world rather than soteriology. Observance of the mitzvot (commandments) and study of the religious law are the major means or expressions by which Jews sacralize the world. Maimonides was not unusual among Jewish thinkers in stating that the reward for virtuous living is the good life on this earth. In comparison with Christianity and Islam, descriptions of the person or soul's existence after death have been rare and often vague and indefinite in official or rabbinic Judaism. Nevertheless, eschatology was not ignored by Judaism, and rabbinic authorities distinguished three stages: (1) the location of the soul after an individual's death, (2) the messianic age, and (3) the resurrection of the dead and final judgment at the end of the messianic age.

After death the promise for the righteous, those who had observed the mitzvot, was *Gan Eden* (heaven or paradise), whereas the wicked were destined for *Gehinnom* (hell). There were varying conceptions of heaven. One elitist notion was that heaven was where the person could finally understand the conception of God, but heaven was also portrayed as a place of perfect pleasantness where the soul resided with God and his angels, and popular conceptions included tangible, sensual delights. An elitist notion of hell was the extinction of the soul so that the sinful had no afterlife. More popular notions included descriptions of punishments and tortures. In some formulations life in hell lasts for no more than twelve months, and after that the souls, now purified, are transferred to heaven. Notions of the resurrection of the dead and the nature of what is resurrected to reside in "the world to come" also varied. The dominant rabbinic scenario was that both the bodies and souls of the righteous dead would be resurrected at the beginning of the messianic age, and when this came to an end, all the dead would be resurrected to appear before God for the last judgment. There was no consensus on what form immortality would take after the last judgment: of the soul alone or, if both body and soul, what kind of body.

Unlike the predominance of other-worldly notions of the locations and forms of the body and soul after death and after the last judgment, this-worldly components characterized most conceptions of the messianic era or millennium, although these also varied. Maimonides stated the rationalist position: "The only difference between this world and the days of the Messiah is oppression of one kingdom by another."[1] The messiah would restore the kingdom of David, rebuild the Temple, reinstate the ancient laws and sacrifices, and gather the Jews from their dispersion, but there would be no miracles, no changes in nature, no innovations in creation, and no end to history. The rationalist viewpoint was opposed by Jewish scholars who were millenarians as well as messianists: The revival of the kingdom of David was to be accompanied by changes in nature, in the cosmos, and in humankind's moral character.[2]

Whereas scholars of Christian religious movements have distinguished a category of religious movements that they call millenarian or millennial, scholars of Jewish religious movements have tended to use the term *messianic* to refer to a similar category of movements among Jews. Jewish writers may have been hesitant to use the term *millennial* because of its association with Christian belief, as found in the book of Revelation, in a thousand-year reign of Christ on earth before the final judgment. The term *millenarianism*, however, has come to be applied far more generally to movements in many religious traditions. The common feature of such movements is that they look forward to an imminent collective salvation that will occur in a transformed world that will be brought about by or take place under the auspices of supramundane beings or processes. The present world will be replaced by a perfectly good and happy one, in which the terrestrial and transcendental realms will be united. Some writers have distinguished millennialism, referring to a thousand-year period, as a specific form of millenarianism, but the meaning of the millennium is not necessarily limited to the literal sense of a thousand years. It might be conceived of as a shorter duration (the messiah in the fourth book of Ezra will rule for 400 years), or it might be conceived of as an eternal age. In messianic-millennial movements, it is believed that a savior figure will accomplish or take a leading part in the collective salvation and transformation of the world. Not all millenarian movements have messiahs, and some messianic movements have visions of the future that are not strictly millenarian in the sense of an expected transformation in nature as well as society.[3]

It is important to distinguish between millenarian phenomena in general and millenarian movements. The term *movement* has been applied to cover a wide range of phenomena both in the general social-scientific literature on millenarianism and in Jewish studies on messianism. G. W. Trompf, in his general review of the scholarly analysis of millenarianism, noted that millenarian ideas can spread widely without coagulating into a movement or distinct outbreak. Collective ideas and shared rumors do not necessarily become active preparations for a predicted cosmic event, and where some form of organization exists, this may not go beyond a clique or coterie. Trompf warned against a tendency among scholars of millenarianism to "force sociological substance on to activities which can be rather minor in import."[4] Moshe Idel has argued that the term *movement* has been applied inappropriately with respect to both elite and popular forms of messianism among Jews. Messianic calculations that predicted a particular year as the beginning of redemption were often no more that an intellectual activity or literary exegetical activity. Many individuals who possessed a strong messianic awareness failed to create a movement, and it is misleading to designate the modest excitement around certain individuals who proclaimed themselves the messiah or whose activities were attributed with messianic significance as movements.[5]

It is, of course, important to distinguish between elite and popular forms of millenarianism-messianism, although they may overlap and influence each other. Idel distinguished three forms of messianism. The first two, magical and mystical, were elite forms, and the third type, apocalyptic, was popular. Magical procedures in millenarianism included the recitation of incantations to destroy the demonic realms, disrupt the continuum of history, and cause change in the natural order.[6] Magical messianism had its elitist, esoteric elements, but Idel's major comparison is between the mystical messianism of kabbalists and the messianic mass movements that "were controlled by much simpler and cruder apocalyptic images."[7] The sophisticated systems of thought of the kabbalists made them accessible to a small elite, and the type of messianism that they created represented a "dis-apocalyptization of messianic concepts."[8]

Idel was interested primarily in the mystical form, and he argued that this form was mistakenly regarded as exclusive of messianism. In comparison to Idel, who emphasized the empirical interrelationship of messianism and mysticism, I have emphasized the importance of making a conceptual distinction between them. Unlike the millenarian, who envisages visible material change in the world, the mystic seeks an ultimate reality and a transformation of his individual condition not directly perceptible to others. The mystic seeks union, adhesion, or some form of direct contact with the divine or a superworldly state that goes beyond sense perception and intellectual apprehension. Whereas the millenarian takes an activistic or symbolic revolutionist stance toward the world, the mystic attempts to escape or withdraw from the world and is likely to show indifference to its material conditions. The millenarian may see the millennium as an end to history, but he gives a place to history in the events leading up to the millennium. The mystic, on the other hand, takes a timeless stance, seeking the eternal now of the divine. The focus of the mystic on his personal salvation or individual soul contrasts with that of the millenarian, who holds that his individual salvation is bound up with that of the group or the collectivity.[9]

These distinctions between millenarianism and mysticism were intended as ideal types, and on an empirical level they have combined and existed in tension with each other and with thaumaturgy. Idel's discussion of messianic mystics appears to depend on a broad understanding of messianism, which includes individualistic mystical quests for redemption. My focus is on more collective and popular forms of millenarianism that can be distinguished from mysticism. An example of a Jewish religious movement in which mysticism is an important component is Hasidism, and, as noted in chapter 3, part of the explanation of the movement's phenomenal spread among eastern European Jews was its combination of mysticism with thaumaturgy. Hasidism is an example of a movement in which mystics are leaders of collectivities; the leaders' mysticism is a means to thaumaturgy.

Crises have been a common explanation among historians and social scientists for religious movements, including messianic, millenarian, and mystical movements. Millenarian movements in particular have been interpreted as responses to the disruption of social and cultural patterns. One acute instance of disruption is a disaster, such as an epidemic, famine, war, or massacre. Following a disaster, people feel vulnerable, confused, and full of anxiety, and they turn to millenarian beliefs to account for the otherwise meaningless events. They interpret the disaster as a prelude to the millennium; thus their deepest despair gives way to the greatest hope.[10] However, the appeal to crises as an explanation of Jewish religious movements has been questioned by scholars of Jewish history. Glenn Dynner, who doubts that crisis was an important cause of the success of Hasidism, writes, "In the case of diasporic Jewish history, moreover, the currency of crisis is rather cheap: one does not have [to] look far to discover something of a crisis in any and every period."[11]

Idel argued that explanations of historical crises or deprivations cannot account for the mystical or elite forms of messianism that are the focus of his analysis, although he acknowledged that such explanations might be pertinent in explanations of mass movements.[12] Small, local, short-lived messianic outbursts have occurred in Jewish communities that had not directly experienced a serious crisis; the news of an event or series of events elsewhere in the world was sufficient to activate the messianic beliefs. Crises or sociocultural disruptions do appear to be among the necessary causes of large and widespread messianic movements, but such conditions are not sufficient causes. Given the importance of the belief in the messiah in the Jewish religious tradition and the number of disasters and crises in Jewish history, it is surprising that there have been so few important Jewish messianic movements. This might be understood, in part, as a result of the influence of a rabbinic tradition that opposed activistic forms of messianism and held that men should not even attempt to calculate the timing of the Redemption.

In the Diaspora, messianic movements were rarely militaristic, but they represented a challenge to the passive forms of messianism; the messiah was said to have appeared or was about to appear, imminent dates of redemption and the return to the Holy Land were announced, and believers were seen to have an important part in speeding the process of redemption. The fact that messianic movements constituted a break from the dominant rabbinic opinion meant that they were likely to emerge only under exceptional circumstances. Disasters and crises were among those circumstances, but the effects of these events have to be understood in wider cultural and social frameworks.

In the next three chapters I apply the comparative approach to millenarianism, particularly its Jewish manifestations in the medieval and early modern periods. After a brief review of the development of millenarianism and messianism in ancient Judaism, in chapter 4 I compare and explain the differences in levels of millenarianism in the medieval period among Ashkenazic Jews in central and western Europe, Sephardic Jews in Spain, and Italian Jews. In chapter 5 the analysis of millenarianism is extended to those Jews in Spain and Portugal who converted, mostly under duress, to Christianity, and to those conversos, or New Christians, who left the Iberian

Peninsula and "returned" to Judaism. I argue that the forced converts were particularly important in the largest (if we exclude Christianity) millenarian movement in Jewish history: the Sabbatean movement, in the seventeenth century. Chapter 6 widens the comparative approach to an analysis of antinomianism in both millenarian and mystical movements in a number of religions.

4. JEWISH MILLENARIAN-MESSIANIC MOVEMENTS

Comparisons of Ashkenazim, Sephardim, and Italian Jews

Development of Millenarianism and Messianism in Ancient Judaism

The development of millenarian beliefs in ancient Judaism was conditioned by the experience of conquest and exile.[1] Although the prophecies before the Babylonian conquest of Judea and the destruction of the First Temple were based on supramundane premises, they did not present a view of the future as an essentially different order from that of the present. The dualistic conception of two worlds, in which the future hope would be realized in transcendental as well as terrestrial realms, was essentially a postexilic development. The book of Ezekiel, composed by an exile in Babylon, attributed cosmic significance to the return of the exiles and the rebuilding of the Temple. According to Deutero-Isaiah, who is believed to have prophesied in the last years before the conquest of Babylon by the Persians in 539 B.C.E., the demonstration of Yahweh's power was to go beyond the return of the Israelites to Israel and the destruction of their enemies. The people of Israel would be given a glorious position in a transformed world.

The millenarianism of the postexilic prophets was developed further in works to which modern scholars have attached the label apocalyptic. The Greek word *apokalypis* means "unveiling," referring to the revelation of hidden knowledge, hitherto known only in heaven, by God to a chosen prophet, often through the intermediary of an angel. The secret knowledge often included heavenly events, but the focus was on catastrophic events, often conceived of in fantastic imagery, that would occur on earth at the end of this age or at the end of the world as we know it. The book of Daniel has been designated as the first Jewish apocalypse, and it is the only clearly apocalyptic text in the Hebrew Bible. Together with the book of Enoch, the book of Daniel represents a new type of text in that it foregrounds the influence of angels and demons on human affairs and includes a final judgment not only of nations but also of individuals.

The origins of apocalypticism are obscure. Many scholars believe that the apocalyptic chapters in the book of Daniel were written at the time (160s B.C.E.)

of the attack on Judaism by Antiochus IV, a monarch of the Hellenistic Seleucid dynasty, which pillaged Jerusalem, forbade Jewish religious practice, and replaced the worship of Yahweh with that of a Syrian god. A Jewish resistance, known as the Maccabean revolt, fought successfully against the monarch's forces, entered Jerusalem in triumph, and rededicated the Temple to the worship of Yahweh. Doubts have been cast on a connection between the apocalyptic texts and specific historical events. The texts may represent an attempt by an intellectual elite to grapple with the problem of theodicy: a concern to reconcile a transcendent, omnipotent, good god with an evil and chaotic world.[2]

During the classical period of Jewish apocalyptic works, from the second century B.C.E. to the second century C.E., their writers came to envisage a view of the future world that was removed from historical reality. Whereas the ancient prophets knew only a single world in which the events of "the Day of the Lord" would occur, the apocalyptic works made a radical contrast between this world and the next, the reign of darkness and the reign of light, and between sin and holiness, impurity and purity. Concrete hopes for political redemption remained a central feature of millenarian hopes, but in many texts they became subordinate to mythical and cosmic scenarios.

The apocalyptic elements became more pronounced in those works written under Roman domination, which referred to the appearance of monsters, demons, plagues, famines, floods, falling stars, earthquakes, wars, revolutions, and so forth as the "birth pangs of the messiah." In contrast with the book of Revelation in Christianity, these Jewish apocalypses did not become canonic writings, and graphic representations of the end did not achieve the importance that they attained in Christianity. However, the belief arose that the messiah would come at the time of the deepest catastrophe of the Jewish people, and the apocalyptic literature provided subsequent generations with a frame of reference for interpreting their experiences of crises as signs of the coming of the messiah.

In the Israelite and early Judaic literature the concept of a messiah was either absent or of little importance beside the concept of eschatological salvation. Suggestive words and images in the later works of the Hebrew Bible point in the direction of a messianic figure; certain terms, such as the "suffering servant" in Deutero-Isaiah and "the one like the son of man" in Daniel 7, were later interpreted as referring to a messiah. However, no Jewish text written before the second century B.C.E. describes a messiah in the eschatological sense of a leader at the end of time. Daniel and other early apocalypses do not contain references to a messiah, and it is only from the late 160s B.C.E. that some apocalypses (not all) contain a messiah figure.

During the Second Temple period Jewish writings continued to refer to eschatological salvation without a messiah; still, a variety of savior figures were drawn during that period. The most prominent messianic image was a this-worldly warrior-king of Davidic origin who would restore Israel, inaugurate an age of peace, and die when his kingdom ended. After the destruction of Jerusalem in 70 C.E., the restoration of the Temple became one of the messiah's important tasks, and after the failure of the last revolt against the Romans, apocalyptic writers began to made a distinction between the warrior-messiah of the house of Joseph, who would die in the final battle against Gog and Magog, and the more spiritual messiah of the house of David, who would rule the future kingdom. From this time on, a number of texts combine messianism with apocalypticism, and the messiah comes to be seen by some as a superhuman, eschatological king.

Even when the Jewish notion of the messiah took on superhuman attributes, it remained radically different from the Christian conceptions of Jesus as God or the son of God and as a major actor in the apocalypse. In addition, of course, there was the difference that Christians believed that their messiah had already come and that they were to await his second coming. The Jewish messiah was yet to come, and the variety of messianic notions, images, and expectations in the religious literature opened up the field to widely divergent claimants. In the years before the destruction of the Second Temple, a number of messiahs appeared who emphasized deliverance from the Romans, but it would be mistaken to attribute messianism to the rebels of 66–73 C.E. Messianism has been associated with the revolt in 132–35 C.E., particularly because its leader, Bar Kochba, was acclaimed as the messiah by the renowned Rabbi Akiva. Paucity of information makes it difficult to interpret the rabbi's declaration, which may have been an attempt to revive the Davidic dynasty.[3] If there were messianic expectations among the rebels, their defeat appears to have put an end to messianism for a lengthy period.

The disastrous consequences of the revolts against the Romans and the precarious position of Jews in Diaspora communities may explain the tendency of Talmudic or rabbinic Judaism to neutralize imminent expectations and activist forms of millenarianism and messianism. Later rabbinic literature tended to moderate and minimize the catastrophic or apocalyptic elements, and, with the exception of the book of Daniel, the apocalypses of the Hellenistic and Roman periods were not preserved by the rabbis as canonic texts. No Jewish text approaches the centrality of the book of Revelation in Christianity, which accords far more importance to graphic representations of the end of time than Judaism.

Rabbinic literature presented the messiah as an earthly redeemer, the instrument by which the kingdom of God would be established, as well as the future ruler of that kingdom. However, rabbinic scholars were suspicious and sometimes openly hostile toward popular millenarianism with its more militant and apocalyptic elements. The rabbinic elite sought to incorporate millenarianism into an eternal sanctification of life to be attained by religious observance and study, and they encouraged Jews to accept their suffering and resign themselves in a humble and passive manner to their political subordination. It was not rebellion but repentance that would bring the messiah. Thus the coming of the messiah and dramatic change were dependent on obedience and keeping things as they were.[4]

Rabbis and scholars in the medieval period never formed a consensus with respect to the importance of the messiah and the nature of the millennium.[5] The twelfth principle of the best known formulation of Jewish religious doctrines, Maimonides' "Thirteen Principles of the Jewish Faith," reads, "I believe with complete faith in the coming of the Messiah, and even though he should tarry, nevertheless, I shall wait for his coming every day." The famous scholar Nahmanides (1194–c. 1270) did not share this view of the centrality of the messianic belief in Judaism, and other Jewish sages in Spain, although they did not dispute that the messiah was a true doctrine, did not consider it a "first principle" or "cornerstone" of Judaism.[6]

Although the dominant rabbinic tendency did not encourage imminent expectations of the coming of the messiah, it was nevertheless an article of faith among Jews in the medieval and early modern periods to hope constantly for the advent of the messiah. Affirmation of this belief was a persistent theme in Jewish prayers: in a number of daily benedictions, in the prayers after meals, during the wedding ceremony, and on festivals and fast days. Family and business letters, holiday wishes, and expressions of congratulations often concluded with the wish that the correspondents would witness the advent of the messiah and the ingathering of the exiles. Belief in the coming of the messiah and the collective salvation of the Jews in a future, this-worldly, perfect age might therefore be described as normative in traditional Judaism. The question is, Under what circumstances were messianic beliefs activated in the form of messianic movements?

Instances of Millenarianism in the Medieval Period

Messianic hopes arose in the late eleventh century and the twelfth century in places as distant from each other as Spain and Yemen, and it has been suggested that they were all connected in some way with the Crusades. In fact, an examination of the location and the timing of the movements shows that the connection with the Crusades was tenuous at best. In those areas where Jews were massacred by the hordes following the crusading armies, the survivors interpreted their sufferings within a Jewish religious framework, but they did not turn to active messianism. Some Jews did view the persecution in a messianic context,[7] but among the Ashkenazim this did not become the dominant trend, and they took no steps to prepare for such an event.

Jewish chronicles of the period show that Jews understood the persecutions of the Crusades as a continuation of the seemingly endless sufferings that God had chosen them to endure.[8] They saw precedents to the massacres in biblical narratives, and this archetypal mode of thought possibly militated against any tendency to view the events as signifying an end to history. They believed that their suffering was a just retribution for the sins of the Jewish people and their failure to uphold the law of God. Although some declared that their own sins were being justly punished, self-accusation was more a conventional formula than a deeply held belief. Medieval Ashkenazim found little in their own behavior to warrant such punishment, and some concluded that they were being punished for the sins of their ancestors.[9] For them suffering was a test of faith; it was imposed on a religiously qualified generation that was able to withstand the cruel tests and thereby fulfill the hopes of God. Compensation was to come in the form of an immediate personal afterlife in which proof of religious merit was to be rewarded by happiness in heaven.[10] Ashkenazic rabbis also stressed that the righteous would be resurrected and enjoy the splendors of the ultimate redemption, but they did not introduce any apocalyptic interpretations of contemporary events into their millenarian conceptions.[11]

Historical records indicate that active millenarianism did not attract the Ashkenazim in central and western Europe in the medieval period. Most instances of millenarianism occurred among the Jews of Spain and, after the expulsion of 1492, in Italy. Elitist forms appeared among certain kabbalists who proclaimed themselves messiahs and created syntheses of mysticism and messianism in their endeavors to achieve perfection of their human intellect and to restore the Godhead to a state of perfection. One of the most prominent kabbalistic messianic prophets was Abraham Abulafia, who announced that he received his first prophetic call in Barcelona in 1271, presented himself to the Jews of Sicily as the messiah, and predicted that redemption would occur in 1290. Abulafia believed that by achieving self-perfection, he would bring about the redemption of the entire Jewish people. Although Abulafia proclaimed himself to be the messiah and sought an audience with the pope to promote his prophetic mission, his methods of contemplation and his manipulation of divine names and Hebrew letters were those of a mystic rather than a messianic leader of the masses. His mystical approach was unlikely to attract popular support, and he probably influenced no more than a few dozen people.[12]

More popular forms of millenarianism occurred in 1295 in Castile, where considerable excitement centered on two messianic prophets, one in the town of Ávila and the other in the village of Ayllon. In Ávila a reputed illiterate claimed that angels had dictated to him a treatise revealing the imminent future kingdom, whereas in Ayllon a prophet announced that on a specified day of that year a blast of the messiah's horn would summon Jews from exile. Many prepared themselves by fasting, praying, and giving to charity, and on the day they rose early, dressed in white, and went to the synagogue to await the signal.[13]

Ávila had a Jewish population of about fifty families, mainly small shopkeepers and artisans who also had some land under cultivation and owned small herds of sheep and cattle.[14] In a village such as Ayllon the economic character of the Jews could not have been very different. Millenarianism did not appear at that time in the larger urban Jewish communities, which were dominated by wealthy Jewish families.

Nearly a century later, in 1391, a number of Jewish prophets in Spain predicted the imminent coming of the messiah. These prophecies occurred at the time of widespread attacks on Jews, who were often given the choice of death or conversion. Possibly as much as one-third of Spanish Jews were killed and a further third converted.[15] The fragmentary records do not allow us to establish the extent of the messianic enthusiasm among Jews in 1391,[16] and from that time on it was the conversos, rather than those Jews who remained in Spain, who supported millenarianism. The number of conversos increased in the early decades of the fifteenth century as a consequence of coercive missionary campaigns and discriminatory legislation against Jews, and a further wave of conversion followed the expulsion decree in 1492. Millenarianism among the conversos is the subject of chapter 5.

The conquest of Constantinople by the Turks in 1453 stimulated millenarian hopes among both conversos and Jews in Spain and among some Jews in Italy and Palestine. The millenarian interpretation of this event, which is also found among Christians, demonstrates that messianic hopes among Jews could be induced by historical events that did not directly affect them or have any obvious relation to them.[17] The enthusiastic response of some Spanish Jews to the Islamic conquest, however, may have been influenced by the deterioration of their own situation under Christian rule. Idel suggests a connection between the heavy pressures felt by Spanish Jews and the magical form of kabbalistic messianism that was practiced in the circle of Sefer-ha-Mehiv in the last two decades before the expulsion in 1492. This group of kabbalists believed that the time of the messiah was imminent and that they could hasten the redemption by destroying the evil forces that were the only remaining impediment to the final advent. They claimed that their incantations, which they recited to destroy the demonic realms, were dictated by God through the mediation of angels.[18]

The expulsion decree in 1492 clearly had enormous implications for Spanish Jews, both for the exiles, whose number is estimated to be 100,000–160,000, and for those who chose to convert rather than leave Spain, probably numbering 25,000–50,000.[19] The Jews were given four months to leave Spain; many had to sell their property for less than its value, and they were forbidden to take gold, silver, precious stones, and certain specified goods. Pillage on land and sea accompanied the expulsion. Thieves and pirates murdered many; others died of hunger and disease; and some were turned away from the lands where they had hoped to find refuge. Most of the exiles migrated to Portugal, but in 1497, as a result of an agreement with Spain, the Portuguese king ordered their conversion.[20]

The effect of the experience of the exile on the millenarian hopes of exiles has been a subject of controversy among historians. The experience of the exile encouraged millenarian hopes among some of them, but it appears to have had a disillusioning effect on the messianism of others. Some exiles believed that they would be fully avenged in the apocalyptic events to follow, and because many settled in the Turkish Empire, they found solace in the fact that they were closer to the Holy Land.[21] Most exiles, however, paid little attention to messianism and focused their efforts on rebuilding their lives and communities in their new places of settlement.[22]

About 9,000 Spanish exiles settled in Italy, which in the sixteenth century became the center of messianic speculation and activity.[23] Jews of Spanish or Portuguese origins organized themselves into communities separate from those of other

Jews in Italy, and it was not until the 1530s that their presence began to make itself felt.[24] Some Spanish exiles in Italy predicted an imminent redemption, but the expulsion from Spain does not appear to have been a major factor in Italian Jewish millenarianism. Don Isaac Abravanel (1437–1508), an Iberian exile in Italy, wrote a trilogy on the messianic theme, published in Italy in 1496–98. On the basis of his interpretations of biblical and Talmudic literature, historical events, and astrological calculations, he predicted that the process of redemption would begin in 1503 and be completed by 1531. Abravanel did not view himself as an agent of the process of redemption, his day-to-day activities did not indicate an intense messianism, his works were neither widely diffused nor popular, and after his predictions failed, he abandoned the subject.[25] Abraham ben Eliezer ha-Levi, another exile in Italy, predicted that, beginning in 1520, the process of redemption would unfold with the coming of the messiah in 1530 and the rebuilding of the Temple in 1536–37. He composed prayers that were intended to alleviate the sufferings associated with the birth pangs of the messiah, but he did not mention the expulsion as a crucial event in his interpretation of events.[26]

Ha-Levi's fear of Christian reactions made him cautious in propagating his messianic message, and his influence was limited.[27] More influential was Ascher Lemlein, an Ashkenazi and instigator of what Idel called "a modest messianic movement."[28] Lemlein announced in 1502 in Istria, near Venice, that the messiah would come within six months if the Jews repented and prepared for their redemption, and his prophecies spread among the Ashkenazim who had been expelled from parts of Germany and had settled in northern Italy. Lemlein made no reference to the expulsion, and the Spanish exiles do not appear to have had an influence on or to have been influenced by Lemlein, who was active in northern Italy where German Ashkenazim far outnumbered Spanish exiles. The extent to which "Italian" Jews (a category distinguished from the Ashkenazim and Sephardim), who lived in regions around Rome, supported Lemlein is not clear, but Lemlein's disciples carried his prophecy to many parts of Italy, and widespread repentance was recorded so that long after 1502, the year was known as the year of repentance.[29]

Italian Jews had not themselves experienced any disaster or persecution, and during the Renaissance, a period of greater social acceptance of Jews, Italian Jews may have shared in the millenarianism widespread among the Italian population.[30] Many Christian millennialists knew of the expulsion from Spain, attributed the Jews with a cosmic role in their eschatologies, and shared with their Jewish counterparts millennial interpretations of astrological portents and historical events. Millennial tension and expectations built up in Italy in the 1480s and 1490s, when a number of prophets appeared in various parts of the country, including Venice, proclaiming imminent destruction and the end of the world. This excitement was related to the expectations of invasion and the actual French invasion in 1494 by Charles VIII. In France Charles VIII was seen in the millennial role of a second Charlemagne, and Charles saw himself as an apocalyptic reformer of the church, a new crusader who would conquer the Islamic world. The prophecy that Charles VIII would conquer the Muslims and convert them to Christianity circulated in Italy as well as in France, and at first his Italian conquests appeared to fulfill the prophecies.[31]

The invasion had a particular impact on the Jews. The second entrance of the French into Rome in 1495 was accompanied by an anti-Jewish outbreak, but once Charles assumed control of the city, he put the Jews under his protection. This together with the fact that the pope and his cardinals had fled Rome gave rise to the belief among some Jews that a new era was about to begin. The arrival of the French in Naples in 1495 brought with it the pillage of its numerous and influential Jews, but one Jewish prophet saw Charles's entry into Naples as a sign of the imminent advent of the messiah. In a somewhat confused fashion he calculated that 1490 had been the beginning of the period of sufferings, that 1495 ended this period, and that 1503 would mark final deliverance.[32]

The most important focus of millennial excitement in Italy was Florence, where Savonarola, a prior of the Dominican convent of San Marco, preached the coming advent to enthusiastic crowds. Before the French invasion Savonarola had preached great suffering for Florence and Italy, and after the invasion, when he spoke more of the coming millennium, he spoke with the authority of a prophet whose former predictions had come true. For Savonarola the tribulations of Florence were a sign of its election as the chosen city, the new Jerusalem, the center of the millennium, and he saw the Florentines as latter-day Israelites who would reach new spiritual heights and enjoy great riches, power, and a large empire.[33] We do not know how much impact Savonarola's campaign had on Italian Jews, but Netanyahu argues that Abravanel, a courtier at Naples who had to flee the French, must have been aware of Savonarola.[34]

The activities of David Reubeni and Solomon Molcho also stirred messianic hopes among some Italian Jews. Arriving in Venice in 1524, Reubeni claimed that he was a prince from one of the ten lost tribes in the "Wilderness of Harbor" and that he had been sent to seek assistance from the pope and the European powers to conquer Palestine. Through the influence of a wealthy Jewish banker, Reubeni received an audience with the pope, who in turn gave him a letter of recommendation to the Portuguese king. The king received Reubeni, but the enthusiastic reception given to him by conversos threatened his relations with the Christian powers, exposed him to the Inquisition, and compelled him to leave Portugal. Three years after his return to Italy, Reubeni went with Molcho to the Imperial Diet in Ratisbon to ask the emperor to arm Jews in order to regain Palestine from the Turks. The emperor imprisoned them, and Reubeni was taken back to the Iberian Peninsula, where he died, probably in an auto-da-fé.

Reubeni's intentions, at least at first, were not messianic. He claimed to be neither the messiah nor his prophet but rather a statesman with political and military proposals. Nevertheless, some Jews saw his mission in a messianic context, an interpretation to which Reubeni gave some encouragement. Although he spoke to Christians of joint military action against the Turks, to the Jews he spoke of returning to Jerusalem as part of the process of salvation. He maintained that God had ordained him to wage war to redeem the Jews, but he upheld the traditional view that the final act of redemption would be achieved by a miracle.

The romantic nature of Reubeni's career and his contacts with high Christian dignitaries have led many to exaggerate his influence on Jews and his importance in Jewish millenarianism. His appearance in Portugal caused great excitement among the conversos there, but his influence among Italian Jews was not so great. He appeared at a time when rumors about the ten lost tribes were common in Italy, but many Italian Jews regarded him as an imposter or a madman. In both Venice and Rome the Jewish communities were divided over how to treat him. In Rome the leaders refused to support him, but he did convince some wealthy Jewish families, who gave him their patronage and financial support. His influence peaked after his audience with the pope, but, after failing to obtain the help of the king in Portugal, support and belief among Italian Jews waned.[35]

While Reubeni's influence was declining, Solomon Molcho was gaining a considerable reputation as a messianic prophet. Born into a converso family in Lisbon, Diogo Pires took the Hebrew name Molcho, circumcised himself, and fled to Salonika, where he studied kabbalah. His prophecies, which included the destruction of Rome and the prediction that redemption would begin in 1540, became known in Italy, and, following the sack of Rome in 1527, which appeared to give credence to his prophecies, he went to Italy. He came to believe that he was the messiah, and, in conformity with a Talmudic legend about the sufferings of the messiah, he sat as a beggar for thirty days at the gates of Rome. Molcho met opposition from leaders of the Jewish community but gained an audience with the pope; his reputation was further strengthened when certain prophecies that he was said to have made—a flood in Rome and an earthquake in Portugal—did, in fact, occur. He went to Venice, where he had the support of a large section of the community, but his opponents denounced him to the Inquisition in Rome, and only the protection of the pope saved him at that time from the fire. He was burned in 1532 in Mantua after the failure of the mission with Reubeni to the emperor.[36]

Messianic expectations appear to have declined after Molcho's death, but they were renewed in Italy in the 1560s. A number of dates for the imminent coming of the messiah were announced, but the year that was most widely and strongly believed to be the year of redemption was 1575. When that year passed, a leading believer in imminent redemption recalculated the year to be 1608, but he expressed himself with less certainty than before.[37] This revival of millenarianism among Italian Jews in the last decades of the sixteenth century coincided with anti-Jewish measures of the Counter-Reformation. Beginning in the 1560s an increasing number of harsh restrictions were imposed on Italian Jews: They were expelled from many areas, their occupations and economic pursuits were severely limited, they were forced to wear a distinctive badge and live in ghettos, and the Talmud was publicly burnt and prohibited. Reduced to poverty and a precarious existence, some emigrated from Italy.[38] The economic and social deterioration of Italian Jews did not, however, produce messianic movements. The messianic calculations were a type of intellectual activity or literary exegetical activity that was undertaken in good times as well as bad.[39]

Explanations

Gerson D. Cohen argued that the differences between the "messianic postures" of the Ashkenazim and Sephardim in the medieval period encompassed both the rabbinic elites and the Jewish masses. At the elite level, on those rare occasions when Jewish scholars in France and Germany speculated on messianic issues, they did so esoterically and in restricted circles. Unlike their Ashkenazic counterparts, Jewish scholars in Spain paid little attention to past rabbinic injunctions against messianic speculations; they frequently and openly discussed messianic issues, and the date of the coming of the messiah was made the subject of a long series of tracts. In contrast, among the Ashkenazim the constraints on messianic speculation percolated down from the intellectual elite to the laity and lower strata. Both Ashkenazic and Sephardic rabbis opposed popular messianic activism or movements, but their different perspectives on messianism were paralleled by differences at the popular level. Although no large-scale messianic movement in any European country arose during this period, Jewish messianic pretenders and cases of messianic enthusiasm were almost all confined to Spain and, after the expulsion, to Italy.[40]

Elisheva Carlebach has disputed Cohen's comparisons by arguing that the difference between the Sephardim and Ashkenazim is to be found in their historiographies and not in their levels of messianism. Whereas Sephardic chroniclers did not hesitate to record the messianic character of events, the Ashkenazim tended to minimize the messianic element or to omit it altogether. For evidence of messianism among the Ashkenazim we have to rely far more on Christian writers, who were only too happy to record the failures of false messiahs among the Jews. As evidence of the differences in reporting, Carlebach notes that, in contrast to the Sephardic reports on Molcho, which emphasized his messianism, the Ashkenazic chroniclers did not use the word *messiah* and made no overt references to a messianic mission.[41] One problem with Carlebach's account is that most of her non-Sephardic examples of messianic fervor occurred in Italy, and, although there were Ashkenazim in northern Italy, Italian Jews were regarded as a separate category from both the Ashkenazim and the Sephardim. More important, Carlebach suggests that the reason that the Ashkenazim were less prone to record and remember expressions of messianism was their intellectual and political quietism, the very reason that Cohen gave for the relative absence of messianic activities among the Ashkenazim.

Cohen contended that no discernible connection existed between the persecution of the Jews and Jewish messianic movements and that all such movements appeared in areas and periods of relative stability. It would be more accurate to say that there was no consistent relationship between Jewish millenarianism and crises or disasters. Among the Ashkenazim persecution was not followed by millenarianism. Among the Sephardic and Italian communities a crisis was not a necessary condition of a messianic outburst. Disaster did not immediately precede the incidents in Castile in 1295; in fact, no clear historical or social factor can account for these events. Millenarianism among Italian Jews in the early decades of the sixteenth century had no obvious link to crises. However, incidents of millenarianism did accompany or follow tragic events in the history of Spanish and Italian Jewry: the massacres in 1391, the expulsion of 1492, and the persecution by the Italian Counter-Reformation. The extent of this millenarianism was limited, and it did not develop into millenarian movements, but the relative absence of millenarianism among the Ashkenazim, who were subjected to a greater number of disasters and periods of persecution, requires an explanation. The Ashkenazim were massacred in large numbers during the Crusades, at the time of the Black Death, and on a number of other occasions. They were subject to a number of expulsions, particularly in the fourteenth, fifteenth, and sixteenth centuries, and their livelihoods were increasingly restricted by anti-Jewish decrees.[42] Although the Ashkenazim's faith in the eventual coming of the messiah was often strengthened during these periods of persecution, there were no influential predictions of or preparations for his imminent coming.

The different levels of and responses to millenarianism of the Sephardim and the Ashkenazim were part of more general differences in their cultural and religious orientations. The Ashkenazim emphasized sin, guilt, humility, and asceticism; their quiescence and passivity were not conducive to millenarianism. The Sephardim emphasized pride, nobility, self-assertiveness, and, in some cases, Epicureanism. They put great emphasis on the noble status of their families. As among the Ashkenazim, descent from scholars was important, but Sephardic notions of nobility were closer to those of Christians; nobility was seen to be inherent in the families themselves, and claims were made of descent from the nobility of ancient Jerusalem, including, toward the end of the Middle Ages, the house of David.

Cohen traced the differences between Ashkenazic passivity and Sephardic self-assertion to their different beginnings. He argued that Palestine provided the cultural roots of the Ashkenazim and that after the failure of the Bar Kochba revolt, the Jews in Palestine remained relatively quiescent; their leaders taught submission and passive waiting for the intervention of God. On the other hand, the cultural roots of Iberian Jews were in Babylonia. There they held two political stances: (1) the cooperation of Jewish leaders with the Gentile rulers and (2) the rebellion of dissatisfied groups.[43] This is not a convincing argument. It is true that in the early Middle Ages Franco-German Jewry came under the influence of Palestine through Italy, whereas Spanish Jewry had links with Babylonia through North Africa. It is also true that differences between Ashkenazic and Sephardic rituals stemmed, in part, from their separate beginnings in Palestinian and Babylonian rituals, respectively.[44] But there is no evidence of a transmission of different political and cultural orientations to the Jewish populations, and it is clear that these orientations developed over time, becoming distinctive only in the later Middle Ages.

CHAPTER 4

The different cultural orientations of the Sephardim and Ashkenazim have to be seen in relation to the differences in the societies in which they lived and, in particular, to differences in their relationships with them. Feelings of superiority among the Sephardim stemmed not only from their Judaism and Jewishness, as was the case among the Ashkenazim, but also from their status and power within the larger society. Because they felt secure in and strongly identified with the dominant culture, any reversal in their situation was bound to create disorientation. Among the Ashkenazim, who rarely identified with the host society and culture, pogroms and expulsions created suffering but less fundamental disorientation. Their tradition of martyrdom reminded them that persecution was an integral part of their history and that it was sensible to keep their assets in liquid form, ready to move.

When they were expelled from Spain, the Sephardim felt that they had been torn, violently and cruelly, from their homeland. For the Ashkenazim expulsion was a tragedy in the sense that they lost their property and were forced to migrate and resettle, but it little affected their attachment to a particular society and culture or to focal elements of their identity. For the Sephardim, many of whom regarded themselves as among the cultural elite and who took great pride in their history and achievements in Spain, exile was a great blow to their identity and pride, and it gave rise to enormous resentment and a desire for revenge. Some exiles expressed their concern that they had accepted expulsion without attempting armed resistance; some found consolation in the belief that the punishments of the "end of time" were near.[45]

For an exile such as Isaac Abravanel who had enjoyed wealth, status, and power in Spain, messianism can be interpreted as a response to rejection by a society into which he had formerly been highly integrated, culturally and socially. He had served as diplomat and financier to six kings, associated freely with kings and nobles, and participated comfortably in both Jewish culture and the culture of the Christian upper stratum. On three occasions, in Portugal, Spain, and Naples, Abravanel was separated from his property, stripped of his honor, and forced into exile. He shared the false optimism of Spanish Jewry, and although his immediate reaction was to despair of redemption, he came to interpret the expulsion as part of the birth pangs of the messiah. In his messianic works he emphasized revenge: The redemption of the Jews would emerge from the punishment of the Gentiles, especially of the Christians.[46]

The change in the situation of Italian Jewry in the sixteenth century replicates, in some respects, the change that had occurred earlier in Spain. During the Renaissance, in the fifteenth century and the first half of the sixteenth, Italian Jews mixed freely with Christians and adopted aspects of the dominant culture. Christians, including clergymen, visited synagogues to hear Jewish preachers, and Jewish-Christian friendships, which were especially prevalent among the humanists, were sometimes found between rabbis and priests. As had been the case in Spain, Gentile friends served as godfathers at circumcision ceremonies. The Jews of Renaissance Italy emphasized courage and self-esteem; attracted to pomp and solemnity, they concerned themselves with titles, family coats of arms, and the right to bear arms.[47] Counter-Reformation measures in the second half of the sixteenth century were a sharp reversal for Italian Jews; like the Spanish Jews before them, they experienced a sudden fall from wealth and honor and the rejection of a society that had formerly accepted them and whose culture they had, in many respects, accepted.

All European Jews experienced persecution, but Spanish and Italian Jews underwent a deeper disruption of their social expectations and cultural order. They experienced a greater deprivation, relative to their past state, in their economic position, social status, and political influence. However, millenarianism was never the dominant response to the disruption of their lives. Their responses included hopeless despair, self-blame for their failure to keep the religious law, and acceptance of Christianity. Most of the survivors of the 1391 massacres in Spain and most of the exiles from Spain put their energies into rebuilding their lives and communities.[48] Similarly, millenarianism was a relatively minor response of Italian Jews to their ghettoization and deterioration in economic situation and social status in the second half of the sixteenth century. Despite their residential segregation in ghettos, Italian Jews retained their contacts with non-Jews, and their ghettoization did not lead them to cultural impoverishment, as some past historians supposed, but to cultural innovations.[49]

Crises and Millenarianism

Crises preceded millenarian occurrences in Jewish history, but not all crises gave rise to millenarian outbursts. In fact, only a few did so. An analysis of the relationship of crises and millenarianism requires an examination of the nature of the crises and of the cultural framework in which they were understood. Many widespread messianic outbursts arose during or following instances of acute persecution, massacre, or exile, but the influence of these disasters on messianic outbursts was variable and depended on other factors. One important cultural dimension that influenced the association between persecution and millenarianism was the presence or absence of other established explanations of and compensations for persecution. Messianic beliefs were as much a part of the religious tradition of the Ashkenazim as they were of the Sephardim, but in the medieval period the Ashkenazim were far less prone to use those beliefs to account for the disasters that befell them. The Ashkenazim attributed their fate to the sins of the Jewish people and found solace in the belief that in accepting death rather than conversion, they were proving their righteousness and would be rewarded by a blissful afterlife. Some Sephardim and the Italian Jews explained the exile from Spain and persecution as part of the birth pangs of the messiah and looked forward to the revenge that would be exacted by his forces.

The different responses of the Sephardim and Ashkenazim to persecution were related to more general differences in their cultural orientations toward the countries in which they lived and to the whole notion of *galut* (exile). During most of the medieval period the situation of Jews in the Iberian Peninsula was considerably better than elsewhere, and although the Sephardim accepted exile from the Holy Land as part of their religious tradition, they formed a strong attachment to the Spanish kingdoms and their culture. Exile was less prominent in their consciousness, and thus some turned to messianism when their pride and identity were shattered. On the other hand, the Ashkenazim felt little or no attachment to their host societies, and thus, precisely because they experienced exile as normative, they were less attracted to active millenarianism. Exile was a state of being to which they had to adjust so that sometime in the unforeseen future they would be redeemed.

The type of crises that have engendered Jewish millenarianism are those that have threatened or destroyed important elements of previously held identities, and millenarianism has represented an attempt to reintegrate identities by focusing on a single core element. Before the crises, identities may have contained ambiguous and possibly contradictory elements, and the crises may have motivated Jews to adopt beliefs in an imminent redemption that canceled ambiguity and stood for a wholly Jewish identity. The predicaments of identity were felt most acutely by the New Christians, or conversos, those Jews who converted to Christianity.

5. MILLENARIANISM AMONG CONVERSOS (NEW CHRISTIANS) AND FORMER CONVERSOS (RETURNEES TO JUDAISM)

Three large waves of Jewish conversions to Christianity occurred in Spain: (1) at the time of the riots against Jews in 1391, (2) in 1412–14 as a result of the campaign of the preacher Vincent Ferrer and anti-Jewish legislation, and (3) after the expulsion decree in 1492. Scholars differ widely in their estimates of the number of converts. David Gitlitz evaluated the various estimates and concluded that about 225,000 converted before the expulsion and that a further 25,000–50,000 converted in 1492. Of the exiles, more than half moved to Portugal, but in 1497 those who remained in Portugal were forced to convert, and in 1542 about 60,000 conversos remained in Portugal.[1]

Some conversos defended their conversion by pointing to the "senselessness" of Jewish messianic hopes, but millenarianism found many enthusiasts among conversos, especially among the crypto-Jews or "Judaizers" who continued to practice at least some Jewish rituals. Some of those who converted in 1391 tried to leave Spain for the Land of Israel, believing that their migration would help bring the messiah. A further migration of converts, also stimulated by messianic hopes, occurred after the conquest of Constantinople by the Turks in 1453. Stories circulated among conversos that the messiah had already been born. One New Christian in Valencia told of a miraculous young boy who lived on a mountain near Constantinople; apparently only circumcised Jews could look upon him without being blinded.[2]

The first recorded millenarian incident among conversos after the exile occurred in 1500 in the small town of Herrara in northern Castile. In the fifteenth century Herrara had a Jewish community of substantial size and wealth. Inés Esteban, the teenage daughter of a shoemaker, proclaimed that she had been led by her mother, a boy who had just died, and an angel to heaven to a place where she heard the voices of souls who had been burned "in sanctity of the name." Most conversos in Herrara believed that Inés was a prophet of the messiah, and many converts came from elsewhere to see her. They ceased work, fasted, and prepared themselves in holiday clothing for the imminent arrival of the messiah, who would take them to the Holy Land. Some said that a town created in heaven would be brought down to earth and that the converts would dwell there, eating off golden plates.

There were similar occurrences elsewhere. Maria Gómez, a prophetess in Chillón, a small provincial town in Ciudad Real, claimed that she had ascended to heaven, where she was told that all the conversos who fasted, observed the Sabbath, and kept other commandments would be taken to the Holy Land. The older women who followed Gómez were familiar with Jewish practice, but her younger female followers apparently did not have such knowledge. Women were prominent in these movements as both prophets and followers. In contrast to converted men, who had lost the center of their Jewish life when public Jewish institutions disappeared, the center of Jewish life for the women was domestic rituals that they could continue to observe, albeit in an attenuated fashion. There were, however, male prophets who promised imminent redemption. One claimed that he had ascended to heaven, where he met God, Elijah, the messiah, and the prophetesses of Herrara and Chillón. He said that Elijah would come to Spain to collect the conversos who believed in the law of Moses and had kept the Sabbath and other precepts. His followers dressed in holiday garb in readiness for the messiah.

Popular prophecy among the converts occurred in other parts of Spain, such as Córdoba and Valencia. Signs in the sky, political events, and wars were taken as signs that 1500 was the year of the Redemption. Most prophetesses and prophets who appeared at the time predicted that Elijah and the messiah would soon appear and take the converts who believed in redemption to Israel on clouds or angels' wings. Several communities of converts in Castile lived for weeks in a state of exaltation and excitement, leading ascetic lives, fasting regularly, and adhering as rigidly as possible to Jewish observances. The Inquisition learned of the movements and imprisoned and burned many of those involved.[3]

Not all converso millenarians in postexpulsion Spain were crypto-Jews. Some were devout Christians who were influenced by Spanish Christian millenarianism. Vincent Ferrer, the preacher who took a leading role in the conversion of Jews, was himself a millenarian who, together with other Spanish theologians, saw the conversion of the Jews as a decisive event before the imminent second coming of Christ. Francesco Ximines de Cisneros, the leader of the reformed spiritual Franciscans and the queen's confessor, founded a university to prepare an elite for the coming millennium.[4] The Franciscan Fray Melchior, born into a converso family in Burgos, prophesied in 1512 imminent revolutionary changes: The Holy Roman Empire and the papacy would be overturned; all the clergy would be killed, apart from an elect who would be preserved to accomplish the work of renovation, the church would be transformed and situated in Jerusalem, and all of humanity would live in virtue and happiness. He started conventicles of followers and found disciples among the conversos.[5]

In Portugal, millenarianism attracted many conversos. When David Reubeni arrived in Portugal in 1528, he found more support among conversos than he had in the Jewish communities of Italy, and he tried to persuade them that he was a warrior and not a miracle worker. When Diogo Pires, who would change his name to Solomon Molcho, first encountered Reubeni in the court of John III of Portugal, he believed that Reubeni would take on the role of the commander of the forces of the messiah.[6] Reubeni and Molcho's activities continued outside Portugal. Within Portugal perhaps the most influential converso messiah was Luis Dias, an unlettered tailor who lived in Setúbal, a seaport south of Lisbon. He attracted a considerable following of conversos who believed that he worked miracles, and they gave their children to him to be circumcised. Together with eighty-three of his followers, he was burned at the stake in Lisbon in 1542.[7]

Conversos also contributed to the Portuguese millenarianism in its royal form. In the 1530s, in the province of Beira, a cobbler, Gonçalo Eannes Bandarra of Trancoso, prophesied the reappearance of a hidden king, the redeemer of mankind. Bandarra was in close contact with many conversos who believed in his prophecies. His prophetic verses were later interpreted as predicting the death of the young king San Sebastian in 1578 and his future return. The king's body was never recovered after his death in battle in Morocco, and many Portuguese would not accept that he had died. Conversos contributed to the belief in Sebastian as the national messiah who would return and liberate his people.[8]

The Background to Converso Millenarianism

Until the late 1440s, the position of the conversos in Spain was comparatively good. They were not fully accepted into Christian society, but they were able to enter occupations closed to the Jews. Many experienced rapid social mobility; they entered the professions and obtained important offices in the municipal councils, the church, and the state. They provided the chief financial officials at court, and many assimilated into the nobility. Many "Old Christians" resented the success of the "New Christians," and tension arose, especially in Toledo and the cities of Andalusia where the power of the throne was weak. In 1449, mobs attacked conversos in Toledo, and from then until 1474 conversos had to endure a series of riots and popular uprisings against them. Their troubles increased with the passing of the "purity of blood" statutes, which were intended to exclude them from public administration, academic life, religious orders, and cathedral chapters. At first only a few towns and institutions adopted the statutes, but discrimination became pronounced after the establishment of the Spanish Inquisition, which began its operations in 1480.[9]

The Inquisition directed its activities against the conversos and instilled fear into the lives of even the most sincere converts and their descendants. The category of New Christians included not only the converts themselves but also their children and grandchildren—anyone in fact with known Jewish ancestry. All of them, including the second and third generations of pious Catholics, were subject to suspicion of Judaizing and accusations of heresy.[10]

In Portugal, as in Spain, a period of relative tolerance and social mobility preceded one of persecution and a rapid fall in fortune. From the mass conversion of the Jews in Portugal in 1497 to the late 1530s, however, the situation was far better in Portugal than in Spain. As in Spain in the first half of the fifteenth century, conversion to Catholicism in Portugal eliminated the legal disqualifications that applied to Jews and lifted many barriers to social mobility. The Portuguese conversos became physicians, financiers, and commercial entrepreneurs, and they entered the army, the universities, and the church. In the first decades of the sixteenth century they almost monopolized finance and high commerce in Portugal. Some acquired enormous wealth and intermarried with the nobility.

A few conversos in Portugal were killed in mob attacks on them in the late 1520s, but the major blow for the Portuguese conversos came with the establishment of the Portuguese Inquisition in 1536. The first auto-da-fé took place in Lisbon in 1540, and in 1547 a bull bestowed great authority upon the Inquisition. Thus in both Spain and Portugal a period of relative security and economic and social success was followed by discrimination and persecution. The "fall of fortune" became a common experience of the conversos; many who had successfully pursued wealth and honor lost their property, became targets of the Inquisition, or lived in fear of that persecution.[11] Millenarianism appealed more to the poorer conversos, who had not experienced wealth and status, but they were no less affected than their richer brethren by mob attacks and persecution by the Inquisition.

Historians have disagreed over the extent to which the conversos continued to identify themselves as Jews and to practice the Jewish religion. I. F. Baer and Haim Beinart have argued that most Spanish conversos, including their children and grandchildren, were crypto-Jews or Marranos and that the Inquisition correctly evaluated the character of the conversos when it prosecuted thousands for continuing to practice Judaism.[12] An opposite view, expressed by B. Netanyahu and Norman Roth, is that most conversos had become detached from Judaism by the time the Spanish Inquisition began its operations in 1480.[13] Stephen Haliczer distinguished three broad groups of conversos in the kingdom of Valencia when the Inquisition began its operations in the mid-1480s. One group did everything to maintain a Judaic style of life and maintained close relationships with the local Jewish communities; another believed in and practiced Judaism and Christianity simultaneously, and a third saw themselves as true Catholics. The proportions of these categories are difficult to determine, but there can be little doubt that the Inquisition thwarted the process of assimilation and strengthened a converso identity.[14]

An important distinction should be made between the conversos of Spain and those of Portugal. For a whole century in Spain, from 1391 to 1492, a substantial converso population lived in a society with a substantial Jewish population. Some Jews had little sympathy for the conversos, and the harsher Jewish critics denied them a share in the Redemption.[15] Others received the conversos in their synagogues and provided occasional instruction. Most Jews were reserved toward conversos, neither encouraging their crypto-Judaism nor openly rejecting them as apostates.[16] The expulsion of the Jews and the persecutions, spoliations, and emigration of conversos left only small, isolated crypto-Jewish groups in Spain. In Portugal, the whole Jewish population, including the most tenacious Jews who had chosen exile from Spain, was converted in one sweep, and all Jewish energies were immediately directed to the organization of a converso community. The fact that conversion was the norm in Portugal increased the cohesion of the Portuguese converts, and their crypto-Judaism was stronger and lasted longer than in Spain.[17]

The levels of Jewish observance among conversos varied greatly, but it is evident that by rabbinic standards the overwhelming majority of conversos, including the most loyal crypto-Jews, came to deviate substantially from Judaism. Judaism, a strongly ritualistic religion, was not easy to keep secret, and although some possessed Hebrew prayer books as well as Jewish religious books in Spanish, the conversos became increasingly dependent on oral transmission. Knowledge of Hebrew declined until it was lost completely, the absence of prayer books reduced the stock of prayers to a few, only vestiges of the dietary laws remained, the observance of the Sabbath came to be limited to one or two rites, and most religious holidays were forgotten or neglected.[18]

The influence of Catholicism and the syncretic nature of converso religion were obvious at many points. Worshipers no longer covered their heads; kneeling during services was prevalent; Catholic prayers were used with only slight modifications and omissions, and prayers were recited rather than chanted in the traditional manner. In some instances crypto-Jews adopted Catholic forms in order to strengthen their Jewish identity. In reciting that salvation was possible only through the Law of Moses and not through the Law of Christ, crypto-Jews used the language of Catholicism to confess their Jewish faith. The victims of the Inquisition were revered as saints according to Christian models: They were incorporated into the liturgy; candles were burned in their honor; and their intercession with heaven was sought.[19]

The attenuation of Judaism led many conversos to center their religion on a few doctrines, especially the denial of the Christian claim that Jesus was the messiah. The belief in a Jewish messiah who was yet to come became a major, sometimes the only, Jewish principle of many conversos. The desperate desire of some to retain their Jewishness, despite the dangers and fear of the Inquisition, led them to believe in the miraculous appearance of the messiah as their only hope. Their suffering made no sense if the messiah had already come; if Jesus was the messiah, they asked, why had they not been able to assimilate and find peace and honor? They were saved from despair only by their belief in redemption. The Marranos sang, "Has the redeemer already come? No—*this one* is not the redeemer; the redeemer is yet to come."[20]

Although crypto-Jewish conversos often defined their religious identity by denying the messiahship of Jesus, their messianism was nevertheless influenced by their Catholicism. They used Christian terminology, referring to their messiah as the Antichrist or the true Christ, and in place of the Jewish concept of a human, politically oriented messiah, they envisaged a messiah who worked miracles and whose mission included the saving of souls. Their messianic scenarios deviated from those of both Judaism and Christianity and focused on their salvation, their resettlement in Zion, and the punishment of their enemies, the Old Christians, and the inquisitors.[21]

Former Conversos and the Sabbatai Zvi movement

Large numbers of Spanish and Portuguese Jews had chosen conversion under duress, including the threat of death or the choice of expulsion, but even those who became devout Christians faced discrimination, suspicion, and possible persecution by the Inquisition. After Portugal was annexed by Spain in 1580, some conversos migrated to Spain to escape the Portuguese Inquisition and the country's declining economy. The activities of the Spanish Inquisition were renewed against the "Portuguese," the term by which New Christians came to be known in Spain, and Portuguese conversos became the inquisitors' principal target in the seventeenth century.[22] Many left the Iberian Peninsula, and, where possible, they returned to Judaism.

The emigration of conversos from Spain began after the forced conversions of 1391, but that was a short-lived movement. Emigration increased in the second half of the fifteenth century, especially after the establishment of the Inquisition in 1481. A larger emigration of conversos from Portugal began after the forced conversions of 1497, increased after the introduction of the Inquisition in 1536, and accelerated with the intensification of persecution after 1630.[23] Some conversos settled in Morocco, but at the end of the fifteenth century, most settled in the Ottoman Empire, particularly in the larger towns of Turkey, Syria, and Palestine. The Ottoman rulers welcomed the conversos as innovative entrepreneurs, and they had no objection to their returning to Judaism. In Christian Europe the conversos first migrated to a number of Italian cities (Florence, Ferrara, Ancona, Livorno) that were willing to accept conversos who openly reverted to Judaism. In other European cities in which they settled, particularly Hamburg and Amsterdam, the conversos had at first to proclaim themselves to be Catholic while secretly practicing Judaism, but after they came to be accepted openly as Jews, their numbers increased. Most who settled in these cities were not, in fact, conversos who had "returned" to Judaism but rather the descendants of converts who had undergone baptism more than a century before.[24] These former conversos were among the most fervent believers in Sabbatai Zvi as the messiah in 1665–66.

The Sabbatean movement was the largest and most widespread messianic outburst in Jewish history. It began in Gaza, Palestine, where in the spring of 1665 Nathan Ashkenazi, a young mystic, convinced a number of Jews that he had had a prophetic vision and that it had been revealed to him that Sabbatai Zvi, a rabbi from Izmir (Smyrna), resident at that time in Palestine, was the messiah. Sabbatai had previously made known his messianic pretensions, but it was Nathan's announcement that generated support. Enthusiasm grew among the communities in Palestine, and when Sabbatai returned through Syria to his former home in Izmir, he was greeted in a number of towns as the messiah. Sabbatai contributed to the spread of the belief in his messiahship by his travels through communities in Palestine, Turkey, the Balkans, and Egypt, but he did not travel outside the Ottoman Empire or to a community in Europe. Sabbatai and Nathan sent delegates to a number of communities, but the messianic tidings spread far beyond the area of activities of Sabbatai, Nathan, and their immediate circle, first to many communities under Islam and then, in the last months of 1665, to communities in Europe. In 1666 many Jewish communities were greatly excited by letters and rumors that told of miracles and apocalyptic events that were believed to presage an imminent return to the Holy Land and redemption.[25]

News traveled fast from one Jewish community to another, particularly through the wide network of Sephardic communities, including former conversos and networks of kin, friends, acquaintances, and tradesmen. Letters from Palestine took only ten to twenty days to arrive in Turkey or Italy. The development of printing in the sixteenth and seventeenth centuries had quickened communication, and news of the messiah appeared in news sheets read by a wide public, Jewish and Christian. Much of the information on Sabbatai was relayed within elite groups, including rabbis, priests, diplomats, and traders, but letters and rumors also circulated among lower strata. It was important to the spread of the movement that a small circle of mostly Sephardic rabbis became convinced and spread their belief by person and by mail. Their opinion carried sufficient authority to convince a large number of Jews, including other important rabbis. The most important opponents were from the rabbinic elite, but the belief in Sabbatai crossed the social strata in many Jewish communities.[26]

Matt Goldish has argued convincingly that the prophecies of ordinary Jews, including those from the lower strata, were critical to the spread of Sabbateanism in the winter of 1665–66. Sabbatai, Nathan, and their early followers lost control of the messianic message as prophecy shifted from the learned elite to that of ordinary Jews, including women and children. Nathan proclaimed that belief in Sabbatai was not to be dependent on signs or wonders, but believers supplied their own miracles and visions, including pillars of fire, portents in the sky, and sightings of the prophet Elijah. Descriptions of pillars of fire, first reported around Sabbatai, were taken up by believers who saw them everywhere, adding their embellishments. Penitential exercises, including intense fasting and self-flagellation, were widely performed, and spiritual possession, following a standard pattern, was common. A visionary would enter a trance, a voice issued from his or her mouth pronouncing the messiahship of Sabbatai, and the person would wake up from a faint with no memory of what he or she had said. The popular prophecies were a target of the movement's opponents, who were contemptuous of the prophecies of ignorant people, including women and children, who had none of the qualifications and had done nothing to prepare themselves for communication from God.[27]

CHAPTER 5

Expectations of an imminent redemption reached a pitch early in 1666 when Sabbatai sailed from Izmir to Istanbul. Many expected that he would remove the crown from the sultan, assume rulership over the Ottoman Empire, and inaugurate the messianic era. Sabbatai was imprisoned for insurrection, but with the help of bribes he managed to meet with his followers and hold court in some style for several months. News of Sabbatai's miraculous actions, such as his resurrection of the dead and his passing through locked doors, continued during his imprisonment. In September 1666 Sabbatai was given the choice between execution and conversion to Islam. Sabbatai chose conversion, and after clear confirmation of his apostasy, the great majority admitted that they had been mistaken in believing him to be the messiah.[28] A minority continued to believe, and the movement continued to develop in a number of sectarian forms. The focus here, however, is on the widespread millenarianism among Jews in 1665–66.

Gershom Scholem's explanation for the ready acceptance of Sabbatai Zvi as the messiah was the diffusion throughout the Jewish world of a messianic form of kabbalah formulated by Isaac Luria Ashkenazi (1534–72) and his disciples in the town of Safed in Palestine. According to Scholem, the decisive innovation that gave the Lurianic kabbalah its great appeal was the transposition of the central concepts of exile and redemption from the historical to the cosmic plane. The terrestrial exile of the Jewish people had its counterpart in a primordial cosmic event, the shattering of the "vessels" that had contained God's spheres of holiness. Since the breaking of the vessels, which had resulted in the mixing of God's lights with the realm of exile, exile had been a fundamental aspect of all existence. The all-important goal was to purge the divine lights of its impurities and to restore the ideal spiritual order, and Jews had a major part in this process of *tikkun* (cosmic mending).

By performing the mitzvot and through their mystical worship, Jews contributed to the progressive separation of good and evil and the perfection of their maker. The Lurianic ideas were mediated to the masses in the seventeenth century by popular preachers who proclaimed that the process of cosmic repair was almost complete and that following the Lurianic teaching was a means of bringing the messiah. Once the preachers had successfully implanted the doctrine of *tikkun* into the popular consciousness, "the eschatological mood was bound to grow." Thus Scholem's contention was that "the growing dominance of the kabbalah on the popular consciousness of the time, and particularly among the fervently religious, must be seen as the general background which made the movement possible."[29]

Scholem's explanation of the appeal of Sabbateanism is basically an idealist one. It is an outcome of developments in kabbalah. Nonreligious factors were of little consequence. Scholem did not adequately address the question of why Lurianic kabbalah became widely diffused and popular, but he noted a relationship with the expulsion from Spain. Although the messianic expectations following the expulsion had been disappointed, the event and its consequences were recast by the Lurianic kabbalists, who assimilated them into their notion of exile, which was a cosmic as well as human event.[30]

Scholem presents no evidence to show that the notion of *tikkun* had spread beyond small groups of Jewish mystics, and when he discusses the support for Sabbatai among unscholarly Jews, he admits that they were far removed from kabbalistic speculations.[31] The influence of Lurianic kabbalah on the reception of the masses to Sabbatai Zvi is unlikely because few Lurianic writings had been printed before the messianic outburst, and it is doubtful whether many would have understood them.[32] Sabbatai himself was a "classical" rather than Lurianic kabbalist, conversant more with the Zohar than with Lurianic ideas, which he opposed. Jacob Barnai notes that Sabbatai was expelled from Jerusalem, a town where Lurianic kabbalah was important, and was accepted as the messiah in Izmir, a town where Lurianic kabbalah was unimportant.[33]

Moshe Idel argues that the messianic element was only a minor element in Lurianic kabbalah and that Scholem exaggerated its importance by too strongly projecting the notions of exile and redemption into kabbalistic metaphysics and ritual.[34] Idel also questions any connection between Lurianism and the expulsion from Spain by noting that there is not a single reference to the expulsion in the whole of Lurianic kabbalah.[35] David Biale argues that the Lurianic kabbalists were antimessianic because they conceived of *tikkun* as a gradual process that depended on the religiosity of generations and not on the coming of the messiah.[36] Goldish gives more credence to the importance of messianism among the kabbalists of Safed, but he notes that, among the Jewish masses, tales of the kabbalists' miracles were more important than their mystical ideas. Although few Jews in the 1660s had studied Lurianic kabbalah, the hagiography concerning Luria and the Safed mystical circle was widespread. Nathan augmented his authority by successfully presenting himself as following the prophetic-mystical path of Luria and the Safed kabbalistic circles.[37]

The influence of Lurianic kabbalah may have been a contributing factor to the messianic outburst, but it cannot be regarded as a sufficient or even major cause. The centers of Sabbatean enthusiasm in 1665–66 show a closer correspondence with another factor: the geographic distribution of the Iberian exiles and, in particular, the distribution of the former conversos. Scholem did not ignore the former conversos, but because he argued that the belief in Sabbatai was widespread among a large proportion of Jews throughout almost the whole Diaspora, he did not perceive the former conversos as a major factor. In fact, Scholem's own data demonstrate that the Jewish communities could be distinguished by their levels of support and that these corresponded in large part with the distribution of former conversos. Three categories of Jewish communities can be distinguished with respect to their differences in the proportion of believers in Sabbatai, the strength of the community's commitment, and the forms of messianic activities. In the first category the great majority were believers, commitment was high, and individuals participated in mass ecstatic behavior. In the second category a majority or a substantial minority were believers, commitment varied, and repentance was the main expression of the beliefs. In the third category, only a small minority were believers, and, as in the second type, repentance was the main activity. For a number of communities sufficient evidence to place them firmly in one category or another is lacking.

Most of the communities in the first two categories had high concentrations of former conversos and their descendants. The first category is composed principally of towns in the Ottoman Empire, in Turkey, Syria, and Palestine, that had become major settlements of former conversos. The communities in Istanbul, Aleppo, and Izmir can be placed firmly in the first category; the communities of Gaza, Hebron, Safed, and Damascus were possibly closer to category 2. The second category is composed principally of those European towns with large proportions of former conversos. The communities of Salonika, Livorno, Ancona, Venice, Amsterdam, Hamburg, Tripoli, and Alexandria can be placed firmly in category 2; somewhat less firm in their placement are the communities of Frankfurt, Vienna, Prague, Yemen, Cairo, and some parts of Morocco, Persia, and Kurdistan. The communities in the third category, with no or few former conversos, are in Poland, Bohemia-Moravia, Hungary, France, and most of Germany. For the communities in the third category, the evidence that Scholem presented did not support his general statements of majority support. Certainly, some in these areas were fervent believers, but for most the happenings in the Middle East were simply a matter of news.[38]

A direct connection between former conversos and Sabbatai Zvi was present from the beginning of the messianic activities in Izmir, Sabbatai's hometown. A Jewish community had been established in Izmir in the sixteenth century, when the town became an international trading center. The town's Jews were mostly from Spain and Portugal, descendants of those who had been expelled from Spain and conversos from Spain and Portugal who had returned to Judaism. Former conversos and their descendants continued to settle in Izmir in the seventeenth century, and they became one of the strongest and wealthiest groups in the city. Several of Sabbatai's closest childhood friends came from converso families, and they had a marked influence on him: He spoke Spanish, studied in Sephardic yeshivas, and loved to sing Spanish romances. When Sabbatai returned to Izmir as the messiah and took over the Jewish community's government, he appointed former conversos to special positions in his inner circle.[39]

Izmir was one of the towns where reports of popular prophecies originated. Reports also came out of Safed, Aleppo, and other locations in Turkey and Greece in the winter of 1665–66. When the names of the prophets were mentioned, most were Sephardic names. How many of these were former conversos is difficult to estimate, but the converso background of some can be traced from documents. Indications of Christian influences, such as the prominent part played by women and children and the readiness to allow faith in the messiah to override rabbinic law, also point to the importance of former conversos in the movement.[40] Former conversos were conversant with Christianity from their background, and after their return to Judaism, many continued to have extensive contacts with Christians.

Scholem completely rejected the possibility of Christian influence on the Sabbatean movement, but his arguments were mainly directed against the view that

Sabbatai's father, Mordecai, heard rumors from English merchants about the millennial date of 1666 and passed them on to his son. Scholem wrote that propaganda for the date 1666 appeared in Dutch and English literature only in the 1650s.[41] In fact, as early as 1597 one English writer had fixed on 1666, calculated from the number of the Beast (666) in Revelation, as the date when the anti-Christian Rome would fall; moreover, there was widespread discussion in England on the date both before the 1650s and continuing up to 1666, and elsewhere in Europe hopes were focused on that year.[42] Sabbatai was a well-traveled man, and he might have heard about the Christian millenarian beliefs from a number of sources;[43] but speculation regarding Christian influence on Sabbatai is largely beside the point. More important is the possible influence of the widespread millenarianism among the Christian contacts of the former conversos and other Sephardim.

Scholem noted that, whereas most Christian writers disparaged the movement, some Dutch Christian millenarians were enthusiastic and contrasted the penitential revival of the Jews of Amsterdam with the laxness of Christians. Peter Serrarius, a leading Flemish millenarian who had contacts with Protestant circles all over Europe, expected the conversion of the Jews, but he also sympathized with the Sabbateans and had visions of Israel's glory in the new kingdom.[44] Serrarius had many Jewish friends in Amsterdam, but Scholem does not infer from such facts that Christian millenarians may at least have provided a stimulus to Jewish millenarianism. To recognize such a factor would be to go against his consistent emphasis on "the immanent development of eschatological traditions in rabbinic and kabbalistic Judaism."[45]

Many former conversos were familiar with intellectual developments, scientific and religious, among Christians. Although a direct causal connection between Christian and Jewish millenarianism may not have existed, the fact that the largest messianic movement in Jewish history occurred at a time of widespread millenarianism among Christians, especially Protestants, cannot be ignored. Protestant Reformers, such as Martin Luther and Ulrich Zwingli, had rejected expectations of a literal paradise on earth, and in 1530 the Lutheran Confession of Augsberg denounced millenarianism as a "Jewish doctrine." But millenarianism was integral to radical reformers, such as Thomas Müntzer and Melchior Hoffman, and Protestant millenarianism continued in strength throughout the sixteenth and seventeenth centuries.

Millenarianism in England was especially prominent around the time of the execution of Charles I in January 1649, and during Cromwell's republic many believed that Christ's return was imminent. Radical forms of millenarianism, advocating social revolution, appeared in such movements as the Fifth Monarchists, the Diggers, and the Levellers, and, although these movements were short-lived, their millennial expectations were shared in large part by surviving movements such as the Baptists and Quakers, who accommodated themselves to the social and political order. Millennial expectations were also widespread among Protestant groups in the Netherlands, Germany, Bohemia, and Switzerland. Catholic millenarians had seen the Protestant break with Rome as one of the negative signs of the end of time, but as the Protestants became more millenarian and denounced the pope as the Antichrist, official Catholic circles became suspicious of millenarianism in any form. However, the Thirty Years' War was widely regarded by Catholics as well as Protestants as a struggle marking the last days, and Catholic and Protestant monarchs were commonly allocated messianic roles.[46]

Conversos contributed to the Catholic millenarianism of Sebastian in Portugal. A contribution to Christian millenarianism in France was made by Isaac La Peyrere, a son of a wealthy New Christian family resident in Bordeaux. Like many conversos from Portugal who settled in the south of France, La Peyrere was raised as a Calvinist. He moved to Paris in 1644, where he became the secretary and confidant of the Prince of Conde, a powerful nobleman with pretensions to the French crown. La Peyrere wrote works in 1643 and 1655 in which he argued that the Jewish messiah was about to appear and join forces with the king of France. The king would gather the Jews in France, convert them, and lead them to the Holy Land from which he would rule the world together with the messiah and his Jewish Christians.[47]

Interest in Sabbatai Zvi was expressed by Christians, both pro- and antimillenarians. Pamphlets appeared in England telling of miraculous events that indicated that the restoration of the Jewish people in their homeland was imminent, and some writers sought to denigrate English millenarians by claiming that Sabbateanism was derived from their millenarianism.[48] Parallels between the behavior of believers in Sabbatai Zvi and the Quakers were recognized by contemporaries, and it is worth noting that Quaker missionaries were present in Izmir, Istanbul, and Jerusalem in 1657–58. However, similar behaviors associated with visions and prophecies could be found among a number of Christian groups, such as the Spanish spirituals, mainly women, both nuns and beatified laypersons.[49] Parallels could also be found in the Islamic world, especially in Sufi groups and among Bektashi dervishes, who were numerous in the Ottoman Empire. Islamic millenarian groups gathered around the figure of the Mahdi close to the time of Sabbatai Zvi, but Mahdism was less prominent in the seventeenth century compared with previous centuries, and although Islamic messianic influence on Jews cannot be ruled out, the evidence of contacts between millenarians from different religions is confined to Jews and Christians.[50]

A prominent example of a former converso who had many Christian contacts was the fervent messianist Menasseh ben Israel (1604–57). Menasseh was baptized in Madeira, a Portuguese territory, but when his family moved to Amsterdam, they openly returned to Judaism and Menasseh eventually became a rabbi and the head of a yeshiva. In addition to his knowledge of rabbinic and mystical literature, Menasseh was widely read in classical literature and Christian theology. His friends included not only the elite of the Jewish community but also Christian theologians and other scholars in Holland, Sweden, Germany, and France.[51] Like many Christian millenarians, Menasseh believed in the importance of the ten lost tribes in the process of redemption, and he expressed his views in *The Hope of God*, a book published in Amsterdam in 1650. A Spanish edition of the book was published in Izmir, where former conversos read it and wrote poems in its honor.[52]

Menasseh was encouraged in his belief that the messiah was imminent by a report of a Portuguese explorer who claimed he had found members of the lost tribes in the Andes Mountains. Menasseh believed that redemption required the dispersal of the Jews in all parts of the world, and because the formal admission of the Jews to England appeared to him as a vital prelude to the Redemption, he traveled to England in 1655 to petition Cromwell to readmit them. The massacres of Jews in Poland in 1648 and other events, such as the Thirty Years' War, the revolt in England, and the execution of the king, were interpreted by Menasseh as birth pangs of the messiah, a view shared by many of his Christian friends. But the tragedy that Menasseh felt most closely was that of the conversos. Not only his own family but also most of his Jewish friends in Amsterdam were former conversos and their descendants, and the reports of autos-da-fé in Spain, Portugal, and other dependencies made a deep impression on him.[53] Like many other former conversos, Menasseh lived in conditions of relative freedom and prosperity, but the past sufferings of the conversos and the continuing suffering of those who remained in the Iberian Peninsula still posed problems of religious meaning. In the 1640s and 1650s the Inquisition accused hundreds of conversos of being secret Jews and burned dozens at the stake. The converso Diaspora learned with great pain of the persecutions and killings.

An understanding of the success of Sabbateanism requires an examination of the religious, social, and psychological problems of the former conversos. Scholars have noted the contradiction that many conversos encountered between their expectations of Judaism before their return to Judaism and the reality that they found after it. For most former conversos their return was the espousal not of a religion in which they had previously been members but of the religion of their ancestors; they had been baptized, and most had had a Catholic upbringing. Many had been introduced to the Marrano religion in their adolescence; others had turned to Judaism only when they were persecuted by the Inquisition or were discriminated against. Most knew little Hebrew, the Talmud, or the rabbinic traditions, and the limited knowledge that they did have was often distorted.[54]

It was not an easy or simple matter to step over the religious gulf between Catholicism or the converso religion and rabbinic Judaism. Males had to undergo circumcision, and they had to acquire a considerable knowledge of ritual practice and religious law. Some accepted without question their new religion. Others resented the elaborate system of rituals, many of which appeared to be irrational and unjustified, as did the authority of the rabbinate. The more educated former conversos, many of whom had been students and teachers in Spanish universities—at that time among the most advanced scientific and philosophical centers of Christendom—particularly resented these strictures. They had rejected the authority of the church and the priesthood, and they were now expected to accept the discipline of the Jewish community and its rabbis, to whom many educated former conversos felt intellectually superior.[55]

Most former conversos remained in Judaism, but just as the first-generation conversos, whatever their commitment to Catholicism, were not able to be ordinary Catholics, so their descendants who adopted Judaism could not be ordinary Jews and take either their Judaism or their relationships with other Jews for granted. In a number of communities, such as Istanbul, where the Jewish community was substantial even before the converso influx, Jews were suspicious and distrustful of the former conversos. They were offended by the ignorance of the former conversos regarding Jewish rites and customs, and they often treated them with sarcasm or pity. Some Jews accused the former conversos of secretly remaining Christians and hiding their crucifixes. Others defended them, arguing that the Marranos had never been true Christians and that their faithfulness to Judaism should not be questioned.[56]

Even in communities such as Salonika and Amsterdam in which the former conversos formed the dominant section of the Jewish community and other Jews did not question their status, their experiences as former conversos gave rise to perplexity, self-questioning, and deep problems of identity. The former conversos had gone through the experience of what Peter Berger has termed alternation: They had passed between logically contradictory meaning systems. Alternation is a phenomenon of the modern world, when people are able to choose between varying and sometimes contradictory intellectual universes.[57] What was peculiar about the former conversos was that they experienced alternation in a largely traditional society, a society of closed and binding worldviews in which people were assigned definite and permanent identities. The Christian and Jewish worlds in the seventeenth century were separated by legal, cultural, and social barriers; Jews and Christians had little contact beyond formal economic and political relationships, and each group regarded the other as another species of being. In such a society alternation caused acute problems of identity and location in society. Many former conversos retained a nostalgia for the land of their births, and a few returned despite the dangers. Some retained a fondness for Catholicism, and a few returned to the religion of their childhood. Others, identifying strongly with Judaism, felt an overwhelming sense of guilt and sought pardon for their Catholic past by such practices as wearing hair shirts.[58]

The society of the former conversos, with its conflicts, tensions, and problems of identity, produced both heretics, such as Uriel da Costa and Baruch Spinoza in Amsterdam, and a high level of millenarianism. Having rejected one religious system, a few former conversos rejected another and chose to remain outside or on the margins of both Christian and Jewish societies.[59] The majority committed themselves to Judaism,[60] and in 1666 many found an immediate cure for their problems of doubt, the conflicts they felt between their childhood socialization and their adult resocialization, their feelings of guilt over their Christian past, and the

Millenarianism Among Conversos and Former Conversos

tensions involved in adopting a new religion and a new identity. By their belief in Sabbatai, the former conversos declared their full commitment to Judaism and immediately put behind them the problems of adopting a complex system of religious rituals. The commitment to the Jewish messiah was the decisive test; their past was to be forgiven and forgotten, and they were now assured of redemption.

The contention here is that the Sabbatean movement would not have been so widespread and important without the former conversos, but in many communities the major support came from Jews who had not been conversos. In some cases these Jews may have been influenced by the enthusiasm of the former conversos, but the latter were not always present in numbers that would achieve such an impact. Additional factors that might have contributed to the millenarian outburst must be considered.

In the past many historians emphasized the importance of the 1648 massacres of Polish Jews. Ukrainian peasants and Cossacks led by Bogdan Chmielnicki swept through large areas of Poland, killing Polish nobles, Catholic clergymen, and Jews. The uprising was an expression of religious, ethnic, and economic class divisions and conflicts; the Orthodox Ukrainian peasants were rebelling against the Polish Catholic landowners and their Jewish administrators and middlemen. The Jews often bore the major brunt of the attacks, and it has been estimated that 40,000–50,000 Jews (20–25 percent of the total Polish Jewish population) were killed.[61]

Scholem wrote that the 1648 massacres could not explain the messianic enthusiasm among Jewish communities that were far from Poland and had heard little of the events.[62] Barnai has argued that the disturbances continued longer and that their effects were more widespread than Scholem had acknowledged. The uprising and wars in Poland and Lithuania and the accompanying destruction continued for eighteen years (1648–67). Before the 1648 massacres, the Thirty Years' War (1618–48) in Germany and central Europe resulted in many Jewish refugees, and after the massacres the war between Sweden and Poland (1655–60) led to further expulsions, persecutions, and killings of Polish Jews. Jewish refugees from Poland arrived in Italy, Germany, Holland, the Ottoman Empire, and even as far as the Maghreb. Jewish communities were well informed about the massacres, and some organized help for the refugees. The massacres made an impression on Sabbatai, who married a refugee from Poland in Egypt in 1664.[63]

Barnai admits that there is no direct link between the massacres in Poland and Sabbateanism, but he argues that the massacres were an important background factor.[64] It should be emphasized, however, that the Polish Jews themselves demonstrated the traditional nonmessianic responses of Ashkenazim to persecution: They condemned the perpetrators of the killings and identified the victims as martyrs, but they also stated that the moral and religious deficiencies of the Jewish people had unleashed the wrath of heaven. There were warnings concerning the observance of the mitzvot, further restrictions were placed on dress, penitential prayers were composed, and additional fasts were instituted.[65]

CHAPTER 5

A more general background factor was what many historians have termed the "crisis of the seventeenth century." The crisis included economic decline, especially in the Mediterranean area, a fall in banking profits and prices, political instability, and social revolts. There is a wide consensus among historians that the economic boom of sixteenth-century Europe came to an end during the first half of the seventeenth century and was followed by a period of economic stagnation. About midcentury, even Holland, which was enjoying a position of economic hegemony in Europe, began to experience economic contraction.[66]

The Sephardim, including the conversos and former conversos, were especially involved in the commercial developments of the sixteenth century, and their position made them particularly susceptible to the economic and political crises of the seventeenth century. The most dramatic economic declines occurred in the Ottoman Empire and Italy, two major areas of Sephardic and former converso settlement. The Ottoman Empire reached the limits of its expansion in the sixteenth century, and the Sephardim were among the important builders of its commercial and industrial structures. A network of Jewish merchants stretched over the whole empire, Jewish industrialists built up the cloth trade, and Jews were prominent among the tax-farmers, physicians, diplomats, officials, and courtiers of the sultans. The decline of the empire began in the last decades of the sixteenth century; it suffered naval defeats, revolts of the army, a shrinking economy, struggles of power, palace intrigues, a corrupt administration, and the increasing ineffectiveness of central control. The town of Izmir was an exception; it developed economically in the years preceding Sabbateanism, when the empire as a whole and the Jews within it were undergoing economic decline.[67]

Italy, the European center of late medieval and early modern commerce and manufacture, fell into a deep decline. At the beginning of the seventeenth century, central and northern Italy were still among the most highly developed regions in Europe, but by about 1680 industry had collapsed, leaving a backward region. Competition from nations that were expanding their industrial, banking, and maritime activities led to a drastic decline in Italy's exports and a consequent withdrawal of investment from industry, banking, and shipping. Venice and Livorno, which were among the towns where former conversos had concentrated, were exceptions in the last decades of the seventeenth century insofar as the Jews enjoyed a prosperous existence and friendly relationships with Gentiles. However, neither town was immune from the decline of the Italian economy, and after they reached their peaks in about the middle of the century, they too began to decline.[68] Thus, although many of the centers of Sabbateanism in the Ottoman Empire and Italy were comparatively prosperous communities, they had passed the height of their economic prosperity, political freedom, and social accomplishments and had experienced often sharp and drastic declines in their situations.

Not all centers of former conversos suffered from economic decline. Hamburg and Amsterdam remained prosperous communities despite a decline in the overall German economy and problems in Holland's trade and colonial expansion.[69]

However, the crisis in the wider society was not confined to economic matters but was evident also in an effusion of competing intellectual systems and in a series of revolts and political conflicts over the issues of local autonomy and centralization. Holland's economic prosperity did not make it immune to tensions over political centralization, and the country's comparative tolerance encouraged the expression of intellectual controversies over fundamental matters of religion and philosophy.[70]

Some communities that were caught up in the messianic excitement in 1665–66 had neither former conversos nor other Sephardim present in any number or at all. A common element in these communities (Yemen, Morocco, Frankfurt, Prague, Vienna) was their economic distress and persecuted state during this period.[71] Of course, other poor and persecuted communities were not conspicuous in their support of Sabbatai, and other factors, such as geographic location and the communication networks of Jewish communities, were no doubt relevant. Vienna, for example, was close to the Ottoman border.

I do not claim to have accounted in full for the distribution of messianic support and enthusiasm in 1666, but I do claim to have gone some way in explaining the general pattern. There was no one cause but a convergence of factors. The importance of the former conversos appears to me to be the single most important consideration. The locations of many former conversos made them particularly susceptible to the crisis of the seventeenth century, but even where this was not the case, their cultural anomie and social and psychological strains made them particularly responsive to millenarianism.

Following Sabbatai Zvi's Conversion to Islam

Like other Jews, most former conversos abandoned the movement after Sabbatai's conversion to Islam, but because they had been among the most highly committed, many were ready to accept an explanation that justified Sabbatai's action. The common explanation was that Sabbatai's messianic role made it necessary for him to enter the evil realm represented by Islam. This explanation appeared independently in several places, but it was Nathan and his disciples who gave it a theological foundation by relating it to kabbalistic concepts and beliefs. Nathan argued that only the messiah could complete the extraction of the remaining divine sparks from the *kelippot* (literally shells or husks), or powers of evil, and that in order to do this, he had descended into the realm of the *kelippot* and assumed the form of evil. Outwardly, the messiah had to submit to the demands of the realm of impurity, but actually he was conquering the *kelippot* from within and rescuing the sparks that were imprisoned there.[72]

The former conversos were particularly ready to accept a religious interpretation of Sabbatai's conversion because his action was a repetition of their own biographies and family histories. If Scholem underestimated the importance of the former conversos in the movement in 1666, he fully acknowledged their prominence in the movement after the conversion. He wrote that the key to Sabbateanism at that stage was the paradoxical religious feelings of the former conversos and their children; without their disposition, he wrote, it is doubtful that the doctrine of the apostate messiah would have been adopted. They could easily accept that the conversion was not real but was the mask of a converso; they had also led a double life—the religion that they had professed was not the one that they believed. "The idea of an apostate messiah could be presented to them as a religious glorification of the very act which continued to torment their own conscience."[73] At first it was argued that the conversion occurred under such pressure that Sabbatai was left with no choice but to become a convert. This was, of course, how many former conversos had seen their own conversion to Christianity. At a later stage, the paradox was declared more openly. It was argued that the messiah had become a convert of his own free will. This interpretation enabled the former conversos to reinterpret their own conversions and to assuage their guilt still further; perhaps, like Sabbatai, their conversion had not represented an admission of weakness or cowardice but had been part of a cosmic process working toward redemption.[74]

6. THE SACREDNESS OF SIN

Antinomianism and Models of Man

Following the conversion of Sabbatai Zvi to Islam in 1666, a number of his followers interpreted Lurianic concepts to support an antinomian position: Only the descent of the messiah into evil would exhaust the full potential of evil and lead to its collapse. Scholem wrote, "Once it could be claimed that the Messiah's apostasy was in no way a transgression, but was rather a fulfillment of the commandment of God . . . the entire question of the continued validity of the Law had reached a critical stage."[1]

A central issue was whether the believers should follow Sabbatai in his descent into evil in order to redeem the divine sparks. The "moderate" Sabbateans drew a circle around the concept of "strange holiness": the apostasy of the messiah was not intended to serve as an example to others, and so long as Israel remained in exile and the exterior world remained unchanged, no commandment of the Torah could be violated. The "radical" Sabbateans believed that all the believers had to convert and descend into the evil realm to conquer evil from within and hasten salvation. The violation of the Torah became its true fulfillment; by outward transgression of the commandments, the spiritual elite were destroying the *kelippot* (shells or husks) by filling them with holiness. Alongside this idea, another somewhat contradictory notion was presented in support of antinomianism: It was impossible for those whose souls were already in the messianic world to sin. In the world of redemption, which the spiritual elite already inhabited, all is holy and everything is permitted; the Torah of the unredeemed world was cancelled, and its violation expressed a truer Torah that had been concealed in the premessianic world.[2]

Sabbateans disagreed about the appropriate behavior of the higher world and its Torah, but many radical Sabbateans put the antinomian ideas into practice.[3] The secret rituals of one of the subsects of the Sabbateans in Salonika included eating forbidden food, and the transgression of sexual prohibitions was used as an initiation rite. Ceremonial ritual fornication took place mainly during the ritual of the "extinguishing of the lights," celebrated at the beginning of spring.[4]

Antinomianism in Judaism has been coupled with messianism; with the coming of the messiah or the advent of the messianic era, a "higher" law is understood to nullify the Halacha, and believers may demonstrate this by deliberate transgressions. An earlier case of Jewish messianism was early Christianity, and Paul, its major propagandist to non-Jews, has been called the first Jewish antinomian. Paul's teaching that the Mosaic law had been abrogated by the "law of the Spirit" in Christ was ambiguous because he did not clarify the nature and boundaries of the new law or the extent to which it retained elements of the old law. This teaching has been interpreted as containing the seed of antinomianism, and a number of antinomian thinkers and movements can be found throughout the history of Christianity.[5] Antinomianism is not, however, confined to messianism in the monotheistic faiths. It has also been associated with mysticism and can be found in the nonmonotheistic world religions.

An important question here is whether antinomianism is an abnormal religious phenomenon with little or no relationship to prevailing religious, sometimes orthodox, conceptions, or whether it is one possible rational outcome of those prevailing, sometimes orthodox, systems. The answer to this question is an important preliminary to a consideration of the applicability of sociopsychological models. If we counterpose two models derived from the works of Sigmund Freud and Emile Durkheim, we might ask the following question: Is antinomianism an expression of man's basic sexual and destructive drives in revolt against the constraints of society, or is it a product of processes of learning and socialization within particular social and religious milieus? Is antinomianism a product of a normally latent but unalterable human nature, or does it demonstrate the phenomenal modifiability of human nature?

Antinomian ideas have been associated with dualistic metaphysical systems. Three types can be distinguished. First, radical dualism asserts that two supramundane forces or principles are in complete opposition to each other. Second is a metaphysical system that distinguishes a dualistic plane of existence that is false and relative from a monistic plane that is true and absolute. And the third idea is that an antithesis of the spiritual and material realms is confounded by the immanence of God or the Spirit in worldly phenomena or individuals. These metaphysical systems are more likely to provide a context for antinomian behavior when they are accompanied by certain soteriological beliefs: millenarianism (the belief in an imminent or current transformation of the cosmos) and mysticism (the belief in the individual's achievement of unity with the divine).[6]

Radical Dualism

The relationship between radical dualism and the antinomian idea can be illustrated with two historically unrelated movements: (1) the gnostics, who were centered in the eastern Mediterranean in the first centuries C.E., and (2) the Frankists, who were centered in a number of Jewish eastern European communities in the eighteenth century.

Gnosticism presented a radical dualism of God and the world, spirit and matter, soul and body, light and darkness, good and evil, life and death. It was not God who created and governs the world but rather the Archons, tyrannical demonic powers who imprison men and obstruct their knowledge of the absolute transmundane deity. Man's body and soul are products of the evil cosmic powers, but his spirit, or pneuma, contains a portion of the divine substance that has fallen into the world. The Archons created man in order to imprison this spirit, and in its unredeemed state, immersed in the soul and flesh, the pneuma is unconscious of its true quality.

The goal of the gnostics was to release the spirit from its material prison, and this was to be attained through revelation, knowledge of the way, allowing the spirit to force a passage through the spheres of matter and impurity. By reuniting with the divine, each individual contributed to the restoration of divine unity that had been impaired in precosmic times. After the completion of the process of divine unification, the cosmos, deprived of the elements of divine light, will come to an end. In this life the pneumatics, the possessors of the gnosis, are set apart from other men, and they show their elite status by their contempt for all mundane ties.

As Hans Jonas showed, two contrary conclusions were drawn from the gnostic doctrines: the ascetic and the antinomian. The ascetic emphasized the dangers of contamination from the world and reduced his contact with it to a minimum. The antinomian emphasized that conventional morality did not emanate from the hidden God but was part of the Archons' tyrannical bondage. It was necessary to thwart the evil designs of the Archons and seek salvation through violation of their moral law. Apart from what Jonas called a brief period of revolutionary extremism, the trend in gnosticism was in the direction of asceticism. Even when the antinomian idea was advanced, it is doubtful whether many gnostics practiced what they preached.[7]

Accusations of antinomian behavior were made against Christian dualist movements in the medieval period, but most accusations appear to have had little foundation. The major dualist heresies were Bogomilism, which arose in Bulgaria in the tenth century and spread to the Byzantine Empire, and its western offshoot, Catharism, which spread in France and Italy in the second half of the twelfth century and died out in the fourteenth. These movements began by professing a moderate dualism: The phenomenal world was the creation of Satan, but both Satan and Christ had been fathered by the one God. Beginning in the mid-twelfth century, the Bogomils moved to an absolute dualism: There were two coeternal principles of good and evil, and it was the evil principle that had created the phenomenal world. Absolute dualism spread to western Europe and gained many adherents in southern France. Because both moderate and absolute dualists believed that Satan had created the material world and held men captive in their flesh, they preached that they could attain perfection and become one with God by freeing their human spirits from materiality.⁸ Once perfect, the believer was no longer subject to worldly constraints, but, as John Passmore has noted, the meaning of "perfection" is ambiguous. The perfect man may no longer perform acts that men call sinful, but this may be taken to mean that whatever the perfect man does, however immoral in the eyes of other men, his acts cannot be counted as sins.⁹ The opponents of the dualist heresies argued that the dualists believed and acted on the second interpretation, but the evidence points to a scrupulous asceticism among most Bogomils and Cathars.

Jacob Frank, the leader of the Frankist movement in eighteenth-century eastern Europe, taught that the world had been created by an evil force that enslaved men by unjust laws and blocked the way to the hidden "Good God." The road to the divine was through the rejection of all religions and morals and the performance of "strange deeds" that violated the accepted standards of purity and decency. Frank wrote, "I have come to redeem it [the world] from all the laws and customs that have ever existed. It is my task to annihilate all this so that the Good God can reveal Himself."¹⁰ As with most antinomian movements, the extent of antinomian behavior in the Frankist movement is difficult to assess. There is evidence that Frank himself was not far from living up to his antinomian theory, and a number of Frankists admitted before a rabbinic court that they had had adulterous and incestuous relationships. Certain Frankist rites included orgiastic elements, but after Frank's death both the theory and the practice of antinomianism were discarded.¹¹

Scholem wrote that neither Frank nor his disciples knew that they were renewing the gnostic tradition but that the similarities are not surprising because both developed their thought within a biblical framework. Dualism can be interpreted as a response to the problem of theodicy within the monotheistic, biblical tradition; if God is both omnipotent and all-benevolent, then why does he allow evil and injustice? The dualistic solution to this ubiquitous problem was one that created an opening for the development of antinomianism.

Dual Planes of Existence

The metaphysical framework of the Free Spirits, a mystical movement that spread over a large area of Europe in the fourteenth century, was provided by neo-Platonism: Ordinary existence had emanated from God and had become divorced from Him, but there was ultimately a single essence, and at the end of time everything would be reabsorbed in God. The central feature of the belief system of the Free Spirits was their claim to deification through mystical experience of the divine. The adept had to detach himself from daily life and divest his self of all internal will and desire in order to allow for the miraculous penetration of God. It was at the point of mystical union that the antinomian belief was expressed: The Free Spirit was unable to sin.

Historians disagree over the question of whether the Free Spirits were antinomian in practice. Norman Cohn called the Free Spirits a self-proclaimed elite of amoral supermen and claimed that they practiced a "promiscuous and mystically colored eroticism."[12] Robert Lerner challenged this view by questioning those sources that reported on amorality and promiscuity; they were either written by opponents of the movement (and similar accusations were made against many other heretical groups) or based on confessions extracted by the inquisitors. A number of cases demonstrate that at least some Free Spirits countenanced the theoretical possibility of behavior unrestrained by conventional morality. Conrad Kannler, for example, agreed with his inquisitors that a Free Spirit could have sexual relations with his mother and sister, but he added that God would not let such a thing occur for one so perfect. Such qualifications were lacking in the testimony of John Hartmann of Ossmannstedt, who was tried in 1367. He said that the "truly free" were not subject to any authority; they could take whatever they please and kill whoever tries to stop them. Without prompting, Hartmann claimed that the Free Spirit could have sexual intercourse with his sister or mother in any place, even on the altar. Hartmann's deliberate outrageousness was probably atypical, but even he never said that he acted in such a manner.

Lerner shows that the authentic Free Spirit literature does not provide evidence of the encouragement or practice of sexual behavior freed of normative constraints. He deals in some detail with Marguerite Porete's book *The Mirror of Simple Souls*. Porete was condemned in Paris in 1310 as a relapsed heretic. Lerner argues that the book reveals Porete to be the first identifiable Free Spirit.[13] A somewhat different estimation is provided by Eleanor McLaughlin, who writes that the Mirror stands in the ambiguous middle ground between orthodox mystical spirituality and the heresy of the Free Spirit.[14] Both scholars are in agreement that Porete's book does not advocate antinomian practice.

The Mirror presents the mystical path as seven stages of grace leading to union with God. The seventh stage is attainable in the future life, but in the fifth and sixth stages the "annihilated" or "liberated" soul can be compared to the angels. At this point the soul, united with God, has no independent needs or desires and takes leave of the virtues. Porete was careful to note that, although the soul has passed beyond any concern with such matters as virtues, the virtues remain with the soul; it is now God who carries them out.[15]

Lerner notes the differences between Free Spirit mysticism and orthodox mysticism. The Free Spirits believed in total rather than partial identity with God on earth; they believed that this identity would be lasting and not momentary; and they rejected all religious authority, perceiving the church as an obstacle to salvation. Lerner also emphasizes that in their bodily austerities and spiritual abnegation the Free Spirits were typical of the medieval search for God.[16] The continuity between the Free Spirits and orthodox mystics is stressed by McLaughlin; they all sought the ideal of deification and spiritual freedom when the soul is free from all material considerations. The differences are to be found in the orthodox mystics' careful qualifications concerning the temporality of the mystical union and the essential virtuousness of the person who had reached such heights. Thus the Free Spirit was not a perversion of Catholic medieval mysticism but one outcome of that kind of search for Christian perfection.[17]

Connections between mysticism, asceticism, and antinomianism can also be found among the dervish groups that emerged from Sufism in the twelfth and thirteenth centuries. A prominent example was the Qalundariyah, a loosely organized movement of itinerant dervishes in Syria and Egypt, but similar groups appeared in most Islamic societies by the end of the thirteenth century. The dervishes believed that their salvation required their withdrawal from and renunciation of society, and this required mendicancy and itinerancy. However, it became common for mendicancy and itinerancy to be practiced for a large part of the year and for the dervishes to spend some time in the communal life of their hospices. The negation of the norms of society was signaled by wearing a simple loincloth or nudity, shaving all their bodily hair, and, in certain cases, dwelling in cemeteries. Some openly disregarded Islamic ritual practices and would neither pray nor fast. They rejected marriage, and some embraced celibacy, but they were accused of sexual libertinism and perversions.[18]

Outside the monotheistic traditions, Tantrism provides an example of an antinomian outcome of a metaphysical system that presents a monistic cancellation of dualism. The term *Tantrism* was introduced by European Orientalist scholars in the nineteenth century; they used it to characterize a wide array of texts and practices. For Westerners Tantrism represented the quintessence of Oriental idolatry, polytheism, and licentiousness—the Oriental Other in its most extreme form. Within the framework of the New Age, Tantrism is now praised by Westerners as an art of "Sacred Sexuality," a cult of ecstasy that combines sexual pleasure with liberation, hedonism with transcendence.[19]

The Hindu and Buddhist metaphysical systems, which are the basis for what is now called Tantrism, present absolute reality as a unity of all the dualities and polarities that are experienced on the inferior plane of existence. Creation represented a shattering of the primordial unity, the separation of the One into opposing principles. This state of being is one of suffering, illusion, and bondage, and the goal of the Tantric adept is to return to the primordial state of nondifferentiation, a motionless, timeless unity that existed before the rapture.

Tantrism developed, in particular directions, the Hindu and Buddhist metaphysics of separating the self from material existence and entering a form of existence in which categories such as time and space are transcended. Wendy Doniger O'Flaherty has shown that in the Hindu myths the ambivalent image of Shiva, a symbol of both chastity and eroticism, can be seen to represent a reconciliation of opposites, but the extreme contradictions are presented in a single image to show that they are untenable and immoral. The myths avoid compromise and instead stress and exaggerate the contradictions until the extremes can be said to have been exhausted. But whereas the Hindu mythology did not normally seek a true synthesis, the Tantric solution was to equate the extremes. A number of solutions to the equation of chastity and passion have been proposed. The sexual impulse could be transformed into chastity by exposing the self to temptation, such as lying in bed with a beautiful woman without giving way to one's passion. A further development was to allow a man who had conquered his desires to penetrate the woman but to retain his seed. It was believed that the seed would rise through the spinal cord to the brain, rendering the yogi immortal. Finally, the antinomian solution was to perceive the conquest of desire as the satisfaction of desire; the correct ritual performance of sexual union would transform the natural animal function into an act of worship.[20]

A Hindu movement singled out by critics as a degenerate Tantric cult was the Kartabhajas, or Worshippers of the Master. This movement spread throughout the Calcutta area during the late eighteenth and the nineteenth century. Its beliefs and rituals centered on the bipolar sexual symbolism of the male principle or deity (Perusa, or Krishna) and the female principle or deity (Prakrti, or Radha). In accord with the belief that the male deity had generated the female from himself to create the universe, the goal of the *sadhana* (male adept) was to reunite the two principles within his body by reabsorbing the female back into himself. By techniques of the reversal of flow, the adept sought to suck the male and female sexual fluids, the semen and the menstrual blood, back out of the female and into his own body. The adepts, both male and female, were expected to engage in intercourse without carnal desire and thereby transmute base physical love into pure spiritual love. For some this required the deliberate transgressions of the laws of caste and of marriage, so that even adultery was permitted.[21]

The dialectic of opposites was a frequent theme in Mahayana Buddhism, and Tantrism multiplied the opposites found in the Buddhist texts. The orthodox response to the Buddhist metaphysics of the meaningless, valueless, and illusory nature of material reality was an ascetic withdrawal from the world. Ascetic otherworldliness was a prerequisite for achieving nirvana, the annihilation of suffering by canceling the illusionary phenomenal self of mundane existence. Buddhism has always had a strong anti-ascetic countercurrent, and it is in certain forms of Tantrism that this opposite flow was most strongly expressed. Tantrism emphasized that the state of pure spirituality, of nonconditional existence, could be reached by transcending the dualities. The major means, which were formulated more precisely in Buddhist than in Hindu Tantrism, were the immobilization of thought, breath, and semen. These techniques, which could be learned under the guidance of a teacher, bound the dualities together and liberated the divine powers of the adept.

Tantrism postulated the fundamental unity of nirvana and samsara, of the decisive mystical experience with the world of sensual experience. Right-handed Tantrism placed an emphasis on the transmutation of the imperfect into the perfect; the sensual love of a woman should not be suppressed but could be transformed into a universal and all-embracing love. It was in some of the left-handed Tantras that the antinomian idea was expressed; the identification of nirvana in samsara was taken to mean that the adept would devote himself to the enjoyment and indulgence of his desires. Perfect enlightenment was attained through the enjoyment of the five M's, which were forbidden or restricted to others: alcohol (*madya*), meat (*mamsa*), fish (*matsya*), hand gestures (*mudra*), and sexual intercourse (*maithuna*). Once the yogi had placed himself in a state of nonduality, everything was of equal value and all his actions were pure. One text stated that the man who had reached Buddhahood could kill and eat any animal, lie, steal, and commit adultery. Some Tantric sects made such acts part of their initiation process.[22]

Immanentism

The Protestant belief that assurance of salvation was not gained by obedience to the religious law but by faith alone reintroduced the ambiguities in the teaching of Saint Paul and made possible an antinomian interpretation. The antinomian claim was that those individuals in whom the spirit dwelled were entirely free from the law and in some sense without sin. Protestant theologians sought to forestall such reasoning. John Calvin proclaimed that, although works do not bring about salvation, the sanctified individual will naturally act in accord with the moral law.[23]

Antinomian thinkers among Puritans in seventeenth-century England and North America were frequently accused of libertinism, but few extended the doctrine that they were free from sin to the belief that they were free to sin, and even fewer appeared to have carried this belief into practice.[24] The most radical form of antinomianism, combined with a social millenarianism, appeared in England during the Interregnum (1649–60) among a loose association of groups and individuals who came to be known as Ranters. The antinomians did not refer to themselves as Ranters, but it was a popular pejorative and its widespread use contributed to the mistaken impression among an earlier generation of historians that the Ranters constituted a sect or movement with a common identity. A lively debate ensued among historians in response to the thesis of James Colin Davis that the Ranters were a fabrication of sensationalist journalism in 1650–51.[25] The critics of the thesis acknowledged that it was inappropriate to refer to the Ranters as a sect or movement, but they argued that a number of groups, some of whom were loosely linked, shared antinomian views based on a belief in divine immanence.[26]

The emphasis of the Ranters on the indwelling of God was expressed in an apparent pantheism: "All the creatures in the world . . . are but one entire being"; "God in all in one, and so is in everyone"; and God is "the Being and Life of all" or "the Being and Operation of all things." In accord with this view, mankind could not be divided into saints and sinners; "rogues, thieves, whores and cut purses" were "every whit as good" as the saints. For some Ranters the infusion of God in all creatures excluded the possibility of personal immortality, the resurrection of the body, or a heaven or hell. Hell was only a state of mind, and some proclaimed the same for sin: "Devil is God, Hell is Heaven, Sin Holiness, Damnation Salvation";

"sin hath its conception only in the imagination; therefore, so long as the act was in God, or nakedly produced by God, it was holy as God."[27]

The historian Jerome Friedman substantiates his argument that the Ranters were not pantheists but dualists by quoting from such Ranters as Richard Coppin, who believed that the conflict between spirit and matter characterized all existence and that humans were torn between two warring principles. Another Ranter, Jacob Bauthumley, wrote that God had two sides, the light and the dark, and that man shared the qualities of both and was caught between them. Immanentism was reconciled with dualism: God was found in everything only insofar as phenomena belonged to the realm of spirit. The same spiritually infused persons also belonged to the realm of matter and, as such, had nothing to do with God.[28]

The implications for conduct that Ranters drew from their immanentism were not uniform. One view was that because evil could not derive from the good that was God, a scrupulous code of behavior was required. Another view was that because sin did not exist, men should not act in ways that were normally regarded as sinful. However, some Ranters, for example, Lawrence Clarkson, were prepared to face the logic of their position: "There is no such act as drunkenness, adultery and theft in God. . . . What act soever is done by there is light and love, though it be the act called adultery." Because sin was only in the imagination, "none can be free from sin till in purity it be acted as no sin, for I judged that pure to me which to a dark understanding was impure: for to the pure all things, yea all acts were pure."[29] Clarkson practiced what he preached, but he drew the line at murder.[30]

In accord with the dualist view, it was Satan as God who created the world of matter, including religious institutions, doctrines, and restrictions. It was therefore necessary to reverse or overturn the creations or representations of the devil. Aliezer Coppe believed that one could be liberated from evil matter only by becoming it, and he wrote that everything that was normally considered base or in poor taste was good and redeeming. He expressed a preference for coarse gypsy women over beautiful ladies, and he described dancing with them, touching their breasts, and kissing them. Clarkson wrote that all prohibitions against sinful behavior were the product of evil humanity, that the disregard of prohibitions was essentially righteous, and that the only way to overcome sin within this world was to sin.[31] Thus, like the Sabbateans, redemption was to come through evil.

Immanentism does not necessarily give rise to antinomian beliefs and conduct, but it is likely to pose antinomianism as a possible implication that has to be neutralized in some way. It is instructive to compare Ranterism with Hasidism, a movement that arose a century after the Ranters among Jews in southeastern Poland. Immanentist tendencies were present among the early Hasidim, but their beliefs were not formulated in such a radical fashion as the Ranters. As with the Ranters, scholars have argued that it is misleading to refer to the Hasidim as pantheists. Some scholars prefer the term *panentheistic*: God and the universe are not identical, but God's divine power emanates into the world so that everything is included and embodied within God. But although it was expressed in a different language of divine symbols and was hedged by many qualifications, Hasidic immanentism was not so distant from Ranter immanentism; every object and activity contained a spark of divinity, absolute evil had no independent existence, and the conceptions of sin, punishment, hell, and the devil were minimized.

The Hasidic doctrine of "worship through corporeality" (religious achievement through involvement in the concrete, material world) bears some similarity to Ranter beliefs. The early Hasidic leaders believed that, as a spiritual elite, they were able to cleave to God not only through specifically religious acts, such as prayer and study of the Torah, but also through everyday activities, such as eating, drinking, sexual relations, earning a living, storytelling, and traveling. Any act, including those concerned with physical pleasure and the achievement of material needs, became a religious act if the intention was to cleave to God. Like the Ranters, the Hasidim used tobacco, alcohol, and dance for spiritual purposes, but unlike the Ranters, their communal feasts were not occasions for the expression of freedom from moral restraints. Although Hasidim were influenced by a number of radical ideas in the Jewish religious writings of the time, they were successful in inhibiting the antinomian implications.[32]

One theme in the Jewish religious milieu was that of transforming evil traits into good. A relatively nonradical interpretation of this motif was that of turning carnal love into love of God. It was argued that if a man with a strong carnal lust was able to transform his urge into love of God, his love and enthusiasm for God would be greater than those of men with weaker inclinations. A more radical suggestion was that one should endanger oneself to the extent of lying in bed with an unmarried woman. Desire would be stimulated in an extreme fashion in order to control it and redirect it for religious purposes. Finally, there was the antinomian position: One should sin to conquer evil from within and rescue the divine sparks from captivity in the *kelippot*. The sole limitation here was that only a few special people were qualified for this task.[33]

The early Hasidic teachers dealt with the problem of transforming evil into good when they considered the raising of "strange" or "alien" thoughts, such as those of a sexual nature, during prayer. They believed that such thoughts were fallen sparks that should not be repulsed but "mended" and raised to their divine root. Visions of a beautiful woman, for example, could be traced to the divine root of beauty, and it was with this absolute beauty that the Hasidim would seek to unite. It was possible to conclude that it was legitimate to deliberately arouse such thoughts in order to contribute to the process of redemption, and one Hasid, Lieb Melamed of Brody, argued that it was suitable during prayer for the worshipper to think of a woman standing before him. Most Hasidic teachers, however, warned against intentional strange thoughts. They argued that the worshipper might not be able to raise them and would descend further into evil. Thus the beliefs of the Hasidim brought them to the border of antinomianism, but the great majority were careful not to cross that border.[34]

Antinomian Sabbateans justified the transgression of the religious law by the appearance of the messiah. The leaders of the Izbica/Radzin Hasidim, in contradiction to rabbinic tradition, acknowledged that extra-halachic behavior may point to the imminent arrival of the messianic era, but they did not claim that that era had arrived and they did not, therefore, condone any permanent abrogation of the religious law. They did, however, believe that there were "messianic persons" or sanctified souls living in the protomessianic age and that the mystical illumination of these individuals transcended the fragmentary world of which the Halacha is part. They suggested that the unification or alignment of the illuminated individuals with the divine justified their transgressions from the religious law, but strict limits were set on the antinomian implications of this belief. Before the coming of the messiah, the sacredness of the halachic system was to remain intact, even for those individuals whose mystical illumination had gone beyond it. Although the messianic individuals had overcome the need for Halacha, they remained externally bound by it. They lived in a state of tension between their antinomian illuminism and their conformity to normative Judaism. Shaul Magid argues that the antinomian Hasidic thinkers served to strengthen the Halacha because they showed that the law's boundaries were transparent and permeable and that it existed in a state of liminality and instability.[35]

Antinomian Beliefs, Behaviors, and Boundaries

It is clear that antinomianism cannot be explained by a psychological reductionism that would dismiss it as a religious mask for sexual promiscuity and antisocial impulses. Antinomian beliefs were not intentional outcomes of the metaphysical beliefs and soteriologies from which they emerged. This is not to argue that antinomianism was an inevitable development of immanent change within a belief system. In most cases it was only one of a number of ideological developments from a single metaphysical system or soteriology, but it was no less a logical or rational deduction than, say, asceticism. In some cases antinomianism appears to have been the most logical inference, but many refused to draw this inference and presented somewhat tortuous arguments to avoid it. The logical implications of the belief system and the desire to conform to conventional morality were in tension. Even when the antinomian idea was accepted intellectually, fear of sanctions or internalized inhibitions often prevented antinomian practice.

The historical evidence rarely allows an unequivocal judgment regarding antinomian behavior. In some cases, such as the Free Spirits, no reliable evidence supports the accusations of antinomian practice, and in those cases, such as the Sabbateans, where there can be little doubt of antinomian behavior, the accusations were often exaggerated and directed against people who were innocent, such as "moderate" Sabbateans.

Accusations of antinomianism, like witchcraft accusations, served to define and condemn an antisystem and thereby reinforce the orthodox system. The importance of identifying and persecuting an antinomian heresy was especially great when antinomianism was a possible inference within orthodoxy itself. For example, it is plausible that the notion of perfectionism in orthodox Christian mysticism strengthened the concern of medieval churchmen to identify antinomian "heresy" with a group that the church could clearly delineate and condemn. The Free Spirits did not constitute a coherent sect or organized movement, but in the decree Ad Nostrum the Council of Vienne listed eight errors of "an abominable sect" of boghards and beguines. The first error in the list was the central one: the belief that man could attain such a degree of perfection in his earthly life that he was incapable of sin. This decree provided the framework for subsequent investigations and trials of Free Spirits and for the association of the heresy with boghards and beguines. These were men and women who sought the apostolic life of poverty, mendicancy, and preaching outside or on the margins of the institutionalized church. Without fixed rules, organization, or final vows, they often faced the hostility of both the established orders and the parish clergy. There is no reliable evidence to connect mystical antinomianism with the boghards and beguines, and many Free Spirits were found outside their ranks, but their ambiguous position and status made them vulnerable to suspicion and persecution.[36]

The severe persecution of antinomians was a response to a belief system that went beyond a denial of orthodoxy; it challenged the fundamental categorizations in society of good and evil and purity and sin. Mary Douglas has shown the complexities of the contrasts between dirt and defilement and cleanliness and purity. She wrote that "it is part of our human condition to long for hard lines and clear concepts" but that experience is not always amenable to logical categories of noncontradiction. A strict pattern of purity leads to discomfort, contradictions, or hypocrisy, and the most complete belief systems "find some ultimate way of affirming that which has been rejected." She gives examples of dirt affirmation in tribal societies; behavior that is normally condemned and avoided is made the focus of certain rituals and attributed with tremendous power. By confronting ambiguity in an extreme and concentrated form, people are able to transcend the distinctions and separations made by their cultures.[37]

The orthodoxies of the great religious traditions appear to be less encompassing than those primitive cultures whose categorization and rejection of filth is in certain ritual frames collapsed in a mixing of categories, a welcoming of filth. Religious orthodoxies, and especially Western monotheism, have persecuted and destroyed those who have identified filth with purity and sin with holiness. In a number of cases it is difficult to know whether a heretical group has actually fused the categories or whether the religious establishment has invented (or at least vastly exaggerated) a heresy in order to confront and deny such a possibility. In either case a process of ritual cleansing is undertaken—excommunications, show trials, executions, and so on—in order to reassert the fundamental distinctions of the society.

Images of Man and Society

Antinomianism might usefully be analyzed from a number of perspectives. I have chosen to restrict my comments here to two models as classically formulated in the works of Freud and Durkheim. The intention at this point is not to explain antinomianism but to compare analytical frameworks.

In his later works Freud presented a general model of the relationship between human propensities and social constraints.[38] He wrote that social cohesion is possible only if peoples' libidinal energy is inhibited and their death instincts are curbed. The sexual and death instincts combine together in varying ways, but society needs to control sexuality so that a surplus libidinal energy will be available to counteract the destructive tendencies of the death drive. Society cannot exist without its members' libidinal energy, but society will crumble if that energy is not sublimated.

Because people learn and internalize cultural values and controls, a fundamental tension within the individual exists between the instinctual energies, which operate according to the pleasure principle, and the internalized culture, which enables the person to act according to the reality principle and to adapt to his environment. The individual's happiness requires that these conflicting forces reach a stable balance. Some limitation on sexuality and destructive aggression is necessary, but if the superego is too harsh and does not allow the expression of instinctual energy, then guilt, anxiety, and neurosis are likely outcomes.

In the framework of the Freudian model, sexual freedom and the negation of morals in antinomianism can be described as a breaking through to expression of the individual's drives. Scholem's view of human nature appears to have been similar to that of Freud. Scholem wrote that "the instincts of anarchy and lawlessness lie buried in every human soul" and that "traditionally Judaism has always sought to suppress such impulses."[39] Within the Freudian framework, when the cultural restrictions are removed, the instinctual impulses are released. An analogy might be made here with Freud's analysis of the crowd; it is a release mechanism that enables the individual to act out his normally forbidden desires.

The Freudian model would hypothesize that antinomianism is most likely to arise in "undersocialized" people or in people who have not balanced inhibition and release, although they have control. In the first case a number of undersocialized people have not internalized the cultural constraints of their society. This may occur among groups with weak agencies of socialization. Attempts by agencies of the wider society to impose strict limitations on sex and aggression may engender an antinomian revolt, a complete rejection of external constraint. The second case is more interesting because antinomianism may arise where people have internalized the cultural controls but have not achieved a balance between inhibition and release. A society's moral code may be too restrictive, and the individual's superego will, in consequence, be too demanding. The religious responses to this tension are likely to take extreme forms: either asceticism or antinomianism. Religion in general draws energy from sexuality, and the sublimation of libidinal energy is found in extreme forms in asceticism.[40] Thus both religious asceticism and religious eroticism draw on the same energy; in religious asceticism there is an extreme sublimation, and in religious eroticism the demands of the superego are entirely rejected and the sexual and destructive impulses are given their freedom. Whatever the truth of the hypothesis, it is the case that ascetic and antinomian tendencies are often found together: Two or more sects in a single society have represented the two extremes, both tendencies have been expressed contemporaneously in a single movement, and some movements have moved in their histories from one extreme to another.[41] The distribution of ascetics and antinomians is not necessarily the consequence of random psychological differences but might be explained by such factors as social networks, channels of communication, and the influence of local religious milieus.[42]

Two different images of man and society can be found in the writings of Durkheim. The image that Durkheim stated in the most explicit fashion is close to that of Freud. Human nature is conceived as dualistic; man's sensual desires and appetites, rooted in the organism, are in tension with his concepts and morals, which he has learned and internalized within society. Durkheim's discussion of man's sensual appetites is undeveloped compared with Freud's analysis. Durkheim gives basic examples, such as hunger and thirst, and he does not deal with sex in this context. However, clear parallels exist between the Freudian and Durkheim models: The individual's sensual appetites incline him toward egoistic, irrational, and immoral ends, whereas the socially determined part of the self inclines him to altruistic behavior and impersonal, moral ends. The opposition between the two parts of the self is expressed in religious thought by the dichotomies of body and soul, the profane and the sacred.[43]

As with Freud's model, it is difficult to interpret antinomianism within the framework of Durkheim's dualism. Durkheim argued that the sacred was an expression of collective forces, imposing respect and love for others, whereas the profane was often associated with the egoistic passions of the organism. How, then, does one deal with religious beliefs that justify the expression of antisocial individual desires and may even urge the destruction of the society's moral code? In terms of the first model antinomianism can be interpreted only as a pathological phenomenon that emerges when a breakdown of the normative system permits an unregulated expression of human passion.[44]

Durkheim presented another model, however, in which there was no sharp line between the individual and the society or between the two parts of human nature. In this model Durkheim was more consistent in his sociocultural determinism: The individual's desires and needs, including his egoism and self-interest, are socially generated and historically variable. This perspective was never set out as explicitly as the first, and Durkheim's simultaneous use of the two models produced conceptual confusion and inconsistency. For example, Durkheim analyzed anomie as a state of normlessness that permitted the unrestrained passions of the organism to come to the fore, but he also saw it as a cultural product of a particular type of

The Sacredness of Sin

society.[45] In his polemics, Durkheim often accepted the conceptual framework of his opponents. Instead of a thoroughgoing rejection of the individual-society dichotomy, he was inclined to turn his opponents' schemes on their heads and assert the primacy of society over the individual.[46]

Durkheim's second model allows for the conceptualization of conflict or tension between two or more sets of socially produced phenomena. Durkheim himself did not extend his analysis in this direction; he did not delve deeply into conflict among normative systems or into the paradoxes and tensions that emerge within a single normative or religious tradition. My examination of antinomian movements in relation to their religious contexts suggests that this may be the most fruitful starting place for the study of antinomianism. It is a starting point that rejects a statically conceived human nature and emphasizes that people are naturally adapted to change. As Norbert Elias wrote, "One unique aspect of humanity is that human beings are in certain ways changeable *by nature.*"[47] Antinomianism is no more or less in conformity or in conflict with human nature than asceticism or a conventional moral standpoint is.

Coda: Antinomianism and Nihilism

Gershom Scholem wrote that the Jewish antinomian Jacob Frank taught "a religious myth of nihilism."[48] Hans Jonas emphasized the analogies of antinomianism and nihilism when he compared gnosticism and the modern philosophy of existentialism. He found a parallel between Nietzsche's statement that "God is dead" and the gnostic rejection of the god of the cosmos. He argued that the transcendent god of the gnostics was a nihilistic conception because he was not related to any normative order that is found in this world.[49] There are, however, important differences between religious antinomianism and modern nihilism. The nihilist slogan "Nothing is true, therefore everything is justified" can be applied only to antinomianism, with important qualifications.

Antinomians may believe that everything is justified because nothing that ordinary men believe is true or because their special spiritual status means that they are beyond good and evil. Nevertheless, they believe in fundamental truths. The gnostic, for example, believes that the hidden god is true and that their gnosis of that god is true. It is because of certain truths that the antinomian believes himself beyond good and evil, and it is because of certain truths that he may feel obliged to violate morality. The antinomian does not face the self-defeating relativism of the nihilist. If there are no truths, then the statement that "nothing is true" is itself not true. As Johan Goudsblom has noted, pure nihilism can have no practical consequences; it justifies nothing, not even suicide.[50] It justifies neither morality nor a violation of morality.

Whereas antinomianism arose in many different cultures and periods, nihilism was a product of nineteenth-century Western society. The emergence of a multiplicity of competing belief systems and the possibility of freely choosing between them were prerequisites for the diffusion of the "nothing is true" doctrine. An extensive cultural pluralism of widely different and contradictory subcultures existing side by side provides the background to the reversal of the nihilistic slogan from "Nothing is true, therefore everything is justified" to "Everything is justified, therefore nothing is true."[51] Some antinomian movements arose in periods when the religious establishment was undergoing a crisis and there were attacks on it from a number of different groups, but these contexts were still a far cry from the cultural pluralism of modern society.

AFTERWORD TO PART 2

As in part 1, I began part 2 with "internal" comparisons of Jewish communities and then widened the discussion to include "external" comparisons of a particular religious phenomenon in Jewish and other religious contexts. In chapter 4 I compared millenarianism in the medieval and early modern Jewish communities of central and western Europe, the Iberian Peninsula, and Italy. The focus in chapter 5 on the millenarianism of the conversos and former conversos of Spain, Portugal, and the Sephardic Diaspora led to a comparison in chapter 6 of antinomianism in the world religions.

Rodney Stark has drawn on my previous work on Jewish messianic movements to criticize the social-scientific approach that explains religion in terms of something more "basic" or material than religion. He argues that the idea that religion is a mask for more fundamental factors has been popular among social scientists and that sociologists have been prone to ignore the fundamental truth that religious motives cause religious developments and that religion can have far-reaching consequences. My work on millenarianism is one of the cases he uses; the Crusades, the Great Awakenings in the United States, and post–World War II Japanese religious movements are used to show "the immense capacity of religion to motivate and direct human action."[1]

Stark qualifies his appreciation that I recognized that a disaster was not a necessary condition of a messianic outburst by noting that I "made this concession very reluctantly" and that in some passages I seem "to have forgotten it."[2] Stark omits to note that, with respect to the effects of such factors as disasters, social dislocations, and anomie on millenarianism, I made a distinction among the outbursts in terms of their scale and diffusion. I wrote that small, local incidences of millenarianism occurred in communities that had not directly experienced persecution, deprivation, or disruption, but a comparison of Jewish millenarian outbursts suggests that social factors were among the causes of large, widespread outbursts.

Stark wrote that his aim was not to deny that "humans often *do* turn to religion in times of trouble and crises . . . but only to reject it as a necessary condition and to recognize that religious phenomena can be caused by other religious phenomena."[3] I have no quarrel with such an evenhanded statement, but Stark has a tendency to set up explanations as exclusive alternatives: to criticize materialist in favor of idealist explanations and to criticize "demand (for religion)-side" in favor of "supply-side" explanations. I take a more pluralistic approach in explaining religious phenomena. Certain religious developments may have been caused to some extent by other religious developments and they are likely to have their own consequences, but it would be unwise to ignore the possibility that the major causes of certain religious phenomena can be found in economic and nonreligious social and cultural factors.

My nonreligious explanations of Jewish millenarianism go beyond a simple one-to-one linkage with crises. The comparative approach provides an invaluable aid in showing that the influence of the persecution of the Jews on millenarian outbursts was variable and dependent on other factors. Of particular importance were differences in religious conceptions among Ashkenazic, Sephardic, and Italian Jews—their established explanations of persecution and their conceptions of *galut*. However, these religiocultural differences were, in turn, related to the differences in the historical trajectories of their socioeconomic locations in those countries.

One common explanation of millenarian movements is social dislocation and anomie. Such an explanation appears to be appropriate to the millenarian movements of indigenous peoples whose way of life was disrupted by invasions and colonialization. Examples include the Melanesian "cargo cults" and the Ghost Dances of the Native Americans in 1870 and 1890.[4] The disruption of the Spanish and Italian Jewish communities was partial compared with such instances as the Melanesians and the Native Americans. The persecution and expulsions affected the Jews' social relationships with and cultural orientations to the dominant non-Jewish society, but the Jewish culture remained intact. Elements of anomie and a more pervasive social disruption were found among the conversos and former conversos, who demonstrated a greater adherence to millenarianism than most Jewish communities. Some conversos became crypto-Jews and practiced an attenuated Judaism that in a number of cases focused on the Jewish messiah. The task of the Inquisition was to root out the Judaizers, but even those conversos who adopted Catholicism wholeheartedly found themselves subject to suspicion and persecution. The problems of the conversos and their descendants did not cease when they returned to Judaism in the Sephardic Diaspora; they were unfamiliar with the complex system of Jewish ritual, and they experienced problems of assimilation into the established Jewish communities. Millenarian movements appeared to offer an end to problems of social integration and cultural confusion.

Stark's idealist explanations are formulated in a general fashion: "What people believe influences what they do."[5] In my analysis of the messianic enthusiasm around Sabbatai Zvi, I considered Scholem's idealist explanation that it was the spread of Lurianic kabbalah that accounts for the widespread belief in Sabbatai as the messiah. The evidence for Scholem's explanation was found wanting. I proposed the greater relevance of the social and psychological strains of the former conversos and "the crisis of the seventeenth century," which particularly affected a number of Jewish communities with many former conversos in their populations.

Sabbatai's totally unexpected conversion to Islam and his death ten years later were apparent disconfirmations of the messianic prophecies and Sabbatai's messianic role. The rationalizations for these events and the continued enthusiasm of at least a minority of the believers have been analyzed within the conceptual framework of cognitive dissonance provided by the classic work by Festinger and colleagues, *When Prophecy Fails*.[6] Scholem argued that all Sabbatean beliefs after Sabbatai's conversion were directed toward enabling believers to live in the state of tension produced by the messianic beliefs and their apparent disconfirmations.

The disconfirmation of prophecy has arisen more recently within the Chabad (Lubavitch) Hasidic movement. A messianic campaign to spread the belief in the imminent coming of the messiah began among the Lubavitch in the early 1980s. The campaign increased in momentum and was given a major boost in 1991 when the movement's rebbe, Menachem Mendel Schneerson, encouraged his followers to act to bring about the coming of the messiah, which, he later indicated, was imminent. Although the rebbe never identified himself as the messiah, he did not refute those Lubavitch who proclaimed that he was. The stroke suffered by the rebbe in 1992, which rendered him speechless and paralyzed on the right side of his body, served only to increase the messianic expectations. One belief was that divine intercession would work a miracle to restore the rebbe's health, but some believed that the rebbe had chosen this path, taking on himself the sufferings of the Jewish people. Another stroke in 1994 rendered the rebbe comatose, and he died three months later.

Even when the rebbe was alive, some Lubavitch opposed the belief that the rebbe was the messiah, and some messianists admitted that they had been mistaken after his death. Messianism has persisted in the movement, in some cases with even greater enthusiasm, and social scientists have once again drawn on the cognitive dissonance perspective to analyze the techniques used by believers to neutralize their dissonance and reinforce their faith. Some spoke of the resurrection of the rebbe or believed that he was "concealed" and "hidden" from human eyes and would return to reveal himself to the world. A common theme was the rebbe's spiritual presence and that, without the hindrance of his physical body, the rebbe had greater spiritual powers to enable him to bring about the Redemption.[7] It has been argued, however, that the rationalizations create new challenges for believers, who are required "to see" the rebbe beyond his invisibility. The transition from dissonance to consonance is unclear, and the process of defining and constructing the messianic "reality" continues.[8]

Critics of the Lubavitch messianists have pointed to Sabbateanism as a warning of the disastrous antinomian consequences of such beliefs. Messianism and its apparent disconfirmations were important contexts for the antinomianism that developed in the more radical forms of Sabbateanism, particularly in the Doenmeh, composed of converts to Islam in Salonika, and the Frankists in Poland. However, as I show in my comparison of antinomian tendencies and movements in the world religions, antinomianism has emerged in a number of religious contexts, mystical as well as messianic. At this level of comparison, the analysis takes a more idealistic direction. The emphasis is on those particular religious perspectives, particularly dualistic systems accompanied by millenarianism or mysticism, that have been favorable to antinomian developments.

Antinomian ideas did not necessarily lead to antinomian behavior, although this has been a common accusation against such groups. The possibility of separating the accusations from the "truth" are limited for the historical movements, but the justifications for antinomian behavior, even if rarely practiced, are of considerable interest. The readiness to broach the possibility of antinomian behavior, despite the severe sanctions that the antinomian believers knew could be brought down on them, points to the influence that religious beliefs can have on behavior. However, just as particular socioeconomic conditions might be favorable or necessary but never sufficient causes of millenarian outbursts, particular religious perspectives might be favorable or necessary but never sufficient causes of antinomianism. The search for more comprehensive explanations continues.

PART 3
Jewish Identities

INTRODUCTION TO PART 3

From the focus on premodern and early modern Jewish communities in parts 1 and 2, in this part I move to an analysis of modern and contemporary Jewish communities, especially the two largest: the United States and Israel. With respect to the analytical focus, we move from comparisons of religious practice to Jewish identities and, in particular, the relationship between religion and ethnicity (or nationality) in those identities.

The distinction between the religious and ethnic components of Jewish identity and the discourse on their relationship are modern phenomena. The distinction was made a public issue when Napoleon convoked the Assembly of Jewish Notables to endorse his goal of assimilating the Jews of France into a united French nation. When they declared their French nationality and validated only their practice of Jewish ritual, the assembly recognized a new definition of Jewish identity. Jewishness confined to religion became a widespread form of identity among western and central European Jews in the nineteenth century, and it was challenged in the last decades of that century by nonreligious ethnic or national forms of Jewish identity, especially among Jews in eastern Europe. What had been fused in a taken-for-granted fashion in the traditional Jewish communities was differentiated, and many Jews who continued to adhere to both the religious and the ethnic or national elements of their identity did so in a self-conscious fashion.

Before I discuss Jewish identities in the modern era, I would like to consider how religion and ethnicity came to be fused in Jewish identities in antiquity. Attempts by historians of antiquity to trace this fusion have been complicated by debates over the appropriateness of using the terms *ethnic group* and *religion* as well as debates over the issue of when it becomes appropriate to use the terms *Jew* and *Judaism*. The appropriateness of using the English term *ethnic* has been acknowledged because it is derived from the Greek *ethnos*, a term that was widely used in antiquity in ways similar to our classifications of peoples as ethnic or national entities. Max Weber's definition of an ethnic group, which many sociologists have followed, appears to encompass the understanding of ethnos in antiquity: "those human groups that entertain a subjective belief in their common descent because of similarities of physical types or of customs or both."[1] Thus Herodotus, a Greek author writing in the fifth century B.C.E., presented Greekness as consisting of kinship and common cultural items, including shrines of gods and sacrifices. Similarly, ancient Jewish writers assumed that they had a group identity based on kinship and culture, and an outsider who wished to become one of them was required to adopt both their culture and a new kinship relation.[2]

Unlike *ethnic group*, no word in antiquity approximates the meaning of our word *religion*. The peoples of antiquity did not differentiate what we now understand as religion from conceptions of kinship, ancestry, and geography. In my view, though, the absence of a one-to-one correspondence between modern and ancient vocabulary does not prohibit the use of our terms. The use of the term *religion* is necessary when we acknowledge that ethnicity and religion were fused in antiquity, and its use allows us to trace the development of this fusion in what came to be designated as the Jewish people.

The people in antiquity who were known in Hebrew as *Yehudim* (singular, *Yehudi*) and in Greek as *Ioudaioi* (singular, *Ioudaios*) constituted an ethnos, a people with an attachment to a specific territory who believed that they had common ancestors and who possessed a number of distinctive cultural characteristics. Shaye Cohen writes that the correct translation of *Ioudaios* before the middle of the second century B.C.E. is Judean, not Jew. The Judeans inhabited their ancestral land, but in Diaspora settings, where many joined associations or corporations that were ethnic in character, the geographic meaning of *Ioudaios* became attenuated. Cohen argues that a semantic shift from Judean to Jew is justified from the latter part of the second century B.C.E., when the term *Ioudaios* came to be applied to people who were not geographic or ethnic Judeans but who had come to believe in the God of the Judeans. A non-Judean could become an *Ioudaios* by joining the Judeans in worshiping and venerating the God whose temple was in Jerusalem. The change from "ethnos to ethno-religion" permits the use of the translation "Jew" in place of Judean and "Jewishness" in place of Judeanness.[3]

Critics of Cohen have argued that the semantic change from Judean to Jew is only justified at later dates. Philip Esler suggests that to refer to Jews is justified after 135 C.E., when there was no longer hope of rebuilding the Temple,[4] and Steve Mason argues that the use of the word *Judaism* to refer to a comprehensive system and way of life is appropriate only from about the third century C.E.[5] These writers have focused on the appropriate translation of Greek terms. David Goodblatt extends his discussion to Hebrew terms, particularly *Yehudi*, and his justification of the term *Jewish* is that the Judeans also thought of themselves as Israelites. *Yehudi* was derived from the name Judah, who was believed to be one of the twelve sons of Jacob who had acquired the name Israel. At first, *Yehudi* referred specifically to the tribe of Judah, as distinguished from the other tribes of Israel, but the name came to designate anyone resident in or originating from the kingdom of Judah. Goodblatt writes that an Israelite identity continued among the Judeans after the division of the single kingdom into the two kingdoms of Israel and Judah and after the destruction of the northern kingdom of Israel in the eighth century and the conquest of the southern kingdom in the sixth century. The exiles from Judah and their descendants continued to invoke the name Israel as an identity, and this identity continued from the Persian period into the Hellenistic era.

INTRODUCTION TO PART 3

Goodblatt acknowledges that the name Israel was almost entirely restricted to Jewish literary sources in pre-Christian times; in the non-Jewish Greek and Latin literature the name Judeans was in standard use. The name Judah was used by both the Hasmoneans and their successors, the Herodians, to designate their states, and the name Israel was used only by the rebel regimes of 66–70 C.E. and 132–35 C.E. Goodblatt speculates that the rebels were averse to the name Judah because of its use by the Romans.[6]

Goodblatt uses the term *Jewish* because it can imply either Judah or Israel, and just as the Judean and Israelite overlapped in antiquity, so did the Jewish and Israelite identities in subsequent history. Whatever name the "Jews" of antiquity used to refer to their group, its meaning included belief in a common ancestry and a common culture or religion. Sociologists of ethnicity have followed Weber in pointing to the belief in a shared ancestry as a central feature of an ethnic group. Andreas Wimmer writes that the degree of stability of ethnic groups is linked to modes of transmitting ethnic membership and that the most stable boundaries are found among peoples who identify their members through multigenerational, unilineal descent ties. It is a genealogical membership criterion rather than behavioral criteria that make for stable boundaries, and Wimmer gives the Jews as the most prominent example of an ethnic category that has survived over "thousands of years."[7] The biblical account clarifies the genealogy of the "Israelites" by referring to the grandfather and father of Jacob, Abraham and Isaac, as the ancestors of other peoples (Ishmaelites, Edomites) as well as the Israelites. It is on Jacob that the new name of Israel was bestowed, and his twelve sons, including Judah, became the ancestors of the twelve Israelite tribes.

The Bible allows for the full assimilation of non-Israelites into the Israelite people through intermarriage, but in the Second Temple period some groups promoted genealogical purity as the distinguishing characteristic of Israelite identity. Ezra, a priest from Persian Babylonia in the late fifth century, proposed that Israel and other peoples were two distinct seeds, one holy and the other profane. This formulation drew an impermeable boundary between Israel and other peoples, and the groups that adopted Ezra's approach in the Second Temple period insisted that "Gentiles" could not be assimilated by conversion or intermarriage. This was the position of a minority. All Jewish groups in the Second Temple period held that genealogical filiation was sufficient to establish Jewish identity, but most did not make it an indispensable or necessary condition. Foreigners who renounced idolatry and immorality could adopt Jewish identity.[8]

Goodblatt qualifies Cohen's thesis that the ancient "Jewish" (Judean/Israelite) identity shifted from kinship to religion by insisting that the ethnic component did not disappear and that in some sources it remained dominant.[9] The difference between these writers appears to be a matter of emphasis. Cohen did not write that the ethnic component disappears, and he clarified his position when he compared changes in the meanings of the words *Judean* and *Hellene*. The changes were somewhat parallel, as *Hellene* changed in the fourth century B.C.E. from an ethnic-geographic term to a cultural one. A person could become a Hellene by speaking Greek, adopting the Greek way of life, and worshiping the Greek gods. Cohen notes, however, the differences in these developments. One was the relative importance of language. Whereas "to Hellenize" required speaking Greek, "to Judaize" did not require the adoption of Hebrew. Another difference was that *Judean* retained the ethnic component far more than *Hellene*; although the greater emphasis on the religious component made conversion possible, the myth of common ancestors and the covenantal link of God, people, and land were not conducive to proselytization.[10]

The argument that the trajectory of Jewish identity became an increasingly religious one cannot be separated from interpretations of the changes from Israelite religion to Judaism. Debates continue among historians over how much (if any) of the Bible antedates the Babylonian exile. One position is that the Bible or some of its books were compiled in the period of the Babylonian exile and the Persian era to formulate or reinforce a Judean/Israelite identity that was believed to be under threat. A minority position among historians is that the Bible was the creation of the Hellenistic era. Goodblatt assumes that the contents of the Bible were available by early Second Temple times, but he poses the question of whether the beliefs in a shared descent and culture were limited at that time to a small elite. The vast majority of Judeans were illiterate, and it is not until the first century C.E. that there is clear evidence of public readings of the scripture.[11]

A general and perhaps oversimplified summary of the changes after 70 C.E. is that Israelite religion, centered on the sacrificial cult, was transformed into Judaism, centered on the written and oral Torah, by the rabbis who replaced the priests as the religious elite. The rabbis constructed a complex system of religious markers of Jewish identity, but some of what became the most distinctive markers were already contained in the twenty-four books of the Hebrew Bible (Tanakh): circumcision of male infants, avoidance of pork, and observance of the Sabbath. In some respects the foundations of a Judaism without a temple, priesthood, and sacrificial cult were laid during the Second Temple period,[12] but the transformation of Second Temple Judaism into rabbinic Judaism was a fundamental one. One aspect of that change was canonization. Some historians trace the process of canonization as early as the Babylonian exile, but the boundaries of scriptural authority remained fluid during the Second Temple period, and although a "canonical consciousness," a sense of a need to delineate the bounds of the written scripture, may have begun at an early date, it was no doubt strengthened by the destruction of the Temple.[13]

Seth Schwartz writes that the authors of the ancient Jewish literature belonged to a tiny elite that was decimated by the repression of the revolts of 66–70 C.E. and 132–35 C.E. The religion that Schwartz believes was shattered by the failure of the two revolts became for most Jews "a vestigial identity" with only "bits and pieces [that were] incorporated in a religious and cultural system that was essentially Greco-Roman and pagan." The texts created by the rabbis under the pagan Roman state were a "world apart" from the majority of Jews, and it was only when many synagogues were built in the period of the Christianized empire, 350–640, that rabbinic texts came to influence the way of life of the majority of Jews.[14]

Schwartz indicates that the Jews continued to believe in their common ancestors after the repression of the revolts, but he does not emphasize shared genealogy in the reconstructed Judaism, centered in the synagogues and local religious communities, that emerged in the fourth century. Goodblatt writes that it is possible to interpret Schwartz as claiming that, with the exception of the marginal elite of rabbis, the "cultural" (I prefer "religious") component of Jewish identity was considerably weakened after 135 C.E. and that the survival of the kinship component served as a basis for the revival of the religious component after 350 C.E.

A consensus among historians of antiquity is unlikely to be forthcoming over questions of the continuities and discontinuities of the religion that emerged as Judaism and the dating of the compilation and canonization of its core texts. There can be little doubt, however, that ethnic and religious elements of Jewish identity came together and received canonical authority in rabbinic Judaism, which took shape in the first seven centuries of the Common Era. A useful analysis of the rabbis' formulations of Jewish identity in the first centuries of the Common Era is provided by Gary Porton, who examines the Mishnah, the basic compilation of the Oral Law put together around 200 C.E. and the Tosefta (supplement or addition), possibly from the mid- to late third century. Porton writes that there was an inherent tension in the rabbinic documents in defining Jews as an ethnic group and a religious community, but the two categories were brought together in a way that allowed them to be mutually important.

The rabbinic texts defined a Jew as a person who belongs to a particular descent group, "the children of Israel/Jacob." The common ancestors were linked, however, to a religious event. The "people of Israel" had entered into a unique relationship with Yahweh through the covenants with Abraham, Isaac, and Jacob, and that relationship was more sharply defined through the covenant at Sinai, an event that, according to the rabbinic tradition, defines Israel. According to the rabbinic formulation, the souls of all Jews, including converts, stood at Sinai and signed the covenant.[15]

The rabbis of the second century C.E. standardized the conversion process by requiring that all converts accept the commandments of the Torah, that male converts be circumcised, and that all converts should undergo ritual immersion.[16] This standardization provided a group identity with permeable boundaries that was removed from the emphasis on genealogical purity characteristic of Ezra, the Jubilees, and Qumranic sources. The rabbis' emphasis was on moral rather than genealogical purity, and the prohibition of intermarriage with unconverted Gentiles was predicated on the moral dangers this represented for the Jewish partner. Gentiles who renounced idolatry and immorality could enter the Jewish community as converts.[17]

It was also in the second century C.E. that rabbinic law established the matrilineal principle: Only the offspring of a Jewish mother were recognized as Jews. This ruling was surprising in the context of the patriarchalism of Israelite and Judean laws and culture. Cohen considers a number of explanations for the matrilineal ruling and writes that we do not have a full explanation, but he notes that the development of conversion procedures for women facilitated the matrilineal principle. This principle, together with the prohibition on intermarriage, expressed the rabbinic concern for "proper pedigree and genealogical purity."[18]

The fusion of religion and ethnicity formulated by the rabbis came apart in the modern era, when rabbinic hegemony came to an end and Jews were freed from enforced segregation by non-Jews. In the following chapters I deal with Jewish identity when it is the differentiation rather than the fusion of religion and ethnicity that is taken for granted. Chapters 7 and 8 deal principally with American Jewry. Chapter 7 is a critical review of how American sociologists have conceptualized and theorized the relationships between the religious and ethnic components of the identity of American Jews. Chapter 8 has a more empirical compass, and in it I analyze the changes in the relationships between religion and ethnicity among Jews in the modern and late modern (or postmodern) world. The focus remains on American Jews, but I include a wide historical perspective on the changes in identities of Western Jews in the modern era and compare American Jewish identities with those of Jews in Europe and Israel. The focus in chapter 9 is on Jews in Israel, and in it I compare the combinations of ethnic identities that are found among Israeli Jews of different origins. Variations in religiosity and secularity are shown to be an important determinant of the variations in ethnic identities among Israeli Jews.

7. FORMULATIONS OF ETHNICITY AND RELIGION REGARDING AMERICAN JEWS IN THE WRITINGS OF AMERICAN SOCIOLOGISTS

Religiosity Symbolizing Ethnicity

A common argument among American Jewish sociologists has been that Jewish ethnicity is the major basis of the religious behavior of American Jews. This argument was particularly persuasive when religious pluralism was far more legitimate in American society than ethnic pluralism. In his classic work, *Protestant, Catholic, Jew,* Will Herberg noted that the considerable increase in church and synagogue membership in the late 1940s and 1950s, which some referred to as a religious revival, paralleled migration to the suburbs in the late 1940s and 1950s. Herberg viewed the increase as an attempt by those who had moved from ethnic neighborhoods to combine their identities as Americans with loyalties to their ethnic backgrounds. He believed that the "return" to religion was especially common among third-generation Americans. They had grown up in families that had adopted American secular culture, and because ethnic culture was unacceptable as a basis for identification in America, religion became the focal point of their identity, both as Jews (or Catholics or Protestants) and as Americans. However, a number of facts, such as the absence of an increase in religious observance, appeared to point to ethnicity, not religiosity, as the real foundation of the religious revival among Jews. That many Jewish parents joined a synagogue only when their children reached the age for Sunday school appeared to demonstrate that an important function of the synagogue was to instill a Jewish identity into the next generation and lessen the chances of intermarriage.[1]

Ideas similar to those of Herberg were expressed by Nathan Glazer in his book *American Judaism*, published in 1957. According to Glazer, the real basis of the "religious revival" that focused on the synagogues and temples after World War II was not a "strong religious drive" but ethnic Jewishness. The ancient notion that the people of Israel exist to serve the religious law had been reversed; it was now the law that served the people.[2] The turn to the synagogue to express ethnicity followed the decline, beginning in the early 1930s, of the secularist Jewish movements of socialism, Socialist Zionism, and Yiddish culturalism. In the interwar period, the rise of nonreligious Jewish educational and social centers appeared to support the view that future Jewish life in America could be built on a variety of Jewish expressions, secular as well as religious. However, the demands of the wider society for ethnic integration, together with the general decline in America of socialist and atheist ideologies, left religion as the only way for American Jews to express their ethnicity.[3]

Ethnic pluralism appeared to gain more legitimacy in the late 1960s, but the theme of Jewish religious behavior as an expression of Jewish ethnicity continued into the 1970s. Marshall Sklare, the most prominent sociologist of American Jewry at that time, wrote that it was a general characteristic of the American social structure "for ethnic differences to be expressed and sustained as religious differences" and that this was especially so for American Jewry. The Jewish religion may be "the prototype of an ethnic religion," and therefore it was hardly surprising that in the American context "the specific character of American-Jewish religious energy is more ethnic than religious."[4]

If religion was an expression of ethnicity among American Jews, it was not always clear what dimensions of ethnicity religion was expressing. It was not an ethnic culture, because only remnants remained of an ethnic culture that had been differentiated from religion and based primarily on the vernacular Jewish language (Yiddish). Two interrelated dimensions were more important than ethnic culture: ethnic social ties (sociation) and ethnic identity. Ethnic social ties were emphasized by Charles Liebman, who wrote about what he regarded as the ambivalent American Jew. Liebman regarded the essence of what he called the folk religion of American Jews to be their social ties to each other. The distinguishing mark of Jews in American society was not how they behaved or what they believed but the fact that they associated with other Jews. Religious observances that required regular practice and that would have been obstacles to the integration of Jews into American society, such as Sabbath observance, a strict observance of the Jewish dietary laws, and family purity rules, had been abandoned. American Jews desired both their survival as a distinct group and their integration into American society. The dominant meanings of the few practices that continued to be observed by most American Jews, the Passover seder, the rites of passage, and observance of the High Holy Days, were practices entailing family celebration and affirmation of Jewish peoplehood. In Liebman's view, "One does not have to believe with Durkheim that all religion is celebration and ritualization of communal ties to observe that this is the major function of Jewish folk religion in America."[5]

The Durkheimian theme was taken up by Jonathan S. Woocher in his thesis of the rise of an American Jewish "civil religion." Liebman, Sklare, and others argued that for most American Jews religion was the vehicle of ethnicity or the external form that was filled with ethnic content, but they did not argue that ethnicity was sacralized in the Jewish religious denominations. Woocher's thesis can be understood as implying a sacralization of Jewish ethnicity, although he tried to avoid this implication. He argued that the "secular" organizations of American Jews, and, in particular, the welfare federation movement, "have achieved unity, purpose, and identity as a moral community which transcends (without excluding) the overtly religious ideology and practice of the denominational movements of American Judaism."[6]

An institutional complex that has the Jewish collectivity at the center of its meaning system might well be described as a sacralization of ethnicity, and Woocher's delineation of the major traits of the civil Jewish faith reinforce this impression. Along with the belief in Americanness as a virtue and American society as benign, the major social reference of the beliefs and myths of the civil religion are the Jews as a people or nation: the unity of the Jewish people, mutual responsibility, Jewish survival, the centrality of Israel, and the enduring value of Jewish tradition, philanthropy, and social justice.[7]

In a paper published in 2005 Woocher wrote that, since the publication of his book in 1986, the centrality of the American Jewish civil religion in defining the content of American Jews' Jewishness had declined, perhaps dramatically.[8] It is doubtful, however, whether the American Jewish civil religion ever had the centrality that Woocher proposed. Only a small, albeit influential, sector of American Jewry had been regular participants in the organizations and rituals of the civil religion described by Woocher. It might be argued that the beliefs, myths, and rituals of the American Jewish civil religion could be publicly propounded and performed only in a society where the trend toward legitimate ethnic pluralism no longer required that ethnicity be expressed through a conventional religious facade. Nevertheless, the synagogue remained the most important institutional context of group identity and formal Jewish American activities.

If synagogues have retained their centrality in American Jewish life, the ethnicity that they are purported to express and support appears to have changed, because the sociation of Jews has become less exclusively Jewish. In the early 1970s sociologists such as Sklare and Liebman could still argue that, although American Jews had accommodated their religious behavior to American society, they retained their group boundaries by associating with and marrying predominantly other Jews. Later surveys showed that the friendship networks of Jews had become ethnically more heterogeneous and that the intermarriage rate had increased substantially. The 1990 National Jewish Population Survey reported that 45 percent of those who stated that they were Jewish by religion described their friendship networks as "all or mostly" Jewish. The 2000–01 survey reported 20 percent.[9]

Gans's Symbolic Ethnicity and Symbolic Religiosity

The ethnic churches that arose among the groups who migrated from Europe to the United States in the mass migration from the 1880s to the early 1920s have long disappeared. The decline of religiously informed ethnic cultures and the trends of intermarriage across both ethnic and religious (Protestant-Catholic-Jew) boundaries have been common phenomena among these groups. In response to these developments, Herbert Gans presented in 1979 the concept of symbolic ethnicity,[10] which he later defined as "the consumption and other use of ethnic symbols . . . intended mainly for the purpose of feeling or being identified with a particular ethnicity, but without either participating in an existing ethnic organization (formal or informal) or practicing an ongoing ethnic culture."[11]

Studies by Richard Alba and Mary Waters supported Gans's arguments that the ethnic identities of white Americans had become "symbolic." First, they provided evidence that the cultural foci of ethnicity had become limited to such symbolic aspects as food, attending a yearly ethnic festival, and using certain words or phrases from the language of origin. Second, they showed that the communal bases of ethnicity had eroded; predominantly ethnic neighborhoods had disappeared or become far more heterogeneous, ethnic groups were no longer concentrated in particular occupations, and intermarriage had become commonplace. And third, they demonstrated that ethnicity retained subjective meanings. Despite an increasingly complicated ancestry (two-thirds of Alba's sample had mixed ancestry, and of these nearly half had three or more ethnic groups represented in their background), approximately two-thirds continued to identify themselves ethnically, many in terms of a single group.[12] As a source of pleasure and meaning, which gives people the feeling of being unique and of belonging to a collectivity, ethnicity is not quickly relinquished, but without structural underpinnings, ethnicity can become merely a vague sense of family origins with few or no demands on the individual.

In an article published in 1994 Gans formulated symbolic religiosity as a notion parallel to but yet separate from symbolic ethnicity.[13] Gans's conceptualization of symbolic ethnicity can be viewed as an alternative to both the positing of an inevitably total, or straight-line, assimilation on the one hand and portrayals of a continuing strong ethnicity or even ethnic revival on the other. Similarly, his conceptualization of symbolic religiosity can be viewed as an alternative to both straight-line secularization and arguments for the steady or increasing strength of religiosity.

Both straight-line assimilation theories and theories of the disappearance of religiosity have long been out of favor among most sociologists of ethnicity and religion in the United States. Among American sociologists of religion an antisecularization position has become prominent in recent years.[14] Gans's formulations, however, can be understood as suggesting caution, viewing these latest theories as overreactions to previous portrayals of linear declines. Thus his arguments can be understood as correctives directed primarily to theories of ethnic and/or religious revivalism among third- (or later) generation descendants of white immigrant populations.

In any event, Gans viewed American Jews as a major example of symbolic religiosity. Such a view is understandable because Gans first developed his notion of symbolic ethnicity in an early article on symbolic Judaism.[15] However, the example compounds problems of empirically separating the religious and ethnic dimensions of identity and behavior. Gans is aware of the complexities involved in disentangling religious and ethnic dimensions, especially among Jews. Nevertheless, I contend that the problems in making a case that religiosity has become symbolic in a way parallel to that of ethnicity led Gans to slip into another meaning of symbolic religiosity: making religiosity symbolic of ethnicity. After Gans's emphasis moved from symbolic religiosity as parallel to symbolic ethnicity to religiosity as symbolic of ethnicity, he then followed the tendency among many sociologists of American Jews up to the early 1990s to explain the importance of Jewish religious institutions and religiosity in terms of their ethnic functions.

Symbolic Ethnicity and Symbolic Religiosity: Parallels and Differences

Gans's definition of symbolic ethnicity stressed what it is not as much as what it is. Moreover, the inclusionary factors (feeling, identity) cited in the definition are primarily subjective, whereas the exclusionary factors (ethnic organization, ethnic culture) are objective. Gans's initial definition of symbolic religiosity as "a form of religiosity detached from religious affiliation and observance,"[16] similarly stressed what it is not, or at least what it is "detached" from. In other words, symbolic religiosity is parallel to symbolic ethnicity in that, although it includes the practice of a few, selected religious rites or customs that express religious feelings and identity, it is detached from the traditional, comprehensive religious culture and from participation in religious organizations.

Gans drew on surveys conducted by American Jewish sociologists, especially those of Steven Cohen,[17] to demonstrate that the religiosity of most American Jews was minimal, confined to using a few religious objects, such as the mezuzah, observing a few yearly practices, such as the Passover seder and lighting Hanukkah candles, and attending synagogue on the High Holy Days and for certain rites of passage. The decontextualization of these practices from the comprehensive system of religious law and ritual of traditional Judaism parallels the selection of objects and practices of symbolic ethnicity among Jews, such as "Jewish" or kosher-style foods (bagels and lox for Sunday brunch), the use of certain Yiddish words and phrases, the acquisition of art objects from Israel, reading books and going to films of Jewish interest, and occasional contributions to Jewish charities and the financial support of Israel. However, when Gans's analysis moved from religious culture to participation in religious organizations, the parallels he wished to make between symbolic ethnicity and symbolic religiosity become far more problematic.

Surveys conducted in 2000 and 2001 indicate that the proportion of American Jews affiliated with a synagogue or temple is about 40 percent, and it is likely that more than half become members during at least part of their adult lives.[18] Although most attend religious services infrequently, many make use of or participate in the various functions and activities of the synagogues, such as classes and social activities for children, the celebration of rites of passage, and a wide variety of educational, club, and social events. About twice as many American Jews are members of a synagogue or temple than are members of a nonreligious or ethnic

Jewish organization, and although membership in nonreligious or ethnic organizations is higher for Jews than it is for most other American ethnic groups, a case for symbolic ethnicity based on the absence of majority participation in ethnic associations would appear to be far more persuasive than a case for symbolic religiosity.

The differences between the social supports of ethnicity and religion in the United States pose a problem for the claim that the development of symbolic religiosity is similar to the development of symbolic ethnicity. Gans noted that religion, unlike ethnicity, does not require affiliation and may be a truly private activity: "American religious individualism [has] no ethnic equivalent."[19] It is, however, the connection between individualism and voluntary affiliation that has been a major strength of religion in America[20] and that points to important differences between the social structures of religiosity and ethnicity in the United States. The social foundations of ethnicity have tended to be more informal than formal, more gemeinschaft than gesellschaft. The family, including the extended family, and the neighborhood or local community have been important social anchorages. These bases have been greatly weakened by intermarriage and residential distribution, and formal ethnic organizations have not attracted sufficient support to replace them. Religion also has its informal social bases (Gans emphasized the importance of home-centered religion among Jews), but religious organizations, churches, synagogues, denominations, sects, and cults constitute the major social basis of religion in America. Once ethnicity comes to depend primarily on voluntary association, its future is uncertain, but, as a long line of observers of American religion have argued, one principal strength of religion in the United States has been its voluntarism.

Gans recognized the importance of the associational dimension of American Jewish religiosity. However, rather than noting that the difference in the importance of associations indicates a lack of parallel between symbolic ethnicity and symbolic religiosity and undercuts the claim that symbolic religiosity is a suitable description with respect to most American Jews, he extended his definition of symbolic religiosity. The extension incorporated those purposes that are "purely secular." Thus Gans defined symbolic religiosity as "the consumption of religious symbols apart from regular participation in a religious culture or religious organization, for the purpose of expressing feelings of religiosity and religious identification."[21] The suggestion here is that symbolic religiosity is a suitable term for the minimally religious, but it would not encompass that minority of American Jews who are highly observant in their religious practices. Debra Kaufman objects to this meaning because it appears to measure the authenticity of religious practice by its distance from orthopraxy. She argues that there is no single measure of religiosity and that religiosity has to be understood from the different perspectives of the Jewish denominations. From a Reform Judaism perspective, fewer religious observances do not make religiosity less authentic.[22]

For Gans, however, minimal religiosity indicated a cover for ethnicity. He wrote that, although Jews are able to express their ethnicity in Zionist groups and affiliations, the synagogues and temples are important contexts for ethnic identification, especially in small communities. Synagogues are places where Jews can meet and make friends with other Jews and where parents can send their children to instill and reinforce in them a Jewish identity with the proviso that this should not include too much religion. Gans was suggesting that, despite its differences from symbolic ethnicity with respect to the dimension of association, the term *symbolic religiosity* is appropriate because the major purpose of the association of American Jews with synagogues is not to express religiosity and religious identification. Moreover, it is not just the association with synagogues that is interpreted in terms of ethnicity; the decontextualized religious rituals are interpreted as performed in order to express feelings of ethnicity and ethnic identification as well as feelings of religiosity and religious identification.

The effort to support the notion of symbolic religiosity by noting the nonreligious references and purposes of ostensive religious activity echoes Gans's defense of the appropriateness of symbolic ethnicity as a descriptor for white ethnicity in the United States by interpreting the apparent ethnic revival in the late 1960s and early 1970s as principally a class phenomenon.[23] However, Gans did not make the "American tradition" of using ethnicity as a surrogate for class part of his definition of symbolic ethnicity as he did the nonreligious uses of religion in the definition of symbolic religiosity. It is important to note in this context that the ethnic revival involved a coalition of a number of ethnic groups for class purposes. The strategy of extending the meaning of "symbolic" to include references other than the apparent ones appears to go much further in the analysis of symbolic religiosity. The *symbols* of symbolic ethnicity (foods, festivals, ancestral memorabilia, vacation trips to the old country) have generally been considered nothing more than symbols of ethnicity. The *symbols* of symbolic religiosity, in contrast, are interpreted as having important references and purposes, ethnic and familial, other than those of religion.

Just as I would not want to suggest that Gans reduced ethnicity to class, I also do not intend here to suggest that Gans presented a reductionist interpretation of American Judaism in terms of American Jewish ethnicity. He indicated that in the 1950s and 1960s, when the taboo on intermarriage was greater among American Jews than it is today, parents were concerned with religious preservation as well as with ethnic group continuity. The taboo has lost its force, and concern about the long-term demographic viability of American Jewry because of the high intermarriage rate came to overshadow the debate on whether Jews are a religio-ethnic group or an ethnoreligious one. Gans did not resolve the issues in this debate. He did, however, suggest that "the best way to conceptualize what is happening is through a joining of the concepts."[24] Unfortunately, his suggestion was hardly enlightening, given his intention in the symbolic religiosity article to separate religious and ethnic dimensions. In fact, Gans's analysis of Jewish religious objects and practices gives the impression that it is the nonreligious purposes, particularly the ethnic and familial ones, that are predominant.

CHAPTER 7

Ethnic Acculturation and Religious Acculturation

Gans acknowledged that the associational functions of the synagogues complicated his attempts to compare religious acculturation and ethnic acculturation. The denominalization of American Judaism was itself a form of acculturation.[25] However, because the pace of acculturation depended on the level of formal organization, the strength of the synagogues should have resulted in a slower acculturation in religiosity than in ethnicity. One piece of evidence for religious acculturation is the decline in the observance of religious practices from the immigrant generation to the third and later generations. Yet, whereas all indicators of communal (ethnic) activities had declined, not all religious observances had done so. Another piece of evidence for religious acculturation was the changes in the religious services, such as the introduction of English to partly replace Hebrew and the adoption of the democratic and communitarian trappings typical of the Protestant denominations.

It would be useful at this point to make a more explicit distinction between the quantitative and qualitative dimensions of acculturation than that made by Gans. Gans described ethnic acculturation mainly in terms of the decline of ethnic practices. Although he indicated qualitative change by noting that the constructed ethnicity of later generations is more acculturated than that of earlier generations, he gave little indication of the content of the (re)constructed ethnicity. Instances of qualitative religious acculturation, such as changes in the themes of prayers, are perhaps easier to delineate, but it is not evident that the trend among American Jews in recent decades has been in the direction of acculturation.

Among the major Jewish denominations, religious acculturation has been most extensive in Reform Judaism. In some respects, Reform Judaism took more acculturative forms in the late nineteenth century and early twentieth century than it has in recent decades. Early, "classical" Reform Judaism in America omitted references to the return to Zion, transformed the messianic message to one of universal progress, and, in some temples, forbade male head covering and transferred the major Sabbath service to Sunday.[26] These indicators of a high level of acculturation were accompanied by a self-conscious distinction between a Jewish religious identity, which was adopted, and a Jewish ethnic or national identity, which was rejected.

Changes in American Reform Judaism since the 1930s, such as more Hebrew, the restoration of references to Zion, and the use of head covering and *tallit*, are instances of deacculturation, and they were accompanied by a reaffirmation of the integral relationship between Judaism and Jewish ethnic identity. These changes can be explained in part by the entrance of second-generation Jews of eastern European origin into the Reform denomination, which had previously been the preserve of the more established and more acculturated American-born families of German Jewish origin. The deacculturation of the denomination was accomplished by new members whose affiliation with Reform Judaism represented a process of acculturation compared with their former Orthodox or Conservative Judaism background.[27] In some respects, however, the process of deacculturation continued even as the third and subsequent generations became numerically predominant. The reappropriation of tradition in Reform Judaism has been made more explicit in recent years by the encouragement of the performance of mitzvot, albeit in a manner consistent with Reform Judaism's emphasis on religious autonomy.[28]

Gans suggested the term *bumpy-line process* to depict the ups and downs of expressions of ethnicity in the United States. With respect to American Jewry, the process of deacculturation appears to make religious acculturation an even better case for such a depiction than ethnicity does. However, American Jewish sociologists might argue that religious deacculturation really expresses a bumpy-line development of ethnicity, because the reappropriation of traditional forms does not make the religious behavior less symbolic (it may make it more so) in the sense of providing appropriate symbols for ethnic feelings. When the most acculturated religious forms were adopted in the latter part of the nineteenth century, ethnicity was rejected. The readoption of traditional practices may provide feelings of greater ethnic distinctiveness.

Comparisons with Other Ethnic Groups

Despite expressions of uncertainty about whether symbolic religiosity and symbolic ethnicity can be analyzed or explained separately, Gans focused on Jews, a group for whom the problems of empirically differentiating religion and ethnicity are particularly acute.[29] A comparison of the symbolic ethnicity and religiosity and of the ethnic and religious acculturation of, say, Italian Americans would appear to present fewer problems. Greater problems present themselves in the cases of what Gans called ethnoreligious groups, such as the Greek Orthodox and the Apostolic Armenians, who are, as Gans noted, closer to the Jews than the Italians with respect to the relationship between religion and ethnicity. Gans recognized the differences between these groups and Jews when he described Jews as a "religio-ethnic group."[30] However, the implications of putting *ethno-* or *religio-* first are not made clear by Gans. A major difference is that the relationship of ethnicity, or nationality, and religion is more integral and less historically contingent for the Jews than for, say, the Armenians, who, although they have an ethnically bounded church, are nevertheless part of a religion, Christianity, that is not nationally or ethnically bounded.

The studies by Alba and Waters of ethnicity among white ethnic groups in America do not give special attention to the Jewish case, but their analyses of trends of ethnicity among American whites point to an important difference between the Jews and other ethnic groups. They argued that Jews are distinctive among American white ethnic groups with respect to the anchorage of ethnic identity in ethnic social structures. The most important Jewish ethnic organizations, those encompassing the majority of American Jews, are the synagogues and temples.

Alba noted that the evidence for religion sustaining ethnicity is not convincing *except* for those groups who represent a fusion of religion and ethnicity. The sustaining of religion is still far less problematic than the sustaining of ethnicity in the American context. The American credo continues to emphasize that everyone must have a religion, and whereas ethnicity may no longer be proscribed, neither is it prescribed. The contribution of religious institutions to ethnicity was recognized by Gans in a comment on the Greek American community, one of the few groups that approximate the Jews in their fusion of religion and ethnicity: It appears "almost as if the church is a means to a secular ethnic end, except for the important fact that the Orthodox church is the major agent assuring the persistence of Greek ethnicity."[31]

Jews were singled out by Alba as the outstanding instance of a group that had not been swept along by the assimilatory tide. Unlike other groups, Jews still thought they were discriminated against, were still involved in political issues as an ethnic group, and maintained friendship networks that were still far less ethnically heterogeneous than other groups. What the Jews had, and what other groups such as the Italians rarely had any longer, was ethnically homogeneous religious congregations and other religiously related institutions, such as schools, colleges, and summer camps. These institutions informed and reminded members of the beliefs and practices of their heritage. Moreover, within these institutions and within the informal networks that often developed from meetings in these institutions, the contacts of Jews with other Jews sharpened the perception of the group's social and cultural boundaries.

Religiosity and Ethnicity in the Works of Optimists and Pessimists

Following the sharp rise in intermarriage beginning in the 1970s, American Jewish sociologists hotly debated its implications and the demographic changes in general for the future of American Jewry. The pessimists, who maintained that American Jewry was undergoing substantial assimilation, were opposed by the optimists, who claimed that American Jewry was maintaining its viability through a process of transformation. The most prominent optimists among the sociologists in the 1980s were Calvin Goldscheider and Steven Cohen. Some twenty years later, Goldscheider appears to have retained his optimism more than Cohen. However, my intention is not to adjudicate the arguments over the future of American Jewry but rather to focus on how both optimists and pessimists have presented the relationship between ethnicity and religion.

Goldscheider's position was that structural rather than cultural or religious factors have always provided the bases of Jewish cohesion, and he suggested that Judaism is a weaker element in Jewish continuity than in the past. In his analysis of the data on the Boston Jewish community, published in 1986, Goldscheider found signs of weakening religiosity, such as declines in religious observance, synagogue affiliation, and Orthodox and Conservative identification. These signs of weakening religiosity were not taken to mean that religion was no longer of any importance in the continuation of the Jewish community; the great majority continued to practice at least a few rituals, few never attended synagogue, and there appeared to be greater generational continuity in religious identification and behavior than in the past. Goldscheider's contention was that religion had lost its centrality. Other sources of group cohesion, such as occupational concentration in prestigious occupations and a concern with Israel, emerged, he claimed, as alternative Jewish expressions and conveyors of Jewish continuity.[32]

Goldscheider contended that the inference that secularization among Jews is an indicator of the decline of the Jewish community confuses Judaism with Jewishness. He admitted, however, that the available data could not answer the following questions: "How much secularization and erosion of traditional religious practices can occur without having a major impact on the Jewishness of the younger generation?" and "Are the new forms of Jewish ethnicity able to balance secularization?"[33] In his more recent work Goldscheider questions the validity of the secularization thesis and writes that the changes that Judaism has undergone in the modern period should be described as a "transformation" rather than a secularization of Judaism. In its transformed state, Judaism is no longer a source of generational conflict because, unlike the immigrants and their children, the third and fourth generations have common religious expressions that reinforce the bonds created in the home. Nevertheless, Goldscheider still refers to the Judaism of the third and fourth generations of American Jews as secularized, and his understanding of the extent of Judaism's contribution to Jewish continuity is that religion is no longer a source of generational conflict within the Jewish family.

Goldscheider continues to emphasize the contribution of interrelated ethnic and structural factors, especially the connection of family and communal institutions, to Jewish identification and continuity. Concentrations of Jews in particular occupations, neighborhoods, schools, and universities have, according to Goldscheider, resulted in powerful new forms of Jewish networks and institutions. Educational and occupational achievements have contributed to Jewishness by enhancing the choices that Jews can make in its expressions. He writes that the major source of Jewish identification among American Jews tends to be ethnic or communal rather than "narrowly religious" and that "the key indications of Jewish continuity" are not religious practices but rather "family, communal and associational *networks.*"[34]

Steven Cohen, another prominent sociologist of American Jewry, has not dealt directly with the secularization thesis, but he has presented his data in a way that minimizes secularization and its effects. In an analysis of data from a 1981 survey of Jews in the greater New York area, Cohen argues that, although levels of religious observance had declined from the first to the third generation, there were indications of a stemming of the secular trend. A comparison of the religiosity of respondents and their parents (as reported by respondents) showed that an increasing number of respondents with highly observant (or Orthodox) parents were retaining high levels of observance and that children of the least observant did not report further reductions (some respondents reported increases).[35]

Cohen continued the same line of argument when he drew on data from the 1990 National Jewish Population Survey, and his emphasis on the stability of ritual practice made him less concerned than Goldscheider with finding alternatives to Judaism in dimensions of Jewishness.[36] More recently Cohen has suggested that, for a large proportion of American Jews, religious stability has been accompanied by a decline in ethnicity. The data Cohen gathered from a 1997 survey of just over 1,000 Jews throughout the United States showed that, whereas younger and older Jews did not differ in their levels of religious practice and commitment, in nearly all measures of Jewish ethnicity (commitment to Jewish peoplehood, support of endogamy, proportion of Jews among close friends, affiliation with nonreligious Jewish institutions, support for Israel), younger respondents scored lower than older respondents. Intermarriage, which was higher among younger respondents, was associated with some lower religious scores, but it was associated with diminished ethnicity far more. The growth in intermarriage could account only partly for the decline in Jewish ethnicity.

Cohen admitted that the ethnic dimensions of Jewish identity could be more salient than was indicated by his data. Respondents could have been influenced by the general tendency among Americans to denigrate ethnicity and to exaggerate socially approved religious behavior. A further reservation of his religious stability/ethnic decline position was that popular religious practices, such as lighting Hanukkah candles and attending a Passover seder, could well be socially acceptable vehicles of ethnicity. Nevertheless, Cohen wrote that, with the decline of ethnic particularism, Jewish identity was becoming more like American religious identity in general.[37]

In a book co-authored with Arnold Eisen, *The Jew Within: Self, Family, and Community in America*, Cohen suggested that many American Jews are displaying a new "spirituality of seeking," a form of religiosity that they share with an increasing number of non-Jewish Americans. To discover the meanings attributed by American Jews to their Judaism and Jewishness, Cohen and Eisen conducted in-depth interviews with fifty "moderately affiliated" mostly Conservative and Reform Jews who belonged to at least one Jewish organization. They found that the meanings attributed by their subjects were focused on the private sphere, and they referred, with some hesitation, to a "postmodern" Jewish self, for whom the "grand narrative" of the Jewish people and its destiny is replaced by "local narratives" and "personal stories" of the individual and the nuclear family. The Judaism of the postmodern Jews is personalist, focused on the self rather than the group, and voluntarist, with an emphasis on freedom to choose selectively (and perhaps only temporarily) from the repertoire of Jewish religious beliefs and practices. The question of what is correct is supplanted by what is meaningful, and the quest for Jewish meaning is perceived as never-ending, because it is the journey more than the arrival that is valued.

The emphasis on personal meanings and spirituality, on private rather than public forms, favors the religious dimensions, albeit expressed in a transformed

Judaism rather than in the ethnic dimensions of Jewishness. Indications that Jewish ethnicity has become less important include the increase in non-Jewish friends and the decline of interest in and emotional ties to Israel. Commitment to Jewish organizations has declined, but the synagogue is a partial exception to this trend because much of the "new spirituality" takes place within it. When the Jews studied by Cohen and Eisen attend religious services, the content of the liturgy is less important to them than the opportunity the synagogue provides to reflect on and explore personal meanings. Religion is privatized within the collective frameworks of the family and the synagogue.[38]

The institutional basis of the strength of the religious dimension of Jewishness among American Jews was supported in a separate analysis by Cohen of membership in congregations, based on the 2000–01 National Survey of American Jews. Cohen reported that 89 percent of those American Jews who identified as Orthodox belonged to a congregation and that the figures for those who identified as Conservative and Reform were 63 percent and 52 percent, respectively.[39] As I have noted, one argument for an ethnic basis of American Jewish religious behavior is that American Jews tend to join a congregation when their children reach school age and abandon their membership after their children's bar or bat mitzvah. Cohen's data show that this assertion should be modified. The Orthodox demonstrate a lifelong synagogue membership. Conservative Jews tend to join a congregation after they marry and have children but retain their affiliation after the children's bar or bat mitzvah. Only Reform Jews exhibit a child-centered congregational affiliation, but even among the Reform it is only a minority (albeit a substantial one) who join at the time of their children's bar or bat mitzvah preparation and leave afterward.[40]

Cohen modified his optimistic portrayal of the future of American Jewry, but his position remained one of relative optimism compared with that of Charles Liebman, who proffered a pessimistic portrayal of American Jewry bound up with his concern about the relationship between Judaism and Jewishness. Liebman did not believe that the observance of a few mainly yearly ceremonies, shorn of their transcendental religious meanings, provided grounds for optimism. The high proportion of Jews who participate in the Passover seder has little significance when it may mean little more than a family meal.[41]

Goldscheider and Zuckerman were a direct target of Liebman's critique.[42] Their optimistic assessment was based on a tacit approval of the minimization of Judaism and its substitution by Jewishness or ethnic Judaism. Much of Liebman's critique was based on his religious assumption that there is an essential Judaism against which changes in the Jewish community can be evaluated. However, it is not necessary to accept Liebman's religious position in order to question the long-term functional viability of the sources of group cohesion emphasized by Goldscheider and Zuckerman. The concentration of Jews in high-status white-collar and professional occupations may provide an important basis of social interaction among Jews, but if Jews constitute only a small percentage of those occupations in which they are concentrated, the importance of this factor for Jewish cohesion is doubtful.

Israel became an important focus for Jewish identity, especially after 1967. However, Israel's drawing power has become attenuated in recent years. Visiting Israel can hardly be said to be taking the place of religious belief and ritual, especially when it is the more ritually observant who are the most pro-Israel.

In an early work, Liebman argued that folk Judaism was primarily an expression of the association of Jews among themselves.[43] The increase in social ties with non-Jews, as reflected in the much higher intermarriage rate, weakened this argument. The ethnicity that came to be expressed by the continued widespread practice of selected rituals was seen to be related less to the actual sociation of American Jews and more to their feelings of ethnic identity. Symbolic religiosity was symbolizing symbolic ethnicity, as indicated in Liebman's distinction between ritual and ceremony. Ritual has transcendental implications for participants; ceremonies represent assertions of membership within an existing social order. The popular rituals carried out in non-Orthodox contexts, such as Hanukkah candle lighting in the home and havdalah prayers marking the end of Sabbath in public settings of Jewish organizations, are ceremonies in that they do not follow the prescriptions of Jewish law and/or they do not chronologically precede or follow other appropriate parts of the ritual. For example, the havdalah benediction is often performed without the Ma'ariv, the ritually prescribed evening prayer that should precede it.[44]

Liebman's emphasis on the performance of a few decontextualized ceremonies as an expression of group membership was similar to Gans's portrayal of American Jewry in terms of symbolic religiosity: Judaism had become a narrow superstructure of a Jewish ethnicity, which itself had become focused on feelings and identity. In his later works, in response to privatized forms of Judaism of the type described in the study of Cohen and Eisen, Liebman emphasized the importance of Jewish ethnicity for Judaism and Jewish survival. According to Liebman, the adoption of the values of personalism and voluntarism among American Jews had two interrelated consequences: a decline in ethnic commitment and a privatized religion that replaced the performance of Jewish ritual as an obligatory system.[45]

Liebman was critical of a new wave of studies of Jewish identity that challenged the notion that there is an entity or essence called Judaism. Bethamie Horowitz, for example, wrote that it was no longer appropriate to measure Jewish identity solely by a "canon" of religious behaviors and practices and that it should now include whatever is personally meaningful for the individual. Jewishness was changing, and it was necessary to examine the subjective inner experience of being Jewish in addition to Jewish practices and involvement in Jewish life. Horowitz wrote that investigators of Jewish identity had tended to overlook "subjectively engaged" Jews who carry out few if any "conventional" Jewish observances. The personally meaningful terms in which Jewish identity had come to be expressed meant that it was founded less in terms of either religion or ethnicity.[46]

Like Horowitz, Debra Renee Kaufman has emphasized the importance of investigating identity as an "inner thing" that is not necessarily expressed or enacted in regular activity. Kaufman collected narratives from a sample of seventy young Jewish adults, mostly fourth generation, who "are highly committed to Jewishness, but not necessarily to those things Judaic." Like the respondents in the study of Cohen and Eisen, Kaufman's subjects emphasized that Jewishness or Judaism was primarily a subjective experience and that it was possible to pick and choose the expressions of one's identity without a worry about their so-called authenticity. Kaufman found that religion and ethnicity moved in and out of her subjects' narratives and that expressions of religiosity and ethnicity were combined in many ways. It would be a distortion, therefore, to categorize her subjects' identities into those of ethnicity and religion.[47]

Kaufman, in a co-authored piece with Harriet Hartman, wrote that the use of narratives to explore the construction of "meaning-making" in identity studies offers the possibility of moving beyond the dualities of ethnicity and religion.[48] Liebman, in comparison, expressed his concern with those developments that represented an unraveling of the "religion-ethnicity package." The ethnically based religion was retreating before a privatized religion that emphasized individual rather than collective meanings. Ethnic Judaism, according to Liebman, posed the Jewish people as a transcendent presence, and this made the notion of a transcendent God meaningful and real. A personalized religion, focusing on individual spirituality, does not provide such a basis for a strong commitment to Judaism as a differentiated religion. It can easily lead to spiritual questions outside Judaism. It provides no intrinsic justification for boundaries, and the notion of an unbounded Judaism undermines its basis as a religion.[49]

Conclusion

The differentiation of ethnicity from religion pursuant to the emancipation of Western Jewish communities raised the problem of articulating the relationship between them. Efforts to deal with the problem generated numerous formulations and continue today in Jewish communities, both in the Diaspora and in Israel, and among sociologists of the Jews. The manner in which the relationship is formulated depends on the point of comparative reference. For many American Jewish sociologists the point of reference has been a traditionalist or orthoprax community in which religion provides a comprehensive way of life. When they have noted the minimal level of religious observance of American Jews, they have assumed that it cannot be taken seriously as religion and that ethnic identity provides its real basis. The subjective feelings of ethnicity appear to determine the objective existence of religious institutions and behavior. However, when the comparative focus turns to accounting for the relatively strong ethnicity of Jews compared to other white American ethnic groups, the importance of the structural foundation provided by religious institutions becomes evident. The ethnicity of American Jews is now based less on sociation and has moved in the direction of symbolic ethnicity.

However, as ethnicity becomes more a matter of feelings and identity, the social supports of the religious institutions assume importance for the salience and continuation of those feelings and identity.

Among American Jews, ethnicity and religion are in a relationship of symbiosis or complementarity; each is comparatively weak where the other is comparatively strong. Ethnicity is strong with respect to identity and feelings of belonging to a group of purported common ancestry and history, but it is weak with respect to a structural basis. Religion is weak in the sense that feelings of belonging to a community of shared religious beliefs and practices are declining, but it is strong in that it provides a firm structural basis. From an idealist perspective, ethnicity is the subjective component that provides the real reasons for joining synagogues and carrying out religious practices. From a materialist perspective, religious institutions are the objective conditions that make possible the persistence of a relatively strongly held ethnicity. My suggestion, therefore, is that greater attention be given to the symbiosis of religion and ethnicity rather than to viewing religion as a symbolic superstructure of ethnicity.

8. JUDAISM AND JEWISH ETHNICITY

Changing Interrelationships and Differentiations in the Diaspora and Israel

Descent Versus Consent

One feature of what many call postmodernism and what others call late modernity is that cultural identities are no longer structured and regulated by the constraints of descent but are structured and transformed by the freedoms of consent. The language of descent—of hereditary qualities, liabilities, and entitlements—is being replaced by the language of consent—of agents who freely choose not only their occupations and spouses but also their religions and even their ethnicities.[1] The transition from traditional to modern societies included the change from ascription to achievement, but this affected mainly occupations, classes, and socioeconomic statuses. Modernization also included the process of nation building, which involved distinguishing groups in terms of descent. Terms such as American, French, and German were understood to signify unified cultures to which minority religious and ethnic descent groups might acculturate and dominant groups into which minorities might assimilate.

The multiplicity of differentiations in extensively pluralistic postmodern societies, together with processes of globalization, has weakened these distinctions. Cultural diversity (both religious and ethnic) has obscured the notion of a dominant culture associated with purportedly nonethnic carriers; in the absence of a normative standard or reference group, cultural identities come to be perceived as freely chosen and constructed by consent.

The change from descent to consent has not affected all cultural identities in equal measure. One cultural identity that has undergone considerable transformation in the direction of consent is religion. An identity previously passed on in most cases from one generation to the next has become in some Western societies, especially the United States, a matter of consumer freedom, of private preference and taste.[2] Two interrelated changes have contributed to the religion of consent. One change is the substitution of the autonomous self or inner spirituality for the external voices of authority. The other is an ever more extensive religious pluralism, which provides the religious consumer with a wide range of choices.

Nowhere is there more emphasis on the right of the individual to choose his or her religious preference than in the United States, and nowhere is the number of religious alternatives so great. The triple melting pot of Protestant, Catholic, and Jew, which apparently became entrenched in the 1950s, has been superseded by a religious pluralism that also includes Islam, Eastern religions, and New Age religions.[3] Religious privatism is occurring in other societies, but making the self the locus of religion has fewer implications for religious choice if the choice is made within a society with few religious alternatives. Such is the case for Jews in Israel, where the high social boundaries between national groups associated with Judaism and Islam and the state-supported near monopoly of orthoprax Judaism are highly restrictive of choice among religious traditions.

Ethnic identities are also undergoing a transformation from descent to consent, but this is a slower process and is not yet so encompassing as in the area of religion. The definition of ethnicity includes references to descent or inheritability, and the development of ethnic choice is likely to depend more on intermarriages than religious choice has. An increasing number of ethnic intermarriages produces multiple ancestries from which children can choose their preferred ethnicity.[4]

In the past the constraints of descent meant that a religious intermarriage was often accompanied by one spouse's adoption of the other spouse's religion; but the understanding of ethnicity as inherited made the adoption of a spouse's ethnic identity problematic. The principle of religious preference has made partners in intermarriage feel less obligated to adopt the religion of their spouses—but conversion of one spouse to the other's religion is still more likely than the adoption by one spouse of the other's ethnic identity. Where religious and ethnic identities are associated with each other, it is possible that a religious conversion will be seen as an ethnic act as well as a religious one.[5] However, it is also possible for the spouse who converts to differentiate between religion and ethnicity and adopt the partner's religion without the accompanying ethnic identity.

Compared with religious identities, which may even become more salient when adopted, the choice of ethnic identities provided by multiple ancestries is likely to be accompanied by a decline in the salience of ethnicity. Recent studies of white Americans have shown that, although most Americans desire a sense of ethnicity, this identity is of middling salience, without a deep commitment to special behaviors or social ties.[6] Where ethnicity and a particular religious tradition are associated, the decline in the salience in ethnicity may affect loyalty to the religious tradition. Phillip Hammond and Kee Warner present evidence that appears to show that among Catholics a decline in ethnic religious loyalty followed a decline in ethnic identity and that in the past the same process may have occurred among Protestants.[7] The relationships of ethnic and religious identities among most Catholics and Protestants are understood to be different from those among most Jews, and the question arises as to the effects of ethnic intermarriage and religious choice on Jews.

Hammond and Warner follow Harold Abramson's categorization of three patterns of ethnic-religious relationships in the United States. Jews are given as an example of the first pattern, a fusion of religion and ethnicity, together with other groups such as the Amish and Mormons. In the second pattern religion may be one of several bases of ethnicity so that ethnicity extends beyond the religion, as, for example, in the cases of Greek Orthodox and Dutch Reformed. In the third pattern a number of ethnic groups are linked to the same religion so that the religion extends beyond ethnicity, as, for example, in the cases of Irish or Italian Catholics. In the second pattern it is possible to claim an ethnic identity without the religious identity, whereas in the third pattern the religious identity can be claimed without the ethnic identity. Such differentiations are claimed to be exceptional in the first pattern, where religion and ethnicity are merged; the denial of the religious or the ethnic identity involves the denial of the other.[8]

Ethnic Versus Religious Identity Among Jews

Since the entrance of Western Jewry into modernity at the end of the eighteenth century, the number of Jews and Jewish movements claiming a religious or an ethnic identity without the other are too numerous to be designated as exceptions to the pattern of religious-ethnic fusion. Placing the Jews in a category together with the Amish and Mormons as a case in which "religion is the major foundation of ethnicity" is problematic. A person born and brought up as an Amish or a Mormon who refutes the religion does not remain an Amish ethnic or a Mormon ethnic. A person born Jewish who refutes Judaism may continue to assert a Jewish identity, and if he or she does not convert to another religion, even religious Jews will recognize the person as a Jew. Unlike the Amish and the Mormons, Jews may differentiate between religion and nationality or ethnicity on the basis of their core sacred book, the Tanakh, or Old Testament. A history-*cum*-mythology tells of a people who became the exclusive carriers of a religion through their covenant with God, and because the religious ceremonies recall and celebrate the history of a people, they lend themselves to secularized reformulation.

According to tradition, the Jewish people existed to serve the Torah, the Jewish religious law, and because no other people ascribed to that law in all its essentials, it was evident that Judaism could not survive the disappearance of the Jewish people. However, in contrast to Christianity, with its focus on the life and teachings of the founder, the Tanakhic focus on the history of a people meant that once the process of secularization began, it became possible for Jews to identify with the people without the religion. The traditional formulation could then be reversed: The Torah existed to serve the Jewish people. Within secularized contexts, Jews might better be categorized with such groups as the Greek Orthodox, among whom ethnicity extends beyond the religion, than with the Amish or Mormons.

Apart from the secularist ethnic identity, some Jews, such as Jewish Christians, claim that their adherence to another religion does not invalidate their Jewish identity. On the other hand, many Jews in the modern period, primarily during the period before World War II, have identified religiously as Jews and claimed a non-Jewish national identity. Both of these types of differentiation have been associated with individuals who are recognized as having been "born Jewish." What is new in recent decades, especially in the United States, is the number of people recognized as not having been born Jewish who have converted to Judaism or who participate in Jewish religious ceremonies. This development opens up the possibility of different ethnic identities becoming conjoined with Judaism, somewhat similar to Irish, Italian, and Polish Catholics. A brief historical summary can provide perspective on the differences between Jewish ethnic and religious identities that have emerged in recent decades and those that emerged in the late eighteenth and nineteenth centuries.

Toward the end of the eighteenth century, new patterns of Jewish identity developed in Europe and North America in response to secularization and the construction of new collective identities of modernizing nations. The construction of boundaries of citizenship and identity involved formulating terms for the Jews' inclusion or exclusion. Where secularization was accompanied by willingness to include the Jews—often conditioned on the Jews' adoption of the dominant culture and national identity—many reinterpreted their Jewish identity as a purely religious one and eschewed any Jewish national, or what came later to be known as Zionist, identity. Proclaiming that they differed from their non-Jewish compatriots only in terms of religious persuasion, the Englishmen, Frenchmen, Germans, and Americans of the Jewish or Mosaic faith developed forms of Judaism that they believed would allow them to both participate in the wider society and retain an identity associated with Judaism. Such self-designations indicated a break from the past and a separation from coreligionists who still embodied the characteristics associated with the term *Jew* in the public mind. Although identity was attributed with a differentiated religious meaning, in most cases involvement in Judaism was limited to rites of passage, infrequent visits to the synagogue, and a few yearly observances in the family setting.

In eastern Europe, where the construction of national and ethnic identities involved marking the Jews as unassimilable outsiders, the inroads of secularism and the breakup of traditional communities led to many Jews' adopting a nonreligious national, ethnic, or cultural Jewish identity. This type was, in some respects, the converse of the type that had become common in central and western Europe and the United States. A greater proportion of secularized eastern European Jews believed that their problems required radical solutions (a socialist revolution or an autonomous Jewish state), and religion was seen as an irrelevance or obstacle in the attainment of such solutions.[9]

The ideologically secularist Jewish movements attracted only a minority of eastern European Jews, but a number of the secularists joined the mass migration to the West beginning in the 1880s and transplanted their socialist, nationalist, and Yiddish cultural movements to those communities. In the United States the secularist movements of these eastern European immigrants continued to find support among the second generation, in the years between the two world wars; secularist ethnic identities remained the preference of a minority, but antireligious Zionists, secularist Yiddish culturalists, and a number of anarchist, socialist, and communist Jewish organizations could still be found.[10]

Secularist nationalists, especially socialist Zionists from eastern Europe, were prominent in the first modern waves of Jewish migration to Palestine, and the construction of the national identity of "New Hebrews" or "Israelis" involved attempts to make a clear differentiation between nationality and religion. The emphasis on nationality rather than religion was signaled by substituting the "people of Israel" for "God" when drawing on biblical and traditional literature. The dissociation from Judaism in formulations, such as "Canaanites," was intended to contrast between the "Hebrew" and the "Jew," the latter being associated with the negatively evaluated condition of exile.[11]

Both the religious antinational or anational Jewish identity espoused by Reform Judaism and the national antireligious or areligious Jewish identity of secularist Zionism were expressions of an acute preoccupation with the boundaries of identity and were cast in highly ideological forms. They were examples of modernist movements in their rejection of the traditionalist religious societies, their conceptions of progress, and their reinterpretations of the Jewish past to legitimize their endeavors and visions of the future. Reform Jews found their values of social justice in the teachings of the ancient Jewish prophets, and secularist Zionists pointed to the Hebrew kingdoms of antiquity as expressions of the primary ties between the people and the land and the importance of political autonomy. Finding an appropriate link with a distant past and unburdening themselves of the deadweight of tradition, both Reform Judaism and secularist Zionism presented themselves as carriers of a mission that would bring further enlightenment and freedom in the future.[12]

A number of events and social processes have resulted in the decline of the modernist ideological forms of the denationalized religious Jewish identity and the dereligionized national Jewish identity. The exclusively religious identity that was given ideological and ritual expression in classical Reform Judaism lost its attraction in the face of vehement racial anti-Semitism, the Holocaust, the achievements of the Zionist movement, the establishment of the state of Israel, and the wars between Israel and Arab countries. The second generation of American Jews tended to be drawn to Conservative Judaism, which combined religion and ethnicity and provided, in its ritual forms, an attractive middle road between the old-society Judaism of their parents and the Reform Judaism of the more established American Jews. The third and subsequent generations have shifted more to Reform—but this brand of Judaism no longer attempts to dispute the national component of Jewish identity and places greater emphasis on Israel and Zion.[13]

The Six Day War accelerated the decline of both the nonnational religious identity among Jews in the Diaspora and the antireligious national identity in Israel. The American Council for Judaism, a Reform offshoot that represented the anti-Zionist position of classical Reform Judaism, virtually collapsed,[14] and in Israel ideological secularism was marginalized by the interpenetration of politics and religion that followed the war.[15] In addition to the Six Day War and its repercussions, two longer term processes contributed to the decline of a secularist or antireligious Jewish ethnicity, both in the Diaspora and in Israel. One was secularization. Secularist Jewishness had its high point when the religious worldview was beginning to lose its shared taken-for-granted qualities, but religion still retained a strong influence over a large part of the community. Once the pervasive influence of religion came to be confined to a minority enclave (or a number of enclaves) that rarely impinged on the daily lives of the majority of Jews, secularist Jewishness lost its appeal and was replaced by minimal religiosity.[16] Ideological secularism may appear to have retained some importance in Israel, but it tends to take the form of opposition to the religious establishment and to the political power of the religious sectors, especially the *haredim*, rather than to religion per se.

Another development that contributed to the decline of the antireligious or areligious Jewish identity, especially in the Diaspora, was the decline of ethnic cultural elements (especially the Yiddish language), which in the past provided a cultural basis for nonreligious ethnicity, and the decline of communal and social structures, such as ethnic neighborhoods and industries where Jews provided most of the employers and employees. The destruction of Yiddish culture in eastern Europe and the decline of its remnants in the West undercut the foundations of a Jewish ethnic identity that could draw on rich cultural resources with little regard to or in opposition to religious heritage. Where an all-encompassing religion lost its strength and where nonreligious ethnic cultural sources were no longer available, instead of rejecting religious symbols, secularized Jews tended to reinterpret them, extracting their supernaturalist meanings and making them suitable for familial and ethnic celebrations.

Ethnic Versus Religious Identity Among Jews in the United States

Ideological differentiation and oppositions between religious and ethnic forms of Jewish identity are now rarely made, but among American Jews signs of both a weakened form of Jewish ethnicity without Judaism and a deethnicized religious identity are evident. American Jews are no longer under pressure to proclaim their Americanness by refuting an ethnic Jewish identity, but soon after Jews found that they could openly proclaim their ethnicity without damaging their Americanness, the notion of what it was to be an ethnic weakened. The disappearance of a uniform, stable single notion of what it meant to be American caused the conception of what it meant to be an ethnic to lose its clarity. The emerging de-ethnicized religious American Jewish identity is not, as it was in the past, a consequence of discomfort in proclaiming dual loyalties but rather accompanies the high level of intermarriage within a society that emphasizes religious choice and retains high levels of affiliation to and participation in religious institutions. Although the intermarriage rate of American Jewry is no higher than that of some European Jewries, the implications of intermarriage on Jewish religious identities are likely to be greater in the United States because organized religion, including organized Judaism, continues to thrive in the United States—more so than in most European countries. For this reason, and because it is the largest Diaspora community and will likely continue to provide the clearest contrast with Judaism in Israel, I focus on American Jewry and make only brief comparisons with European Jewry.

The unraveling of the once seamless overlap between Judaism and Jewish ethnicity has posed problems of who is to be counted in surveys of the "Jewish" population. Two recent surveys, the 2000–01 National Jewish Population Survey (NJPS) and the 2001 American Jewish Identity Survey (AJIS) came to similar estimates of the designated "core" American Jewish populations: 5.2 million and 5.3 million, respectively. The adults in the core Jewish population, about 4.1 million in both cases, represented the total of three categories: (1) those born Jewish who named Judaism as their religion, (2) those who were not born Jewish and had converted to Judaism or named it as their religion ("Jews by choice"), and (3) those born Jewish who did not identify with any religion.[17] Another survey, the Heritage and Religious Identity (HARI) survey, conducted in 2001–02, arrived at a higher estimate of 6 million American Jews. The authors of the HARI study argued that other surveys had undercounted the number of American Jews primarily because their questions had not allowed acceptable responses from those who had an explicitly nonreligious or ethnic/cultural Jewish identity and those who practiced Judaism together with another religion.[18]

The core population encompasses nonreligious Jews and excludes people with Jewish parentage and/or upbringing who identify exclusively with a religion other than Judaism. When the latter are added to the core population, the surveys differ in the numbers and proportion of "Jews" in the various categories. The proportion of those adults identifying with Judaism, including the small proportion of Jews by choice, was 64 percent of the total in the NJPS, 57 percent in the AJIS, and 43 percent in the HARI survey. The percentages for the born-Jewish but expressing "no religion" or "ethnic/cultural" Jews were 13 percent, 19 percent, and 27 percent, respectively, and for people who were born or brought up Jewish who identified with another religion, mostly Christianity, the respective percentages were 23 percent, 25 percent, and 30 percent. With the inclusion of the noncore population, one-third to possibly more than one-half of the adults who were born Jewish or had a Jewish upbringing did not identify Judaism as their religion.[19] However, more than one-third of those born Jewish who had adopted another religion found reasons to continue to think of themselves as Jews.[20]

Despite the differences among the surveys, they all showed a decline since 1990 in the number of Jews who were born Jewish and named Judaism as their religion. The comparison is with the 1990 NJPS, which calculated a core population of 5.5 million. There was little change in the number of Jews by choice and a growth of the born-Jewish sector that did not identify with Judaism as their religion. The AJIS reported that 27 percent of the core Jewish population did not identify with any religion and that the number of adults who reported a Jewish parentage or upbringing but professed a religion other than Judaism grew from 625,000 in 1990 to 1.4 million in 2001.

The increase in out-marriage is of clear relevance in accounting for the changes in the categories of Jews. The percentage of born Jews who married individuals who had not been born Jewish rose from 11 percent of those who married before 1965 to 31 percent for those marrying between 1965 and 1974, to 51 percent for those marrying between 1975 and 1984, to 56 percent for those marrying between 1985 and 1990, and finally to 58 percent for those marrying between 1995 and 2000. Thus, more than half of recent marriages involving Jews have been marriages to non-Jews. The AJIS found that 77 percent of the Jews by religion were married to a Jewish spouse, whereas only 16 percent of Jews with no religion were married to a Jewish spouse. Both the secular or "no religion" category within the core population and the noncore categories were more likely to be products of out-marriage than those who were born Jewish and identified with Judaism. The AJIS found that 87 percent of the respondents identifying with Judaism had two Jewish parents; the proportions of secular Jews and Christian Jews were 8.4 percent and 3.8 percent, respectively.[21]

The absence of data makes it difficult to evaluate the salience of the "no religion" Jewish ethnic identification. Lynn Davidson conducted a case study of twenty-eight Jews who did not belong to synagogues and created ethnic as opposed to what they considered religious identities. The subjects did not participate in religious rituals, but they emphasized their pride in Jewish history and culture and the accomplishments of the Jewish people. Although they began by defining Judaism as an ethnic or cultural identity, they went on to state that being Jewish was something a person was born into and they expressed uncertainty about converts being "real" Jews. Despite such statements that indicated a belief in the ascriptive nature of Jewish identity, they recognized in their construction of their own identities that ethnic identities are also achieved. Davidson showed that an ethnic Jewish identity may have considerable salience for some "secular" Jews,[22] but a wealth of data show that indicators of Jewish ethnicity (number of Jewish friends, identity with Israel, etc.) are stronger for those Jews who identify with Judaism.

Most of the core American Jewish population continues to mix religious and ethnic components in their identities. When asked in a 1990 survey what it means to be Jewish in America, 70 percent said it was a cultural group, 57 percent said it was an ethnic group, and 49 percent said it was a purely religious group.[23] It would be interesting to probe what American Jews mean by these labels; meanwhile, it is reasonable to assume that the label "cultural group" encompasses both religious and ethnic elements and that those who say that Jews are an ethnic group do not necessarily mean that they are only an ethnic group. That there is a religious element in the identity of most of the American Jews who prefer the labels cultural, national, or ethnic to purely religious can hardly be doubted: Four-fifths identify with one of the Jewish religious denominations, and many of the remainder who term themselves "just Jewish" are no doubt stating the absence of a religious preference within the orbit of Judaism rather than a Jewish identity without a religious element.[24] We can agree with Samuel Heilman that most American Jews do not associate their identity exclusively with religion;[25] but what is interesting is that nearly half stated that Jews in America were a purely religious group. The religious label is in accord with how most non-Jewish Americans identify Jewish Americans.[26]

Although a majority of the intermarried retain their separate religious identities or choose a "no religion" option, a significant minority have adopted the religion of their spouses.[27] Many non-Jews married to Jews have adopted Judaism as their religious identity without conversion. Of the Jews who married in the 1990s, 40 percent married a spouse of Jewish origins, 9 percent married a spouse of non-Jewish origins who converted to Judaism, and 51 percent married a spouse of non-Jewish origins who, at the time of the survey in 2001, had not converted. The conversion of non-Jewish spouses has been experiencing a long-term decline. In the 1950s, when out-marriage was rare, two-fifths became in-marriages through the conversion of the non-Jewish spouse. The proportion hovered at just over one-third from 1965 to 1974, declined to just over one-fourth from 1975 to 1995, and dropped to 15 percent from 1995 to 2001.[28] In households in which one of the marriage partners was a convert, most of the children were being raised as Jews, and in mixed-marriage households about one-fourth of the children were being raised as Jews.[29]

The Reform movement's outreach to the non-Jewish partners of Jews was in part a response to their low level of conversion, and it represented a remarkable break with the nearly 1,600-year Jewish tradition of discouraging conversion to Judaism. The Reform movement also made an important break with Jewish religious law by passing a resolution in 1983 proclaiming that a child born of a non-Jewish mother and a Jewish father would be considered Jewish so long as the child was raised as a Jew.[30] Reform congregations now treat the children of intermarried members as Jewish so long as the parents do so and are not actively involved in another religion.[31] A survey found that, whereas most Orthodox Jews would be upset if their children married someone Jewish only by patrilineal descent, only one-third of Conservative Jews and one-tenth of Reform Jews said that they would be upset.[32]

Although most non-Jews who marry Jews have neither converted nor chosen to identify with Judaism in recent years, the rapid rise in the intermarriage rate has meant that an increasing number of Jews by choice make up an increasing proportion of the Jewish core population and of synagogue members. This is especially the case in the Reform branch, which has the largest membership of the American Jewish denominations.[33] The Reform movement also has a large minority of members who are in mixed marriages. Jews who were raised in Reform Judaism are more likely than those raised in Orthodox and Conservative homes to marry non-Jews, and Jews who were raised in Orthodox and Conservative homes who marry non-Jews often join Reform congregations or begin to describe themselves as Reform. Many Reform rabbis are willing to perform marriages between Jews and non-Jews, and some are willing to perform a marriage together with a Christian clergyman.[34] Steven Cohen reports that, based on data from the 2000–01 NJPS, overall, in the three major denominations, 72 percent of married members were in-married, 12 percent were from marriages with a non-Jewish spouse who had converted to Judaism, and 17 percent were from mixed-marriages. In-married members made up 90 percent of Orthodox members, 79 percent of Conservative members, and 57 percent of Reform members. The conversionary in-married members were 5 percent of Orthodox members, 10 percent of Conservative members, and 17 percent of Reform members. The mixed-marriage members were 5 percent of the Orthodox, 12 percent of the Conservatives, and 26 percent of the Reform.[35]

Data from a number of surveys indicate that Jews by choice and their children identify with a form of Judaism that has little or no ethnic connotation. We have no data that distinguish Jews by choice who convert from those who do not, but it is likely that the ethnic factor is particularly weak among the nonconverts, those who have not formally joined "the Jewish people." At least 30 percent of Jews by choice have not undergone a formal conversion to Judaism, but in most cases this has not prevented them from participating in the religious and other activities of Jewish congregations. Whereas Conservative synagogues have required non-Jewish wives to convert if they or their children wish to participate in the religious life of the congregation, Reform temples have taken a flexible stance. They have encouraged non-Jewish members to participate in religious services and to serve on committees, and in many congregations this acceptance is not accompanied by pressures to convert.[36]

The 1990 and 2001 surveys found that, on most indicators of Jewish religious practice, Jews by choice tended to be either as observant or more observant than those born Jewish. The 1990 NJPS found that 56 percent of Jews by choice belonged to a synagogue compared with 39 percent of the born Jews who identified with a Jewish religious denomination and 5.6 percent of the secular Jews or born Jews who did not identify with any Jewish religious denomination. Jews by choice and born-Jewish religious identifiers differed little in the observance of the two yearly rituals that the vast majority of Jews observe (participating in a Passover seder and lighting Hanukkah candles), but with respect to other practices there were significant differences: 72 percent of the Jews by choice fasted on Yom Kippur compared with 58 percent of born-Jewish religious identifiers and 6 percent of Jews who identified themselves as secular; 40 percent of Jews by choice had separate meat and milk dishes compared with 20 percent of born-Jewish religious identifiers and 8 percent of secular Jews; and 68 percent of Jews by choice lit Sabbath candles compared with 43 percent of born-Jewish religious identifiers and 11 percent of secular Jews. However, only 11 percent of Jews by choice had visited Israel (which may be considered more an ethnic than a religious expression of Jewish identify), compared with 31 percent of born-Jewish religious identifiers and 11 percent of secular Jews.[37]

A survey conducted in 2005 of Jews in the greater Boston area provides comparisons of in-married households and intermarried households in which the children are being raised in the Jewish religion. Almost half of recently formed Jewish households in Boston are intermarried, but the survey found that in 60 percent of the intermarried households the children are being raised in the Jewish religion and that these households have similar levels of religious observance to those of in-married households.[38] Ninety percent of those intermarried households light Hanukkah candles compared with 87 percent of in-married households who identify with Reform Judaism and 95 percent of in-married households who identify with Conservative Judaism. Regular lighting of Sabbath candles was reported by 36 percent of the intermarried, 10 percent of the Reform, and 25 percent of the Conservative. The observance of the dietary laws at a strict level or "to some extent" was reported by 19 percent of the intermarried, 15 percent of the Reform in-married, and 19 percent of the Conservative in-married. A high proportion of the intermarried households ceased their synagogue membership after their children's bar or bat mitzvah, and a small proportion were members of both a congregation and a nonreligious Jewish organization: 19 percent compared with 33 percent of Reform in-married and 35 percent of Conservative in-married. The relative absence of Jewish ethnicity of the intermarried households was also indicated by the finding that only 1 percent of the children of the intermarried households had visited Israel compared with 15 percent of the Reform in-married and 24 percent of the Conservative in-married.

The meanings of Jewish ethnicity, which include tracing ancestry to common putative ancestors and references to a common history, are not easily acquired by Jews by choice, and the question arises as to whether they are acquired by those with a mixed ancestry—the children of intermarriages. Mayer's 1981–83 survey of 117 children of intermarriages found that children of conversionary marriages were more than three times as likely to identify with the Jewish religion than children of mixed marriages.[39] However, although 84 percent of the children of conversionary marriages affirmed that their current religious identity was Jewish, only about one-half identified exclusively with the ethnic ancestry of their Jewish-born parent. Unlike their religious identity, they were prone to see their ethnic identity as an amalgam of two heritages. They were also likely to have a mixed group of Jewish and Christian friends and to reject particularistic notions, such as that Jews have a greater responsibility to help other Jews in need than to help all people equally.[40]

The de-ethnicizing effects of intermarriage on Judaism are not likely to be confined to Jews by choice and their children. The patterns of religious observance of Jews by choice will affect their marriage partners because most religious practices are observed by the family as a unit. The born-Jewish partners and their children are not likely to deny the ethnic components of their identity, but it is likely to be of only moderate salience and without deep commitments to special nonreligious behaviors or social ties. As Jews by choice come to make up an increasing proportion of Reform congregations, the relatively nonethnicized Judaism of their families and offspring is likely to affect the congregations as a whole as well as the movement. The resolution of the Reform and Reconstructionist movements that proclaims that children are Jewish if they are brought up Jewish regardless of which parent has Jewish ancestry is a recognition of a nonethnicized Judaism. According to the movements' decisions on patrilineal descent, the supposition of Jewishness conferred by birth must be authenticated by the individual's commitment to Judaism. Thus the born-Jewish also become Jews by choice.

In moving toward the position of the majority of Americans that religious identity is chosen rather than ascribed by birth, the Reform movement has also encouraged a personalistic approach to religion that permits each Jew and congregation to choose their own selections from the tradition and religious services.[41] The American Reform movement of the nineteenth and early twentieth century demonstrated its acculturation by rejecting many traditional practices that appeared inconsistent with the values of the Enlightenment and modern culture. Reform Jews today are no longer under pressures from non-Jews to reconcile Judaism with modernity, and there is no longer a self-conscious rejection of Jewish tradition. Since the mid-1960s the Reform movement has made both changes that represent radical breaks with the tradition (such as the ordination of women and patrilineal descent) and changes that draw on the tradition (such as the donning of yarmulkes and prayer shawls, Hebrew usage, and the affirmation of the importance of the mitzvot and religious study). In place of the former modernist ideology of religious changes signifying progress and a break with tradition, the emphasis now is on congregations' and individuals' ability to choose those religious expressions according to their preferences and tastes. Many Reform temples have compiled their own liturgies, and in 1975 the New Union prayer book provided a number of optional services from which congregations and individuals could choose.[42] Jews by choice, many of whom display higher levels of religious observance than born Jews, may well be attracted to a tradition that is not presented as an obligatory system of religious laws but as a rich source of religious behaviors from which members make selections according to what they find personally meaningful.

The selection of religious expressions by individuals and families can extend beyond the boundaries of a single religious tradition, and this is especially likely to be the case in intermarried households. In her study of a relatively small, nonrepresentative sample, Sylvia Barak Fishman found that almost all mixed-marriage households celebrated Hanukkah and Christmas, Easter and Passover. Whereas the 2000–01 NJPS found that only 6 percent of American Jews reported having a Christmas tree in their homes, Fishman found that 60 percent of mixed-marriage families that identified as Jewish by religion had a Christmas tree. Many of the mixed-marriage couples who said that they were raising their children as Jews described their incorporation of Christian activities as "cultural" or "not religious." Blending was less frequent in those households where the non-Jewish spouse had converted to Judaism.[43] Syncretism, however, extends beyond the intermarried, and the initiative sometimes comes from non-Jews. Christian churches have initiated interfaith Passover seders and have invited Jews in their neighborhoods to teach them the holiday recipes and songs. Interfaith synagogues, combining Judaism and Christianity, have appeared. The erosion of religious boundaries between Judaism and Christianity is evident in kabbalah institutes, and there is also a movement that combines Jewish religious traditions with Eastern religions and self-actualization themes.[44]

Ethnic Versus Religious Identity Among Jews in Europe

Jews by choice, nonethnicized Judaism, and movements combining Judaism with other religions are far less evident in Europe despite intermarriage rates that are close to those in the United States. A survey of British Jews carried out in 1995 found that, of those who were married or in a stable relationship, about 30 percent were living with a non-Jewish partner. The out-marriage rate for men was higher than the rate for women, and for Jewish men younger than 40 years the rate was 44 percent. A survey of French Jews from 2002 found that the out-marriage rate was 30 percent for those who married between 1985 and 1989 and 40 percent for those who married between 1990 and 2001. Of those adult French Jews living in a nonmarried cohabitating union, 83 percent had non-Jewish partners. The out-marriage rate for Jews in Russia rose from 66 percent of those who married between 1985 and 1989 to 78 percent of those who married between 1990 and 2001.[45]

The changes within Judaism in the United States were made possible by the general features of religion in that society; the operation of religious movements within an open market, the constitutive pluralism and structural flexibility of institutional religion, and the individualistic tendencies in American religion are as evident in American Judaism as they are in American Christianity.[46] Judaism in Europe is far less pluralistic and flexible; Orthodox synagogues are the dominant type in most European societies, with a much smaller contingent of Conservative and Reform synagogues than in the United States.

Jewish identity varies greatly among the various European communities, but apart from the small ultra-Orthodox communities, which continue the relatively un-self-conscious fusion of religion and peoplehood, Jewish identity in Europe appears to be expressed in secular ethnic rather than religious forms. The survey of British Jews in 1995 found that, although more than 60 percent were members of a synagogue, 44 percent chose options of Jewish identity with no religious connotations: 26 percent chose "secular" and 18 percent chose "just Jewish." Of the religious identity options, 31 percent chose Traditional, associated in Britain with mainstream Orthodoxy; 15 percent chose Progressive, associated in Britain with Reform and Liberal Judaism; and 9 percent chose strictly Orthodox. On all measures of identity and participation in the Jewish community, the Traditional and strictly Orthodox had far higher scores than the secular, but it was found that levels of ritual observance were far more closely related to strength of ethnic identity than to strength of religious belief. Affiliation with a mainstream Orthodox synagogue in Britain is not a strong indicator of orthoprax religious observance or a belief in even the most basic doctrines of Judaism, and many of those unaffiliated with a synagogue are actively involved in Jewish life in other ways. These data indicate that most British Jews, whether they are affiliated with a synagogue or not, tend to identify on an ethnic level.[47]

Religious identities are stronger among French Jews because the population of approximately half a million, the largest Jewish community in Western Europe, includes a large proportion of Sephardim (about 70 percent) who migrated from North Africa (half of French Jews were born outside France) or were born to parents from North Africa. A survey in 2002 found that 65 percent of in-married French Jews described themselves as Traditional, 7 percent as Orthodox, 11 percent as religiously liberal; only 18 percent described themselves as nonpracticing. In contrast, 24 percent of the out-married described themselves as Traditional and 54 percent as nonpracticing.[48]

In strong contrast to French Jews are the Jews in Russia and Ukraine, most of whom conceive of their Jewishness as a matter of descent with little, if any, connection to religion. The Soviet regime's imposition of a Jewish nationality, as indicated in internal passports or identity cards, its anti-Jewish policies, and its destruction of Jewish organizations and culture left Russian and Ukrainian Jews with a Jewish identity that was largely divorced from specifically Jewish cultural content. For many Russian Jews of the 1970s and 1980s, Jewishness took on the meanings of cosmopolitan intellectualism and a strong achievement drive to overcome the barriers of occupational mobility.[49] Today, the Russian and Ukrainian governments no longer impose an official national identity, they do not pursue anti-Semitic policies, and Jewish cultural activities are no longer restricted. Jews have taken advantage of this unprecedented freedom within the Russian context and have established a wide variety of Jewish institutions, including community centers, clubs, schools, and kindergartens. Although religious institutions and congregations have been provided by Chabad and the Movement for Progressive Judaism,[50] few Russian Jews have incorporated religious elements into their Jewish identities. A survey conducted in 1993 in the towns of Moscow, Kiev, and Minsk found that 57 percent of the 1,000 Jews interviewed said that Jewish culture had been nonexistent in their families of origin and only 15 percent said that they were raising their children in the spirit of the Jewish tradition; 65 percent had never attended synagogue, and only 1 percent went regularly or often to synagogue.[51]

Surveys of Jews conducted in Russian and Ukrainian cities in 1992–93 and 1997–98 found that few made a strong connection between being Jewish and the Jewish religion. Almost none believed that religious observance was an integral part of being Jewish, and only 26 percent of the Russian Jews and 30 percent of the Ukrainian Jews participated in a Passover seder in 1997. For many, Judaism no longer provided even a boundary of their Jewish identity. They stated that Christianity does not preclude the acceptance of a person as Jewish and that descent, either matrilineal or patrilineal, together with a feeling of oneself as a Jew were sufficient bases for Jewishness.[52]

The trend among European Jews toward secular ethnic rather than religious forms has been reinforced by the transformation of many Western and Central European societies from relatively homogeneous national societies—in which the Jews were often the most prominent religious or ethnic minority—to multiethnic and multireligious societies. In this context of ethnic pluralism and weak religious institutions and identity among the majority, few non-Jews who marry Jews convert and most of the children of mixed marriages are not raised within the Jewish religion. A de-ethnicized religious Jewish identity is not a likely development, and ethnic Jewish identities are also likely to decline in salience.

Ethnic Versus Religious Identity Among Jews in Israel

In Israel, intermarriage with non-Jews, which is largely confined to Russian immigrant couples, is not a factor in the transformation of identity among Israeli Jews, and the de-ethnicized Jewish religious identity that is emerging in the United States has no basis in Israel. A dereligionized ethnonational Jewish identity may be an appropriate designation for that part of the Israeli Jewish population who say that they are "totally unobservant" of the religious tradition (21 percent in a survey carried out in 1999) and also for some of those who say they observe the tradition "somewhat" (43 percent), as opposed to those who say that they observe the tradition to "a great extent" (20 percent) or strictly, in all its particulars (16 percent).[53] It is true that ideological expressions of secular identity have lost their intensity and appeal and that, especially after the 1967 war, there was an interpenetration of Jewish and Israeli identities, but these developments should not be taken to signify a strengthening of a Jewish religious identity among most Israeli Jews. The greater readiness among Israeli Jews to proclaim a Jewish identity probably reflects changes in the Israeli civil religion, with its more extensive nationalization of traditional religious symbols after 1967. Few Israelis have increased their religious observances, and most continue, as before, to participate in highly secularized forms of popular observances, especially the Passover seder and the lighting of Hanukkah candles.[54]

The 1991 and 1999 surveys of Israeli Jews found that the average levels of religious observance among them are relatively high and that most, including those who define themselves as nonobservant, carry out certain practices from the religious tradition. However, from the replies to questions on the reasons for their practices, it is evident that the nonobservant and many of the "somewhat observant" Jews see themselves as observing national or family customs and ceremonies rather than religious commandments.[55] When asked in 1991 to what extent various factors influenced their feelings of being part of the Jewish people, the four highest ratings were given to the establishment of Israel, living in Israel, upbringing in parents' home, and the history of Jewish settlement in modern Israel. These were followed by participating in the Passover seder and celebrating Hanukkah, holidays whose traditional religious meanings have been superseded among many Israelis by their national historical meanings and as family gatherings. The "Jewish religion" received a lower rating, toward the bottom of the list. There were no significant differences between the religiously observant and the mildly or nonobservant with respect to their beliefs that the establishment of Israel influenced their feelings that they were part of the Jewish people, but only 8 percent of the nonobservant and 33 percent of the mildly observant said that the Jewish religion influenced a lot their feelings of being part of the Jewish people compared with 72 percent of the greatly observant and 79 percent of the strictly observant.[56]

Israeli Jews have not been untouched by the trends of religious self-determination and self-selection of postmodern societies, but in the Israeli context religious preference or the religion of your choice has little meaning in the sense of choosing among religious traditions or denominations. Many Israelis have, however, chosen to be clients of religious or quasi-religious cults and human potential organizations, such as Transcendental Meditation, I Am, and Landmark Education.[57] These are client cults that provide various forms of therapy and teachings that are believed to allow the clientele to come to a deeper understanding of themselves and the world, maximize their potentials, improve their social relationships, and advance their careers. Client cults do not require formal membership or organization among the clientele, and participation, which for most is limited and temporary, is not seen to pose any problems for the participants' Jewish identity. Cult movements, which require far greater commitment and regular participation, are seen to pose a danger to Jewish Israeli identity, and a movement such as the Emin has a hard time trying to persuade other Israelis that there is no contradiction between Emin beliefs and Israeli identity. Such movements attract few Israelis, and those concerned with self-realization and self-expression are more likely to do their spiritual seeking among the ephemeral cultural forms of client cults. These can be constituted as their privatized religion, albeit of a fragmentary kind, whereas Judaism remains important for them in providing public expressions of their national identity.

Conclusion

To conclude, the disappearance of the ideological differentiations between religious and ethnic or national Jewish identities in both the Diaspora and Israel has not meant a convergence of those identities. In the Diaspora the boundaries of the Jews as a discrete ethnic group are breaking down, and in the United States signs of a nonethnicized religious Jewish identity are emerging. In Israel public expressions of the religious components of Jewish identity are strong, but a large part of the population has a weak religious Jewish identity at the private level; Jewish identity as a national identity tends to become encompassed by the Israeli national identity. It would appear that the two major centers of the Jewish population, the United States and Israel, will pull farther apart with respect to the differentiations between religion and ethnicity or nation in their Jewish identities.

9. JEWISH AND OTHER NATIONAL AND ETHNIC IDENTITIES OF ISRAELI JEWS

Jewish identity in Israel, like Jewish identity elsewhere, is an ethnic identity. It is an identity with a people that meets the criteria of most recent definitions of an ethnic group. These criteria are distinctive cultural and symbolic characteristics (in the Jewish case the major element is religion) and a sense of kinship and community, the "we" feeling that relates to a belief in a common ancestry and group history. This ethnic identity is a national identity in the sense that the relationship of the group to a particular territory, a homeland, is also emphasized.

Jewish identity in Israel is differentiated from but interpenetrates and overlaps with other national and ethnic identities. In this chapter I look at the interrelations between Jewish identity and Israeli identity, identities based on countries of origin, and identities based on a broad distinction between Jews from the European Diaspora and Jews from the North African and Asian Diaspora.

Among Israeli Jews the Israeli identity has both a civic component and an ethnic-national component. The civic component relates to the legal definition, rights, and obligations of all citizens, Jews and non-Jews, of the Israeli state, a legal-geographic unit. However, when Israeli Jews emphasize their Israeli identity, the ethnic-national component is normally the most prominent in their consciousness. When they think of the term *Israeli*, more than half of Israeli Jews do not include Arabs,[1] and the fundamental distinction made between Jews and Arabs at the level of national identity is reflected in the use of different terms when referring to the plurality of non-Jewish and Jewish ethnic groups in Israeli society. The term *miutim* (minorities) is used with respect to non-Jewish groups, whereas the term *edot* (plural of *edah*) is used to denote Jewish populations from particular counties of origin or regions within countries. However, *edah* is used more commonly by Israelis to refer to Jewish groups from North Africa and Asia (Moroccan *edah*, Yemenite *edah*, etc.), who are often referred to collectively as *edot ha'Mizrach* (communities of the East), *Mizrachim* (Easterners), or Sephardim. Less commonly, the term *edah* is applied to Israelis from Europe and America (Poles, "Anglo-Saxons," etc.), who are collectively known as *edot Ashkenaz* or Ashkenazim.

Identities with particular *edot*, *edot ha'Mizrach*, or Ashkenazim are identities with Jewish populations from particular geographic-cultural backgrounds and are not identities with the countries or continents of origin, their non-Jewish populations, and their cultures. Some Israeli Jews do identity with their countries of origin or have at least a positive orientation toward certain cultural components of those countries, and some hardly differentiate between identity with the country of origin and identity with the Jewish group from that country. But where a differentiation is made, several patterns of identity are possible. Where high levels of segregation and tension existed between a comparatively cohesive and culturally distinctive Jewish community and the non-Jewish population in the country of origin, a negative orientation toward the country of origin may coexist with a strong identity with the Jewish group of origin. Where there was little segregation of Jews, cultural distinctiveness, or community organization or where Jews were relatively assimilated, an Israeli Jewish identity may coexist with a positive orientation toward the country and culture of origin and little special identity with the Jews from that country. Identity with Jews from a particular country of origin may relate to their common participation in that country's wider culture rather than to any distinctiveness they might have had as Jews.

Whereas identities of Israeli Jews with their countries of origin may be similar to ethnic identities in other societies of immigrants, the *edah* ethnic identity is of a special kind. It is of a type particular to a "returning Diaspora," of a people who, before their immigration, felt bound to and part of the nation linked to the country or state in which they wished to settle. The special nature of *edah* identity has made some sociologists question the translation of the term *edah* into English as "ethnic group." Ernest Krausz, for example, admits that *edot* are characterized by primordial attributes, particular sociocultural features, and a consciousness of constituting a group different from others in the same setting, but he argues that, with respect to all three attributes, what unites Israeli Jews is stronger and more important than what divides them. He notes that Israeli Jews share a common religion, trace their origins to a common source, and, in addition to the ancient history of their common ancestors, share parallel historical experiences of dispersion and persecution. These commonalities represent the deepest level of primordialism on which are superimposed differences in communal histories, languages, and culture that were brought from the more immediate countries of origin.[2]

Krausz implies that the common Jewish ethnic identity of Israeli Jews rules out the possibility of ethnic identities based on communities of origin. My position is that people may have more than one identity based on common descent. National and ethnic identities contain cultural definitions of kinship, and they can vary, like biological kin, in terms of closeness and distance as well as their relative importance with regard to loyalty, pride, social activities, and cultural orientations. National-ethnic identity, encompassing the entire extended family, may readily coexist with ethnic or subethnic identities that encompass branches of that family.

Within the more encompassing Jewish identity, Israeli Jews may feel a close kinship to members of their own *edah*. As Israelis they may feel closer ties to other Israelis than to Jews in the Diaspora, including those Jews who remain in their country of origin. Indeed, many Israeli Jews report that their Israeli identity, in its ethnic-national sense, is more important to them than their Jewish identity. The extent to which Israelis distinguish their Israeliness from their Jewishness and from the relative importance of one or the other is not always clear, and certain expressions such as *am Yisrael* (the people of Israel) are often understood to encompass all Jews. The emphasis placed on these interpenetrating and overlapping identities (Jewish, Israeli, *edah*, and *edot ha'Mizrach* or Ashkenazim) will vary from context to context, but certain generalizations can be made about their relative importance among different sectors of the Jewish Israeli population.

Few studies of ethnic and national identities among Israeli Jews have investigated the relationships between the identities that I have distinguished. Most have focused on either the relationship between Jewish and Israeli identities or the relationship between Israeli and *edah* identities. The studies of Simon Herman are an example of the Jewish-Israeli identity relationship. Herman reported on the identities of high school students (16–17 years old) in surveys carried out in 1964 and 1974 and of an adult sample (over age 20) in 1985. Most Israeli Jews were found to have positive feelings toward both the Jewish and the Israeli identities. Herman wrote that the exceptions, small in number, were the "Canaanites," who rejected a Jewish identity in favor of a new Israeli or "Hebrew" identity, and the ultra-Orthodox, anti-Zionist Neturei Karta, who rejected any Israeli identity. He found that most Israeli Jews say that, when they feel more Jewish, they also feel more Israeli. Few Israeli Jews feel that their Jewish and Israeli identities are incompatible, but a significant minority (over one-fifth) reported that there was no relationship between their feelings of being Jewish and their feelings of being Israeli.

The Israeli Jews who compartmentalized their Jewish and Israeli identities displayed somewhat weaker orientations to both identities and were found more frequently among those who defined themselves as nonreligious rather than as traditional or religious. In fact, the crucial variable in Jewish identity was religious observance as operationalized by self-definition as religious, traditional, or nonreligious. Israeli Jews from North Africa and Asia had a stronger Jewish identity than those from Europe because they included greater proportions of the religious and traditional respondents. However, when respondents were faced with a question in which they had to favor one identity over the other, a greater proportion of religious and traditional students originating from North Africa favored the Jewish side in comparison with religious and traditional students originating from Europe.[3]

Yasir Auron also found that religiosity was the crucial factor in accounting for the relative emphases on Jewish and Israeli identities in a survey, carried out in 1990, of students in teacher-training colleges. Sixty-six percent of those who identified themselves as nonreligious put their Israeli identity before their Jewish identity compared with 19 percent of those who identified themselves as traditional and less than 1 percent of those who identified themselves as religious. Auron found that the Israeliness of this sample of young Israelis (most were between the ages of 21 and 26) was expressed *principally* in relation to the Israeli state and to the Land of Israel, whereas Jewishness was expressed *principally* in relation to the religion of Judaism and to the people of Israel. The majority of the *haredim*, or ultra-Orthodox, did not accept an Israeli identity and had negative feelings toward the Israeli state, but the "nationalist religious" and the traditionalists expressed strong positive feelings for the Israeli state and for the Jewish religion and people. The nonreligious expressed either lack of interest or negative orientations toward religion and only weak feelings in their belongingness to the Jewish people. The meaning that they attributed to the *people of Israel* appeared to be restricted to those Jews who lived within the boundaries of the state of Israel, whereas among the traditionalists and the religious the term referred to the worldwide Jewish people.

Like Herman, Auron did not find that differences in origin (North Africa and Asia or Europe and the United States) had an effect on identity beyond the differences in religiosity between the two categories. Jewish identity tended to be stronger among North Africans and Asians because this category included the majority of traditionalists. An intergenerational decline in religiosity, which was especially evident in the North African/Asian category, suggests a decline in the importance of Jewish identity, but this might be balanced out by a trend among the nonreligious to put a greater emphasis on their Jewish identity.[4] The significance, if any, of this trend is difficult to interpret. The pattern among secular Israelis up to the Six Day War of denying a Jewish identity in favor of an Israeli or "Hebrew" identity has almost disappeared, but Auron suggests that Jewishness may have only appeared to have strengthened because of a weakening of Israeliness. Although the Holocaust has become a central element in the Jewish consciousness of all Israelis, among the nonreligious this does not appear to have changed attitudes toward Diaspora Jews or Jewish Diaspora history. Most of the nonreligious expressed their differences from Diaspora Jews when they argued that, although religion should not play an important part in the public and private lives of Israelis, it should play an important part in the lives of Diaspora Jews.[5]

The disappearance of the self-proclaimed non-Jewish Jewish Israeli should not be taken to signify a revival of Jewish consciousness. The greater readiness to proclaim a Jewish identity may reflect changes in the Israeli civil religion with its more extensive nationalization of traditional religious symbols. This does not mean either deeper understandings of what it means to be a Jew in Israel or growth in the existential meaning and value of Israel as a Jewish state.[6]

Studies of the relationships between Jewish and Israeli identities have tended to be quite separate from studies of identities based on country or continent of origin. The origin-based studies have focused on either an *edah* identity or an identity with the broad categories of *edot ha'Mizrach* or Ashkenazim. In general, those who have focused on the *edah* identity have been anthropologists who approached the subject from a perspective that emphasizes the cultural, primordial, expressive, nonrational components of ethnicity.[7] Those who have focused on the *edot ha'Mizrach* identity have been sociologists who have emphasized the socioeconomic, political, instrumental, rational components of ethnicity. Neither of these approaches has paid much attention to the ethnic identities of Israelis of European origin. The cultural-anthropological perspective finds little interest in them because they do not emphasize distinctive cultural heritages of their communities of origin. From the socioeconomic perspective, Shlomo Swirski argues that the need to analyze Ashkenazic consciousness is less than that for the *edot ha'Mizrach* consciousness; the Ashkenazic consciousness is expressed openly in the mass media, in literature, in the educational system, and by official propaganda. Swirski argues that, although there are clear signs of mutual recognition among Ashkenazim, they do not express their commonality in particularistic terms but by such terms as the *state* or *society*.[8]

A prominent example of the cultural-anthropological approach is to be found in the work of Shlomo Deshen, who presents persistence and change of religious and cultural practices as outcomes of a conflict between an identity with the *edah* and an identity as an Israeli. The tension and accommodation of the *edah* and Israeli identities was the focus of a study of ritual changes in a synagogue of Jews from Tunisia. Deshen wrote that the Tunisian immigrants were bound by the cohesive factors of common culture and origin but that they also wished to acknowledge the new bonds of Israeli nationhood. Israel has seen some change from a melting pot to a more pluralist ideology, "yet ethnic loyalties and adherence to ethnic practices remain uneasy bedfellows with Israeli nationalism, patriotism, and citizenship."[9] Deshen showed how changes or adjustments in the prayers and symbols of the synagogue represented an infusion of new content that related the immigrants' evolving Israeli identities to traditional themes. For example, a memorial prayer that was traditionally confined to deceased rabbis was said for two nonlearned men who had died when they tried to save a girl from drowning. The original reference of this symbol of commemoration was the traditional criteria of scholarship and piety, but it was bestowed on men who were evaluated according to new criteria of universal human virtues. Over some issues, particularly those that encroach on focal aspects of cultural heritage, a separatist stance was taken; but in most cases compromises were made that allowed for the continuation of a separate *edah* identity within the broader compass of the national Israeli identity.[10]

When the Tunisian Jews lived in Tunisia, they identified themselves principally as Jews and conceived of their religious culture as *the* Jewish religion (rather than as one particular local version of it). Their identity as an *edah*, as Tunisian Jews, developed in Israel, and their concern in preserving their heritage took on the meaning of the preservation of a specific Tunisian Jewish heritage. This newly formed identity could not be divorced from or seen to be in conflict with their continuing identity as Jews. Deshen's analysis implies, therefore, that tension between *edah* and Israeli identities is a tension between Jewish and Israeli identities and that, in contrast to the works of Herman and Auron, religious Jews rather than secular Jews experience tension between Jewish and Israeli identities.

An exception to the focus of Israeli anthropologists on the ethnicity of Jews from North Africa and Asia is Rina Neeman's study of an ethnic association founded in 1980 by veteran immigrants from Romania. Unlike the Tunisian Jews, whose identity as Jews and as an *edah* were anchored in their religious heritage, the members of the Romanian association, who were all age 55 or older, defined themselves as irreligious and were reluctant to use ethnic terminology to identify themselves and their association. They referred to Romanian Israelis not as an *edah* but as an *aliyah*, an immigration or literally "ascent," a term with clear positive connotations in Israel. The members' orientation toward their country of origin or the Romanian people as a whole was ambivalent; references to Romania as motherland and nostalgia for the scenery and culture of their youth existed alongside feelings of antagonism and hostility toward a people whom they saw as their oppressors and persecutors. The feelings of ambivalence that association members also expressed toward Romanian Jewry, both in the past and in contemporary Israel, were related perhaps to their perceptions that Romanian Jewry lacked solidarity and that Romanian Jews were ignored and discriminated against in Israeli society, especially compared with other Ashkenazic populations.

Neeman interprets the activities of the association as the means by which members are able to transform their identity as Romanian Jews from one with negative associations to one they can be proud of. The concerns of the association to promote the cultural distinctiveness, sociocultural integration, and status of Romanian Jewry are seen as ways of bridging their identities as Romanian Jews and as Israelis. Members are deeply committed to the state of Israel, but their problems with the Hebrew language and with Israeli patterns of behavior, including those of their children, are seen by them as indications of their lack of integration into the society. Within the association they are able to feel belonging and solidarity, restructure their personal biographies around ethnic themes, and integrate their Romanian ethnicity into both the Jewish and Israeli identities.[11]

The relationships between *edah* identities and the broader Jewish and Israeli identities have tended to be ignored by those sociologists who are inclined toward socioeconomic interpretations of ethnicity in Israel. Shlomo Swirski has presented the most explicit socioeconomic interpretation of *edot ha'Mizrach* as the basis of an emergent ethnic identification in Israel. He argued that the common experiences of Jews from North Africa and Asia created a new ethnoclass and identity. Their subordinate position within the ethnic division of labor, their subjection to discrimination, and the "colonialist" orientation of the Ashkenazim have erased the differences among the *edot* from North Africa and Asia and created a common consciousness.[12] In this analysis Swirski simply takes the wider Jewish and Israeli identities for granted; they do not appear to impinge on the *edah* identity or the *edot ha'Mizrach* identity.

The relationship between Jewish identity and *edah* identity is a central part of

Eliezer Ben-Rafael's analysis of ethnicity in Israel. In his *Emergence of Ethnicity: Cultural Groups and Social Conflict in Israel* (1982), he treated ethnicity primarily as a cultural phenomenon and argued that the form it has taken in Israel was the consequence of an encounter between the cultures of Jews originating from Europe and those from North Africa and Asia. Ben-Rafael wrote that an *edah* identity did not develop among the dominant category of Jews from Europe. Their cultural orientations were largely formed by Zionists who emigrated from Eastern Europe to Israel before the establishment of the state. They had already undergone a process of secularization before their migration, and they understood their migration as "a denial of history," as a break from the religiocultural and social features of the Jewish communities of the Diaspora. They were committed to a secular notion of nationhood that was justified in terms of the universal right of all nations to autonomy and emancipation. Religion, their Judaism and Jewishness, was but a reflection of the national principle. Ben-Rafael did not explicitly discuss the relationship between the Jewish and Israeli identities, but his arguments imply that for the Ashkenazim the Israeli identity is the most encompassing one.

Most immigrants from North Africa and Asia underwent comparatively little secularization, and they conceived of their immigration as a fulfillment of messianic prophecies or as a means of expressing and continuing their sacred culture. They did not distinguish Judaism from their "parochial" cultural legacy, and therefore they were not ready to abandon those cultural attributes that they had adhered to in the Diaspora. Their contact with secularized Jews in Israel came as a shock to many, and their consciousness of the need to defend their primordial attributes led many to strengthen their traditional ways during their first years in the new society. This meeting led to the emergence of the *edot* as distinct sociocultural entities and distinct identities (Moroccan, Yemenite, etc.), even though these identities continued to be bound to the broader identity of Jew. Although not explicitly stated, this implied that for Jews from North Africa and Asia, the Jewish identity would continue to be more encompassing than the Israeli identity.

Ben-Rafael denied that the term *edot ha'Mizrach* referred to an ethnic group or identity. It is, like the term *Ashkenazim*, a term referring to a sociocultural category and emerged to signify the de facto pluralism between the two Jewish sociocultural categories. The term does not denote a major focus of ethnic self-identity because, unlike the *edah* identity, it does not have an ascriptive basis or have much meaning within the wider framework of Jewish identity.

The absence of an awareness of kind based on country or community of origin among European immigrants was congruent with the ideology of *mizug ha'galuyot* (fusion of the exiles). In its traditional formulation, the gathering and amalgamation of Jews from different parts of the world referred to the future messianic kingdom, but this idea was secularized as part of the modern Zionist ideology. This fusion was to be implemented by the unconditional acceptance of all Jewish immigrants as full citizens of Israel. Among North African and Asian immigrants, the absence of differentiation between Jewishness and the cultural legacy of the community of origin meant not only that they were concerned with maintaining their particular religiocultural expressions but also that they conceived of themselves as part of a larger whole in which they would amalgamate. In comparison with European immigrants, Middle Easterners experienced a tension between the belief in the fusion of the exiles and their emergent ethnic identities.

Ben-Rafael drew on his samples of middle-class Moroccan and Yemenite Jews in Israel to demonstrate that the fusion ideology, when combined with the openness of the dominant European category, encouraged mobile Jews with North African and Asian origins to assimilate and undergo a process of "de-ethnization." At the same time, the openness of the European category contributed to the continuation of cultural distinctiveness in the "ethnoclasses" of the lower strata of Jews from North Africa and Asia. Because the upwardly mobile from the *edot* assimilated into the predominantly European middle class, they distanced themselves from their origins and exerted little cultural influence on the majority of their edot, who remained in the lower strata. Thus ethnicity is likely to remain an important feature of the "truncated ethnoclasses" in Israel.[13]

The restriction of Ben-Rafael's sample to middle-class Jews from Morocco and Yemen meant that he was not able to substantiate that the *edah* identity among Israelis from North Africa and Asia was far more important, especially among the lower strata from those origins, than the *edah* identity among Jews from Europe. Nor was he able to show that an identity based on the label *edot ha'Mizrach* had not emerged among at least the lower strata of Israelis from North Africa and Asia.

In the book that I coauthored with Ben-Rafael and in the articles that we wrote together with Hanna Ayalon, we analyzed a large and more comprehensive sample of middle-aged males, most of whom had migrated to Israel in their childhood or youth, from four countries of origin: Morocco, Iraq, Poland, and Romania. The sample was stratified so that in each group of origin half of the respondents were in blue-collar work and half were in white-collar work. Among the hypotheses we tested were those suggested in Ben-Rafael's previous book: that an *edah* identity is more important among North Africans and Asians than among Europeans; that this identity is convergent with the broader Jewish and Israeli identities; and that this identity is more important among the lower strata of North Africans and Asians.

However, we revised Ben-Rafael's former expectations with respect to an identity of *edot ha'Mizrach*. We recognized that the term *edot ha'Mizrach* was not related to a cultural entity that existed before immigration and that the communities in North Africa and Asia varied greatly with respect to their Judeo-Arabic dialects, religious customs, and other cultural features. However, in their confrontation with Israelis from Europe, many North African and Asian Israelis felt that, despite their differences, they were closer culturally to other *edot ha'Mizrach* than to Ashkenazim. The label *edot ha'Mizrach* may have originated as a stereotypical device used by Israelis from Europe, but North Africans and Asians appear to have rejected its negative connotations and adopted it as a source of identity. Insofar as it was based on a feeling of cultural similarities, we did not expect it to be an alternative to the *edah* identity (as Swirski suggested) but rather to accompany and possibly reinforce it.

We did not expect the Ashkenazim identity to have as much meaning for the European Israelis as the *edot ha'Mizrach* identity had for North African and Asian Israelis. However, the integration of the European groups in Israel and their perceptions of differences, both cultural and socioeconomic, between themselves and North Africans and Asians may have made the Ashkenazim identity more significant than the more specific *edah* identity.

To tap ethnic identities, we asked respondents to rank four identities in order of their importance for them: (1) community of origin (*edah*), (2) Ashkenazim or *edot ha'Mizrach*, (3) Jewish, and (4) Israeli. The great majority of respondents placed the Jewish and Israeli identities in first or second place. The Moroccan and Iraqi respondents were split evenly in placing Israeli or Jewish identity in first or second place. In contrast, two-thirds of the Poles and Romanians placed the Israeli identity before the Jewish. Regarding the *edah* and Ashkenazim or *edot ha'Mizrach* identities, more than twice as many Poles and Romanians (greater than 40 percent in these groups) as Moroccans and Iraqis refused to accept these identities. Of those who did rank the labels, most placed the *edah* identity in fourth place. Moroccan and Iraqi respondents were split in about equal proportions in placing the *edah* or *edot ha'Mizrach* identity in third place.

A second set of questions on ethnic identity asked respondents to indicate their level of pride, if any, in the four identities. On all four identities, the Moroccans and Iraqis indicated greater pride than the Poles and Romanians, and only on the Israeli identity was there little difference. Consistent with the data on the hierarchy of identities, Moroccans and Iraqis did not indicate a clear preference for the Israeli or Jewish identities, and Poles and Romanians tended to express greater pride in the Israeli identity. Differences were especially prominent with respect to the orientations toward the *edah* and Ashkenazim or *edot ha'Mizrach* identities: Many more Moroccans and Iraqis expressed pride in these identities than did Poles and Romanians.

Levels of pride in Jewish and Israeli identities were highly correlated for all four groups. There was also a high correlation for all groups, but especially for the Moroccan and Iraqis, between the *edah* and Ashkenazim or *edot ha'Mizrach* identities. However, only the Moroccans and Iraqis demonstrated high correlations between their Israeli-Jewish identities and their *edah* and *edot ha'Mizrach* identities. Among Poles and Romanians these relationships were weak or nonexistent. We found, as expected, that both the *edah* identity and the *edot ha'Mizrach* identity were more important among the lower stratum of Moroccans and Iraqis than among the higher stratum. However, class differences within the Moroccan and Iraqi groups with respect to ethnic identity were of a lower magnitude than the differences between the Moroccans and Iraqis and the Poles and Rumanians.

In analyzing the prominent division in the level of ethnic identity between North African and Asian Israelis and European Israelis, we pointed to an avenue of investigation that has been neglected not only in Israel but also in the general literature on ethnic identity: the relationship between ethnic identities and the wider identities of nationality and citizenship. The finding that Israelis from Europe were disposed to place their Israeli identity before their Jewish identity and to reject or place only minor importance on the identity associated with the Jewish community of origin may indicate the continuing influence of the cultural orientations of the early Zionist "pioneers" who viewed their Zionism and the Israeli state as rebellions against the Jewish tradition and the way of life of the Diaspora. Such negative orientations toward Diaspora Jewishness were less important among later Ashkenazic immigrants, and they have lost the prominence they once had, but there has been no ethnic revival of the Ashkenazic *edot*, and it is clear that associations of elderly immigrants, such as the one studied by Rina Neeman, will not continue into the second generation. Among North African and Asian Israelis, Israeliness is a source of great pride, but it has not overtaken Jewishness as the most encompassing identity; and the wider identities have not become differentiated from the subethnic identities of the communities of origin.[14] This fusion of the broader and specific identities among *edot ha'Mizrach* is demonstrated by the revival of ethnic festivals (the largest and best known is the *mimuna* of the Moroccans), which are multigenerational and celebrate both the specific customs and the Jewishness-Israeliness of the *edot*.

This research bears implications for the evolving identities among immigrants from the former Soviet Union. Three categories of immigrants from the former Soviet Union should be distinguished: (1) those from the Baltic countries and other areas that were annexed by the Soviet Union in the west; (2) those from Georgia and the Islamic republics; and (3) those from the Russian heartland, a large proportion of whom lived in Moscow and St. Petersburg (Leningrad).

The Baltic Jews had been subjected to a process of secularization that started later and was less intensive than the process in the Russian heartland. Although distinctive Jewish cultural forms became highly attenuated, many retained a contact with Judaism and a positive Jewish identity.[15] Their emergent pattern of ethnic identities in Israel should resemble what we found among Polish and Romanian immigrants. The Israeli identity will become the somewhat more prominent identity of the interrelated Israeli and Jewish identities, and their identities as *edot* or as Ashkenazim will not be as strong. In contrast, the pattern of ethnic identities among Israeli Jews from Georgia and the Islamic republics appears to resemble that of *edot ha'Mizrach*. They had been less exposed than the Jews in the European parts of the USSR to anti-Semitism and to the regime's suppression of Jewish culture, and they had succeeded in retaining a number of Jewish traditions, such as the celebration of Jewish religious holidays. The greater opportunities for religious practice in Israel have allowed a significant minority to increase the number of their religious observances. Few admit to becoming less religious in Israel, but it is probable that the second generation will follow the *edot ha'Mizrach* pattern of intergenerational decline in religiosity.

Before their emigration, the Jews from Georgia and the Islamic republics were strong supporters of Zionism. As among the Jewish communities from North Africa and Asia, Zionism did not take predominantly secularist forms but fitted well into the religious tradition of praying for a return to Zion. In Israel the strong Jewish identity continues as the more encompassing of the interrelated Jewish and Israeli identities. Other Israelis identify them as members of a distinctive Jewish group of origin ("Georgian" or "Bukharan") and this pattern contributes to the emergence of a strong *edah* identity that is not differentiated from their Jewish identity. In addition to their Jewish identity, Georgian Jews have a strong sense of Georgian patriotism, and in Israel some maintain an identity and cultural ties with Georgia.[16]

As noted in chapter 8, the policies of the Soviet regime left Russian Jews with little cultural content for a Jewish identity. The negative associations of Jewishness as imposed by the state and by popular anti-Semitism were countered somewhat by the pride associated with the Israeli victory in 1967, and Soviet propaganda unintentionally reinforced Jewish identity by blurring the distinction between Zionism and Jewish peoplehood.[17] After 1967, learning Hebrew and becoming a Zionist became the most common ways to express a Jewish identity among Russian Jews, and in the early 1970s an increasing number of Soviet Jews sought permission to emigrate to Israel. Many of those who managed to emigrate chose to come to Israel, but this changed in 1977, when most Jewish emigrants chose other countries. Soviet restrictions from 1980 severely cut the number of emigrants, but a mass migration followed the removal of restrictions in 1989. Between 1989 and 2003 about 900,000 Jews and their non-Jewish close relatives migrated to Israel, and the number of Israeli citizens from the former Soviet Union now numbers 1.1 million, constituting about 20 percent of Israel's Jewish population.[18]

The immigrants from Russia in the early 1970s were Zionists who made Hebrew their primary language and successfully integrated into Israel society. Most of the immigrants from 1989 were motivated by a desire to improve their economic situation and provide better opportunities for their children. If Western countries, particularly the United States, had not imposed restrictions on the number of immigrants, it is likely that most Russian emigrants would not have made Israel their country of destination. A 1993 survey in Moscow, Kiev, and Minsk found that, although Israel was the intended destination of one-third of the sample who intended to emigrate, only one-fifth said that Israel was their historic homeland.[19]

The predispositions of the Russian immigrants contrast with both the secular Zionism of the early aliyot from Eastern Europe and the traditionally informed Zionism of Jews from North Africa and Asia. In some respects the Russian immigrants are similar to many of the Jews who fled Germany and settled in Palestine in the 1930s; they are highly educated, have middle-class occupations and aspirations, are largely removed from Jewish culture and Jewish nationalism, and are strongly committed to their native language and culture. The Holocaust struck a blow to anything associated with Germany, and Zionism won over the young with parents from Germany. Today, in post-Zionist, multicultural Israel, immigrants have far more opportunities to preserve their language and establish their institutions and homogeneous social networks.[20]

The flourishing Russian institutional complex and subculture in Israel includes an extensive array of mass media (newspapers, radio stations, and a television channel); consumption markets, such as supermarkets, grocery and meat stores, restaurants, cafes, and bookshops; schools; cultural venues, such as clubs and theaters; and political parties. Russian culture in Israel is reinforced by the immigrants' familial, social, and professional contacts that extend beyond Israel's borders, not only to their country of origin but also to the transnational Diaspora of Russian Jews. A survey conducted in 2001 found that 75 percent of post-1989 immigrants read Russian fiction, 97 percent watch Russian television channels, 65 percent listen to Russian radio stations, and more than half attend Russian cultural events and tours of Russian artists. However, Russian economic venues, such as the supermarkets, cater to the wider Israeli public, and Russian cultural and educational institutions, such as the Gesher Theater and Mofat school system, have become or are becoming Hebrew-speaking. The penetration of Hebrew beyond instrumental spheres is clearly indicated, especially among the younger cohort, and it is likely that the Russian language will be largely lost by the third generation.[21]

Surveys of the national and ethnic identities, Russian, Israeli and Jewish, of the immigrants have found different patterns between adolescents and adults. A study carried out in 1992 of adolescents who had arrived in Israel during the previous two years found that they saw themselves first as Russian, second as Israeli, and third as Jews. The investigators wrote that the upheaval of immigration had underscored the feeling of Russianness and that the Israeli identity was selected as second because of the adolescents' desire to be accepted by the Israeli peer groups.[22] A study conducted in 2001 of adolescents who had been in Israel for at least six years and no more than eleven years did not find a single dominant pattern of self-identity, although both the Russian and Israeli identities were reported to be stronger than the Jewish identity.[23]

A consistent finding is that adult Russian immigrants emphasize their Jewish identity most of all. A study conducted in 1992 of adults who had arrived in Israel about two years earlier found that 72 percent chose the Jewish identity as first in importance, 19 percent put Israeli identity in first place, and only 9 percent put their Russian identity in first place. However, more than half of the respondents did not answer the questions concerning identity.[24] A survey conducted in 2003 found similar patterns: The majority considered their first identity to be Jewish, 20 percent chose Israeli identity as first in importance, and 18 percent chose Russian identity as first in importance. The choice of Jewish as the primary identity was positively correlated with the number of years in Israel and with arriving in Israel at an older age: 80 percent of respondents older than 55 years marked their first identity as Jewish compared with half of those respondents age 18 to 55.[25]

A study carried out in 2005–06 of Russian immigrants age 18 and older who arrived in Israel between 1990 and 2006 found that Jewish identity was their most common primary or exclusive identity (39 percent), Israeli identity was slightly less common as their primary or exclusive identity (34 percent), and Russian identity was the least common (26 percent). However, Israeli identity was the most common exclusive or primary identity among those age 18 to 44 and peaked (58 percent) in the youngest cohort, ages 18–24. The longer the respondents had been in Israel, the more they felt Jewish and Israeli and the less they felt Russian, and a comparison with earlier studies showed a particular strengthening of the Israeli identity. Almost 23 percent identified themselves as exclusively Israeli, and among those who identified as primarily Jewish, the Israeli identity was the most common secondary identity. An exclusive Russian identity was reported by only 7 percent of respondents, who were mostly non-Jews, and only in the 60-plus age group was the Russian identity the most common secondary identity. Although as a reported identity the Russian identity had significantly weakened, Russian origins remained of great importance with respect to language, culture, and friendship networks.[26]

Like other immigrations, Jews from Russia are identified by other Israelis by reference to their country of origin. In the former Soviet Union, Russianness and the state-imposed Jewish national designation had been viewed by many as mutually exclusive, and it is not surprising that many of the older immigrants at first rejected being labeled as Russian. The immigrants began to adopt the label as they came to understand that this was just one of many country of origin terms that were tied to a Jewish identity in Israel.[27] The Russian Jewish identity could not, however, refer back to memories of a Jewish culturally distinctive or communally organized group; its cultural references are the Russian language and Russian, especially "high" culture. The 2002 survey found that respondents attributed Russian identity as meaning sharing Russian culture (72 percent), whereas being Jewish meant belonging to the Jewish people (52 percent), and being Israeli meant either living in Israel (44 percent) or belonging to the Israeli people (41 percent). This and other studies found that immigrants cherish their Russian cultural heritage and believe it to be superior to Israel culture, which is considered Levantine and provincial. Feelings of cultural superiority are expressed especially toward Jews from North Africa and Asia, who are seen to resemble the "uncultured" Asian peoples of the former Soviet Union.[28]

The Jewish identity of the Russian immigrants is largely divorced from Judaism. Estimates of the proportion of non-Jews among the Russian immigrants vary from one-fourth to one-half. The halachic definition of a Jew is a person born of a Jewish mother who does not proclaim another religion, but the Law of Return has been modified so that one Jewish grandparent has been sufficient to obtain Israeli citizenship. Although some immigrants may have invented a Jewish ancestry, the degrees of Jewish ancestry are not necessarily indicative of identity because even most of the halachic Jews have had little experience with Judaism or a distinctive Jewish culture.[29] Most of the non-Jewish immigrants are similar to the Jewish immigrants in their secularism. The 1999 survey of religious identities and religiosity among Israeli Jews found that only 2 percent of Russian Jews in Israel identified themselves as religious, 22 percent identified themselves as traditional, and 76 percent identified themselves as nonreligious. In comparison with the almost total absence of religious observance in Russia, a large minority said that they light Hanukkah candles (40 percent) and fast on Yom Kippur (41 percent). Such practices are not seen as having religious significance but as indicating belonging to the Jewish state.[30]

To conclude: As a consequence of different religiocultural backgrounds and socioeconomic encounters in Israel, five distinguishable patterns of national and ethnic identities have emerged.

1. Rejection of a Jewish identity and any *edah* or ethnic identity based on country or region of origin in favor on one national identity, Israeli or Hebrew. This was the Canaanite position and is rarely found today.

2. Rejection of Israeli identity and an overlap and mutual reinforcement of Jewish identity, a wider categorization (Ashkenazim), and, possibly, a more specific religious community of origin (e.g., the Litvak *mitnagdim*). This pattern is common among ultra-Orthodox or *haredim*, especially those from Europe.

3. Rejection of or relatively low attachment to specific *edah* or ethnic identities in favor of a broad Israeli-Jewish identity, with the Israeli component being the greater source of pride. This is common among Israelis who define themselves as secular, especially those of European origins.

4. Overlap and mutual reinforcement of identities based on Jewish community of origin (*edah*), a wider categorization (*edot ha'Mizrach*), and Jewish-Israeli identities with the Jewish identity being the most encompassing and greatest source of pride. This pattern is particularly common among Jews who describe themselves as religious or traditional from North Africa and Asia.

5. Compartmentalization between an ethnic (but not *edah*) identity, based on language and certain additional cultural components of the country of origin, and Jewish-Israeli identities related to feelings of belonging to a people. This is common among recent immigrants from Russia.

Not every group from a particular country of origin can be fitted neatly into this categorization. Not only will different groups from a particular country of origin be found in different categories, but certain groups will demonstrate a combination of patterns. Ambiguity of ethnic identities is no doubt pervasive. However, I hope I have shown that an understanding of Jewish identity in Israel requires that it be investigated and analyzed in relation to other national and ethnic identities of Israeli Jews.

AFTERWORD TO PART 3

All three chapters in part 3 focused on the interrelationships in the modern era between the religious and ethnic components of Jewish identity. Chapter 7 was a critique of those American sociologists who have interpreted the religiosity of most (mainly non-Orthodox) American Jews as an expression of their ethnicity. At first, religion was seen to express an ethnicity anchored in the continuing strength of social ties among highly acculturated American Jews, but as those ties weakened and intermarriage increased, the religion of American Jews was seen to express their symbolic ethnicity. Somewhat contrary to the view of religion as an epiphenomenon of ethnicity, I emphasized the importance of religious institutions as the "material" basis for ethnic feelings and identity. A number of developments over the last decades would appear to be unfavorable to the epiphenomenon arguments. Whereas measures of religiosity in the identity of American Jews have stabilized, measures of ethnicity have weakened. The "new spirituality," with its emphasis on subjective experiences and individual rather than collective meanings, has come to encompass many American Jews, and this supports the religious rather than the ethnic dimensions of Jewish identity.

The data presented in chapter 8 reinforced the argument for the growing importance of religion over the ethnic components of Jewish identity among American Jews. It is true that secularization has produced a pattern of a weakened form of Jewish ethnicity without Judaism among some American Jews, but in a society where descent has given way to consent, a de-ethnicized religious Jewish identity may become a prominent type. This is largely the consequence of the de-ethnicizing effects of intermarriage, which has grown considerably in recent decades, together with the personalistic approach to religion among Americans. The de-ethnicized Jewish religious identity is found particularly in the Reform movement in the United States, but in the more secular and different religious contexts of European countries this type of identity is unlikely to become a chosen option. Reform and other progressive forms of Judaism have been far less successful in Europe, and it is the ethnic component that tends to be more prominent in the Jewish identity of European Jews. Many Russian Jews take the view that Jewish identity can be divorced entirely from Judaism, and they are willing to accept the combination of Christian faith and Jewish identity.

For a large proportion of Israeli Jews who describe themselves as secular or nonreligious, the religious component in their Jewish identity finds expression on the public rather than the private level. This is relevant to the relationship between the Jewish and Israeli identities of Israeli Jews, and I tried to show in chapter 9 that the religious factor largely accounts not only for the relative emphases that Israeli Jews put on their Israeli and Jewish identities but also for the relationships between these identities and the *edah* and *edot* ha'Mizrach or Ashkenazim identities. Significant differences are evident in the forms and expressions of Jewish identity in the two largest Jewish populations in the world: Israel and the United States. These differences are related to differences in the characteristics of religion and the processes of secularization in these two countries, subjects that are taken up in part 4.

PART 4

Judaism in the Sociology of Religion

INTRODUCTION TO PART 4

In part 4 I deal with subjects that have been prominent in the sociology of religion: secularization and fundamentalism (or, the term I prefer, neotraditionalism) (chapter 10) and public religion (chapter 11). If secularization and neotraditionalism occur together, polarization, a process I discuss in chapter 10, is possible.

Perhaps no subject has been as contentious in the sociology of religion as secularization, but the multiplication of definitions, dimensions, and measurements of secularization has made it increasingly difficult to single out "the secularization thesis."[1] Among the multidimensional frameworks for the analysis of secularization, the framework suggested by José Casanova is particularly helpful for my purposes because it was formulated with particular reference to the importance of public religion, which I discuss in chapter 11. Three dimensions of secularization are distinguished: (1) the differentiation of secular spheres from religious norms and institutions, (2) a decline of religious beliefs and practices, and (3) the marginalization of religion to a privatized sphere. The first dimension, differentiation, is common to all Western societies, but of particular relevance here is the variation among societies with respect to the differentiation of nationalist ideologies from religion and the differentiation of state and religion. The second dimension, the decline of religious beliefs and practices, is less encompassing of Western societies than differentiation, and, as Casanova notes, the more the religious institutions resisted differentiation, the more religion declined. The third dimension, privatization, has been a historical trend in many societies, but Casanova emphasizes that, unlike differentiation, it is not a modern structural trend. It is a "historical option" found particularly in those societies that have experienced religious decline, and in recent decades there have been important trends of deprivatization.[2]

The subsuming of the privatization of religion under the rubric "secularization" has been challenged,[3] but the greatest dispute among sociologists of religion has been over whether religious beliefs and practices in Western societies have declined (Casanova's second dimension). The authors of a number of discussions of the secularization thesis have begun by noting that the conventional view among sociologists is to support the thesis and that by questioning the thesis, the author is questioning and doing battle against accepted wisdom.[4] However, readers of the sociology of religion since the 1970s might easily obtain the impression that, at least in the United States, it is the antisecularization thesis that has become the accepted wisdom and that the supporters of the secularization thesis are now in the minority. The antisecularization thesis is not new,[5] but the number of its proponents among sociologists of religion grew considerably in the 1970s and 1980s.[6]

Among Western societies the United States appears to be among the most religious, and American sociologists have been prominent in refuting the secularization thesis. With one exception, indications of religiosity among Americans appear to have changed little since 1990. Recent polls continue to show that close to 90 percent of Americans continue to proclaim their belief in the existence of God and almost 60 percent say that they believe that religion is important in their lives. Church membership and attendance, after reaching peak figures in the 1950s, declined after 1960, but most of the decline took place in the 1960s and 1970s, and since then the decline has been small. However, the proportion of Americans who do not espouse a religious identity has markedly increased, from one-tenth in 1990 to nearly one-sixth in recent surveys. More Americans say that they have no religion or describe themselves as atheist, agnostic, secular, or humanist.[7] Few American sociologists of religion see this as a significant indicator of secularization. They tend to argue that many Americans have become skeptical of conventional religious institutions and have become highly subjective and selective in their approaches to religion.

The secularization thesis is held to be refuted empirically by studies that show that religion is alive and well in the modern world and has not been affected adversely by dimensions of "modernization," such as urbanization and the development of the mass media.[8] The growth of conservative religious movements, the success of television evangelism, and the proliferation of new religious movements are believed by many American scholars to demonstrate the invalidity of the secularization thesis.[9] This conclusion has been challenged by those who have argued that the growth of conservative movements has been negligible in proportion to the population, that conservative religious growth has been internal and has not attracted the growing numbers of unaffiliated, and that the membership of new religious movements is relatively small and has not provided an alternative for the majority of those who have disaffiliated from the mainline denominations.[10] These and other arguments are found in the extensive defense of the secularization thesis by Steve Bruce, although his most convincing evidence tends to come from Europe.[11]

Supporters of the secularization thesis have tended to be European scholars, and it has been suggested that the relative secularity of Europe is an exception in the global context. European countries vary considerably with respect to their levels and patterns of secularity, but, from the perspectives of such countries as England, France, the Netherlands, and Denmark, it is the religiosity of the United States that appears to be the exception among Western societies.

British sociologists, particularly Bryan Wilson and Steve Bruce, have provided excellent analyses of the causes of the differences in the patterns of secularity and religiosity in England and the United States.[12] These comparisons focus on the Christian populations, and it cannot be assumed that the differences in levels of religiosity and secularity among the Jewish populations in the Diaspora will simply reflect those of the dominant non-Jewish populations. In the American context, most American Jews appear to be particularly secularized compared with their non-Jewish fellow Americans. Forty-four percent of American Jews who identify as Jewish by religion describe their outlook as secular or somewhat secular compared with 15 percent of Episcopalians, 13 percent of Catholics, 10 percent of Lutherans, and 6 percent of Methodists. When asked whether they agree or disagree with the statement that God performs miracles, 28 percent of American Jews disagreed strongly or somewhat compared with 9 percent of Episcopalians, 7 percent of Lutherans, 6 percent of Methodists, and 5 percent of Catholics.[13] With respect to the indicators of religiosity and secularity, the differences among the Western Jewish communities (including Israel) appear to be considerably smaller than the differences among the Christian populations.

One religious trend of recent decades that many observers believe contradicts the secularization thesis has been the rising importance of conservative or "fundamentalist" movements in a number of religious traditions, including Judaism and Christianity. It should be noted, however, that many fundamentalists portray themselves as battling against secularization and secular ideologies. American fundamentalists, for example, perceive "secular humanism" as the greatest cultural threat that they face; it has replaced modernist theology as their major enemy. Although they question the secularization thesis, the sociologists Anson Shupe and Jeffrey K. Hadden argue that global fundamentalists represent a resistance in many societies to secularization or the process in which religion becomes institutionally differentiated and loses its relevance in the general culture. They define fundamentalism as "a proclamation of reclaimed authority of a sacred tradition which is to be reinstated as an antidote for a society that has strayed from its cultural moorings."[14]

Movements that have been designated as fundamentalist include the Muslim Brethren and its more radical offshoots and successors among the Sunni, the Shiites in Iran, Protestant conservative and evangelical movements, ultra-Orthodox Jewish communities, and the messianic Gush Emunim movement in Israel. The term *fundamentalism* has been used frequently in recent years, both in the mass media, where it is often used to denote religious extremism or fanaticism, and in scholarly works. The wide variety of understandings and definitions that have accumulated has led some scholars to question whether the extensive use of the term is likely to lead to analytical precision or explanations.

My preference is to adopt the term *neotraditionalism* to refer to religious movements that self-consciously attempt to represent or reassert what they regard as their authentic religious tradition against what they perceive as threats in modern developments. A past society is believed to have embodied the authentic tradition, and this provides a model to be reconstituted or emulated. Understood in this way, neotraditionalism encompasses movements that are often called fundamentalist (Protestant fundamentalism, Jewish ultra-Orthodoxy, and Islamic radicalism) as well as others that have been rarely so called (e.g., the Catholic opposition to Vatican II). It excludes, however, Pentecostal and millenarian movements that have also been labeled fundamentalist.[15] I would exclude them because neotraditionalism does not constitute the core of their self-definitions, although the groups might include elements of neotraditionalism. The distinctive characteristic of Pentecostal movements is their focus on the gifts of the Spirit in the here and now, and that of millenarian or messianic movements is their belief that the time of redemption is under way or will begin in the near future. Neotraditional movements may have messianic beliefs, but these are of much less immediate concern than the rebuilding in "normal times" of a society that conforms to what is believed to be the authentic religious tradition.

It has been common to refer to Gush Emunim (Bloc of the Faithful), the religious nationalist movement in Israel, as fundamentalist, and it has been argued that it is similar in type to Islamic movements such as the Muslim Brethren and its radical offshoots.[16] It is true that there is some similarity of Gush Emunim to the Islamic movements in that its members condemn the intrusion of materialism from Western culture, but this is a relatively minor theme in the movement's ideology and is not emphasized when it seeks support among secularized Jews. In fact, the movement's interpretation of modern history in the framework of the process of redemption includes positive evaluations of certain secular developments among Jews. Because it was secular Zionists who were the principal historical actors in the early modern Jewish settlement in the Land of Israel and in the establishment of the state and its institutions, Gush Emunim see them as having played an important role in the process of redemption, paving the way for the religious Zionists who now have the principal role in the process.

The sacralization of Zionism by Gush Emunim and its interpretation of events, particularly the foundation of the Israeli state, the Six Day War, and the settlement of "Judea and Samaria" within the framework of the process of redemption, are in radical contrast to the understanding of recent historical events by the neotraditionalist or ultra-Orthodox, Neturei Karta and the Satmar Hasidim, who condemn Zionism and the Israeli state as blasphemous abominations and even blame the Holocaust on Zionism. Gush Emunim should not be classified as a fundamentalist or neotraditionalist movement because it does not proclaim that the remedy for certain modern cultural developments that it opposes can be found by attempting to approximate a society of the past. The First and Second Jewish Commonwealths (thirteenth to sixth centuries B.C.E.; and second century B.C.E. to second century C.E., respectively) are important positive historical references for Gush Emunim, but these do no more than foreshadow the Third Commonwealth that is believed to be emerging in the messianic process.[17] It is true that Gush Emunim seeks to promote the sacred texts, the Torah, in the determination of public policy and that it sees the laws embodied in these texts as absolute and indivisible, but unlike neotraditional movements, Gush Emunim has not so much emphasized the need to implement the sacred texts as it has emphasized the sacred meaning of historical events and processes in recent times. Its sacralization of Zionism and the Israeli state indicates that its orientation toward modernity is, in some important respects, one of appropriation rather than rejection.[18]

It is also important in the Jewish context to distinguish between the Orthodox, which I would not categorize as neotraditional, and the ultra-Orthodox or *haredim*, for whom the neotraditionalist label is appropriate. Both reject the incorporation of modernist themes within Judaism, but they differ considerably both in the nature of their response to modernity and in their sociohistorical origins.[19] The Orthodox movement in Judaism was a response to religious modernism in the form of Reform Judaism that began in Germany in the first half of the nineteenth century. The characteristics and context of Jewish religious modernism were quite different from those of Christianity. The centrality of postbiblical writings in Judaism meant that Orthodox Jews felt much less threatened by source criticism than Orthodox Christians. The disputes between Orthodox and Reform Judaism were, in contrast with the disputes over doctrine within Protestantism, focused on the form and content of the synagogue services and have to be seen in the context of the acculturation and assimilation of many Jews to the wider society. In its emphasis on decorum, its replacement of Hebrew by the vernacular, and its abolition or reformulation of traditional prayers referring to the messiah and the return to Zion, Reform Judaism represented an attempt to accommodate the wider, more "modern" non-Jewish cultural and national environment.[20] Orthodox Judaism would not countenance any change in the traditional prayers, but in Germany a more compartmentalized response developed in what came to be known as neo-Orthodoxy or modern Orthodoxy, which combined an adherence to the traditional religious laws with an accommodation to what were considered the nonreligious aspects of the wider culture.[21]

A Reform or modernist religious movement did not penetrate most Eastern European communities (Hungary was an exception), and in those areas the ultra-Orthodox represented a reaction to general secular trends and to the secular Jewish socialist and Zionist movements.[22] The ultra-Orthodox rejection of Jewish accommodation to secular Western culture was strengthened after the major centers of traditional Jewry were destroyed in the Holocaust, and in the post–World War II period they have continued to represent a rejection of the wider secularized culture more than religious modernism. This is particularly the case in modern Israel, where the Reform and Conservative movements are small and uninfluential.

10. SECULARIZATION, NEOTRADITIONALISM, POLARIZATION

Secularization and Differences Among Religions

The debate on secularization has been confined mainly to the Christian context, and there has been disagreement on whether the term *secularization* is useful as a cross-cultural concept.[1] I extend the debate in this chapter by showing how secularization can be conducted within the Jewish context, and I suggest that differences among religions should be brought into the discussion of the effects of modernity on religion.

Most sociologists of religion are likely to acknowledge that the relationship between religion and the processes of modernity is an interactional or, as many prefer to call it, a dialectical one. But although the effects of Western religion, especially Protestantism, on the modern world have been endlessly debated, there has been little consideration of whether the effects of the processes of modernity (industrialization, urbanization, etc.) on religion depend on the characteristics of the religions. Religions are understood here to include all systems of beliefs and practices that are anchored in notions of the supramundane, and in its barest formulation the secularization thesis states that the processes of modernity are accompanied by or result in a decline or contraction of such beliefs and practices.[2]

Both proponents and opponents of the secularization thesis have supported their arguments mainly with data from the Christian context, but they have generally assumed that their arguments are applicable to other religious contexts. Peter Berger wrote that the seeds of secularization can be found in ancient Judaism and Protestantism but that the modern industrial economy is the major secularizing "carrier" in the contemporary West and that the spread of Western civilization involves the spread of secularization. Even though other religions may never have carried within themselves the seeds or the potential of secularization, Berger implied that they would be similarly affected by the forces of modernity.[3] Bryan Wilson wrote that certain characteristics of Christianity, such as its effective circumscription of the sacred, have made a difference with respect to the secularization process, but he argued that the model of secularization was intended to have general validity, and he expected that similar technological, economic, and political changes would have similar effects on religion in societies with different religious traditions.[4]

Problems of comparing possible secularization patterns among societies with different religious traditions are compounded not only because the different religious contexts might make a difference but also because the many factors, such as industrialization, urbanization, growth of science and technology, and political developments, that many believe produced secularization in the West also vary enormously in their relative importance and patterns. Sociologists have long questioned the thesis of a uniform process of modernization, and if neither the "dependent variable" (religion) nor the "independent variables" (the various dimensions of "modernization") are strictly comparable, then the problems of extending the secularization debate beyond its current Western Christian focus do appear formidable.

The comparative problems in this area do not appear to me to be insurmountable or of such a magnitude as to make comparative analysis worthless, but where should we begin the comparisons? Although a case could be made for a number of comparative strategies, I believe one profitable strategy is to begin with Judaism. This may not take us very far outside the Western context, but it takes us out of the Christian one, and it has the advantage at this stage of widening the comparative range while retaining Western patterns of modernization as parameters. The minority position of Jewish communities has meant that modernization has affected Judaism in special ways, but the comparative analysis can include the case of Judaism in Israel, where Jews are in the majority.

Two characteristics of Judaism that differentiate it from Christianity are likely to be relevant in considering the effects of modernity on religion or on patterns of secularization: (1) the integral tie between the religion and a particular people and (2) the emphasis on practice. In his comparison of Christian societies, David Martin showed that where religion had become an important component of ethnicity or nationality, as in Poland and Ireland, religiosity continued at relatively high levels.[5] The importance of religion in such cases was contingent on factors in the nations' histories, but where there is an essential identity of religion and peoplehood, as signified by the covenant in Judaism, the implications for secularization may well be different.

The differentiation in the modern period of what are now termed ethnic or national components of Jewish identity from religious elements may itself be considered one aspect of the secularization of Jewish communities. In the traditional society, there had been no consciousness that Jewishness was made up of elements that could be distinguished in this way, and their differentiation in the postemancipation period made possible a Jewish identity in which there was a self-conscious focus on either the religious or the ethnic component. The reformulations of Jewish identity in the nineteenth and early twentieth centuries included those identities with an exclusively religious or nationalist basis, but these are rarely found today (see chapter 8). The ethnic or national component of Jewish identity can be the focus for a large proportion of Jews in both the Diaspora and Israel, but it is expressed through symbols taken from the religious heritage. Rather than reject religious symbols, most contemporary secular Jews tend to reinterpret them, and this means that a level of religious observance continues even among atheists and agnostics.

The core of Talmudic Judaism is not theology but the Halacha (religious law) and its practice, and it has been argued that the absence of a theology helps account for the rapid secularization of Jews once they entered open societies and were exposed to modern scientific beliefs. Nathan Glazer wrote, concerning the Jewish immigrants from Eastern Europe in the United States, that "Jews lost their faith so easily because they had no faith to lose; that is, they had no doctrine, no collection of dogmas to which they could cling and with which they could resist argument."[6] Jews had observed a complex system of practices within the segregated society, but once the first step had been taken and certain practices that were felt to limit participation in the open society had been abandoned, no religious principle could stem the abandonment of further practices. Religious practice fragmented into a great variety of levels and patterns of observance, but, as suggested, the majority were likely to retain a few common practices that appropriately expressed their Jewish identity.

If the combination of an ethnic identity and the absence of a theology results in an attenuated religiosity among the majority who accommodate to Western norms, then for the minority of Orthodox Jews who reject such accommodation the halachic system of religious practices (mitzvot) provides a clear boundary between themselves, the pious who observe the mitzvot, and those who do not. Jewish Orthodoxy is better termed an *orthopraxy*, and its boundaries, based on the distinction between observance and nonobservance or partial observance, are clearer and easier to defend than Christian orthodoxy, whose beliefs are subject to various interpretations.

Scientific and secular ideologies have posed threats to the traditional beliefs of both Christians and Jews, but they are likely to pose a more direct threat to a conservative religion whose core is theology than to one whose core is practice. The defense of Christian evangelicalism or fundamentalism by its theologians and other members of its intellectual elite involves clarifications and reinterpretations of their doctrines and an adoption of the scientific tools of their adversaries.[7] The Jewish ultra-orthoprax elite may feel much less need to defend their practices; scientific and secular beliefs have little relevance for the core of their religion, and they can be ignored or compartmentalized and relegated to a relatively unimportant sphere of human knowledge.

Both Christian conservatives and Jewish traditionalists emphasize moral boundaries, but these boundaries may be subject to greater erosion when doctrine rather than practice is the core of the religion. Among Christian evangelists, the loosening of the strict moral, ascetic regimen of the past followed a decline in their consensus over beliefs and an increasing vagueness about their basic doctrines.[8] In Christianity the legitimation of moral codes by core beliefs implies some differentiation of morality from theology, but in Judaism religious practices are the moral codes. For example, family purity is constituted by rules that regulate such matters as sexual relations and attendance of the *mikveh* (ritual bath). A more stringent ritual observance, therefore, means a more stringent morality.

A comparison of the educational institutions of Christian orthodoxy and Jewish orthopraxy reinforces the argument that, whereas modernity may weaken traditionalist doctrine, it can strengthen traditionalist practice. James Davison Hunter writes that, although the universities of evangelical Protestantism were founded as a defensive response to secular trends in higher education, the very nature of the education, in which students are introduced to more ambiguous and complex ideas, has weakened evangelical orthodoxy. A strict indoctrination into the truth of doctrines does not appear possible in the context of modern higher education.[9] In comparison, the Jewish yeshivas (advanced religious educational institutions) can strengthen orthopraxy; they need be concerned much less with the interpretation or defense of a few basic beliefs than with the interpretation of the vast corpus of the Talmud or religious law. The emphasis on interpretation and application in Talmudic study enables yeshiva students to engage in sharp and lively intellectual debates without challenging the validity of fundamental beliefs.[10] Individual and original thinking can be channeled into finding and justifying the most stringent interpretations of the law.

Thus, insofar as the effects of modernity are channeled or mediated by these particular characteristics of Judaism (the ethnic factor and the focus on practice), divergent patterns are possible: A highly stringent, encompassing pattern of Jewish practice could emerge alongside a highly attenuated one. I now turn to a review of the evidence of Jewish religious practice, setting it within the framework of the debate on secularization. The most relevant means to test the secularization thesis in a number of societies is to use the most salient dimension of religious commitment in each society.[11] In most Jewish communities the most salient dimension is the observance of the mitzvot, and in the following section I use the mitzvot to present the evidence for secularization. I consider objections to this approach in the subsequent section, in which I review a number of antisecularization arguments.

Secularization Among Jews: Ethnicity and Patterns of Religiosity

Compared with the traditional community, in which the great majority observed a comprehensive system of mitzvot that guided their everyday life, Jewish religious observance today is highly selective and fragmented. Rituals that were observed by most Jews in the past, such as donning tefillin (phylacteries) during weekday morning prayers or following the many dietary laws, are observed today by only small minorities. Attendance at synagogue has also become a highly selective practice. The 2000–01 National Jewish Population Survey (NJPS) found that 23 percent of American Jews said that they attended synagogue once a month or more, and 61 percent said that they had attended services at least once over the last year.[12] A somewhat more detailed picture of synagogue attendance was provided by a 1997 survey of American Jews conducted by Steven Cohen. Cohen reported that 26 percent attended once a month or more, 33 percent attended only on special occasions such as weddings and bar mitvahs, and 16 percent attended only on Yom Kippur (Day of Atonement) and Rosh Hashanah (New Year).[13]

The historical identity of Judaism and the Jewish people has meant that a predominantly ethnic Jewish identity can be expressed only through religious symbols and practices, but the symbols and practices that were chosen by secularized Jews are those that relate the individual and his or her family to the themes of the continuation of the Jewish people and its historical emergence and struggles for survival.[14] The rites of passage—circumcision, bar or bat mitzvah, religious marriage and burial—can be interpreted in this way, and they are observed by most Jews, who also signal their Jewish identity by placing a mezuzah on the doorposts of their homes. The two most popular ritual occasions in all Western communities and Israel are the seder at Pesach (Passover) and the lighting of candles during Hanukkah. The Passover meal is a family occasion, often of the extended family, that celebrates the deliverance from Egypt. More than two-thirds of American Jews, as reported by the NJPS, and nine out of ten Israeli Jews, as reported by a national survey of Israeli Jews conducted in 1999, participate in the Passover seder. Hanukkah commemorates the successful struggle against Syrian-Greek rule and the rededication of the desecrated Second Temple. Eighty-three percent of American Jews (in the 2000–01 NJPS) and 81 percent of Israeli Jews (in 1999) reported that they lit candles on the nights of Hanukkah.[15]

The Passover seder and Hanukkah candle lighting meet the criteria listed by Marshall Sklare for the continued observance of certain rituals among American Jews: (1) They can be effectively redefined in modern, nonsupramundane terms; (2) they do not demand social isolation or the adoption of a unique lifestyle; (3) they accord with the wider religious culture and provide a "Jewish" alternative when such a need is felt; (4) they are centered on the child; and (5) they are performed annually or infrequently.[16] With respect to the first factor, it should be emphasized that the rituals are redefined not so much in the sense of giving them new meanings but rather by diminishing or removing the traditional focus on God and his law and giving precedence to the traditional themes of kinship and peoplehood.[17] The fourth criterion, child centeredness, reflects a general characteristic of modern Western culture, and it can also be said to connect the family to the perpetuation of the Jewish people.

With respect to Sklare's third factor, it is relevant for American Jews that Passover and Hanukkah fall close to Easter and Christmas. Advertising and consumer and entertainment industries have promoted the Jewish holidays alongside the Christian ones. An increasing number of Christians hold a Passover seder as an ecumenical ritual and as a recognition of the Jewish origins of Jesus, and many non-Jews light Hanukkah candles to signify their solidarity with the Jewish people.[18] Hanukkah, in particular, has become incorporated by schools and other public institutions into the festivities of the Christmas season, and practices such as Hanukkah cards and presents have enabled Jews to participate in the season's festivities in a Jewish fashion. This consideration is not relevant for the popularity of the holiday in Israel, but it should be noted that, whereas in the United States Hanukkah has become the major children's festival, in Israel other ritual occasions (e.g., Purim and Lag b'Omer) have become the major celebrations that focus on the children (fancy costumes and bonfires, respectively).

No other religious practices come close to the almost universal observance of the Passover seder and Hanukkah candles, but another yearly ritual, fasting on Yom Kippur, is observed by more than half of the American Jewish population and by more than two-thirds of the Israeli Jewish population.[19] It is somewhat misleading to compare the American and Israeli populations because Israeli Jews include a large proportion of first-generation immigrants from the more traditional communities of North Africa and Asia. A more appropriate comparison is with Israeli Ashkenazim who were born in Israel: The 1999 Israeli survey found that exactly half of this category reported that they fasted on Yom Kippur.[20] These are still high proportions, and it could be argued that Yom Kippur cannot be fitted into the interpretation that emphasizes that only rituals whose central theme is Jewish peoplehood are observed by the majority. The major themes of Yom Kippur are confession, repentance, and judgment of the individual for his or her acts over the year. The meaning of fasting on Yom Kippur among contemporary Jews has yet to be investigated, but in Israel, where even the most secular of Jews refrain from travel on Yom Kippur, the major meaning of fasting among many does appear to be an expression of solidarity with the Jewish people. It is possible that the Yom Kippur War reinforced this tendency. Many fast without any ritual participation, such as attendance at synagogue, and it should be noted in this context that the proportion who fast in Israel is greater than the proportion who say that they believe in God (65 percent).[21]

Only a small minority observe the Sabbath in a fully traditional manner. Few refrain from working or shopping on the Sabbath, but like another traditionally important ritual area, dietary regulations, certain selected practices continue to be observed by larger minorities. The 2000–01 NJPS found that 28 percent of American Jews regularly lit Sabbath candles on Friday evening, and 21 percent said that they kept a kosher home.[22] "Keeping a kosher home" is open to a wide interpretation, and most Jews retain some dietary regulations in a highly selective manner. Some buy kosher meat but are prepared to eat nonkosher meat outside the home. Others eat nonkosher meat in the home but draw the line at pork or bacon. Cohen reported (in 1997) that 18 percent of his respondents said that they have separate meat and dairy dishes.[23] The 1999 Israeli survey found that 51 percent of Israeli Jews lit Sabbath candles with a blessing and that 46 percent kept separate meat and milk dishes; the respective figure for separate dishes for Ashkenazim born in Israel was 30 percent.[24] Data on European communities indicates similar patterns of Sabbath and dietary practices as those found in the United States.[25]

It has been suggested that a more appropriate term for the rituals observed by most American Jews is ceremony. Ceremonies, such as lighting Hanukkah candles or attending synagogue on the High Holy Days, are the more collective expressions of religious observances. They typically take place in public or extended family settings, and they reinforce the sense that a social order exists and that the individual is part of it. Rituals, in comparison, are performed by the individual or the nuclear family in private contexts in abeyance to the commandments of God, who is believed to be pleased when the rituals are performed correctly. The ways that particular ceremonies, such as the Passover seder, are observed vary considerably, whereas rituals are stylized and repetitive forms of behavior. Ceremonial behavior has flourished among American Jews, especially among the nonorthoprax majority, and, until recently, ritual behavior has declined. The higher proportions of Israeli Jews who observe such practices as lighting Sabbath candles and separating meat and dairy dishes indicate that the distinction between ceremony and ritual is less encompassing for Israeli Jews than it is for American Jews. Among Israeli Jews the distinction is most relevant for those who identify as secular and confine their religious observances to a few, mainly yearly, ceremonies.[26]

The notion of ceremonies as focusing on the collective and connecting the individual and nuclear family to the perpetuation of the Jewish people has been modified in a recent study of "moderately affiliated Jews" who make up the majority of American Jews. Steven Cohen and Arnold Eisen, the investigators, found that the themes of the historical destiny and survival of the Jewish people have become less important in the celebration of the religious holidays and that their respondents perceive the holidays to be occasions when, together with their families and friends, they can find personal spiritual meaning. This is part of a shift in American Jewish identity from the public to the private domain, from a grand narrative that exalts the story of Jewish peoplehood and destiny to local narratives and personal stories of the family and the self.[27]

Objections to the Secularization Thesis

No writer has disputed the evidence of a decline of religious practice among most Jews in the postemancipation period, but it is possible to distinguish three countersecularization arguments that either question the use of the term *secularization* or point to recent developments among Jews that challenge the secularization thesis. Definitional issues are central to the first two arguments. The first argument disputes the criterion of a decline of practice by pointing to a transition from practice to beliefs or ethics, and the second argument redefines the religion of Jews in nonsupramundane terms. The third argument admits secularization within Judaism but claims that many Jews are finding an alternative supramundane form of religion outside Judaism.

The First Argument: Transition from Practice to Beliefs or Ethics

An objection to equating a decline in practice with secularization can be made by defining nonsecularity in terms of minimal religious requirements. N. Kokosalakis, for example, rhetorically asks whether it is correct to refer to recent generations as secular Jews because they are so distant from the ritual practices and cultural values of their eastern European forebears. He writes, "For purposes of analysis any Jew who acknowledges belief in God and practices even a few rituals will be assumed to be religious."[28] If, on the basis of such all-or-nothing formulations, a secularized society is taken to mean either one in which the majority do not believe in God and there is no religious practice or one in which religious practice has shrunk to a tiny minority, then most Jewish communities would not qualify. The abandonment of particular religious practices need not be classified as secularization when there is no indication of a decline in the importance of the supramundane in the life of the community,[29] but if it is possible to make judgments regarding the relative importance of supramundane beliefs and practices in societies, then it would be difficult to avoid the conclusion that most Jewish communities today are relatively secularized compared with those of the past.

A further objection to labeling a decline in religious practice as secularization is that such an equation makes orthopraxy synonymous with sacredness and thereby religiously devalues forms of modern Judaism, such as Conservative and Reform Judaism. There is evidence that some Reform Jews in the United States have defined their Jewish religious commitment in terms of moral directives rather than religious observance.[30] In so doing, they have adopted the characteristic moralistic orientation of religion in America with its equation of good deeds with the religious life. The abandonment of many religious practices has been legitimized in Reform Judaism by viewing Judaism as a self-transforming faith whose single enduring essence is the principle of ethical monotheism, and "classical" Reform Jews have pointed to a contradiction between the ritual prescriptions of traditional Judaism and their commitment to an activist social ethic.

Thus, if the test of secularization is the most salient dimension of religious commitment in each community or congregation, without regard to whether it relates to supramundane notions or not, then we would need a different test for each Judaism. In her study of a classical Reform congregation, Frida Kerner Furman showed that many members expressed a social activistic ideology with little actual involvement in social action programs, but even if there were high involvement, the application of the term *secularization* might still be considered appropriate if it referred to a decline in religious beliefs and practices anchored in supramundane notions. Furman wrote, "God forms no active part of the motivational base for its [the Reform congregation's] ideology, nor is God used in a justificatory way." God-language is absent: "When God is mentioned, even by the rabbis, the referent is usually the God of history—ancient history—and not a transcendent reality, which potentially confronts people today."[31]

The Reform Jews in Furman's study give their political liberalism a Jewish legitimation by linking it to the prophetic tradition, but although this link is passionately held, it is made without reference to a supramundane source. And it is because the "reality of God is an uncertain proposition"[32] that ritual is attenuated and devalued. The main manifest motive of collective prayer is not communication with God but the experience of community. Thus, if we adopt the supramundane definition of religion, this type of Reform Judaism would have to be described as an expression of secularization. This does not imply that Reform Judaism is any less sacred than orthoprax Judaism, because the sacred, a system of beliefs and practices anchored in ultimate concerns, is not necessarily identical with the religious, a system of beliefs and practices anchored in supramundane notions.[33]

The Second Argument: Redefinition in Nonsupramundane Terms

The second argument against secularization also turns on a conflation of the sacred and the religious. It differs from the first position insofar as it points to the emergence of a system of Jewish sacred beliefs and practices that are, at least in part, a functional alternative to all forms of synagogal or temple Judaism (or Judaisms). Jonathan Woocher, in his book *Sacred Survival: The Civil Religion of American Jews*, did not directly confront the secularization thesis, but his analysis is the best example of this type of countersecularization thesis. Woocher's central thesis is that "the religion of American Jews may be found not only in the realm of synagogue and denominational life, but in the activity and ideology of the vast array of Jewish organizations which are typically thought of as 'secular.'" He focused on the welfare federation movement, "the central core of the American Jewish polity," and argued that through these organizations American Jews "have achieved unity, purpose, and identity as a moral community which transcends (without excluding) the overtly religious ideology and practice of the denominational movements of American Judaism."[34] The division of American Jews along denominational lines (Reform, Conservative, Orthodox, etc.) means that "traditional" religion does not fully express, sustain, or direct American Jewry as a united moral community. This function and task is performed by a civil religion that endows the commonality with a transcendent significance. Transcendence does not refer here to God or to the supramundane but to the meanings and values of the collectivity that go beyond the individuals who compose it.

Woocher delineated the central myths and rituals of the American Jewish civil religion. The myth "from Holocaust to rebirth" recounts a process of destruction followed by a rebirth or redemption in which the state of Israel is a symbol of a new era and a new power of the Jewish people. Another myth emphasizes that America is different: It has provided American Jews with unprecedented opportunities and a unique security (anti-Semitism in America is regarded as an aberration from the "true" America). A third myth is that of Jews as a chosen people with a special destiny and mission. The rituals of the civil religion include those that are appropriated from traditional Judaism and those of the polity itself: the "missions" to Israel and the rituals of the fund-raising campaign and the General Assembly of the federations. These beliefs, myths, and rituals embody a particular religious sensibility, "the conviction that the meaning of Jewishness is located centrally in the experience of Jewish peoplehood."[35]

By describing the myths and rituals of civil Judaism as sacred, Woocher appears to mean that they are referring to a transcendent phenomenon, but he was wary and hesitant about the meaning of transcendence. He wrote that God or "some form of transcendent reality" is insignificant in the American Jewish civil religion. The collectivity is at the center of its meaning system, and the antagonism of supporters is avoided by remaining silent on the role of God in Jewish history and destiny. Civil Judaism differs from "traditional Judaism," in which the notion of the Jewish people as a religious entity, a "holy nation," is derived from the people's covenantal relationship to God. An emphasis on such a difference between traditional and civil religion would support a secularization thesis, but Woocher writes that, although the symbols of civil Judaism "do not have obvious transcendent referents," it is necessary to look below the surface of the stories and ceremonies to determine "whether they serve as functional equivalents of traditional myth and ritual for the civil religion's adherents, indeed whether their secularized language may even mask a genuine transcendent dimension."[36]

But what is this genuine transcendent dimension? On the one hand, Woocher did not want to imply that civil Judaism is a case of collective self-deification; he wrote that civil Judaism acknowledges that the values of the Jewish tradition transcend the characteristics of the people. On the other hand, he wrote that because the ultimate source of the tradition is left unclear, the source of accountability is often history or the people. Woocher was critical of the absence of a serious theology in civil Judaism that would actively affirm "vertical transcendence," as opposed to the "horizontal transcendence" of the people in time and space,[37] but I would argue that it is the absence of a clear notion of a supramundane transcendence that is an indication of secularization.

It is appropriate to note the difference between Woocher's thesis and Herberg's thesis of three decades earlier. Herberg argued that the "return to religion" of the immediate postwar and 1950s period was related to the identification problems of the third generation. The third generation grew up in homes that had adopted American secular culture, and because ethnic culture was unacceptable as a basis for identification in America, religion became the focal point of their identity, both as Jews (or Catholics or Protestants) and as Americans.[38] In fact, the only unambiguous evidence of a return to religion among Jews in that period was a rise in synagogue affiliation, and because the synagogue became an important center for secular social activities and the transmission of an ethnic identity, it appeared legitimate to refer to the secularization of religious institutions.[39] In the 1980s, when ethnic identity required less of a religious facade, Woocher argued that the unity of American Jewry was to be understood in terms of the sacralization of its "secular" institutions.

The Third Argument: Alternative Supramundane Forms

Secularization has also been denied by writers who have retained an approach to religion that emphasizes its distinctive supramundane beliefs and related practices. One variation of this approach, as represented in the work of Rodney Stark and William Sims Bainbridge, is to acknowledge that Judaism has been eroded by secularization but to argue that this is being offset by the movement of Jews into cults or new religious movements. Although they gave little space to an analysis of the Jewish case, Stark and Bainbridge saw it as providing excellent evidence for their thesis that secularization, in the sense of a long historical trend, is impossible because religion is the unique supplier of compensators for ubiquitous desires.[40] They wrote that Jews' relatively low formal religious affiliation and attendance at synagogue showed that secularization had eroded Judaism more than Christianity. A relatively high proportion of Jews have not had a religious socialization, but because the demand for the compensators that only religion can supply does not disappear and Jews are reluctant to adopt Christianity, Jews are "extraordinary overrepresent[ed]" in the new religious movements.[41]

In the 1980s Jews composed about 15 percent of the members of Krishna Consciousness, 9 percent of the Church of Scientology, 6 percent of the Unification Church, and about 20 percent of the Rajneesh movement.[42] The fact that the proportion of Jews in new religious movements was three times or more the proportion of Jews in the population is a significant one, but it is hardly sufficient to discount a secularization trend among Jews. Jews may be overrepresented in new religious movements because they are also overrepresented in the social strata, the educated middle and upper-middle class, from which most converts to new religious movements are recruited.[43] They constitute only a small proportion of Jews who are not affiliated with a synagogue or who do not identify with a particular Jewish denomination. From what we know about the age composition of new religious movements and the life cycle religious patterns among Jews, it is likely that those in the new religious movements are mainly youth or young adults and that many will return to at least a nominal affiliation or identification with Judaism at a later stage in their life cycle.

Diminishing Decline of Religiosity

The increased strength of Jewish Orthodoxy or orthopraxy in recent years, which is discussed later in this chapter, might be seen as a reversal of secularization, but with respect to the majority of American Jews, the evidence indicates a process of stabilization of religious practice rather than a reversal of secularization. A process of a diminishing decline of religiosity was already evident from comparisons among the first three generations; the decline of religiosity from the second to the third generation, although significant, was of smaller magnitude than the decline from the first to the second generation.[44] The differences between the third and fourth generations appeared to be minor or insignificant.[45]

The usefulness of comparing generations has become attenuated as an increasing proportion of American Jews are fourth or more generation or have forebears who are from a number of different generations. Trends in religious observance can be examined by comparing age groups and by comparing the data from the national surveys carried out every ten years. From a comparison of age cohorts in a 1997 survey, Steven Cohen reported that, although the decline of ethnic measures of Jewishness was age related, an age-related decline in religiosity was not supported. Measures of religiosity, such as participation in the Passover seder and lighting Hanukkah candles, show a near uniformity across the age spectrum.[46] A comparison of the 1990 and 2000–01 national surveys (NJPS) also shows that religious behavior has remained largely unchanged; some practices have dropped a few points and others have risen a few points.[47]

Studies of religious patterns among Jewish populations in Europe and Israel do not include data on a number of generations, but the ritual practice of respondents has been compared with that of their parents and these comparisons have shown the same pattern as in the United States: Only a small minority observe more practices than their parents; the majority observe fewer practices but retain at least a minimal number of mostly yearly rituals.[48] The findings from surveys in Israel are particularly interesting with respect to the secularization debate and Judaism because the situation of a Jewish dominant majority allows some comparative test of whether the Jewish minority position in the Diaspora has an influence on Jewish levels of religiosity over and beyond the effects of involvement in modern industrial, urban society.

Religiosity in Israel: Stable Distributions and Secular Trends

Surveys of religiosity conducted in Israel give a somewhat misleading impression that little has changed over time in the religious practice of Israeli Jews. A survey published in 1963 included some rough measures of religious observance, and the distribution of answers was remarkably similar to the distributions found in subsequent surveys asking similar questions, up to the last large-scale survey conducted in 1999. In all the surveys about one-third of the population reported that they observed all or most of the mitzvot, about one-fourth reported that they did not observe the mitzvot, and about two-fifths reported partial observance. Surveys that asked whether respondents were secular or nonreligious reported higher percentages for those responses than those surveys that asked if respondents were entirely nonobservant. This is congruent with findings that show that many respondents who identity as secular or nonreligious observe certain popular religious holiday practices such as lighting Hanukkah candles or participating in the Passover seder.

Three of the surveys (1979, 1991, 1999) provide more detailed data on identification, observances, and beliefs, and these data reinforce the impression that little has changed over time. A classification of identification with respect to religion, widely used in everyday discourse as well as in surveys, distinguishes *dati* (religious), *mesoriti* (traditional), and *lo-dati* (nonreligious) or *hiloni* (secular). Within the religious sector a further distinction made among Israelis and in some surveys is between the *haredim*, or ultra-orthoprax, denoting a segregative lifestyle as well as a strict level of observance, and the *dati*, or orthoprax. These identifications are generally understood to refer to and have been found to correspond with levels of religious observance: *dati*, a strict level; *mesoriti*, a moderate level; and *hiloni*, a low level or nonobservance. Over the time period covered by the surveys, the percentage of "religious" Jews remains unchanged at 17–18 percent, the "traditional" group appears to have declined somewhat in the 1990s from 43 percent in 1991 to 35 percent in 1999, and the "nonreligious" group (including the "antireligious") has increased somewhat from 42 percent in 1979 and 43 percent in 1991 to 48 percent in 1999.

The distribution and pattern of observance indicates a continuum of religiosity rather than any clear-cut polarization between religious and nonreligious Jews, and this has not undergone any significant change over the years. Certain practices, such as not traveling on the Sabbath, are observed by a minority: 22 percent in 1979 and 27 percent in 1999. As noted, some practices are observed by the majority, such as fasting on Yom Kippur (74 percent in 1979, 67 percent in 1999), lighting Hanukkah candles (88 percent in 1979, 71 percent in 1999), and participating in the Passover seder (99 percent in 1979, 85 percent in 1999). However, if there is a trend, it is in the direction of polarization; the minority with strict levels of observance has increased in size, whereas the practices observed by the majority have become somewhat less popular.[49] Among the nonreligious sector there are indications, although no exact figures, of a decline in the religious observance of the rites of passage. More than 90 percent of Jewish parents circumcise their newborn sons, but an increasing number have only the medical procedure without the religious ceremony. In 2001 the Ministry of Health issued permission for medical practitioners to perform the procedure, whereas previously only a mohel, a religious practitioner, was officially entitled to do so. There are increases in the celebration of the bar mitzvah without a religious ceremony and marriages without a religious ceremony, and a number of nonreligious burial sites have been established.[50]

The distribution of responses to questions on beliefs have remained the same: Sixty-four percent in 1979 and 65 percent in 1999 expressed a belief in God; 36 percent in 1979 and 1999 stated that they believed in the coming of the messiah; 56 percent in 1979 believed that the Torah was given to Moses on Mount Sinai and 51 percent in 1999 believed that the Torah precepts are divine commandments.[51] A survey carried out in 2006 found that religious beliefs corresponded closely with religious identifications. For example, belief in the messiah was stated by all respondents who identified as *haredim*, by 83 percent of the "religious" sector, by 47 percent of the "traditional" sector, and by 10 percent of the "secular" Jews.[52]

What might perplex outsiders is that the percentages of Israeli Jews who observe certain religious practices, such as lighting Hanukkah candles and participating in the Passover seder, are higher than the percentage who believe in God. Many Israeli Jews might be described as conforming to a pattern of religious observance without believing.[53] They carry out a few practices, not because of a belief in their divine origins or because they feel a religious obligation but because they are conforming to common practices that express a Jewish Israeli national identity. However, the way that secular Jews carry out the practices often differs substantially from the observance of religious and *mesoriti* Jews. For example, when secular Israelis celebrate the Passover meal, they do not read all the traditional text; they omit some of the traditional symbols, and they introduce meanings of an ironic or sarcastic nature into the text.[54]

The statistics on religiosity, indicating a continuum of levels of observance rather than a dichotomous pattern, obscure differences with regard to the meanings of practices. Almost all the strictly or mostly observant say that their acceptance of the Halacha (code of religious law) is the source of authority for their observance; they observe "because it is a commandment." The reasons given by the less observant for their observance are instrumental or sentimental in nature: "This is what Jews do." "This is the way it was done in my home." "It is more hygienic." Many who fast on Yom Kippur do not do so to beg forgiveness for their sins but as an identity performance and for a number of idiosyncratic reasons. Ninety-eight percent of Israeli Jews attach a mezuzah to the entrance of their homes, but for many this is a declaration of national allegiance rather than one of faith.

Because many of the somewhat observant respondents do not believe in the divine origin of the commandments, they have no problem selecting a few practices that meet their needs of identity and community, and the ceremonies are performed with little or no reference to what the religious law enjoins. Many who light candles on the Sabbath eve do so after sundown and ignore the religious stipulation that the practice should be carried out before sundown.[55] It should not be presumed, therefore, that we can deny the basis for religious-secular divisions because the boundaries between levels of observance are not clear or because self-defined "nonobservers" actually observe a few practices. An important division exists between those for whom the religious commandments represent an absolute and supreme authority, determining an entire way of life, and those who celebrate a few elements of the tradition as noncompulsory and personally chosen folk customs.[56] However, few nonobservers today justify their nonobservance as a matter of principle or by reference to a militant secularist ideology. They are more likely to explain it by a lack of interest or the absence of observance in their families of origin.[57] It is secularization without secularism.

The statistics that give an impression of a stable distribution of religiosity over the years hide trends of secularization and countersecularization. One secularization trend is the decline in the observance of mitzvot among Jews from North Africa and Asia, from the immigrants to the second generation. With respect to the relationship between religious observance, geographic origins, and generational changes, the 1999 survey reinforces what has been shown in previous surveys.

First, it shows that Israelis born in Africa or Asia have much higher levels of observance and are far less likely to identify as nonreligious or antireligious than those born in the West. Second, there are no significant differences in observance and identity patterns between the Western-born and the Israeli-born with Western-born fathers. With regard to certain popular holidays (Passover, Hanukkah), the second generation of Western origin demonstrates slightly higher levels of observance than the first generation. Third, apart from the most popular holidays, the level of observance of second-generation Israeli-born Jews with African or Asian fathers is lower than that of first-generation African- or Asian-born Jews.[58] Fourth, subsequently, the differences between the second generation of Asian or African origin and the second generation of Western origin are less than the differences between the first-generation categories.[59] Fifth, the levels of practice and belief of the more recent immigrants from the former Soviet Union, who now account for one-fifth of the Israeli Jewish population, are consistently lower than the levels for all other categories. Even the most popular practices are celebrated by 40 percent or less of former Soviet Union Jews.

One might have expected that the intergenerational declines within the Asian and African category and the low observance levels of the more recent immigrants from the former Soviet Union would have reduced the overall levels of religiosity of Israeli Jews over time. In fact, as we have seen, surveys have continued to show a remarkably stable distribution. At least part of the answer to this puzzle is that the decline in religiosity has been in sectors with birth rates that are considerably lower than those in the orthoprax and especially the ultra-orthoprax sector, in which the birth rate is more than three times that of the secular population. It would also be misleading to conclude from the decline of the observance of the stricter mitzvot among Jews from Asia and North Africa that the trend among them is simply one of secularization. It is significant that almost no change in the proportion (about half) who identify as *mesoriti* has occurred from the first to the second generation of Jews of Asian or North African origin. This large sector is often overlooked by Israeli public discourse, which tends to divide the Israeli Jewish population into two camps—religious and secular.

Most of those Israeli Jews who identify as *mesoriti* emphasize their ties to the religious tradition, the tradition of their parents, but they select rituals from that tradition with little concern for halachic standards and consistency. For example, they may go to synagogue on Sabbath morning and travel to the sea or to a park on Sabbath afternoon. The term *mesoriti* has highly favorable connotations for Jews of Asian and North African origin, but it is not presented as an alternative stance to the orthoprax establishment, which they accept as the legitimate religious authority, although they largely ignore its decrees.[60]

For Israeli Jews of Asian and North African origin "tradition" denotes the ties of religion to family and communities of origin. Whereas among Israelis of European origins ethnic synagogues based on country of origin rarely continued beyond the immigrant generation, among Middle Eastern Israelis they have continued in the second generation, especially in the lower strata.[61] The close relationship of religion and ethnic community among Jews from North Africa is clearly indicated in the revival of the veneration of saints and the pilgrimages to the tombs of saints on the anniversary of their deaths.

A secularization trend, which is barely indicated in the statistics on religious observance and belief, is the adoption of secular leisure patterns by a large sector of the younger generation of Jews who identify as *datiim* (religious). In contrast with the ultra-orthoprax or *haredim* who reject the secular world and are either non-Zionist or anti-Zionist, the majority of Israelis who identify as *datiim* support Zionism, particularly in its religious forms, and have adopted a compartmentalized response to the secular world; their observance of the mitzvot is compartmentalized from their acceptance of secular education and modern styles of living. Many religious Jews live in neighborhoods and apartment buildings with secular Jews, and although a study of a mixed Tel Aviv suburb showed that the friendships of religious Jews tend to be restricted to other religious Jews, the younger generation appears to have a greater openness to friendships, including romantic attachments, with secular Jews.[62]

The Zionist or nationalist religious have always been open to the influence of secular culture, but in recent years this influence has widened to secular patterns of behavior, which the religious norms and educational institutions of this sector have sought to avoid. In the past the consumption of secular culture among the nationalist religious population was justified by an emphasis on high culture, such as classical music, and the tendency was to reject frequenting popular places of entertainment. This has changed, as religious youth are seen in cinemas, pubs, and dance halls where, in contradiction to religious norms, the sexes mix and dance together. Certain pubs cater to a young religious clientele who have their own popular music groups and appreciate satires on life in religious society, but others have moved into realms formerly confined to secular youth, such as backpacking in India, Southeast Asia, and South America. One attempt by the religious establishment to keep these trends within their institutional auspices was their encouragement of the formation in the late 1980s of a college of film and television for religious students. The intention of the college's founders was to develop media that would convey religious messages, and when some students' films included critical representations of religious society, such as its treatment of women, a concerned administration imposed a stricter censorship.[63]

Neotraditionalism: The Haredim

The trend of a diminishing decline of religiosity among the majority has occurred at the same time as a growth in the ultra-Orthodox, or, as they are called in Israel, the *haredim*. *Haredi* is a Hebrew epithet meaning a God-fearing devotee. The term was used in the past to denote any Jew who was punctilious about religion, but in the last fifty years it has been increasingly used to designate those Jews who go beyond orthodoxy or, a more appropriate term in the context of Judaism, orthopraxy.

After World War II the future of ultra-orthoprax Judaism seemed bleak; most of the traditionalist communities of eastern Europe were destroyed by the Holocaust, and it was expected that the defections to secular society would accelerate in the open societies of the West and Israel. Instead, the last decades of the twentieth century saw a considerable strengthening and growth of the ultra-orthoprax communities, both in the West and in Israel. By building an enveloping system of socialization and education, separated from the wider society, the *haredim* succeeded in retaining the vast majority of those born within the communities, and, as a consequence of high birth rates, they have grown in numbers. The *haredim* in the United States now represent about one-third of orthoprax Jewry, and they have spread in the New York area from their established neighborhoods in Brooklyn to *haredi* "villages" in the suburbs.[64] In Israel they now constitute 6–10 percent of the Israeli Jewish population[65] and have spread from their centers in Jerusalem and Tel Aviv to an increasing number of neighborhoods and towns.[66]

The *haredim* conform to a comprehensive and enveloping system of religious law that they believe was the way of life of the vast majority of European Jews before the incursions of modernity. Although ultra-orthopraxy in Israel has spread to the Sephardim, or Jews of North African and Asian origins, in recent years, most *haredim* are Ashkenazim and trace their Diaspora origins to the Jewish communities of eastern Europe, which, before the incursions of secularism, provide their models of emulation, an emulation that extends to their distinctive clothes and appearance. The men grow beards and dangling sideburns, and many wear long black topcoats and wide-brimmed black hats. Women's dress is governed by rules of modesty: Arms are covered at least to the elbows, dresses and skirts cover most of the legs, and dark stockings are worn. Upon marriage, women cover their hair or shave their heads and wear a wig. Conspicuous by their appearance, the *haredim* concentrate in particular neighborhoods and conduct much of their lives within the confines of their own institutions, which in Israel have attained an autonomous or semi-autonomous status.

Most *haredim* deny that Zionism and the state of Israel have any positive religious meaning, and a minority are vehemently anti-Zionist, charging Zionism in all its forms, religious as well as secular, as a betrayal of the Jewish people's destiny and covenant with God. Among the more radical *haredim* Zionism is seen as a satanic force that is held responsible for the disasters that have befallen the Jewish people in recent times. They regard the establishment of a Jewish state before the coming of the messiah as a blasphemy that holds up messianic redemption.[67] However, most *haredim* in Israel have accommodated to the state on whose support they depend to finance their institutions and way of life: Their independent educational systems are financed by the state without subjecting them to the requirements of the state educational program; housing in new segregated neighborhoods is subsidized; and because the participation of the *haredim* in the workforce is low, many *haredi* families are dependent on welfare.

The *haredim* are divided into a number of camps, some of which are vigorously opposed to each other. In addition to the general division between Hasidim and Lithuanians or *mitnagdim* ("opponents" of the Hasidim), further subdivisions are based on loyalties to particular religious leaders and Hasidic courts, and in Israel in recent years a division has emerged between Ashkenazic *haredim* and Sephardic *haredim* of North African and Asian origins.[68] All the *haredim*, however, condemn the secular lifestyles of other Jews and seek to distance themselves from them. In Israel separateness is sought even in those realms where the *haredim* are dependent on secular Jews, such as health and public transport. Two hospitals catering only to the *haredim* have been established, and requests have been made for separate buses in which the sexes are separated. One significant development in recent years, reflecting both the influence of the wider society and the concern to maintain a separate culture, has been the growth of *haredi* newspapers and magazines with modern-style graphics.[69]

The *haredim* depict the eastern European Jewish communities of the past as the ideal model and their communities today as a faithful expression of that ideal. In fact, the success of the present-day *haredi* society as a neotraditionalist society can be attributed to its differences from the traditional societies of the past, which are now cast in the mold of the present.[70] From a religiosity in the eastern European communities transmitted by the family and local community, religiosity in the contemporary *haredi* population is rooted in texts and transmitted by the schools and yeshivas, the postschool religious educational institutions that have become the focal institutions of the community. In the eastern European communities, the family and the basic school (heder) taught a rudimentary knowledge of the religious texts necessary for the appropriate observance of the mitzvot. Scholarship was an important value and basis for status, but the yeshivas instructed only a small proportion, the scholarly elite of the community. In contrast, the contemporary community is a "society of scholars" in which a large proportion of the male population attends the yeshivas for many years.

After the Holocaust, when only a few thousand children were in the *haredi* educational system, the yeshivas were seen by the *haredim* as the principal means by which a Torah-based society could be rebuilt and the youth kept apart from the secular world. Unlike the former eastern European communities, the traditional way of life could no longer be taken for granted and had to be constructed on the basis of voluntary communities in which the commitment to a strictly religious way of life was more overt. Within an encompassing framework *haredi* males are expected to devote long years to Talmud learning, a way of life that is presented as requiring great effort and devotion and as absolutely essential for the survival of the Jewish people. Removed from the concerns of earning a living and often sheltered from the pressures of families, yeshiva students stress stringent interpretations of the religious law. The tradition of written codes has gained in strength at the expense of folk traditions anchored in families and local communities, and younger *haredim* often supersede their fathers in their religious knowledge and strict conformity to the Halacha.[71]

Long years in the yeshivas have limited the participation of the *haredim* in the workforce. This is particularly the case in Israel, where government subsidies for the *haredi* way of life are far more extensive that those provided in America. The proportion of *haredi* men (ages 25–54) who are not working because of full-time yeshiva attendance rose from 41 percent in 1980 to 60 percent by 1996.[72] Nurit Stadler has shown that withdrawal from the workforce has been legitimized within the Israeli yeshivas by drawing on and emphasizing particular religious interpretations of work and income earning that were previously considered of little importance in rabbinic interpretative traditions. The traditional rabbinic emphasis on hard work and activism in the world has been replaced by interpretations that stress the role of miraculous events in economic maintenance, the need to abandon profane work in order to worship God, and the devaluation of work as a distraction from the higher calling of study and as an obstacle to salvation.[73]

The *haredim* in Israel are exempt from what most Israelis view as an essential duty for Jews of Israeli citizenship: conscription into the army. An agreement on the "deferral" from army service or nonconscription of a certain number of yeshiva students was reached soon after the establishment of the state, when about 400 *haredim* were of the age of conscription. The provisions for nonconscription were extended in 1977 when Agudat Israel, the principal *haredi* party, entered the Likud-led coalition government. Since then the number of yeshiva students has risen considerably; since the late 1990s more than 30,000 each year, 9 percent of the age group, received deferral, and most of these will probably never serve. The nonconscription of the *haredim* has signaled their apartness from the rest of the Jewish Israeli population. At least until recently, most Israeli Jews have served in the army, and for many men the military extends into many years of reserve service.

Considerable resources are required not only to cover the running costs of the yeshivas but also to cover the living expenses of the students and, when they marry and have children, their families. Wives are often the major income earners during the years when their husbands are studying, but their limited education and frequent childbearing restrict their earnings. There are rich *haredim*, especially in the United States, who contribute to the support of both the American and Israeli yeshivas, but in Israel it is the welfare state that has been a necessary condition for the support of this system.

The elementary nature of the nonreligious education of the *haredim*, their self-segregation, and their concern that their jobs not disturb their lifestyle and study have limited their occupational possibilities. There are religious roles (teachers, ritual slaughterers, circumcisers), small shops and businesses, the diamond trade, and some areas of finance. The rapid expansion of the technology sector has created jobs of midlevel expertise that do not require postsecondary education. In recent years a few *haredi* organizations have been founded to provide nonreligious education and professional instruction, particularly in the areas of computer studies, but such developments have provided opportunities for only a small proportion.

Limited occupational opportunities result in low incomes among the *haredim*, especially in Israel, where *haredi* society is more insular and restrictive. Many *haredi* families in Israel live below the poverty line, and half of the income of the *haredim* comes from public support compared with one-seventh of the income of the non-*haredi* population. Not all young *haredi* males are suited to many years in the yeshiva, and the nonlegitimization of army service together with the related restrictions on entering the workforce have left little alternative apart from idleness and petty crime. At the other end of the social scale in the *haredi* community are what have been termed the yuppie *haredim*, a wealthy sector who live in spacious apartments in new *haredi* areas. This stratum has been in the forefront of the penetration of consumerism and entertainment into *haredi* society.[74]

Polarization

Two trends have been delineated so far: (1) the majority trend of stabilization of religious practice at a minimal level and (2) the minority trend of greater religious stringency. The impression of polarization between the secularized majority and the ultra-orthoprax minority is greater in Israel, where the heightened prominence of the *haredim* in the public sphere, the large sums allotted to their institutions and welfare, their refusal to serve in the army, and their confrontational tactics have been met by anti-*haredi* sentiments. The way that large sectors of the Israeli population identify themselves with respect to religion, as either religious or secular has also contributed to the impression of polarization. In contrast, the context of religious pluralism in America has encouraged American Jews to differentiate themselves along denominational lines, to accept the legitimacy of different forms of Judaism, and to formulate different meanings of a "religious Jew."[75] In Israel, religious movements of religious accommodation to modernity have had little success; there is an orthoprax establishment, and for most Israeli Jews, secular and religious alike, "religious Jew" is understood to mean orthoprax.[76] The depth of this polarization should not be exaggerated, however. Many secular Jews may oppose what they regard as the limitations imposed on them by the orthoprax establishment and its supporters in Israel, but most do not attack religion per se because they define Israel as a Jewish state and this necessarily requires their tacit acceptance of its religious symbols.

The religious stringency of the ultra-orthoprax makes them a group apart, but, with respect to the majority of Jews in both the United States and Israel, the distribution and pattern of observance indicates a continuum of religiosity rather than any clear-cut polarization between religious and nonreligious Jews. A thesis of polarization would be persuasive, however, if it could be shown that the middle part of the continuum is diminishing in comparison with the two extremes. Steven Cohen has drawn on the data from the 2000–01 NJPS to make a case that the proportion of American Jews located in the middle range of the Jewish identity spectrum has been declining and that the proportions located at the two ends of the spectrum have been increasing. Cohen argues that the major division is between the in-married and the intermarried. Larger proportions of the in-married than the intermarried belong to synagogues, attend them on the High Holy Days, observe Passover and Hanukkah, fast on Yom Kippur, and light Sabbath candles. With respect to the ethnic dimensions of Jewish identity, the differences between the two categories are even more evident: Much larger proportions of the in-married than the intermarried report that most of their friends are Jewish, feel that being Jewish is very important to them, have been to Israel, contribute to Jewish charities, and send their children to Jewish preschools and Jewish youth groups.

Cohen notes that the low levels of Jewish religious practice and Jewish involvement among those Jews who intermarried, as well as the fact of their intermarriage, derive from their parents' low levels on the various dimensions. He emphasizes, however, that intermarriage has an independent effect on reducing Jewish religious practice and weakening Jewish identity. As I showed in chapter 8, when a non-Jewish partner converts to Judaism, the couple's levels of Jewish religious observance are likely to be similar to or even higher than those of in-married couples of born Jews. However, most non-Jewish partners do not convert, and Cohen does not view the conversionary marriages as making an essential difference to the development of two distinct populations: in-married and intermarried.[77]

Cohen's portrayal of polarization could be viewed as somewhat at odds with his description of most American Jews as "moderately affiliated." These are the Jews who belong to a Jewish institution, "the average members of Reform and Conservative congregations," who "are not as involved, learned, or pious as the most highly engaged 20–25 percent of American Jews."[78] This suggests another possible type of polarization, that between the moderately affiliated and the highly engaged. One indication of such a polarization in recent years has been the growth of those who identity with Reform Judaism or who express no denominational preference (the "just Jewish" response) on the one hand and the growth of those who identify with Orthodox Judaism on the other. The growth of the Reform and orthoprax sectors has been at the expense of Conservative Judaism. Of those American Jews who express a preference for one of the three major denominations, the proportion favoring Reform Judaism has risen from 38 percent in 1971 to 46 percent in 1990 to 49 percent in 2000–01. The proportion favoring Orthodoxy dropped from 13 percent in 1971 to 7 percent in 1990 but then climbed back to 14 percent in 2000–01. The changes in the proportions of synagogue members show the same trends: Reform members climbed from 29 percent (1971) to 35 percent (1990) to 37 percent (2000–01); Orthodox members dropped from 19 percent (1971) to 16 percent (1991) and then climbed to 23 percent (2000–01); Conservative members dropped from 49 percent (1971) to 43 percent (1991) to 33 percent (2000–01).[79]

A comparison of respondents' denominational identification with the denomination in which they were raised demonstrates the trend toward Reform Judaism and the "just Jewish" response as well as the reversal of Orthodoxy's decline. Although only 26 percent of respondents (in 2000–01) were raised in Reform households, 35 percent chose Reform as their denominational preference. Whereas 33 percent were raised in Conservative households, 27 percent chose Conservative Judaism as their denominational preference. Ten percent chose Orthodoxy as their denominational preference compared with 20 percent who were raised in Orthodox households, but this compares favorably with the 1990 survey, which found that, whereas 22 percent were raised as Orthodox, only 6 percent identified with Orthodoxy.

Reform Judaism in 2000–01 retained most of those raised as Reform: Among those raised as Reform, 78 percent were still Reform, 7 percent were Conservative, 2 percent were Orthodox, and 14 percent were "just Jewish." Among those raised as Conservative, 56 percent stayed Conservative, 28 percent had switched to Reform, 3 percent had switched to Orthodoxy, and 13 percent considered themselves "just Jewish." Among those raised as Orthodox, 42 percent remained Orthodox, 29 percent switched to Conservative Judaism, and 17 percent switched to Reform. The Orthodox rentention rate in 2000–01 was considerably better than in 1990, when only 24 percent of those raised as Orthodox remained Orthodox. The 2000–01 data also showed that among those who were raised as Orthodox, the younger cohort was less likely to leave Orthodoxy than the older cohort.[80]

Although the phenomenon of *ba'alei teshuvah* (literally, those who have returned), that is, Jewish converts to ultra-Orthodoxy, has attracted considerable attention, the data show that relatively few Orthodox Jews were raised as non-Orthodox. On the other hand, the earlier pattern of defection from Orthodoxy has been stemmed and the Orthodox population has grown. Samuel Heilman recently estimated that the number of American Orthodox Jews is 650,000, which represents an increase of 8 percent since 1970.[81] The continuity of allegiance together with the high marriage and birth rates of Orthodox Jews makes it likely that the Orthodox will continue to increase as a proportion of the total denominational population. Although Orthodox synagogue members constitute less than one-fourth of synagogue members, their children represent 40 percent of the youngsters in synagogue-affiliated families.[82]

Commentators have for some time pointed to the development of and increase in Orthodox institutions, especially day schools and yeshivas, as signs of an Orthodox revival. However, it is not so much the increased strength of Orthodoxy that supports a polarization thesis but rather the direction that Orthodoxy has taken in recent years. What used to be called modern Orthodoxy and is now more commonly called centrist Orthodoxy has been giving way to the neotraditionalist forms of ultra-Orthodoxy, or the *haredim*. Samuel Heilman has characterized modern Orthodoxy by its "contrapuntalist" approach to the wider society: the position that there is much to be gained by belonging to plural life-worlds. The modern Orthodox tended to deal with the dissonance and competition between the worlds by compartmentalizing their orthoprax level of observance from their participation in the "nonreligious" institutions and culture of secular society. This position continued for at least thirty years after World War II, but by the last quarter of the twentieth century changes in American society and within Jewish Orthodoxy had made it increasingly difficult to uphold.[83]

The decline in the proportion of Orthodox Jews from the first to the third or fourth generation may have left a core of committed Orthodox Jews, but it was the post–World War II immigrants from Europe, the survivors of the Holocaust and their children, who were in the forefront of the revival of Orthodoxy in the United States in this period. In contrast to the abandonment of Orthodoxy by children of earlier immigrants, the children of the more recent Orthodox immigrants are more likely to maintain the high levels of observance of their parents. Changes in American society were favorable to this development. General prosperity has enabled both modern Orthodox and ultra-Orthodox Jews to develop and expand their institutions, and the greater cultural pluralism has reduced the social costs of Orthodoxy. The modern Orthodox are still concerned with achieving social acceptance in the wider society, but they have found that this is obtainable without abandoning visible expressions of an Orthodox level of observance. The open, pluralistic society makes it easy for Jews to discard their religious practices, but it does not motivate them to do so, and it has permitted the Orthodox to draw sharper boundaries between themselves and the wider society (including non-Orthodox Jews). The replacement of the term *modern Orthodox* by *centrist Orthodox* is an indication of this change, and centrist Orthodox institutions have seen a shift to stricter patterns, such as the elimination of mixed dancing at synagogue functions. Orthodox congregations are now less tolerant toward members who are only nominally Orthodox, and because Orthodox rabbis no longer have to accommodate the varied requirements of communities that are heterogeneous in their religiousity, they are less hesitant to interpret the religious law in a strict fashion.[84]

The questioning of American values by the counterculture beginning in the mid-1960s and the more widespread permissiveness of American society have discouraged the accommodationist stance of modern Orthodox Jews. By the late 1970s many Orthodox Jews saw American society as debased and unredeemable. The aspirations of many modern Orthodox Jews included the education of their children in the elite universities, but they began to have reservations about American higher education as they came to perceive the universities as foci of deplorable values and sinful behavior. To ensure that their children would remain committed to an Orthodox Jewish life, many parents came to depend heavily on the Orthodox day schools. Nearly two-thirds of the Judaica teachers in the day schools are *haredim*, and the trend in the day schools has been to increase the hours devoted to Talmudic studies and to encourage stringent regulations. Some of the young from Orthodox families have rebelled against these trends and have abandoned Orthodoxy, but those who remain are more likely to accept the haredization of Orthodoxy.

Since the 1970s many modern Orthodox parents have sought to reinforce their childrens' Jewish commitment by sending them, after they graduated from the day schools, to Israel for a year's study in a yeshiva. Away from their families and communities and free of the demands for grades and competitive pressures, many youngsters imbibed the emphases of the yeshiva on the study of the Torah as the highest value and the importance of punctitious religious observance. Some decided to forgo or postpone entering a university in order to continue in an Israeli yeshiva or an American yeshiva.

Many Orthodox Jews have adopted the neotraditionalist attribution of supreme authority to the text and tend to accept the views of those who best understand the texts, the yeshiva teachers and rabbis, who discredit the accommodative stance toward the wider society and cooperation with non-Orthodox Jews. The modernist forms of Orthodoxy have been put on the defensive, and many have come to follow the separatism of the ultra-Orthodox. Some Orthodox neighborhoods have become no less ghettorized than those of the *haredim*.[85]

The *dati* (religious) identity in Israel is the equivalent or near equivalent of the Orthodox identity among American Jews. The qualifying terms *modern* or *centrist* are not commonly used in Israel, but, like their American counterparts, many Israeli *datiim* have adopted a compartmentalized response to the secular world. Some of the religious youth in Israel have adopted secular forms of entertainment, but trends within the nationalist religious sector are not in a single direction and many within the sector have sought to strengthen their boundaries with the secular population. Many *dati* families have shown an increased preference to concentrate in their own neighborhoods, and distance from the secular atmosphere of the large cities was one consideration in the establishment of religious settlements in the West Bank. Ariel, a youth religious movement that strictly separates boys and girls, was established as an alternative to B'nei Akiva, the long established religious youth movement that has been criticized for allowing the mixing of sexes. Some parents, dissatisfied with the education provided by the religious sector of the state school system, send their children to elitist religious schools. Class and ethnic factors are also a consideration here; large proportions of the pupils in many of the state religious schools come from low socioeconomic and North African or Asian *mesoriti* backgrounds.[86]

Some of the religious nationalists who have become more stringent in religious practice have become *haredim*. This trend has been encouraged by their disillusionment with secular Zionists, particularly their former allies in the right wing, whose dismantlement of Jewish settlements in the occupied territories is perceived by the religious nationalists as a betrayal of the sacred mission to reclaim the whole of the Land of Israel for the Jews and thereby bring about the process of redemption. Some religious Zionists have concluded that their alliance with secular Zionism was at an end and that a new alliance should be forged with the *haredim*. The haredization of some of the *datiim* together with the move toward radical nationalism of some *haredim* has resulted in a new identity label, *haredi leumi* (nationalist *haredi*).[87]

In addition to attracting a number of the religious nationalists, who are mostly Ashkenazim, the ultra-orthoprax way of life has drawn a small but significant number of *mesoritiim* of North African or Asian origin. What has been termed the haredization of Sephardic Jews of North African or Asian origin has been associated with the success of SHAS (Sephardi Religious Party), established in 1983; SHAS is the first *haredi* party led and supported by Jews of North African and Asian origins. Although the majority of its supporters are not *haredim*, SHAS is a consequence of and has contributed to a process of haredization among Jews of North African or Asian origin. SHAS obtains its highest levels of support in the economically depressed "development" towns with high concentrations of Jews from North Africa. These are the same areas where the most important saint shrines are to be found, but in comparison with the *hillulot*, which represent a renewal of a tradition anchored in family and community, haredization involves the adoption of a tradition of written codes.

In the first years of SHAS's existence a large proportion of its voters were *haredim*, many of whom had transferred their support from the Ashkenazic *haredi* party Agudat Israel to SHAS. The party grew by attracting non-*haredi* voters, especially *masoriti* identifiers who had never previously voted for a *haredi* party. The emergence of SHAS as an independent party was related to the discrimination against and haughtiness toward the *haredim* of North African and Asian origins by the Ashkenazic *haredim*, but the major message of SHAS is that the secular Ashkenazic Zionist establishment took away the heritage of Middle Eastern Jews and drove many into lives of poverty, crime, and drugs. SHAS has canalized social and economic grievances into an ethnoreligious program and has presented itself as the party of a true Judaism, superior to that of the Ashkenazim, and a true Zionism, far superior to that of the secular parties.[88]

SHAS has encouraged haredization among its followers and among the children who are educated within its independent school system and who are encouraged to continue a religious education in yeshivas. The extent of haredization among Jews of North African and Asian origins is difficult to estimate, but it appears that only a minority of SHAS supporters have made the transition from *mesoritiyut* (traditionalism) to either *datiim* or *haredim*. Nevertheless, SHAS's attacks on secular Zionism have contributed to the impression of polarization between the religious and secular sectors of the population.

Discussion

The data presented in this chapter on Jewish populations do not support a simple straight-line secularization thesis according to which there is a continuous decline and foreseeable disappearance of religion. Nor do they support a steady-state model of religion or a model according to which religious declines are countered sooner or later by religious revivals. Although the data point to elements of polarization, they do not support polarization in the sense of two sides moving in opposite directions. There are two trends, both of which have to be understood in terms of the effects of Western patterns of modernization on Judaism. The trend among the majority began with sharp declines in religiosity, followed by a diminishing decline of religiosity, and has now reached a fairly steady state of minimal observance. The trend among a growing minority is toward an even stricter pattern of observance than was prevalent in the pre-emancipation traditional society.

In the United States the Jewish population appears more polarized in its religious and secular patterns than the Christian population. On the secularized side, the proportion of Jews who attend synagogue regularly is considerably smaller than the proportion of Christians who attend church regularly. Jews are also less likely than Christians to assert their agreement with basic religious beliefs or say that religion is important in their lives. If the majority of Jews are more secularized than their Christian counterparts, then the minority of neotraditionalists is less compromising and moving further away from the dominant trends than their Christian counterparts. Whereas Christian evangelicals or conservatives have become less austere and ascetic in recent times, Jewish neotraditionalists have become more severe and militant.

Because Judaism is the closest world religion to Christianity in its involvement in the processes of modernity, explanations for the greater polarization in the Jewish context should be sought in the characteristics of the religion. At least two differences between Judaism and Christianity appear to be relevant. The first is the integral tie between religion and peoplehood or nationhood in Judaism. Accommodation to modernity has been accomplished by focusing on the ethnic component and expressing it symbolically through a few religious rituals. This has meant that the secularized majority and the neotraditionalist minority differ greatly in the meanings that they attribute to the religious symbols and rituals. The second difference, the focus on practice, contributes to the greater polarization of the Jewish population because it lends itself to the establishment and strengthening of clear boundaries for those who wish to defend traditional religion.

In conclusion, the case of Judaism in modern society suggests that the classical thesis of secularization should be modified by attention to polarization. Among most Jews, an often steep decline in religiosity followed the breakup of cohesive local communities, exposure to scientific education and secular beliefs, and an involvement in legal-rational structures. At the same time, the processes of modernization encouraged the countertrend of neotraditionalism. This was not simply a matter of a rejection of modernity, or important aspects of it, by conservatives or fundamentalists who felt threatened by change. The processes of modernity have themselves provided congenial conditions for the growth and strength of neotraditionalism. In Judaism it was the reorganization of traditionalism on the basis of voluntaristic communities and reorganized institutions that produced growth, greater militancy, and a radical alternative to the secularized pattern of the majority.

11. PUBLIC RELIGION, PRIVATIZATION, AND DEPRIVATIZATION IN ISRAEL

Few Israeli sociologists who have written on religion in Israel have attempted to apply concepts and theories from the sociology of religion. They have tended to analyze religion from the perspectives of other subdisciplines, such as ethnicity and political sociology. In an attempt to explain why the sociology of religion has not developed in Israel, Ezra Kopelowitz and Yael Israel-Shamsian argued that American sociologists focus on religion as a private, voluntary realm, whereas most Israeli sociologists conceptualize religion as a public realm, tied to the state.[1]

Israel has no formal state religion, but the state gives its official recognition and financial support to particular religious communities—Jewish, Islamic, and Christian—whose religious authorities and courts are empowered to deal with matters of personal status and family law, such as marriage, divorce, and alimony, that are binding on all members of the communities. The Jewish religious authorities who have the sole state-sanctioned authority to deal with these matters with respect to Israeli Jews are the Orthodox or, a more appropriate term in the context of Judaism, orthoprax rabbinate. As a formally proclaimed Jewish state with Jews making up four-fifths of the population, Jewish religious symbols and ritual are prominent in the public sphere and are generally taken for granted by Israeli Jews, including self-proclaimed secular Jews who practice little or nothing of religion at the private, voluntary level.[2]

Israel does not have civil marriage and divorce, although such ceremonies performed outside Israel are administratively recognized. The absence of such choices is called religious coercion by many secular Israeli Jews, who have negative views of the Orthodox establishment. Surveys show that more than half of Israeli Jews believe that religion and state should be separated in Israel, but the understanding of separation in Israel relates for the most part to removing legislation that limits individual liberties, and it should not be assumed that it extends to desiring a state that is neutral with respect to religious symbols or to opposing public expressions of Jewish religious tradition. A survey conducted in 1999 found that 60 percent of

Israeli Jews favored the introduction of civil marriage, 38 percent would opt for civil marriage if it were available, two-thirds favored the introduction of public transportation on the Sabbath, and 50 percent supported the dismantling of the Chief Rabbinate. However, 52 percent believed that "the state should see to it that public life be conducted according to Jewish religious tradition," and 72 percent agreed that "people should take account of the character of the Sabbath in public."[3] When Israeli Jews were asked about the desired level of religion in public life, half felt that the existing level was as it should be; one-third felt that public life should be less religious than it is, and 16 percent felt that it should be more religious. Thus relatively large numbers, including many who observe few or no religious practices, support the presence of religion, or what is often called Jewish tradition, in public life.[4]

Deprivatization has seldom been discussed in Israel because privatization is not widely recognized. Compared with some Western societies, especially the United States, a significant sector of Israeli Jews identifies as secularist and is highly critical of religious institutions. On the other hand, religion is a major social and political force in Israeli society: Religious political parties and movements have both responded to and had considerable impact on political policies and the Jewish-Palestinian or Jewish-Arab conflict. The prominence of public religion in Israel has been taken for granted by both the Israeli public and most Israeli sociologists. In the following account I attempt to explain how this came about with reference to two dimensions of secularization: differentiation and privatization.

Differentiation and Undifferentiation

The state of Israel was founded by secularized Jews from Europe who established institutions differentiated from religion in accord with Western models, but a number of factors limited the differentiation of national and religious values and political and religious institutions. First, the new state was formed as a Jewish state and, given the integral link between Judaism and the Jewish people, national symbols drew on the religious tradition. Second, the dominant ideology of the state founders included secularized forms of traditional religious ideas, such as messianism. And third, the political strategy of the secular founders included accommodations to the ultra-orthoprax and religious Zionist sectors and, at a later date, to the predominantly nonsecular Jewish immigrants from North Africa and Asia.

A Jewish State and Its Symbols

The most basic reason for the prominence of public religion in Israel is that the Israeli state was founded as a Jewish state, and the vast majority of its Jewish citizens have identified with it on this ethnonational and, because of the historical correspondence of the Jewish people and Judaism, religious basis. The Declaration of Independence left open the interpretation of who is Jewish in the Jewish state. If "Jewish" was interpreted in secular nationalist terms, a person's simple declaration that he or she was Jewish would have been sufficient to secure citizenship. Such a possibility was rejected by subsequent laws and government agencies that have defined a Jew according to the halachic formulation: "a person born of a Jewish mother, or who converted to Judaism, and is not a member of another religion." Although the religious parties have been prominent in equating Jewish nationality with the religious definition of a Jew, this formulation was supported by the secular political leadership who rejected a liberal Western definition of citizenship in favor of a definition that, although religious, provided a primordial foundation for national classification and identity.[5]

Although the formal definition of citizenship includes non-Jews, mainly Palestinian Arabs, when Israeli Jews refer to their "Israeli identification," they generally understand by this their commonality with other Jewish citizens. The state is conceived by many Israeli Jews not as an abstract entity with interests of its own, independent of its citizens, but as a communitarian entity, an extension of the Jewish community.[6] Unlike Western societies, democratic norms in Israel did not emerge from a historical struggle against the constraints of the state, and no traditions uphold a separation between the regulated domain of the state and the voluntary domain of civil society.[7]

The importance of religion in the public sphere in modern Western states was limited by the liberal ideal that religion was irrelevant to membership of the polity, and Jews were politically emancipated on that basis. Although mainstream Zionists thinkers from Theodor Herzl onward stressed that the future state for Jews would follow the liberal principle of extending equal rights to all its citizens, the principle of universal civil equality stated in the Declaration of Independence has been subordinated in practice to the particularistic character of a Jewish state.[8] A fusion of religion and state was signaled by the choice of the state's symbols. As the official symbol of the state, a motif of seven stars, symbolizing secular Enlightenment, was rejected in favor of the seven-branch candelabra that played an important role in the temple rites of antiquity. The colors of the national flag with the Star of David at its center are blue and white, the traditional colors of the prayer shawl, and the flag's blues stripes on a white background follow the pattern on the shawl.[9]

Socialist Zionism as a "Secular Religion"

Somewhat paradoxically, the prominence of public religion in Israel followed from the goal of the most important Jewish groups in the Zionist settlement in Palestine and the establishment of the state to create a Jewish society in which a secularized nationalism would replace religion as an identity and culture. The early Zionist immigrants, who came to be known as *halutzim* (pioneers), were mostly from eastern Europe, where, around the turn of the nineteenth century, they had adopted secularist-socialist nationalist identities. Most had grown up in religious homes and were familiar with the beliefs and practices of the tradition, but they had come to reject religion as a repressive force keeping the Jews in chains. Some accused religion of usurping the true bases of national identity—land, language, and the state—and as they constructed a national identity as "New Hebrews" or "Israelis," they insisted on a clear differentiation between nationality and religion, signaled by substituting "people of Israel" for God when they drew on biblical and traditional literature. Their problem was that, if they were to retain some degree of continuity with the past of the people with whom they identified, they had to acknowledge and deal with the fact that their nation's past was bound to religion.[10]

The modern migrations of Jews to Palestine are conventionally divided into a number of waves or aliyahs ("ascensions"). The settlers of the first aliyah (1882–1903) wished to create a society based on Jewish labor and the absence of economic exploitation, but they were not antireligious and they became conventional farmers. It was among the second (1904–14) and the third (1919–23) aliyahs, which included many individuals and groups who wished to fuse Zionism and various forms of socialism, that we find the most militant secularists. These migrants rejected the "bourgeois" and traditional religious life of the Diaspora Jewish communities and saw themselves as pioneers of an entirely different Jewish society to be based on a life of labor in the Land of Israel. They founded the institutions of what came to be known as the New Yishuv (settlement), including agricultural settlements, especially the kibbutzim, various socialist Zionist political parties, military forces, and the Histadrut (Federation of Labor), which combined trade union activities, building and industry, banking and insurance, marketing, transport, housing, and various social services.

Most of the immigrants of the fourth (1924–31) and fifth (1932–36) aliyahs also came from Poland with a significant minority from Germany, and although most were secularized Jews, their attitudes toward religion tended to be more moderate and less ideological than the second and third aliyah groups. They wished to continue the urban, predominantly middle-class life that they had known in the Diaspora, and a private sector, with accompanying values of individual achievement and private consumption, developed alongside the socialist and public modes of production. Interrelationships among these sectors developed in the 1930s and 1940s and increased considerably after the establishment of the state in 1948. The revolutionary zeal of the earlier aliyahs was not maintained, but Jews from the second and third aliyahs continued to be the most politically dominant and to set the secularist tone of the Yishuv and the early state.

The attempts to differentiate between religion and nation and—once the state was established—between religion and state were beset by forces that limited that differentiation or resulted in dedifferentiation. Secularist Jews felt a tension between their goals of transforming Jewish culture into a secular nationalism and settling Jews within the territory of Zion or Eretz Israel (Land of Israel), which was to be the territory of an independent state.[11] Although some western European Jews had considered other territories, particularly Uganda, as possible areas for a separate Jewish political entity, eastern European Zionists had rejected such schemes and insisted on "Zion" as the only possible site for a Jewish state. The moral right of Jews to immigrate and settle was expressed in the term "Land of Israel," which implied an essential link between a geographic place, "the Land," and the Jewish people, "Israel."[12]

As for other emergent nation-states, the particular territory of the Jewish nation was a pivotal factor and was sacralized in Zionism. The territorial ethos was inculcated in the socialization and educational practices instituted in the prestate Jewish settlement, the Yishuv: an emphasis on nature, geography, and agriculture in the school syllabi and frequent cross-country treks, which were called spiritual journeys. The landscape was mystified in art, and archaeology became an important discipline that located and recovered ancient, particularly Israelite, settlements.[13] Zion, however, was the land that the religion taught had been promised to the Jews by God, and the return to Zion had remained the promise of Jewish messianism throughout the almost 2,000 years in *galut* (exile). The sacralization of the land by secular Zionism was difficult, if not impossible, to dissociate from its sacred status within traditional religion.

One way secular Zionists sought to dissociate their sacred foci from that of traditional religion was their rejection of *galut*. Jews in the Diaspora prayed for the return to Zion, but life in exile, according to the secular Zionists, was a deformed one. Secular Zionists opposed religion, not only because they believed it untrue and repressive but also because they saw it as the core of Jewish life in exile. Some saw traditional Judaism as the principal cause of *galut*, and the deliverance from Judaism was a necessary condition for the deliverance from exile and a true national renaissance. The negation of the Diaspora was synonymous with the negation of Judaism.[14]

For the second aliyah manual labor was an absolute moral value that was to redeem the Jewish people from all the evils of Jewish life in the Diaspora. The religion of labor was to replace the traditional religion of the Diaspora, but in promoting this secular religion, the ideologists of the second aliyah evoked traditional symbols and language.[15] Aharon David Gordon (1856–1922), an elder ideologist of the second aliyah, argued that nationality had a cosmic element, a blending of the natural landscape with the spirit of the people who lived there. As a nation in exile, the Jews had become separated from their corporate and individual souls, and they could become whole again only by returning to a life of nature in their homeland.[16]

The Zionist pioneers saw themselves as realizing, in a secular fashion, the diasporic dreams of redemption, messianism, and the realization of God's kingdom on earth. In place of the passive expectation of redemption that Jews traditionally believed would come with the arrival of the messiah, the pioneers saw themselves as leading the nation in its self-redemption. God and a personal messiah had no part in this epic of national liberation, but metaphysical and deterministic elements remained. The return to Zion was a "miracle" or a "miraculous stage in history," and a "law of redemption" determined the progress of Jewish history. Expressions such as "rebirth," "the dawn of redemption," "the lost generation of slavery and first of redemption" recurred in the writings and speeches of the pioneers, and many believed that they were "building the Third Temple" in the political sense. Holocaust Day, established after the War of Independence, reinforced the theme of redemption. The expression "Holocaust and Rebirth," in addition to being a memorial for the victims, articulated an implicit theme of Zionist redemption.[17]

As the negation of diasporic history, Zionist redemption was viewed as a renewal of the Jewish or Israelite history in antiquity. The Jewish past was divided into two periods—antiquity and exile—and this binary model portrayed antiquity as the positive period when the ancient Hebrew nation fought for its independence and enjoyed periods of autonomous political, social, and cultural life. Zionist historiography focused especially on the period of the Second Temple and on Judea's wars against imperial forces, culminating in the Maccabees' revolt against the Syrians and the Jewish revolts against the Romans. The eighteen centuries of exile were portrayed uniformly as a negative period in which the loss of direct contact with the Land of Israel weakened the Jews' shared experience of nationhood and as a period when the Jews suffered constant persecution as a submissive and cowed people. The common use of the term *Hebrew* during the prestate period implied both symbolic continuity with the forebears of antiquity and a contrast with the "Jews" of the *galut*. When the new state was founded, it was represented as the direct successor to the commonwealth periods of Jewish independence in antiquity.[18]

The major text for the account of antiquity was the Tanakh (Old Testament), which became for secular Zionists part and parcel of their rejection of *galut*. Judaism in the Diaspora had become focused on the Talmud, particularly the Babylonian Talmud and the rabbinic responsa, and the Bible had been relegated to the margins by rabbinic Judaism. For the socialist Zionists, the Bible, stripped of its supernatural elements, told of the glorious past of the Israeli people; it linked that past to their present, and it justified their socialism and the Jewish right of settlement. The recent and contemporary history of the conquest and settlement of the land and the victories over the British and Arab adversaries were presented as actualizations of biblical stories. Non-Marxist Jewish socialists claimed that the origins of socialist ideas could be found in the Bible, especially in the books of Isaiah and Amos.[19]

The basis of traditional Jewish belief, as told in the Bible and celebrated in religious holidays, was that God repeatedly saved the people of Israel from their adversaries. In the Zionist interpretations and retelling of the biblical narratives, the intervention and power of God was replaced by the strength of the Israelites, and the references to God in traditional prayers were replaced by "the people of Israel." The theme of the victory of the few over the many was repeated in the retelling of both the myths of antiquity and accounts of recent Jewish victories over their adversaries. The Masada myth, which was not part of traditional Judaism, told of the fierce defense by a small number of Jewish fighters against a large Roman army and the choice of the fighters to commit suicide rather than be taken prisoners and live as slaves. The site of Masada became a sacred place to which schoolchildren, youth groups, and soldiers would make ritual hikes and ascend on foot to the remains of the fortress where they would swear oaths to the nation and homeland.

Memorials of more recent heroes also became sacred places and sites of pilgrimage. The most important was Tel Chai, which commemorated the stand of Hebrew fighters, led by one-armed Yosef Trumpeldor, against a much larger and better equipped Arab force. Martyred Hebrews such as Trumpeldor were viewed as following in the footsteps of the heroes of antiquity with death as a sanctification of the homeland replacing the sanctification of God's name. These national heroes were glorified in songs and poems, and the anniversaries of their deaths were observed in schools. The theme of sacrifice was transformed from submission to the divine will, as symbolized in the Bible by the story of Abraham and Isaac, to an important means for the realization of Zionism.[20]

The link between the biblical past and the Zionist present was reinforced by the observance of sacred holidays, both traditional holidays refashioned by Zionism and new holidays that celebrated socialist ideology (May Day) and commemorated events of modern Zionist history (Balfour Declaration Day, Tel Chai Day). The most important holidays remained the traditional ones, observed according to their dates in the traditional Jewish calendar but transformed to conform to the secular and nationalist values of Zionism. The adoption of traditional holidays was a selective one; those holidays that dwelled on national conflicts and celebrated the victories of ancient Hebrews over their enemies were the most prominent (Hanukkah, Passover, Purim), whereas important holidays of traditional Judaism that lacked these themes were largely ignored (Yom Kippur, Tisha b'Av). The commemorative accounts of the holidays focused on human rather than divine agency. The traditional Hanukkah (Festival of Lights), which celebrated the rededication of the Temple in 165 B.C.E. and the miraculous resupply of oil sufficient for lighting the Temple's lamps for eight days, was replaced by a celebration of the Maccabees' heroism and victory over the Seleucids.[21]

Whereas important holiday rituals were traditionally observed by families in their homes, in the Zionist versions they became communal rituals that mobilized individuals to identify with the community and nation. The emphasis on communally focused rituals was especially evident in the kibbutzim, the agricultural settlements established on communistic principles. The earliest kibbutz members believed that the "religion of work and pioneering" sanctified their whole lives and that there was no need to set aside days for collective remembrance or special rituals. They thought that observing religious holidays was a reactionary practice that contradicted their desire to be born anew without a past or a tradition. Once the kibbutzim evolved from youth movements to fixed settled communities and the rebellious nature of the "religion of pioneering" declined, traditional holidays were reintroduced in forms that expressed kibbutz values and their way of life with an emphasis on the connection of the holidays to the agricultural cycle. Shavuot, traditionally a celebration of the giving of the Torah, was the first of the holidays to be reinstated in the kibbutzim, where it was renewed as a celebration of the first crops.

Passover, with its story of the Israelites' escape from their Egyptian oppressors and its coincidence with the beginning of the harvest season, would appear to be well suited to secular reformulation, but it was little celebrated by the early kibbutz members. Unlike most holidays, which were traditionally centered in the synagogue, the most central Passover ritual was the first night's family seder, when the Haggadah, the telling of the Israelite flight from Egypt, was read. It has been suggested that fond memories of the traditional meal in the parental homes in eastern Europe might have hindered Passover's transformation by the settlers. New Passover ceremonies appeared only at the beginning of the 1930s with newly composed Haggadot in which references to God were deleted or transformed and the coincidence with spring, together with the theme of freedom, was emphasized. The early kibbutz members had enacted parodies of the traditional seder, but once the communally celebrated seder was well established, the ceremony regained its seriousness.[22] Secular Zionists made little effort to transform rituals that focused on the individual, and many continued to observe the rites of passage, often in their traditional forms. Circumcision was performed on practically all newborn males, although some dispensed with the religious ceremony. Most boys had a bar mitzvah, and no secular versions were devised for the marriage ceremony.[23]

Over the last three or four decades many kibbutzim have made changes to their observance of the festivals and rituals. The agricultural components of the festivals declined as industry became central to the economic activities of the kibbutzim. Some of the more socially radical themes lost their relevance or ability to generate sentiment, and some of the formerly discarded traditional holidays, such as Rosh Hashanah (New Year) and Yom Kippur, which have no relation to nature or important events in the nation's past, were reintroduced. In most cases these changes did not represent a return to Orthodox Judaism but rather a more flexible combination of tradition and modernity. In the case of Rosh Hashanah, few kibbutz members attended traditional prayer meetings; they participated in readings and songs that were drawn from ancient and contemporary Jewish literature.[24]

Compromise and Accommodation: The Ultra-Orthodox, Religious Zionists, and Jews from North Africa and Asia

The distaste of the socialist Zionists of the early aliyahs toward religion was reinforced by their perceptions of the Old Yishuv (old settlement), which they regarded as an extension of exile in the Land of Israel.[25] The Jews of the Old Yishuv, predominantly of European origins, led a life regulated by and devoted to the study of the Torah or religious law. Their immigration had been motivated solely by religious considerations; they sought a way of life that was not threatened by the Haskalah (Jewish Enlightenment) and other secular trends in Europe and could be conducted without the worldly pressures of having to make a living. They depended on a system of economic contributions from the Diaspora communities, and they saw in their economic inactivity and material dependence on others an expression of the highest Jewish values: an opportunity to devote themselves to prayer and religious study. The secularist immigrants saw the Old Yishuv as a deformed and parasitic society, and they were seen in turn by the Old Yishuv as the worst representations of all that was evil and dangerous in Zionism.[26]

During the period of the British mandate, changes occurred in the attitude of many orthoprax Jews toward Zionism, and although many of the ultra-orthoprax remained non-Zionist or anti-Zionist, a modus vivendi developed between the more moderate orthoprax, including an increasing number of religious Zionists, and the secular Zionist leadership. Mizrachi, the political party of the religious Zionists, which later changed its name to Mafdal (National Religious Party), was established in 1902 as a faction within the World Zionist Organization, and in the Yishuv its leaders cooperated with the secular Zionists and gave de facto recognition to the secular-led society. Mizrachi leaders saw their party's main role as upholding the essential precepts of Judaism within the public sphere, and after World War I they formulated the statement, "The private sphere is not our concern, but rather the public violation of religious precepts."[27] Although, at first, the secular Zionist leadership tried to ignore the demands of the religious Zionists, such as obligatory kashrut (dietary laws) in restaurants, they accepted that the Sabbath should be recognized as a day of rest, and they became more compromising in order to preserve unity and avoid alienating religiously observant workers.[28]

The most important party representing the ultra-Orthodox was Agudat Israel (Union of Israel), which was established in Europe in 1912 as an anti-Zionist religious movement with the aim of protecting the semi-autonomous political and legal status of traditional Jewish life and opposing secularization and secularism. Agudat Israel vehemently opposed Zionism as an ideology, but it supported efforts to settle Jews in Palestine as a means of easing the plight of Diaspora Jews, and it entered into negotiation with secular Zionists to ensure the religious autonomy of its sector. This stance continued after the establishment of the state, although they declared that they were still living in exile and that a true Jewish state had to await the coming of the messiah. The more extreme ultra-Orthodox groups, Edah Haredit and Neturei Karta, rejected cooperation with secular Zionists and any recognition of the new state.[29]

Although the secular Zionists were by far the most dominant and powerful sector in the Yishuv, their political leaders sought a compromise with the religious sectors in order to obtain their support, or at least neutralize their opposition, to the founding of the state. Agudat Israel had threatened to appear separately before the United Nations fact-finding commission for Palestine if its demands were not met. In a letter to Agudat Israel, David Ben-Gurion and two others made promises with respect to orthoprax control of religion in the public sphere, and they made assurances that the principal arrangements that prevailed in the Yishuv would be maintained in the new state. These arrangements covered Saturday as the national day of rest, the observance of dietary laws in public institutions, the exclusive jurisdiction of orthoprax religious courts over marriage and divorce, and the autonomy of the religious educational system. The arrangements were enacted into the laws of the new state, such as the Rabbinical Courts Jurisdiction (Marriage and Divorce)

Law of 1953 and the State Education Law, which established two state systems, one secular and one religious, the latter under the de facto control of Mizrachi. The separate Labor Zionist school system was abolished, but the ultra-orthoprax were permitted to continue their independent school systems.[30]

The secular political leaders accommodated the ultra-orthoprax by allowing them considerable institutional, albeit state-financed, autonomy, but they could not hope to include the ultra-orthoprax under a unified symbol system. A unified symbol system to unite most Israeli Jews was considered imperative as the population became more heterogeneous in their cultural backgrounds. Of particular importance was the immigration of large numbers of Jews from North Africa and Asia in the first two decades of the state. During the period of the British mandate, only 10 percent of Jewish immigrants came from Asia and Africa, and, at the time of independence, Jews of Middle Eastern origin made up 10–15 percent of the total Jewish population of 630,000. This demographic ratio began to change radically with the mass immigration that started on the eve of independence and continued for four years. Nearly 700,000 immigrants arrived in Israel in the first three and a half years (1948–51) after statehood, half from Europe and half from Asia and Africa. After a lull in immigration, from 1952 to 1954, there was a renewal: In 1955–1957, 160,000 immigrants, mostly from Morocco, Tunisia, and Poland, arrived, and from 1961 to 1964, 215,000 immigrants, especially from Morocco and Romania, settled.[31]

In contrast to both secular Zionists and non-Zionist orthoprax Jews from Europe, many immigrants from the Middle East saw Zionism and the establishment of the state as affirmations of the religious tradition that they had upheld in their countries of origin. Some interpreted their aliyah in traditional messianic terms. These were communities from the Middle East, such as Yemenites and those from the rural areas of Morocco and Tunisia, whose traditional religious life had remained substantially intact before immigration. Among other communities, secularization had made inroads, but in most cases it was moderate in comparison with the European Jews, and this also meant that there was no militant ultra-orthopraxy that took on the self-conscious task of defending the tradition.[32]

Zionist socialism had been the most important "civil religion" of the New Yishuv, but it held no attraction for immigrants from Muslim countries and it was replaced in the newly founded state by *mamluchtiyut* (statism), which equated the state with the highest moral order and affirmed, in a selective manner, elements of the Jewish tradition. In the first years of the state, class and statist symbols coexisted in Labor Zionist circles, but as statism became the civil religion, the socialist rhetoric was toned down, the symbols of statism (national flag, menorah) replaced the older class symbols (red flag, internationalism), and Independence Day became the major holiday. In an attempt to appeal to immigrants from North Africa and Asia, Mapai, the dominant party, created a religious subsystem within the labor movement, further moderating the Labor Zionist attitude toward religion.[33]

CHAPTER 11

Privatization and Post-Zionism

Privatization in the Israeli context has occurred within the "secular religion" of Zionism and the civil religion of the state. This is a change in the secular sector rather than in the religious sector of the population, and it has been associated with the emergence of post-Zionism, the replacement of the institutions and collectivistic ideology and ceremonies of socialist or Labor Zionism by a market-driven economy and consumer-oriented society. The economic expansion that followed the 1967 war was seen by many as accelerating the decline of the communalism that had characterized the Yishuv and early state, but the term *post-Zionism* has been applied to the period since the mid-1980s, when the institutions founded by the labor movement collapsed, restrictions on markets were lifted, the capitalist stratum improved its position by taking advantage of the greater opportunities in the more open economy, and inequality widened. Western patterns of consumerism rapidly advanced, as signaled by the many new shopping malls, the spread of American franchises such as McDonalds, and the introduction in the 1990s of commercial television channels and cable and satellite television.[34]

Zionist calls for the sacrifice of individual preferences and private needs for those of the collective lost their persuasive power, and the collectivistic rituals of Zionism were no longer appropriate to the new style of life. The turn to individualistic values and a nuclear family focus were particularly evident in those sectors, such as the kibbutzim, where collectivism had taken its most manifest forms. On a more general level, the celebrations of civil religion were transformed into private events. Independence Day, for example, was no longer celebrated by processions and other communal events but by private parties and family barbecues in public parks.[35]

The major constituency of post-Zionism, which includes liberal values and dovish positions with regard to foreign policy and the territories, is predominantly middle class and secular. Higher income encourages a secular lifestyle in some respects; purchasing private cars enables travel on the Sabbath (public transport is not available in most of Israel on the Sabbath), and consumption is now possible in the increasing number of shops, restaurants, and entertainment venues open on the Sabbath.[36] The religious population was not unaffected by the greater consumerism and commercialized leisure, but privatization in religion has not been extensive.

Conservative and Reform Judaism

As indicated, the prominence of public religion in Israel is associated with the orthoprax establishment, and this establishment has used its position to obstruct and delegitimize the Conservative and Reform movements in Judaism. Largely removed from public practice, the Conservative and Reform movements in Israel facilitate the privatization of religion, but their influence in this direction is limited by their small size. In the early 2000s the Conservative movement with fifty-two congregations and the Reform movement with twenty-eight congregations had a combined membership of about 15,000 who took part in congregational activities on a regular basis. In contrast to the United States, where the Reform and Conservative movements are far larger than the orthoprax, the members of the nonorthoprax movements in Israel constitute a minute percentage of regular synagogue worshippers. Whereas in the United States affiliation with a synagogue or temple is the most important means of expressing Jewish identity, most Israeli Jews feel little need to affiliate with a synagogue to identify ethnically or nationally as Jews. Association with a synagogue is mainly confined, therefore, to highly observant Jews, who are mostly orthoprax.[37]

The Conservative and Reform movements have sought to attract Israelis who identify as *mesoritiim* (traditional) or *lo-dati* (nonreligious), but they have met with limited success. For the *mesoritiim*, the dominant identity among Jews of North African and Asian origins, religion is orthopraxy, even though they choose not to be bound by its laws. So long as they can practice orthopraxy in their own way, they support it as the official and public representation of Judaism, and because they hold to the *mesorit* (tradition), the "new" forms of Conservative and Reform Judaism have no appeal.[38] More than 60 percent of Israeli Jews are in favor of giving the Conservative and Reform movements equal status to the orthoprax,[39] and many nonreligious Israelis of European origin are sympathetic toward the nonorthoprax movements as part of their opposition to the orthoprax establishment. Some turn to the movements for the celebration of the rites of bar or bat mitzvah, which, unlike marriage ceremonies, have no implications for civil status, but sympathy and infrequent celebrations rarely extend to membership. For most nonreligious Israelis, the ethnonational and identity functions of religion are sufficiently provided for by civil or public religion.[40]

New Religious Movements

Jewish Israelis retain their Jewish identity and its associations with Judaism even when they seek a privatized form of religion outside Judaism. The attraction of new religious movements to Israeli Jews was a post-1973 development. "Cult movements," requiring high levels of obligation and participation, remained small and marginal; in the early 1980s, when new religious movements in Israel were at their peak, there were about twenty movements with a membership that probably never rose above 3,000. However, "client cults" of a quasireligious character, particularly Human Potential and psychotherapeutic organizations, have attracted large clienteles of mostly nonreligious Jews who observe a few Jewish religious practices in secularized forms. In addition to Transcendental Meditation, which at one time boasted many Israeli practitioners, organizations such as est (Erhard Seminars Training), I Am, and, the successor of est, Landmark Education, have attracted thousands to their encounter groups and psychotherapeutic sessions.[41] Movements with more recognizable religious features and more highly involved and committed memberships, such as ISKCON (International Society for Krishna Consciousness), have met with fierce, sometimes violent, persecution by the *haredim*. Coverage in the secular media has also been almost wholly negative. The movements are perceived not only as threats to the family but also as challenges to the very basis of the Israeli state and society: its Jewish religious and national identity.[42]

Deprivatization and the Religious-Secular Division

Although most Israeli Jews, including most of the nonreligious, continue to support the notion of Israel as a Jewish state, the nature of Israel's Jewish identity has become an increasingly divisive issue among different sectors of the Israeli Jewish populations in recent years, and religion has been central to this division. It makes little sense to refer to deprivatization of religion in Israel because privatization was never extensive, but religion and politics have become even more intertwined in recent decades with the greater overlap between divergent political positions and secular and religious worldviews. Conflicts between religious and secular sectors of the population over the allocation of resources have become secondary to conflicts over fundamental questions of the Jewish identity of the state and its territorial boundaries. Two trends are of importance here: (1) the transformation of the religious Zionist population into a movement emphasizing the Jewish settlement of the occupied territories as the most central part of the messianic process of redemption of the Jewish people and (2) the greater political involvement and political hawkishness of the ultra-Orthodox.

Religious Zionism: Nationalism and Messianism

Religious Zionism presents a prominent case of counterprivatization with its emphasis on the relevance of Judaism beyond the spheres of home and synagogue into the civic and political realms. This is a case of political schemes and policies grounded in religious messianism with far-reaching effects on Israeli society and the Jewish-Palestinian conflict.

The emergence of a radical, activist messianism within religious Zionism provided a solution to the tensions and paradoxes within a movement that attempted to combine orthopraxy and modern Zionism, two ideological streams that were for a long time fundamentally opposed. In the Yishuv the religious way of life of the religious Zionists and their belief that a Jewish state should be founded on the Halacha alienated the secular Zionists, and their support of the secular Zionists in the creation of a premessianic state was condemned by the anti-Zionist ultra-orthoprax as a violation of the covenant. Mizrachi, the religious Zionist party, tried to overcome the religious condemnation by distinguishing clearly between the messianic promise and an independent Jewish state that would provide a refuge for persecuted Jews from the Diaspora. An alternative stream of religious Zionism, whose most important exponent was Rabbi Abraham Isaac Kook (1865–1935), defined Zionism as a wholly sacred phenomenon that was furthering the process of redemption. For Kook, the secularist Zionists who did not keep the mitzvot but who sought to redeem the Jewish people from exile were at a higher level of sacredness than the anti-Zionist orthoprax Jews. The contradiction between the sacred root of the secularists' souls and their religious sins was the inevitable consequence of an attempt to build a perfect world in a premessianic reality. Nevertheless, they were bringing redemption nearer and would finally recognize their true souls and repent.

Kook was appointed by the British mandate authorities, with the consent of the Zionist establishment, as the Ashkenazi chief rabbi (1921–35), but his teachings were not widely known, and even among the religious Zionists he had little influence during his lifetime. Mizrachi continued to be guided by a pragmatic stance, and its focus on securing resources for religious Zionist institutions and upholding the religious character of the Jewish public sphere continued after the establishment of the state and the party's fusion with smaller religious factions to form the Mafdal, or NRP (National Religious Party), in 1956. Mizrachi and then the Mafdal became a virtually permanent coalition partner of the dominant Mapai party (Israeli Workers' Party, later Labor Party), which, although it did not need the Mafdal to achieve a parliamentary majority, chose to include it to neutralize a potential source of cleavage.[43] In its policies and position as a junior coalition partner, Mafdal had little to inspire the religious Zionist youth who thought that their movement had achieved little compared with the secular Zionists. Some religious Zionist youth were attracted to the teachings of Rabbi Zvi Yehuda Kook, the son of the former chief rabbi. The younger Kook headed the Mercaz HaRav yeshiva, which became a core institution in the diffusion of religious Zionist messianism.

Zvi Kook took the sanctification of Jewish nationalism further than his father. He pronounced that the sovereign Jewish state was part of the Redemption, that the state's symbols, such as the flag and anthem, were media for the worship of God, and that the process of redemption required Jewish control over the entire Land of Israel.[44] Before the 1967 war, the influence of Kook's teaching was confined mainly to his yeshiva, but this changed with the conquest of Judea and Samaria (the West Bank), when a new dimension was added to Kook's emphasis on the sacredness of the Land of Israel and its relationship to the messianic hope. Some religious Zionists referred to the 1967 victory as a miracle and the beginning of redemption, and the euphoria following the victory encouraged hopes, soon discarded, that they could convert secular Jews to their beliefs. For most secular Israelis the war served to confirm the image of a society that had undergone successful modernization and whose efficiency and rationality, at both the technological and social levels, had defeated the tradition-bound Arabs. Following the war, massive foreign investment, a rise in the standard of living of large sectors of the population, and changes in consumption patterns in imitation of the West made the socialist Zionist values of pioneering and egalitarianism appear increasingly outmoded, but the effects of economic changes on national symbols and ideology were contained within the triumphalism and renewed feelings of national identity and community that followed the war. Confident in their military superiority and confronted with an enemy that most believed was incapable of compromise, few Israelis seriously questioned the policy of holding onto the territories.

The 1973 war shattered the feelings of confidence and optimism of secular Israelis. The questioning and criticism that followed the war went beyond the loss of authority and credibility of the Labor establishment and extended to new appraisals of the meanings of Zionism and the Israeli state. Religious Zionists interpreted the war as one of the "birth pangs of the messiah" and as a warning to the Jewish people to take their part in the process of redemption. They believed that secular Israelis had failed to continue to energize the redemption process and that it was now the role of the religious Zionists to lead the nation in its divine mission and to act as pioneers in the settlement of the conquered territories. Recognition of the need to organize to promote their goals led to the establishment of Gush Emunim (Bloc of the Faithful) in February 1974. Gush Emunim was an extraparliamentary movement, but it was represented within Mafdal by what became known as the Young Guard, who rebelled against the established leadership and succeeded in replacing the party's moderate politics with policies that focused on settlement and a hawkish, noncompromising stand on the territories. Support for Gush Emunim also came from members of B'nei Akiva, the religious Zionist youth movement, and the nationalist yeshivas, whose expansion facilitated the diffusion of the messianic ideology into wider religious Zionist circles. The knitted skullcap was worn by religious Zionist males, especially the young, as a sign of identity with the movement and its cause of settlement.[45]

The major component in the messianism of Gush Emunim was that Jewish sovereignty and settlement over the whole of the Land of Israel was the present decisive state in the attainment of redemption. It was not so much Gush Emunim's messianic interpretation of the Jewish state that was new but rather the insistence on the importance of the borders in the historical process and the enthusiasm and dedication of its supporters in settling the land, which they saw as a sacrament and a *tikkun*, a mending of the cosmos. The bond between the people and the land was seen to derive from God's election of the Jews and his vision of their destiny in the Holy Land. The appropriation of land from Arab Palestinians was justified as analogous to the conquest of the ancient Canaanites, and peace between Israel and the Arabs was seen as dependent on the Arabs' acceptance of the Jewish right to the land. Gush Emunim had no confidence in peace negotiations and agreements with the Arabs; real peace would be one of the signs of redemption.

The first Gush Emunim settlements in the West Bank during the last years of the Labor government usually started as illegal activities that drew public support and succeeded in obtaining concessions from the government. The movement's settlement activities were legalized and given a boost when the Likud party came to power in 1977. During the first Likud government, Gush Emunim continued to be the major force behind the settlement process, because it established many small settlements thinly distributed over an extensive territory. The second Likud government changed the settlement pattern by building large urban settlements or suburbs that provided inexpensive housing near the high-density central zone. Most residents of the government-sponsored settlements were attracted by the opportunity to improve their quality of life at a relatively low cost and were indifferent to the messianism of Gush Emunim. These developments weakened Gush Emunim as an organization, especially because its leaders had not developed hierarchical structures to link national and local levels or formulated procedures for appointments and decision making. Gush Emunim came to function primarily as a concept symbolizing a firm commitment to the greater Land of Israel and its settlements, but its leaders were appointed to key executive positions in most of the new municipalities and regional councils, and the vast sums of money distributed by the government to the settlement authorities gave them a formidable financial and political base. Amana, the Jewish settlement organization in the territories, was founded in 1976 as an appendage of Gush Emunim, and Gush Emunim sympathizers were also prominent in the settlements' organization, the Council of Yesha, a Hebrew acronym for Judea, Samaria, and Gaza that also means "salvation."[46]

Gush Emunim saw itself as the heir apparent of the pioneering spirit that had characterized secular Zionism in the past, and it continued to reach out to secular Jews, moderating its religious language, to join them in "the restoration of Zionist fulfillment." Secular supporters of Gush Emunim did not share the messianic beliefs, but Gush Emunim's language of redemption and its emphasis on the sacredness of the land resonated with what had been the secular messianism of socialist Zionism. Some secular Jews in the Labor camp, including members of the kibbutzim, looked back on the intense ideological spirit and activism of their pioneering period with nostalgia and saw a revival of that spirit in Gush Emunim. Socialist Zionists had secularized and nationalized religious messianism, and they could find an affinity with the fusion of religious messianism and nationalism in Gush Emunim.[47]

A partial affinity also existed between the religiopolitics of Gush Emunim and what has been termed the new civil religion that developed after the 1967 war and became more important after the 1973 war. The new civil religion emphasized the unity of all Jews, the centrality of the Holocaust, and the Jews as an isolated nation confronting a hostile world. An emphasis on the ties of the Jews to the conquered territories, especially "Judea and Samaria" with its biblical associations, invoked a penetration of religious symbols and holy places, of which the Western Wall was the most important.[48] The incorporation of traditional religious symbols by secular politicians was particularly evident in the Likud party, whose leaders clothed their hawkish politics in religious imagery and language.[49]

The close relationship of religious Zionism with the governing Likud party took a knock when Menachem Begin signed the Camp David accords in 1979 and presided over the withdrawal from Sinai and the evacuation of Jewish settlements along the Yamit strip in northern Sinai in April 1982. The reaction of Gush Emunim was one of shock and betrayal, and although some minimized the significance of the return of territory by stating that Sinai and the area around Yamit were not part of the biblical land of Israel, there was growing anxiety that history was retracting from the movement toward redemption. As has been the case in other messianic movements, responses to the failure or partial disconfirmation of prophecy included a weakening of messianic hopes among some and a more intense messianism among others. One group of what was labeled the Machteret (underground) justified their plan to blow up the mosques on the Temple Mount as a preparation for the rebuilding of the Temple in the process of redemption. Underground members, who were arrested and imprisoned in 1984, had hoped that their action would incite a holy war against Israel in which God would be obliged to intervene on behalf of the Jews and thereby hasten the final stages of redemption. The implicit assumption was that God could be directed by humans, and one member asserted than it was man rather than God who had the central role in redemption.[50]

The rebuilding of the Temple on the Temple Mount continues to be the focal goal of Jewish groups supported by pro-Israel Protestant evangelical, messianic organizations, which multiplied in the United States in the 1970s and 1980s. The evangelicals expect the rebuilding of the Temple to be accompanied by the mass conversion of the Jews, a claim that is disregarded or downplayed by the Jewish temple groups and right-wing Israeli political leaders who accept the evangelicals' political and financial support.[51]

Although most religious Zionists did not support the actions of the Underground, the peace agreement with Egypt began a reformulation among them of the place of secular Jews and the state in the process of redemption. The theology that had been formulated by Rabbis Abraham and Zvi Kook was that the secularists were advancing the divine mission despite their nonobservance of the mitzvot, but the willingness of the secular politicians to withdraw from territory and uproot Jewish settlements contradicted this notion and opened them up to the charge of enemies of God, a charge that developed among the more extreme elements of religious Zionism. The state had been seen as a core factor in the process of redemption, and the question arose of the right to oppose the state if its policy contravened the principle of the greater Land of Israel and the unlimited right of Jews to settle anywhere on that land.

These questions became more acute when the Labor party was returned to power under Yitzhak Rabin in 1992 and the Oslo accords were signed with the PLO followed by a peace treaty with Jordan. Rabbinic rulings that it was a sin to relinquish Jewish sovereignty over the Holy Land were a clear indication that the secular leaders could no longer be considered to be acting according to the divine plan. Further rabbinic rulings that territorial withdrawals were endangering the lives of Jews could be interpreted as an invitation to adopt a Jewish law that stated that someone who put the life of a Jew in danger or handed Jews over to their enemies could be punished or killed. After assassinating Yitzhak Rabin on November 4, 1994, Yigal Amir justified his action in such terms.[52]

The question of the place of the state in the sphere of redemption arose in an acute form with the withdrawal from and dismantling of Jewish settlements in Gaza and northern Shomron. The sense of betrayal among religious Zionists was compounded by the fact that the pullout was initiated by Ariel Sharon, who had been a staunch supporter of settlement and one of the most important secular allies of Gush Emunim. Attempts to prevent the dismantling of the settlements included mass demonstrations and marches, the erection of barricades of demonstrators and burning tires on major roads to stop traffic, calls for soldiers and police to disobey orders, and stigmatization of government policy by comparing the "expulsion" of Jews from their homes with Nazi persecution. These actions came from religious Zionists who had encouraged their children to volunteer for army combat units and who had seen the state as "a foundation of the throne of God in the world."

After the dismantlement of settlements, a number of religious Zionists expressed doubts that the state of Israel represented the beginning of the process of redemption of the Jewish people. The question arose of what takes precedence, loyalty to the state or loyalty to the land, and a survey undertaken after the settlements were dismantled found that half of the religious Jews who had settled in the West Bank now felt "less Israeli." Some religious Zionists continue to sanctify the state but claim that the political and military elites have betrayed that sanctity.[53]

Politicization of the *Haredim*

The proposal among some religious Zionists that they need to form an alliance with the *haredim* is an indication of the changes that have occurred since the period of the Yishuv, when the *haredim* attempted to discredit the religious Zionists by casting doubt on their religious observance and accused them of a false messianism that could only delay redemption.[54] Most *haredim* accommodated to the idea and then the actuality of a Jewish state dominated by secular Jews, and to ensure the religious autonomy of its constituency and the resources necessary for living the religious life, the major *haredi* party, Agudat Israel, participated in parliamentary politics and cooperated with nonreligious Jews. Its stance shifted to hostility when its autonomy or fundamental religious principles were threatened, and in 1952 it withdrew from the coalition after the government decided to draft women into the army. From outside the government, *haredi* politicians continued to trade their support in return for benefits, but they remained largely impassive or neutral toward politics, such as foreign policy, which did not affect their particular interests. Their political influence was also limited by their small representation in the Knesset; in the early decades of the state, Mafdal consistently received ten to twelve seats in the Knesset, whereas the *haredi* parties received only four to six.[55]

Agudat Israel's self-imposed ban on entering the government lasted until 1977, when it entered the Likud-led coalition. The party was in a better position to exercise influence and gain benefits for its constituency because before 1977 the dominant Labor party had not been dependent on its coalition partners to stay in power, whereas after 1977 neither of the two largest parties, Likud and Labor, was generally able to form a coalition without the support of the religious parties. The position of the *haredi* parties improved further when their electoral support grew, overtaking that of Mafdal, which saw a sharp drop in its support. The rise of SHAS added considerably to the *haredi* mandates, and in 1988 the *haredi* parties received thirteen of the eighteen religious mandates. The Ashkenazic *haredi* party, now named Yahadut Hatorah (United Torah Judaism), has in recent elections received five to six mandates, and SHAS's mandates rose from ten in 1996 to seventeen in 1999 and then dropped to eleven in 2003 and 2009.

At the same time as they have increased their representation, the *haredi* parties have undergone a transformation from generally moderate positions on foreign policy and security issues to supporting hawkish positions. Although most *haredim* continue to distance themselves from Zionism and the symbols and rituals of the state, a number of factors have disposed them to hawkishness over territory and relationships with the Palestinians. First, continued Israeli control of the conquered territories ensures access to the holy places such as the Western Wall, the Tomb of the Patriarchs and Matriarchs in Hebron, and Rachel's Tomb.[56] Second, the *haredim* have benefited from the highly subsidized housing in new *haredi* neighborhoods in the occupied territories. Third, the belief that non-Jews are bent on destroying Jews is deeply embedded in their religious culture, and Arab hostility is attributed with theological and even cosmic significance. And fourth, Labor and dovish "left-wing" parties are viewed as the major carriers of secularism and alien non-Jewish values that the *haredim* see as the causes of permissiveness, sinful behavior, and social deterioration.[57]

The improved position of the *haredim* has given them confidence to confront their secular enemies more openly. The Supreme Court is viewed as a major enemy, composed of heretics, and its decisions, including a ruling that local religious councils had to accept Conservative and Reform Jews and that the prevailing arrangements for exempting yeshiva students from the draft could not continue, prompted a mass *haredi* demonstration against the Court in February 1999.[58] The heightened prominence of the *haredim* in the public sphere and their confrontational tactics were met by anti-*haredi* sentiments that found political expression in Shinui (Change), a party with a belligerent anti-*haredi* position that increased its seats in the Knesset from six in 1999 to fifteen in 2003. Shinui failed, however, to make significant changes to the status quo on religious issues, and after a split in the party neither faction succeeded in receiving any mandates in the 2006 elections.

Although Shinui was a centrist-right rather than a dovish party, the political cleavage between hawks ("right-wing") and doves ("left-wing") among Israeli Jews has come to overlap considerably with the division between religious and secular Jews. Of course, this overlap is by no means total. A dovish section of religious Zionists, represented by the political faction Meimad, broke from the Mafdal in the late 1980s; it did not succeed as an independent political party, and in 1999 it joined the Labor party. Secular hawks outnumber religious doves, but the small radical right parties that have attempted to combine secular and religious Jews have had little success, and the most hawkish of the secular parties have remained on the political margins.

The largest right-wing party, Likud, has always been dominated by secular politicians of mainly European origins, but a significant part of its electoral strength comes from the disproportionate support of Jews of North African and Asian origin who identify predominantly as *mesoritiim*. Labor voters, in comparison, are disproportionately secular and of European origins. However, the Likud government's recent policy of partial withdrawal from occupied territories has reinforced the impression of a division within the Israeli Jewish population between secular doves and religious hawks. The struggle between the two camps goes beyond the territorial issue, which can be viewed as one aspect of the wider struggle over the identity of the state. For secular Jews withdrawal from conquered territories is a necessary condition for retaining a Jewish state in accord with Western and democratic values. For religious Jews, whose goal is a halachic state, the loss of what they regard as sacred territory is a diminution of the state's Jewishness.[59]

Conclusion

Secularization in one dimension can contribute to secularization in another, but it can also limit secularization in another dimension. The limited privatization of religion in Israel is, in part, a consequence of the attempts by the secularist founders of the New Yishuv and new state to differentiate their national Jewish identity from religion. The historical unity of Judaism with the Jewish people and the secularists' settlement on religiously defined sacred space limited this differentiation: The secularists' own "secular religion" was expressed in terms of messianism and redemption, and in choosing the symbols of the Jewish state, they had recourse to only a symbolic system grounded in a religious tradition.

Two related consequences followed from the process of differentiation and its limitations: (1) the prominence of public religion and (2) the virtual monopolization of orthoprax religion. The early waves of immigration came from eastern Europe, and Israel followed the eastern European Jewish pattern of a division between secular and religious Jews rather than the Western, particularly American, pattern of division into different religious denominations (Orthodox, Conservative, Reform). Israeli Jews who are only partly observant or who observe a few secularized versions of religious ceremonies have felt no need for alternative forms to orthoprax religion. "Traditionalists," who largely originate from the comparatively tolerant Jewish religious traditions of North Africa and Asia, have not attempted to give ideological legitimation or organizational expression to their nonorthoprax patterns of observance, and the secular or nonreligious, who largely originate from Europe, express their Jewish identity in national-political terms, which include secularized renditions of symbols historically grounded in religion.

CHAPTER 11

The trend toward polarization of religious and secular sectors is largely a consequence of an increasing convergence of religious and political divisions. Among religious Zionists the move toward greater segregation and religious stringency has been combined with political radicalization grounded in messianism. Unlike the religious Zionists, the *haredim* do not attach messianic meanings to the state of Israel or the settlement of the territories, but they have also taken a militant hawkish position on the conflict with the Palestinians. These developments, together with some withdrawal among the secular right wing from the more hawkish positions, have made the political dividing lines between hawks and doves among Israeli Jews increasingly religious versus secular. As political and religious positions have become one, it is not surprising that religious trends representing the privatization of religion remain weak.

AFTERWORD TO PART 4

The debate on secularization has been confined largely to Christian contents, and in chapter 10 I extended the discussion to Judaism. I made comparisons between the Jewish and Christian contexts and between Jewish communities, particularly those of the United States and Israel. Privatization of religion has been part of the larger secularization debate, and the focus in chapter 11 on public religion in Israel provides a further comparison with the more privatized religion of American Jews. These differences are taken up in this afterword.

American and Israeli Jews attribute different meanings to the term *religious Jew*. For Israeli Jews the meaning of *dati* (religious) refers to a Jew whom American Jews call Orthodox: a Jew who makes the Halacha, the system of religious laws, the basis of his or her way of life. Many American Jews believe that there are different ways of being a religious Jew, and the term can be applied to Reform, Conservative, or even nonaffiliated Jews who may observe only a few religious customs.

Data from surveys show that the average levels of religious observance are higher in Israel than in the United States, but the differences narrow considerably when the comparisons are confined to Israelis who were born in the West (mainly Europe) or have parents who were born in the West. Similar percentages of American and Ashkenazic Israelis participate in the Passover seder, light Hanukkah candles, and fast on Yom Kippur. With respect to the less popular practices, such as Sabbath observance and separate dishes for milk and meat, the levels of observance are higher in Israel, even when the comparison is confined to the Ashkenazim.

The lower levels of religious observance among American Jews are related to their greater emphasis on voluntarism or choice in the observance of religious customs. Charles Liebman and Steven Cohen wrote that among American Jews "personal choice is endowed with spiritual sanctity, and contrary to past tradition it is always considered more virtuous than performing an act out of a sense of obedience to God."[1] American Jews live in a society of religious voluntarism and have adopted the market system of denominations; they are free to choose to affiliate (or not) among the religious options. The emphasis in Israel is on the protection of Jewish interests by centralized institutions, which include an Orthodox establishment. Although Liebman and Cohen exaggerate somewhat in writing that Israel has "no alternative religious formulations to Orthodoxy,"[2] the consequence of the almost exclusive state support for the Orthodox is that the Reform and Conservative movements are disadvantaged in competing for the allegiance of the consumers of religious services. The choice that a large proportion of Israeli Jews make is expressed in the saying, "The synagogue I do not attend is an Orthodox synagogue." It is true that there is less legitimacy and institutional support in Israel to choose among religious customs and to interpret them in line with personal needs and interests, but secular Israelis do choose which of the religious holidays to celebrate and how to celebrate them. In other words, the choices made with respect to religious observances in Israel are not so much from among religious options but between a religious (Orthodox) interpretation and secular ones.

In addition to voluntarism, Liebman and Cohen characterized the religious life of American Jews in terms of personalism, moralism, and universalism.[3] Because it is linked to voluntarism, personalism—giving the choices personal meanings—has less scope in Israel, but Liebman and Cohen point out that elements of personalism are present in the religion of Israelis, even among Orthodox Israelis. The opposite of personalism would be to interpret the tradition without regard to its relevance or meaning for the individual. With respect to moralism and universalism, the contrasts between the religious orientations of American and Israeli Jews are clear. Moralism, by which the religious person is distinguished by ethical behavior rather than by ritual observance, has long been common among American Jews, and even the modern American Orthodox reject an unqualified ritualism. Religious Israelis emphasize ritual and religious law, and secular Israelis are likely to consider ethical behavior a sign of a good person, a universalistic notion differentiated from religion.

Whereas universalism, the reformulation of Jewish religious customs and rituals to infuse them with meanings for all humanity, is common among American Jews, religious Israeli Jews tend to define morality in particularistic terms. As shown in chapter 11, the changes in religious Zionism in Israel, particularly the messianic trend, have reinforced particularism. The hawkish policies of religious Zionists with regard to relationships with the Palestinians and Arab states have been supported in recent years by non-Zionist *haredim,* and only a minority within the religious population state a willingness to compromise over the territory and Jewish settlement of the Land of Israel. The moral grounds on which outsiders criticize Israeli settlement in the West Bank are rejected by religious Israelis as the standards of cultures entirely foreign to Judaism. This position of religious Jews has contributed to the polarization between religious and secular Jews in Israel. Polarization trends also exist within American Jewry, but these are mainly confined to religious observance and overlap less with political positions. There are the differences between the in-married and the growing number of intermarried, and both the Reform and Orthodox have gained in strength, whereas Conservative Judaism has lost ground. Polarization has also been sharpened by the haredization of certain sectors of the Orthodox or orthoprax populations, a process that has occurred in both the United States and Israel.

The reasons for the prominence of public religion and the relative insignificance of the privatization of religion in Israel were presented in chapter 11. The Reform and Conservative movements facilitate privatization, but they attract only a small minority of Israeli Jews. Another form of privatization, also limited in its extensiveness among Israelis, can be found in client cults, which provide psychotherapeutic or human potential programs that might be considered on the boundaries of religion. Perhaps the most significant form of privatization in Israel has been the secular religion of Zionism. On the other hand, the trends within the religious Zionist and *haredi* populations have heightened the province of religion in the public sphere.

The separation of state and church is well established in the United States, but the country has not been immune to the religionizing of politics and the politicization of religion. Religion, morality, and politics have intertwined in debates over abortion, prayer in public schools, the teaching of evolution and creationism in public schools, and marriage for same-sex couples. Most American Jews are on the liberal side of the political spectrum; they support the protection and extension of civil liberties, and they defend the separation of church and state. Some have incorporated liberalism into their definition of a good Jew.

Few American Jews have joined Christian religious conservatives in bringing religion into politics and the public sphere. The trend among American Jews has been in the opposite direction. As Steven Cohen and Arnold Eisen have shown in their study of the "moderately affiliated" sector, many American Jews have become less interested in philanthropy, social causes, the fight against anti-Semitism, and support for Israel. Instead, they seek the meaning of their Jewishness and express their Judaism in the private sphere. Rather than participate in collective Jewish causes and secular institutions, they seek personal spiritual meaning. Anti-Semitism is the United States is now of little concern, conflicts between Jewishness and Americanness are no longer issues, and the state of Israel has declined in importance as a part of their Jewish identity. The belief that Judaism is given from birth remains, but what it means to be Jewish is increasingly viewed as a matter of individual experience and choice. One wants to be Jewish not because of the need to ensure the survival of the Jewish people but because of what it means personally. Judaism is personalistic, focused on the self, and increasingly enacted in private space and time, at home with family and friends. Jewish meaning is not necessarily found in a synagogue, and when these Jews go to the synagogue, they engage in personal reflection and pay little attention to the words on the pages of the prayer book.[4]

The retreat from public Judaism among American Jews is far removed from the Israeli scene. Many American Jews are critical of the fusion of religion and nationalism in Israel and the refusal of the Orthodox establishment to recognize non-Orthodox forms of Judaism. It is the religious rather than the secular Israeli Jews who are most removed from the trends among the moderately affiliated American Jews. However, the new spirituality of seeking, which many American Jews share with other Americans, appears to have little in common with cultural trends among secular Israelis. The new spirituality has not been absent among Israelis, as is evident from the popularity of some New Age activities, but such phenomena largely remain outside the recognized boundaries of Judaism. Thus comparisons of the Judaisms of American and Israeli Jews appear to show them moving farther apart.

A FINAL AFTERWORD

Boundaries: Comparisons and Shifts

In a number of chapters in this book I have compared Judaism with other religions with respect to particular religious phenomena and processes: saints, millenarianism, antinomianism, and secularization. I also made a number of brief comparisons with respect to the ethnicity of Jews and other ethnic groups or categories. It could be argued that these external comparisons have been limited because no other people is characterized by the kind of fusion of religion and ethnicity that is demonstrated by the Jews. Ethnoreligious groups and minorities are numerous, but most adhere to a particular branch, denomination, or sect of one of the world religions whose boundaries are vastly wider than that of the particular ethnoreligious group.

Some ethnoreligious minorities adhere to the same religion as the majority; examples are Catholic Basques, Sunni Berbers, Orthodox Ossetians in Georgia, Catholic Hutu in Burundi, and Buddhist Mons in Burma. Others adhere to a religion or religious branch that differs from that of the majority; examples are Orthodox Greeks in Albania, Sunni Chechens in Russia, Copts in Egypt, Shiites in Iraq, and Hindu Indian Tamils in Sri Lanka. Compared with all these groups, the ethnic boundaries of the Jews correspond to the religious boundaries of what is widely considered one of the world religions. Whereas an emphasis on membership in one of the world religions has been used by other groups to undermine ethnic boundaries, such an emphasis among Jews can only strengthen their ethnic boundaries. In the late nineteenth and early twentieth centuries some Jews sought to undermine the religious and ethnic boundaries between Jews and non-Jews by emphasizing the boundaries of class and their identity as part of the proletariat. This option lost its attractiveness, and in the postindustrial society, with its fuzzy class boundaries, it has lost its relevancy.

Judaism would appear to be the only unambiguous ethnic religion among the six religions that are generally counted as world religions. Three of the world religions, Buddhism, Christianity, and Islam, have generally been considered the most universalistic in their inclusion of different ethnic groups and their accommodation of a wide variety of social structures. The three other religions combine elements of universalism and particularism: Confucianism has been tied to Chinese culture; Hinduism has been anchored in a particular social structure, the caste system; and Judaism has been intricately linked to the Jewish people.[1] Hinduism has occasionally been designated an ethnic religion, but, apart from the question of whether Hinduism constitutes a single religious system, there are numerous ethnic divisions within Hinduism in India and elsewhere. Ethnic groups in India also cut across the country's religious divisions; for example, Jats and Rajputs may be Sikhs, Hindus, or Muslims, and an ethnic communality, such as the Jats in Punjabi villages, has muted the barriers among the religious groups. Sikhism is included in some lists of the world religions, and its close ties to its homeland, the Punjab, has given it an ethnic character. However, some Punjabis adhere to other religions, such as Christianity and Islam, and, although the congruence of Sikhism with ethnic identity has been encouraged, the openness of Sikhism to converts has not been conducive to the ethnic label.

As shown in chapter 9, ethnic or subethnic differentiations based on countries and continents of origin are made in Israel among Jewish *edot*, but most Israelis regard the *edot* as no more than branches of the Jewish extended family. The unique fusion of religion and ethnicity in Judaism does not prevent meaningful comparisons with other religions, ethnicities, and religioethnic groups, but it does direct us to analytical frameworks that span the subdisciplines of the sociology of religion and the sociology of ethnicity. A concept that has been extensively applied in the sociology of ethnicity and less so in the sociology of religion is boundary. By distinguishing between religious and ethnic boundaries, we can summarize a large part of the material that has been covered in the chapters of this book.

An anthropologist, Fredrik Barth, was instrumental in making boundary a central concept in the sociology of ethnicity. Barth wrote that ethnic groups can be understood only in terms of boundary creation and maintenance and that a shared culture should be regarded as a result rather than as a primary or definitional characteristic of an ethnic group. According to Barth's conception, ethnicity is a corporate identity that exists independently of any particular cultural features. The cultural features can be used to indicate a boundary, but they are likely to change in accordance with boundary maintenance.[2] Alternative definitions of ethnicity, focusing on culture, have emphasized that phenomena such as religion and culture are "primordial" or "natural" attachments on a par with kinship; they are absolute ties that cannot be reduced to or explained by other factors.[3]

Cultural factors need not be characterized as primordial, but a number of writers, including Barth in later works, have acknowledged that the culture that the boundaries enclose may make a difference to ethnicity. Cultural difference and ethnic boundaries may reinforce each other; cultural differentiations may make a boundary appear quasinatural or self-evident, and boundaries may encourage the formulation of further cultural differences. However, ethnic boundaries do not always coincide with cultural differences, and cultural differences do not guarantee that the ethnic group will have a long history.

The boundary drawn by the rabbinic tradition between Jews and non-Jews was both religious and ethnic. The rabbis did not, of course, make this distinction, and if we search in the rabbinic literature for a formulation that approaches our notion of boundary building, we come across one that relates more to religion than to ethnicity. This is the injunction "to build a fence around the Torah." The precepts of the Torah were to be fenced with additional laws that were to have the effect of preserving the observance of the original commandments. For example, to ensure that Jews would not work on the Sabbath, the rabbis added a further prohibition against handling any tools that could be used for such work. The fence was intended to keep out outside influences that might entice Jews to disobey the law, and it had the added advantage of securing rabbinic hegemony.

The additional religious prohibitions increased the religious differences between Jews and non-Jews and thereby sharpened the social barrier between them. A boundary's sharpness or fuzziness is one of three dimensions of boundaries distinguished by Richard Alba in his analysis of ethnic groups. The other two dimensions are whether a boundary is closed or open to crossing over and whether a boundary is static or shifting.[4] These dimensions were formulated by Alba with respect to ethnic groups, but they can be extended to other categorizations, including religious groups and socioeconomic classes. In fact, similar distinctions have been made in the literature on classes, particularly by Frank Parkin, who applied the concept of closure, a concept derived from the writings of Max Weber on status groups.[5]

Alba writes that ethnicity is a boundary with both symbolic and social aspects and is typically embedded in a variety of social and cultural differences. Religious groups can be distinguished along similar lines. The core of their cultural differences is likely to be religious and, like ethnic groups, they may be distinguished by residential concentrations and occupational and class profiles. In the case of ethnoreligious groups, the cultural differences include religion, but other cultural differences, not necessarily related to religion, might also be evident.

A sharp boundary does not necessarily exclude the possibility of crossing it by individuals, families, or even entire communities. A person may be able to cross over an ethnic boundary and assimilate into the adopted ethnic group or, in the case of religious groups, convert into the adopted religious group. Crossing over from one ethnoreligious group to another may be problematic where the ascriptive nature of the ethnicity is emphasized; religious conversion may not be sufficient to gain acceptance as a member of the ethnic group.

Boundary shifting is a relocation of the boundary when populations once situated on one side of the boundary are incorporated into the other side. In the United States ethnic groups such as the Italians and Jews were once conceived of as distinctive races, distinct from the "white" Americans of western and northern European descent. They have come to be conceived of as part of the general category of "whites," who are distinguished from African Americans, Asians, and Central and South Americans. Boundary shifting has also occurred with respect to religion. Jews and Catholics were excluded by the WASP population as much because of their religion as for their perceived ethnic or racial characteristics, but since World War II they have been incorporated into what is commonly termed the American Judeo-Christian heritage.

As shown in part 1, the boundaries between Jews and non-Jews in the postantiquity, premodern period varied considerably among the civilizations. Sharp religious boundaries were typical in Christian and Islamic civilizations, although in those civilizations the boundaries showed significant variations with the sharpest boundaries in central and Western Europe and the least sharp in certain Islamic countries. In these contexts religious customs that were adopted from the non-Jewish environment were transformed by the Jews in ways that did not blur, and sometimes strengthened, the boundaries between the religions. Some blurring occurred at the level of popular religion, and this was particularly evident in North Africa, where saints were central to the religious cultures of both Muslims and Jews.

Christians and Muslims were forbidden, under penalty of death, to cross over into Judaism by conversion. Jews were able and were sometimes encouraged to convert, but few did except in cases of coercion. When many Jews did convert, as in Spain at the end of the fourteenth century, this did not affect the sharpness of the boundary between the dominant population and the remaining Jewish community, and there was no shifting of the boundary.

Jews entered India as outsiders to the Hindu caste system, and it is possible to speculate that local shifting of the boundary transformed them into insiders of that system. The diffuseness of the boundaries of what came to be known as Hinduism, with its extraordinary diversity of beliefs and practices, together with the internal boundaries drawn by the caste system served to both encompass the Jews and ensure their intergenerational continuity.

The boundaries of religions in China were porous, and, in contrast to Europe, the adoption of customs and symbols from the environmental religions resulted in a blurring of the religious boundary between Jews and non-Jews. Blurred boundaries and flexible identities meant that moving out of the Jewish community did not require conversion, and for the socially ambitious who wished to become part of the literati, the examination and appointments system of the imperial bureaucracy encouraged leaving the community and assimilating into a non-Jewish one. Other structural factors supported the survival of the Kaifeng community until those factors were undermined by the breakup of the empire.

The number of Jews in medieval Europe who crossed over into Christianity was not large until, at the end of the fifteenth century, expulsion decrees resulted in mass conversions in Spain and Portugal. With the absence of Jewish communities, boundaries were drawn between "Old Christians" and the conversos, or "New Christians." The discrimination against the conversos in what came to be known as the "purity of blood" statutes might appear to a modern sensitivity to signify a drawing of boundaries along racial rather than religious lines, but the relevant boundary, as understood both by the conversos and their persecutors, was religious. The conversos were accused of heresy, of being crypto-Jews, and some were guilty. As time passed, the boundary of the Judaism of the secret Jews became fuzzy as Catholic forms and symbols were incorporated into it. The messianic outbursts among the conversos represented a redrawing of boundaries: between the saved (the conversos) and the damned (their persecutors and Old Christians).

Many of the conversos who succeeded in leaving Spain and Portugal settled in more tolerant places, where they and their descendants crossed back over the religious boundary, from Christianity to Judaism. It was not a simple matter to move from Catholicism, or the syncretic Marrano religion, into which many had been born, to rabbinic Judaism. The belief in Sabbatai Zvi as the messiah provided a clear declaration by former conversos of their commitment to Judaism and a restatement of the boundary between Jews and non-Jews. This boundary again became problematic when Sabbatai Zvi converted to Islam and some of his believers followed him. And yet again, crossing over the religious boundary by conversion did not dissolve the religious boundary for the converts. They constructed their own boundaries as Sabbatean sects, and some crossed another line into antinomianism.

The millenarianism and antinomianism among conversos and former conversos were linked to the problems of location and identity when religious boundaries were sharp and reinforced by segregatory measures and socioeconomic differences. Both the religious and social components of the boundary between Jews and non-Jews began to lose their sharpness in some European countries as a consequence of nation building in the eighteenth and nineteenth centuries. The process of nation building in a number of European states involved reformulations of the status of the Jews and their inclusion, albeit qualified in some cases, as citizens. The identification with the nation-state that was required or expected from the Jews resulted in a differentiation between Judaism and the Jews' national identity. The boundaries between Jews and non-Jews could be reformulated as twofold, as religious and as national or ethnic. Hypothetically, one boundary could become fuzzy while the other remained sharp, and it was possible to cross over one without crossing over the other. There were attempts to remove one or the other boundary through strategies of identity in which many Jews in central and western Europe and the United States identified exclusively as a religious group and some Jews in eastern Europe identified exclusively as an ethnic or national group. The strategy of identifying as a religious group and denying a Jewish ethnic or national identity was accompanied by religious reforms that were intended to blur the differences between Judaism and the dominant religion. Others concluded that they could achieve their economic and social aspirations only by crossing over the boundary by religious conversion. This strategy became more precarious in the last decades of the nineteenth century, when many non-Jews redefined the boundary between themselves and Jews as a racial one. The racist reformulation reached its most extreme forms in the first half of the twentieth century with unprecedented tragic consequences for European Jewry.

In the United States in the early decades of the twentieth century the Jews were one of the victims of intensified racism, but religious differences remained as salient as ethnic and racial ones. When, after World War II, the religious boundaries shifted and Judaism was incorporated into the mainstream of American religion, the ethnic boundary continued into the 1950s with respect to the more intimate realms of social interaction. The ethnic boundary began to weaken and blur as the 1960s advanced, and this blurring, as indicated by the considerable rise in intermarriage beginning in the 1970s, resulted in a further blurring of the religious boundary. Although there is some crossing over by conversion in both directions, mainly by spouses in intermarriages, the blurring of the religious boundary has meant that many now regard conversion as unnecessary. Some intermarried couples participate as families in both Christian and Jewish religious customs.

The mainstream cultures of those European countries in which the Jewish communities are sizable are more secular than the mainstream culture of the United States. The religious boundaries are sharper in Europe, but for many secularized Jews and non-Jews they are irrelevant to their social interaction and marriage choices, which cross over the increasingly fuzzy ethnic boundaries. As in the United States, it is only the minority that practice an Orthodox or ultra-Orthodox form of Judaism who voluntarily maintain sharp religioethnic boundaries.

The one country in which religioethnic boundaries between Jews and non-Jews retain their sharpness and salience is Israel. When the Jews succeeded in establishing their own state, they adopted the principle of other nation-states that the ethnonational and political boundaries should coincide. Whereas in many Western states over the last decades this principle has been modified by immigrations of diverse ethnoreligious groups and multiculturalism, Israeli governments have sought to uphold it. The Law of Return restricts the granting of citizenship to Jewish immigrants, although this has been made more flexible to accommodate Russian immigrants, who include a large number of families of mixed marriages. As in Western countries, economic considerations have encouraged the immigration of "foreign workers," but strenuous efforts are made to ensure that non-Jewish workers stay for limited periods and do not become permanent residents. Between the Jewish majority and the Palestinian minority the boundaries are sharp, and although passing from one group to another is possible by conversion, this is rare. A shifting of boundaries in Israel does not appear likely.

The establishment of the Jewish state was, in part, a consequence of the boundaries that non-Jews established against the incorporation of Jews into their nations and society. It is an irony of history that, at a time when the barriers between Jews and non-Jews are weakening and shifting in the Diaspora, it is in the Jewish state that the barriers between Jews and non-Jews are sharp and seemingly entrenched.

Notes

Introduction to Part 1

1. Stuart E. Rosenberg, *America Is Different: The Search for Jewish Identity in America* (New York: Thomas Nelson, 1965); Steven M. Cohen, *American Modernity and Jewish Identity* (New York: Tavistock, 1983); Calvin Goldscheider and Alan S. Zuckerman, *The Transformation of the Jews* (Chicago: University of Chicago Press, 1985).

2. Charles S. Liebman and Steven M. Cohen, *Two Worlds of Judaism: The Israeli and American Experience* (New Haven, CT: Yale University Press, 1990).

3. Amos Funkenstein, "The Dialectics of Assimilation," *Jewish Social Studies* 1 (1995): 1–14.

4. Religious separatism was incorporated into Weber's notion of the Jews as a pariah people. Max Weber, *Ancient Judaism* (New York: Free Press, 1952), 336–55.

5. Todd M. Endelman, "Introduction: Comparing Jewish Societies," in *Comparing Jewish Societies*, ed. Todd M. Endelman (Ann Arbor: University of Michigan Press, 1997), 1–21.

6. Mark R. Cohen, *Under Crescent and Cross: The Jews in the Middle Ages* (Princeton, NJ: Princeton University Press, 1994).

7. Rainer Liedtke, *Jewish Welfare in Hamburg and Manchester, c. 1850–1914* (New York: Oxford University Press, 1998).

8. Michael Brenner, Rainder Liedtke, and David Rechter (eds.), *Two Nations: British and German Jews in Comparative Perspective* (Tübingen, Germany: Mohr Siebeck, 1999).

9. Dean Phillip Bell, *Sacred Communities: Jewish and Christian Identities in the Fifteenth Century* (Leiden, Netherlands: Brill, 2001). Bell's analysis includes both external comparisons of Christians and Jews in fifteenth-century Germany and internal comparisons of Jews in late medieval Germany and Spain.

10. Elisheva Baumgarden, *Mothers and Children: Jewish Family Life in Medieval Europe* (Princeton, NJ: Princeton University Press, 2004).

11. Robin Cohen, *Global Diasporas: An Introduction* (Seattle: University of Washington Press, 1997); William Safran, "Comparing Diasporas: A Review Essay," *Diaspora* 8 (1999): 255–91.

12. Stephen Steinberg, *The Ethnic Myth: Race, Ethnicity, and Class in America* (Boston: Beacon Press, 1981). A work by a historian in this area is Thomas Kessner, *The Golden Door: Italian and Jewish Immigrant Mobility in New York City, 1880–1915* (New York: Oxford

University Press, 1977).

13. Seymour Martin Lipset, "The Study of Jewish Communities in a Comparative Context." *Jewish Journal of Sociology* 5 (1963): 166.

14. Rosalind Shaw and Charles Steward, "Introduction: Problematizing Syncretism," in *Syncretism/Anti-Syncretism*, ed. Charles Steward and Rosalind Shaw (London: Routledge, 1994).

15. Harvey E. Goldberg, *Jewish Life in Muslim Libya: Rivals and Relatives* (Chicago: University of Chicago Press, 1990), 14–15, 54–66.

16. Robert Bonfil, *Jewish Life in Renaissance Italy* (Berkeley: University of California Press, 1994), 102–23, 153–69.

17. Kenneth Snow, *Theater of Acculturation: The Roman Ghetto in the 16th Century* (Seattle: University of Washington Press, 2001), 49–51, 68–98.

18. Funkenstein, "Dialectics of Assimilation," 9.

19. Ivan G. Marcus, *Rituals of Childhood: Jewish Acculturation in Medieval Europe* (New Haven, CT: Yale University Press, 1996).

Chapter 1

1. Some historians of antiquity question the use of the term *Jews* for this period (see the introduction to Part 3), but here I follow the common practice of referring to the Judeans of antiquity as Jews.

2. Nissim Rejwan, *The Jews of Iraq: 3,000 Years of History and Culture* (London: Weidenfeld & Nicolson, 1985), 9–31.

3. Erich S. Gruen, *Diaspora: Jews Amidst Greeks and Romans* (Cambridge, MA: Harvard University Press, 2002).

4. Paul Wexler, *The Non-Jewish Origins of the Sephardic Jews* (Albany: State University of New York Press, 1996).

5. Manahem Ben-Sasson, "Varieties of Inter-Communal Relations in the Geonic Period," in *The Jew of Medieval Islam: Community, Society, and Identity*, ed. Daniel Frank (Leiden, Netherlands: Brill, 1995), 17.

6. Youssef Courbage and Philippe Fargues, *Christians and Jews Under Islam* (London: I. B. Tauris, 1997), 6, 32.

7. Salo Wittmayer Baron, *A Social and Religious History of the Jews*, 18 vols. (New York: Columbia University Press, 1952–1980), v. 3, 99–114.

8. Avraham Grossman, "Communication Among Jewish Centers During the Tenth to the Twelfth Centuries," in *Communication in the Jewish Diaspora: The Pre-Modern World*, ed. Sophia Menache (Leiden, Netherlands: Brill, 1996), 107–11; Kenneth R. Stow, *Alienated Minority: The Jews of Medieval Latin Europe* (Cambridge, MA: Harvard University Press, 1992), 6–7.

9. Benjamen J. Israel, *The Bene Israel of India: Some Studies* (New York: Apt Books, 1984), 11, 61–64, 71; Carl Mark Gussin, *The Bene Israel of India: Politics, Religion, and Systematic Change* (Ph.D. dissertation, Syracuse University, 1972), 7.

10. Michael Pollak, *Mandarins, Jews, and Missionaries: The Jewish Experience in the Chinese Empire* (Philadelphia: Jewish Publication of America, 1980), 260–66, 317–19.

11. Gruen, *Diaspora*, 243.

12. Shaye J. D. Cohen, *The Beginnings of Jewishness: Boundaries, Varieties, Uncertainties* (Berkeley: University of California Press, 1999), 28–68; John Joseph Collins, *Between Athens and Jerusalem: Jewish Identity in the Hellenistic Diaspora* (Grand Rapids, MI: Eerdmans,

19–25, 161, 273–74.

13. Baron, *History of the Jews*, v. 2, 191–209, v. 5, 3–20, and v. 6, 16–27; Raymond P. Scheindlin, "Merchants and Intellectuals, Rabbis and Poets: Judeo-Arabic Culture in the Golden Age of Islam," in *Cultures of the Jews*, v. 2, *Diversities of Diaspora*, ed. David Biale (New York: Schocken, 2002), 18–20; Sophia Menache, "Communication in the Jewish Diaspora: A Survey," in *Communication in the Jewish Diaspora: The Pre-Modern World*, ed. Sophia Menache (Leiden, Netherlands: Brill, 1996), 15–16; Grossman, "Communication Among Jewish Centers," 109–21; Ben-Sasson, "Variety of Inter-Communal Relations," 17; Yom Tov Assis, "The Judeo-Arabic Tradition in Christian Spain," in *Jews of Medieval Islam: Community, Society, and Identity*, ed. Daniel Frank (Leiden, Netherlands: Brill, 1995), 112. The Beta Israel in Ethiopia are excluded from this comparative analysis because the evidence suggests that the development of their distinctive Jewish identity began in the fifteenth century and that their religious system was an outgrowth of the Ethiopian tradition. Steven Kaplan, *The Beta Israel (Falasha) in Ethiopia: From Earliest Times to the Twentieth Century* (New York: New York University Press, 1992).

14. S. D. Goitein, *Jews and Arabs: Their Contacts Across the Ages* (New York: Schocken, 1955), 131–40; Scheindlin, "Merchants and Intellectuals," 25–28; Yosef Tobi, "Challenges to Tradition: Jewish Cultures in Yemen, Iraq, Iran, Afghanistan, and Bukhara," in *Cultures of the Jews*, v. 3, *Modern Encounters*, ed. David Biale (New York: Schocken, 2006), 239–40.

15. Goitein, *Jews and Arabs*, 177–92; Andre N. Chouraqui, *Between East and West: A History of the Jews of North Africa* (Philadelphia: Jewish Publication Society, 1968), 67–79; H. Z. [J. W.] Hirschberg, *A History of the Jews in North Africa* (Leiden, Netherlands: Brill, 1974), v. 1, 175, 165–76; Mark R. Cohen, *Under Crescent and Cross: The Jews in the Middle Ages* (Princeton, NJ: Princeton University Press, 1994), 135–136; Raphael Patai, *The Seed of Abraham: Jews and Arabs in Contact and Conflict* (Salt Lake City: University of Utah Press, 1986), 149–90; Paul B. Fenton, "Devotional Rites in a Sufi Mode," in *Judaism in Practice: From the Middle Ages Through the Early Modern Period*, ed. L. Fine (Princeton, NJ: Princeton University Press, 2001), 364–74.

16. Harvey E. Goldberg, "The Mimuna and the Minority Status of Moroccan Jews," *Ethnology* 17 (1978): 75–87.

17. Tobi, "Challenges to Tradition," 212–19; Scheindlin, "Merchants and Intellectuals," 21; Walter P. Zenner and Shlomo Deshen, "Introduction: The Historical Ethnology of Middle Eastern Jews," in *Jewish Societies in the Middle East: Community, Culture, and Authority*, ed. Shlomo Deshen and Walter P. Zenner (Washington, DC: University Press of America, 1982), 1–34.

18. Dina Feitelson, "Aspects of the Social Life of Kurdish Jews," *Jewish Journal of Sociology* 1 (1959): 201–16; Yona Sabar, *The Folk Literature of the Kurdistani Jews* (New Haven, CT: Yale University Press, 1982), xxv–xxxii; Erich Brauer, *The Jews of Kurdistan* (Detroit: Wayne State University Press, 1993), 17–18.

19. L. C. Briggs and N. L. Guele, *No More for Ever: A Saharan Jewish Town* (Cambridge, MA: Peabody Museum of Archaeology and Ethnology, Harvard University, 1964). Another example of a relatively isolated community whose religious culture remained distinct from that of their Muslim neighbors was the Yemenite community. S. D. Goitein, "Jewish Education in Yemen as an Archetype of Traditional Jewish Education," in *Between Past and Present*, ed. C. Frankenstein (Jerusalem: Szold Institute, 1953), 109–46. A study of the Jewish communities of Jerba, Tunisia, has also shown a high level of religiocultural distinctiveness that has continued to the present. Abraham L. Udovitch and Lucette Valensi, *The Last Arab Jews: The Communities of Jerba, Tunisia* (Chur, London: Harwood

Academic, 1984).

20. The reasons for postulating a Persian origin are mostly linguistic: the repeated use of Judeo-Persian rubrics in the religious manuscripts. Pollak, *Mandarins, Jews, and Missionaries*, 267.

21. Pollak, *Mandarins, Jews, and Missionaries*, 286–87, 296.

22. W. C. White, *Chinese Jews: A Compilation of Matters Relating to the Jews of K'aifeng Fu*, 3 vols. (New York: Paragon Book Reprint, 1966 [1942]); Donald Daniel Leslie, *The Survival of the Chinese Jews: The Jewish Community of Kaifeng* (Leiden, Netherlands: Brill, 1972), chs. 7–9; Pollak, *Mandarins, Jews, and Missionaries*, 274, 292–307.

23. David G. Mandelbaum, "The Jewish Way of Life in Cochin," *Jewish Social Studies* 1 (1939): 123–60; Shalva Weil, "Symmetry Between Christians and Jews in India: The Cnanite Christians and the Cochin Jews of Kerala," in *Jews in India*, ed. Thomas A. Timberg (New York: Advant, 1986).

24. J. B. Segal, *A History of the Jews of Cochin* (London: Vallentine Mitchell, 1993), 17, 22–26, 71–88.

25. Segal, *Jews of Cochin*, 39–45.

26. Ezekiel Barber, *The Bene-Israel of India* (Washington, DC: University Press of America, 1981), 10, 13.

27. Israel, *Bene-Israel*, 54, 58, 60; Shirley Berry Isenberg, *India's Bene Israel: A Comprehensive Inquiry and Sourcebook* (Bombay: Popular Prakashan, 1988), 110–43; Gussin, *Bene Israel*, 2, 26; Joan G. Roland, *Jews in British India* (Hanover, NH: University Press of New England, 1989), 12–13.

28. Israel, *Bene-Israel*, 35–36.

29. Barber, *Bene-Israel*, 61–65.

30. Barber, *Bene-Israel*, 63, 66; Gussin, *Bene Israel*, 135, 147–48; Isenberg, *India's Bene Israel*, 115, 117.

31. Shalva Weil, "Yom Kippur: The Festival of Closing the Doors," in *Between Jerusalem and Benares*, ed. Hananya Goodman (Albany: State University of New York Press, 1994), 85–100.

32. Cohen writes that the pervasive influence of Islamic and Arabic culture on medieval Christian Spain spoils the clarity of a comparison between Christian and Islamic countries. He notes that Italy is too special a case for comparison, but by bringing in Mediterranean France (the Midi) into his comparison, he is able to show that divergent socioeconomic and political conditions could temper religious intolerance. Cohen, *Under Crescent and Cross*, xx–xxi.

33. Jacob Katz, *Exclusiveness and Tolerance: Studies in Jewish-Gentile Relations in Medieval and Modern Times* (Oxford: Oxford University Press, 1961), 22–23, 29–46.

34. L. Rabinowitz, *The Social Life of the Jews of Northern France in the XII–XIV Centuries* (New York: Hermon Press, 1972), 174–78.

35. Haym Soloveitchik, "Religious Law and Change: The Medieval Ashkenazic Example," *AJS Review* 12 (1987): 205–21.

36. Ivan G. Marcus, "Hierarchies, Religious Boundaries, and Jewish Spirituality in Medieval Germany," *Jewish History* 1 (1986): 7–26; Ivan G. Marcus, *Piety and Society: The Jewish Pietists of Medieval Germany* (Leiden, Netherlands: Brill, 1981), 64, 77–83, 89–97; Stow, *Alienated Minority*, 121–34; Katz, *Exclusiveness and Intolerance*, 93–105.

37. Max Weinreich, *History of the Yiddish Language* (Chicago: University of Chicago Press, 1980), 255–62. On the characteristics of the religious literature in Yiddish for women, see Chava Weissler, "The Religion of Traditional Ashkenazic Women: Some

Methodological Issues," *AJS Review* 12 (1987): 73–94.

38. For detailed accounts of the traditional Jewish community in early modern and modern times, see Jacob Katz, *Tradition and Crisis: Jewish Society at the End of the Middle Ages* (New York: Free Press, 1961); and Mark Zborowski and Elizabeth Herzog, *Life Is with People: The Culture of the Shetl* (New York: International Universities Press, 1952).

39. Weinreich, *History of the Yiddish Language*, 182, 186.

40. Herman Pollack, *Jewish Folkways in Germanic Lands (1648–1806): Studies in Aspects of Daily Life* (Cambridge, MA: MIT Press, 1971), 27–28.

41. Pollack, *Jewish Folkways*, 49, 113–45; Joshua Trachtenberg, *Jewish Magic and Superstition* (Philadelphia: Jewish Publication Society, 1961).

42. Theodor H. Gaster, *The Holy and the Profane: Evolution of Jewish Folkways* (New York: William Morrow, 1980 [1955]), 60–63.

43. H. J. Zimmels, *Ashkenazim and Sephardim: Their Relations, Differences, and Problems as Reflected in the Rabbinical Responsa* (Oxford: Oxford University Press, 1958), 188–267; Jonathan Ray, "Beyond Tolerance and Persecution: Reassessing Our Approach to Medieval Convivencia," *Jewish Social Studies* 11 (2005): 10.

44. Yitzhak Baer, *A History of the Jews in Christian Spain*, 2 vols. (Philadelphia: Jewish Publication Society, 1961), v. 2, 245–46, 253–59.

45. H. H. Ben-Sasson, *Trial and Achievement: Currents in Jewish History* (Jerusalem: Keter, 1974), 209–16; Robert Chazan, "The Hebrew First Crusade Chronicles," *Revue des Études Juives* 133 (1974): 235–54; Gerson D. Cohen, "Messianic Postures of Ashkenazim and Sephardim (Prior to Sabbatai Zevi)," in *Studies of the Leo Baeck Institute*, ed. Max Kreutzberger (New York: Frederick Ungar, 1967), 148–56; Leon Poliakov, *History of Anti-Semitism*, v. 2, *From Mohammed to the Marranos* (London: Routledge & Kegan Paul, 1973), 73–95.

46. Pollak, *Mandarins, Jews, and Missionaries*, 318–19.

47. Segal, *Jews of Cochin*, 8–13, 21, 37–45.

48. Israel, *Bene-Israel*, 11, 61–64; Gussin, *Bene Israel*, 7.

49. Menache, "Communication in the Jewish Diaspora," 16–30; Ben-Sasson, "Varieties of Inter-Communal Relations," 18–31.

50. Chouraqui, *Between East and West*, 86–97; Goitein, *Jews and Arabs*, 109–15, 122–23.

51. Stow, *Alienated Minority*, 6–7.

52. Gershon David Hundert, *Jews in Poland-Lithuania in the Eighteenth Century* (Berkeley: University of California Press, 2004), 14–29; Arieh Tartakower, "Polish Jewry in the Eighteenth Century," *Jewish Journal of Sociology* 2 (1960): 110–14; Raphael Mahler, *A History of Modern Jewry, 1780–1815* (London: Vallentine Mitchell, 1971), 279–85.

53. Max Weber, *The Religion of China: Confucianism and Taoism* (New York: Macmillan, 1964), 213–14.

54. Etienne Balazs, *Chinese Civilization and Bureaucracy* (New Haven, CT: Yale University Press, 1964), 22.

55. White, *Chinese Jews*; Leslie, *Survival of the Chinese Jews*, 108–11.

56. Balazs, *Chinese Civilization*, 41–42, 70–78.

57. Song Nai Rhee, "Jewish Assimilation: The Case of the Chinese Jew," *Comparative Studies in Society and History* 15 (1973): 115–26; Pollak, *Mandarins, Jews, and Missionaries*, 307–9, 325–32, 338–43.

58. Max Weber, *The Religion of India* (New York: Free Press, 1958), 9–29.

59. M. N. Srinivas, *Religion and Society Among the Coorgs of South India* (Oxford: Clarendon Press, 1952), 31–32.

60. Bernard Lewis, *The Jews of Islam* (Princeton, NJ: Princeton University Press, 1984),

85–88; Cohen, *Under Crescent and Cross*, 23–27, 52–55, 161.

61. Lewis, *Jews of Islam*, 52, 125–53; Cohen, *Under Crescent and Cross*, 67–74, 163–69, 174–77; Norman A. Stillman, *The Jews of Arab Lands: A History and Source Book* (Philadelphia: Jewish Publication Society, 1979), 41–53, 47–50, 64–77, 87–92; Bat Ye'or, *The Dhimmi* (Rutherford, NJ: Fairleigh Dickinson University Press, 1985), 52–79.

62. Baron, *History of the Jews*, v. 3, 120–72; Chouraqui, *Between East and West*, 42–55; Cohen, *Under Crescent and Cross*, 112; Rejwan, *Jews of Iraq*, 87–91.

63. Amnon Cohen, *Jewish Life Under Islam: Jerusalem in the Sixteenth Century* (Cambridge, MA: Harvard University Press, 1984), 140–219; Lewis, *Jews of Islam*, 28–29, 90–91, 129–39, 142–46; Stillman, *Jews of Arab Lands*, 62–63, 86; Cohen, *Under Crescent and Cross*, 88–103, 125–28.

64. S. D. Goitein, *A Mediterranean Society: The Jewish Communities of the Arab World as Portrayed in the Documents of the Cairo Geniza*, v. 2, *The Community* (Berkeley: University of California Press, 1971), 290–93; H. Z. Hirschberg, "The Jewish Quarter in Muslim Cities and Berber Areas," *Judaism* 17 (1958): 405–21; Lewis, *Jews of Islam*, 135–39, 148–53; Stillman, *Jews of Arab Lands*, 78–91; Cohen, *Under Crescent and Cross*, 125–28.

65. Allan R. Meyers, "Patronage and Protection: The Status of Jews in Precolonial Morocco," in *Jewish Societies in the Middle East: Community, Culture, and Authority*, ed. Shlomo Deshen and Walter P. Zenner (Washington, DC: University Press of America, 1982), 85–104; Moshe Shokeid, "Jewish Existence in a Berber Environment," in *Jewish Societies in the Middle East: Community, Culture, and Authority*, ed. Shlomo Deshen and Walter P. Zenner (Washington, DC: University Press of America, 1982), 105–22; Harvey E. Goldberg, *Jewish Life in Muslim Libya* (Chicago: University of Chicago Press, 1990), 38–39.

66. Lewis, *Jews of Islam*, 125–26.

67. Lawrence Rosen, *Bargaining for Reality: The Construction of Social Relations in a Muslim Community* (Chicago: University of Chicago Press, 1984), 153–62; Shlomo Deshen, *The Mellah Society: Jewish Community Life in Sherilian Morocco* (Chicago: University of Chicago Press, 1989), 27; Goitein, *Mediterranean Society*, v. 2, 298–99; Hirschberg, *History of the Jews in North Africa*, v. 1, 174; Cohen, *Under Crescent and Cross*, 132–34.

68. Feitelson, "Social Life of Kurdish Jews"; Briggs and Guele, *No More for Ever*.

69. Baron, *History of the Jews*, v. 4, 5–12 and 89–149, v. 9, 3–54, and v. 10, 122–91; Leon Poliakov, *The History of Anti-Semitism*, v. 1, *From the Time of Christ to the Court Jew* (New York: Vanguard, 1965), chs. 2–7; Joshua Trachtenberg, *The Devil and the Jews* (Philadelphia: Jewish Publication Society, 1961); Stow, *Alienated Minority*, 102–20, 232–40; Cohen, *Under Crescent and Cross*, 17–24, 139, 169–74.

70. Baron, *History of the Jews*, v. 9, 3–96, and v. 11, 77–121; Stow, *Alienated Minority*, 10–40, 232–59; Cohen, *Under Crescent and Cross*, 32–42, 129–31; Hundert, *Jews in Poland-Lithuania*, 56, 63–78.

71. Baron, *History of the Jews*, v. 6, 150–277, and v. 12, 25–197; Guido Kisch, *The Jews in Medieval Germany: A Study of Their Legal and Social Status* (Chicago: University of Chicago Press, 1949), 318–22, 327–29; David Biale, *Power and Powerlessness in Jewish History* (New York: Schocken, 1986), 60–66; Cohen, *Under Crescent and Cross*, 77–87. Cohen writes that the greater heterogeneity of Jewish economic activities in the Mediterranean Christian areas appears to have tempered anti-Jewish feeling. Cohen, *Under Crescent and Cross*, 102–3.

72. Baron, *History of the Jews*, v. 9, 135–236, v. 10, 41–117, and v. 11, 3–76, 192–283; Biale, *Power and Powerlessness*, 62–66, 74; Stow, *Alienated Minority*, 97–101, 273–77, 281–308; Cohen, *Under Crescent and Cross*, 45–51, 121–24.

NOTES TO CHAPTER 2

73. Jonathan Elukin, *Living Together, Living Apart: Rethinking Jewish-Christian Relations in the Middle Ages* (Princeton, NJ: Princeton University Press, 2007), 8, 117; Anna Foa, *The Jews of Europe After the Black Death* (Berkeley: University of California Press, 2000), 15.

74. Hillel Levine, *Economic Origins of Antisemitism: Poland and Its Jews in the Early Modern Period* (New Haven, CT: Yale University Press, 1991); Hundert, *Jews in Poland-Lithuania*, 30–53.

75. Zborowski and Herzog, *Life Is with People*, 66–67, 151–58; Celia S. Heller, *On the Edge of Destruction* (New York: Columbia University Press, 1977).

76. Stow, *Alienated Minority*, 155–95; Biale, *Power and Powerlessness*, 77–82; Mahler, *History of Modern Jewry*, 229–58, 370–423; I. Levitats, *The Jewish Community in Russia, 1772–1844* (New York: Columbia University Press, 1943).

77. Poliakov, *History of Anti-Semitism*, v. 2, chs. 5–7; Abraham A. Neuman, *The Jews in Spain: Their Social, Political, and Cultural Life During the Middle Ages* (Philadelphia: Jewish Publication Society, 1942), v. 1, 161–69, and v. 2, 182–274; Américo Castro, *The Spaniards* (Berkeley: University of California Press, 1971), 532, 544–47; Thomas F. Glick, *Islamic and Christian Spain in the Early Middle Ages* (Princeton, NJ: Princeton University Press, 1979), 168–69, 207; Chris Lowney, *A Vanished World: Muslims, Christians, and Jews in Medieval Spain* (Oxford: Oxford University Press, 2005), 200–207, 221–23.

78. Ray, "Beyond Tolerance and Persecution," 1–18.

79. Baer, *Jews in Christian Spain*, v. 1, 177–80, 308, 364–68, and v. 2, 24–25, 31; Poliakov, *History of Anti-Semitism*, v. 2, 140–56.

80. Haim Beinart, *The Expulsion of the Jews from Spain* (Oxford: Littman Library of Jewish Civilization, 2002); Foa, *Jews of Europe*, 83–89; Philippe Wolff, "The 1391 Pogrom in Spain: Social Crisis or Not," *Past and Present* 50 (1971): 4–18; Poliakov, *History of Anti-Semitism*, v. 2, 163–48.

81. Baer, *Jews in Christian Spain*, v. 2, 244–51; Jane S. Gerber, *The Jews of Spain: A History of the Sephardic Experience* (New York: Free Press, 1992), 129, 137; Mark D. Myerson, *A Jewish Renaissance in Fifteenth-Century Spain* (Princeton, NJ: Princeton University Press, 2004).

82. Elukin, *Living Together*, 123.

83. Elukin, *Living Together*, 96.

84. Elukin, *Living Together*, 84–85, 92–96.

85. Robert Bonfil, *Jewish Life in Renaissance Italy* (Berkeley: University of California Press, 1994), 1.

86. Ivan G. Marcus, "A Jewish-Christian Symbiosis: The Culture of Early Ashkenaz," in *Cultures of the Jews*, v. 2, *Diversities of Diaspora*, ed. David Biale (New York: Schocken, 2002), 163.

87. Deshen, *Mellah Society*, 23–25.

Chapter 2

1. Xu Xin, *The Jews of Kaifeng, China* (Jersey City, NJ: Ktav, 2003), 17–27.

2. Donald Daniel Leslie, *The Survival of the Chinese Jews: The Jewish Community of Kaifeng* (Leiden, Netherlands: Brill, 1972), 108–11; Xu, *Jews of Kaifeng*, 91–93.

3. Xu, *Jews of Kaifeng*, 67–73.

4. Stephen Sharot, *A Comparative Sociology of World Religions: Virtuosos, Priests, and Popular Religion* (New York: New York University Press, 2001), 71.

5. Max Weber, *The Religion of China: Confucianism and Taoism* (New York: Macmillan, 1964), 216.

6. C. K. Yang, *Religion in Chinese Society* (Berkeley: University of California Press, 1967), 187–203; Richard J. Smith, "Ritual in Ch'ing Culture," in *Orthodoxy in Late Imperial China*, ed. Kwang-Ching Liu (Berkeley: University of California Press, 1990), 303–5; Alexander Woodside, "State, Scholars, and Orthodoxy: The Ch'ing Academics 1736–1839," in *Orthodoxy in Late Imperial China*, ed. Kwang-Ching Liu (Berkeley: University of California Press, 1990), 160–64.

7. Leslie, *Survival of the Chinese Jews*, 80, 93; Xu, *Jews of Kaifeng*, 81–82.

8. Andrew H. Plaks, "The Confucianization of the Kaifeng Jews: Interpretations of the Kaifeng Stelae Inscriptions," in *The Jews of China*, v. 1, *Historical and Comparative Perspectives*, ed. Jonathan Goldstein (Armonk, NY: Sharpe, 1999), 38. Apart from the stone inscriptions, some additional writings, such as prayers, were recovered from the last Kaifeng synagogue, but most of the historical sources on the community were not written by the Kaifeng Jews themselves. References to Jews in Chinese sources are infrequent, and the reports of Western Christian missionaries, beginning in the early seventeenth century, have to be treated with caution.

9. William Charles White, *Chinese Jews: A Compilation of Matters Relating to the Jews of K'aifeng Fu*, 3 vols. (New York: Paragon Book Reprint, 1966 [1942]), v. 2, 19.

10. White, *Chinese Jews*, v. 2, 43–45.

11. White, *Chinese Jews*, v. 2, 69.

12. Michael Pollak, *Mandarins, Jews, and Missionaries: The Jewish Experience in the Chinese Empire* (Philadelphia: Jewish Publication Society, 1980), 300.

13. White, *Chinese Jews*, v. 2, 8.

14. Leslie, *Survival of the Chinese Jews*, 102.

15. Plaks, "Confucianization of the Kaifeng Jews," 41.

16. White, *Chinese Jews*, v. 2, 59.

17. Sharot, *Comparative Sociology of World Religions*, 75; Yang, *Religion in Chinese Society*, 248–49, 272–74; Kwang-Ching Liu, "Socioethics as Orthodoxy: A Perspective," in *Orthodoxy in Late Imperial China*, ed. Kwang-Ching Liu (Berkeley: University of California Press, 1990), 54–55; Jacques Gernet, *China and the Christian Impact: A Conflict of Cultures* (Cambridge: Cambridge University Press, 1985), 37, 195, 204, 211–12, 246.

18. Lawrence I. Dramer Jr., "The Kaifeng Jews: A Disappearing Community," in *Studies of the Chinese Jews: Selection from Journals East and West*, ed. Hyman Kublin (New York: Paragon, 1971), 20.

19. Leslie, *Survival of the Chinese Jews*, 101.

20. Nathan Katz, "The Judaisms of Kaifeng and Cochin: Parallels and Divergences," in *The Jews of China*, v. 1, *Historical and Comparative Perspectives*, ed. Jonathan Goldstein (Armonk, NY: Sharpe, 1999), 134.

21. Leslie, *Survival of the Chinese Jews*, 101.

22. Gernet, *China and the Christian Impact*, 141.

23. Thomas A. Metzger, *Escape from Predicament: Neo-Confucianism and China's Evolving Political Culture* (New York: Columbia University Press, 1977), 60–68, 81, 110–11, 203–4; William Theodore de Bary, "Introduction," in *The Unfolding of Neo-Confucianism*, ed. William Theodore de Bary (New York: Columbia University Press, 1975), 17–21; Julia Ching, "What Is Confucian Spirituality?" in *Confucianism: The Dynamics of Tradition*, ed. Irene Eber (New York: Macmillan, 1986), 70–74; Gernet, *China and the Christian Impact*, 157.

24. Aharon Oppenheimer, *Sino-Judaica: Jews and Chinese in Historical Dialogue* (Tel Aviv: Tel Aviv University, 1999), 12–14.

25. Leslie, *Survival of the Chinese Jews*, 101 (quote); Xu, *Jews of Kaifeng*, 39.

NOTES TO CHAPTER 2

26. Plaks, "Confucianization of the Kaifeng Jews," 43.

27. Emily M. Ahern, *The Cult of the Dead in a Chinese Village* (Stanford, CA: Stanford University Press, 1973), 161–69; Maurice Freedman, *The Study of Chinese Society: Essays by Maurice Freedman*, ed. G. William Skinner (Stanford, CA: Stanford University Press, 1979), 273–312; Yang, *Religion in Chinese Society*, 35–52; Arthur P. Wolf, "Gods, Ghosts, and Ancestors," in *Studies in Chinese Society*, ed. Arthur P. Wolf (Stanford, CA: Stanford University Press, 1978), 162–68.

28. Susan Starr Sared, *Women as Ritual Experts: The Religious Lives of Elderly Jewish Women in Jerusalem* (New York: Oxford University Press, 1992).

29. Yang, *Religion in Chinese Society*, 44–53.

30. Xu, *Jews of Kaifeng*, 115.

31. Yang, *Religion in Chinese Society*, 48–53, 243–77; Anthony C. Yu, "Religion and Literature of China: The 'Obscure Way' of the Journey to the West," in *Tradition and Creativity: Essays on East Asian Civilization*, ed. Ching-I Tu (New Brunswick, NJ: Transaction, 1987), 110–13; Stephan Feuchtwang, "School Temple and City God," in *The City in Late Imperial China*, ed. G. William Skinner (Stanford, CA: Stanford University Press, 1977), 609; Smith, "Ritual in Ch'ing Culture," 281–310.

32. Gernet, *China and the Christian Impact*, 68–71.

33. Cynthia J. Brokaw, *The Ledgers of Merit and Demerit: Social Change and Moral Order in Late Imperial China* (Princeton, NJ: Princeton University Press, 1991).

34. Xu, *Jews of Kaifeng*, 32–34.

35. Raphael Israeli, *Islam in China: Religion, Ethnicity, Culture, and Politics* (Lanham, MD: Lexington, 2002), 99.

36. Raphael Israeli, *Muslims in China: A Study in Cultural Confrontation* (London: Curzon Press, 1980), 32; Israeli, *Islam in China*, 100; Michael Dillon, *China's Muslim Hui Community: Migration, Settlement, and Sects* (Richmond, U.K.: Curzon, 1999), 27–30, 36–37.

37. Dillon, *China's Muslim Hui Community*, 31.

38. Israeli, *Muslims in China*, 29.

39. Dillon, *China's Muslim Hui Community*, 49–50.

40. Israeli, *Islam in China*, 105–8.

41. Leslie, *Survival of the Chinese Jews*, 114.

42. Gernet, *China and the Christian Impact*, 4–5, 22–34, 43, 59, 64–82.

43. Pollak, *Mandarins, Jews, and Missionaries*, 7–84, 87–88.

44. Song Nai Rhee, "Jewish Assimilation: The Case of the Chinese Jews," *Comparative Studies in Society and History* 15 (1973): 115–26.

45. Pollak, *Mandarins, Jews, and Missionaries*, 343.

46. Leslie, *Survival of the Chinese Jews*, 112; Xu, *Jews of Kaifeng*, 134.

47. Xu, *Jews of Kaifeng*, 47–61.

48. Xu, *Jews of Kaifeng*, 154–65.

49. Xu, *Jews of Kaifeng*, 27.

50. Irene Eber, "Kaifeng Jews: The Sinification of Identity," in *The Jews of China*, v. 1, *Historical and Comparative Perspectives*, ed. Jonathan Goldstein (Armonk, NY: Sharpe, 1999), 22–35.

51. Eber, "Kaifeng Jews," 27.

52. Daniel L. Overmyer, *Folk Buddhist Religion: Dissenting Sects in Late Traditional China* (Cambridge, MA: Harvard University Press, 1976); David D. Jordan and Daniel L. Overmyer, *The Flying Phoenix: Aspects of Chinese Sectarianism in Taiwan* (Princeton, NJ: Princeton University Press, 1986); Kenneth Dean, *Lord of the Three in One: The Spread of a Cult*

in Southeast China (Princeton, NJ: Princeton University Press, 1998).

53. Jordan and Overmyer, *Flying Phoenix*, 9–15.

54. Jordan and Overmyer, *Flying Phoenix*, 7–8, 13–14.

55. Eber, "Kaifeng Jews," 28.

56. Overmyer, *Folk Buddhist Religion*, 4.

57. Yang, *Religion in Chinese Society*, 301–40; Michael Saso, *Blue Dragon, White Tiger: Taoist Rites of Passage* (Washington, DC: Taoist Center, 1990), 60–61; R. Ransdorp, "Official and Popular Religion in the Chinese Empire," in *Official and Popular Religion: Analysis of a Theme for Religious Studies*, ed. Pieter Hendrik Vrijhof and Jacques Waardenburg (Hague, Netherlands: Mouton, 1979), 415–17; Sharot, *Comparative Sociology of World Religions*, 98–99.

58. Israeli, *Muslims in China*, 39–41.

59. Israeli, *Muslims in China*, 42.

60. Yang, *Religion in Chinese Society*, 194, 197, 204–9.

61. Israeli, *Muslims in China*, 69–70, 136–42, 208–9.

62. Israeli, *Muslims in China*, 65.

63. Israeli, *Islam in China*, 60, 89–90.

64. Pollak, *Mandarins, Jews, and Missionaries*, 334–36.

Chapter 3

1. Official religion is understood here as those religious elements that the religious elite allow as justified or legitimate within the boundaries of the religion they claim to represent. Popular religion is the overall complex of religion as practiced by the masses or nonelite. For a discussion of these and related terms, see Stephen Sharot, *A Comparative Sociology of World Religions: Virtuosos, Priests, and Popular Religion* (New York: New York University Press, 2001), 10–16.

2. Bryan R. Wilson, *Magic and the Millennium* (London: Heinemann, 1973).

3. For a more detailed account of folk religion and magic in traditional Jewish society, see Stephen Sharot, *Messianism, Mysticism, and Magic: A Sociological Analysis of Jewish Religious Movements* (Chapel Hill: University of North Carolina Press, 1982), 27–44.

4. Immanuel Etkes, *The Besht: Magician, Mystic, and Leader* (Waltham, MA: Brandeis University Press, 2005), 42–47, 67–68, 250; Gershon David Hundert, *Jews in Poland-Lithuania in the Eighteenth Century* (Berkeley: University of California Press, 2004), 148; Moshe Rosman, *Founder of Hasidism: A Quest for the Historical Ba'al Shem* (Berkeley: University of California Press, 1996), 14–15, 19–22; Gedalyah Nigal, *Magic, Mysticism, and Hasidism: The Supernatural in Jewish Thought* (Northvale, NJ: Jason Aronson, 1994), 4–14, 33–49.

5. Etkes, *The Besht*, 79–97, 110–11, 250–52; Rosman, *Founder of Hasidism*, 180–81, 185.

6. Robert L. Cohn, "Sainthood on the Periphery: The Case of Judaism," in *Sainthood: Its Manifestations in World Religions*, ed. Richard Kieckhefer and George D. Bond (Berkeley: University of California Press, 1988), 43–68.

7. Cohn, "Sainthood on the Periphery," 48.

8. Max Weber, *Economy and Society: An Outline of Interpretive Sociology* (New York: Bedminster, 1968), 439–46.

9. Weber, *Economy and Society*, 446–47.

10. Max Weber, "The Social Psychology of the World Religions," in *From Max Weber: Essays in Sociology*, ed. H. H. Gerth and C. Wright Mills (London: Routledge & Kegan Paul, 1948), 287–88.

11. Weber, *Economy and Society*, 1166–73.

12. Weber, *Economy and Society*, 1166–68.

13. Weber, "Social Psychology," 288–89.

14. Weber, *Economy and Society*, 1167.

15. Stanley Jeyaraja Tambiah, *The Buddhist Saints of the Forest and the Cults of Amulets: A Study in Charisma, Hagiography, Sectarianism, and Millennial Buddhism* (Cambridge: Cambridge University Press, 1984).

16. Weber, "Social Psychology," 289.

17. Peter Brown, *The Cult of the Saints: Its Rise and Function in Latin Christianity* (Chicago: University of Chicago Press, 1981); R. Van Den Broek, "Popular Religious Practices and Ecclesiastical Policies in the Early Church," in *Official and Popular Religion: Analysis of a Theme for Religious Studies*, ed. Peter Hendrik Vrjhof and Jacques Waardenburg (Hague, Netherlands: Mouton, 1979), 30–32; Barbara Abou-El-Haj, *The Medieval Cult of Saints: Formations and Transformations* (Cambridge: Cambridge University Press, 1994), 7–8.

18. Brown, *Cult of the Saints*; Peter Brown, *Society and the Holy in Late Antiquity* (London: Faber & Faber, 1982); Peter Brown, "The Saint as Exemplar in Late Antiquity," *Representations* 2 (1983): 1–25; Joyce E. Salisbury, *Iberian Popular Religion, 600 B.C. to 700 A.D.: Celts, Romans, and Visigoths* (New York: Edwin Mellen Press, 1985), 131–63; R. N. Swanson, *Religion and Devotion in Europe, c. 1215–c. 1515* (Cambridge: Cambridge University Press, 1995), 152–54.

19. Richard Kieckhefer, "Imitators of Christ: Sainthood in the Christian Tradition," in *Sainthood: Its Manifestations in World Religions*, ed. Richard Kieckhefer and George D. Bond (Berkeley: University of California Press, 1988), 4–5.

20. William A. Christian, *Local Religion in Sixteenth-Century Spain* (Princeton, NJ: Princeton University Press, 1981), 126–28; Patrick J. Geary, *Furta Sacra: Thefts of Relics in the Central Middle Ages* (Princeton, NJ: Princeton University Press, 1978), 4, 152–59.

21. Adriaan H. Bredero, *Christendom and Christianity in the Middle Ages* (Grand Rapids, MI: William B. Erdmans, 1994), 160–75; Andre Vauchez, "The Saint," in *The Medieval World*, ed. Jacques Le Goff (London: Collins & Brown, 1990), 313–45; Geary, *Furta Sacra*, 21–26.

22. Aron Gurevich, *Medieval Popular Culture: Problems of Belief and Perception* (Cambridge: Cambridge University Press, 1988), 59–60; Vauchez, "The Saint"; Gabor Klaniczah, *The Uses of Supernatural Power: The Transformation of Popular Religion in Medieval and Early-Modern Europe* (Princeton, NJ: Princeton University Press, 1990); Donald Weinstein and Rudolph M. Bell, *Saints and Society: The Two Worlds of Western Christendom, 1000–1700* (Chicago: University of Chicago Press, 1982), 196–202.

23. Victor Turner and Edith Turner, *Image and Pilgrimage in Christian Culture* (New York: Columbia University Press, 1978), 156–58; Peter Burke, "How To Be a Counter-Reformation Saint," in *Religion and Society in Early Modern Europe, 1500–1800*, ed. Kasper von Greyerz (London: Allen & Unwin, 1984), 45–46; Weinstein and Bell, *Saints and Society*, 168–69.

24. Weinstein and Bell, *Saints and Society*, 141–43.

25. Vauchez, "The Saint"; Mary Lee Nolan and Sidney Nolan, *Christian Pilgrimage in Modern Western Europe* (Chapel Hill: University of North Carolina Press, 1989), 138. The distinction between holy man and saint has been emphasized by commentators on Peter Brown's seminal article, "The Rise and Function of the Holy Man in Late Antiquity," first published in 1971 and reprinted in his *Society and the Holy in Late Antiquity*. Howard-Johnston writes that saints were either martyrs or holy men who were singled out for posthumous commemoration and veneration. Just as not all holy men became saints, not

all saints had been holy men. Some saints had been worldly leaders who were manufactured into saints to promote a cause or to serve a vested interest. James Howard-Johnston, "Introduction," in *The Cult of Saints in Late Antiquity and the Early Middle Ages*, ed. James Howard-Johnston and Paul Antony Haywood (Oxford: Oxford University Press, 1999), 5–6.

26. Gurevich, *Medieval Popular Culture*, 74–77; Thomas A. Kselman, *Miracles and Prophecies in Nineteenth-Century France* (New Brunswick, NJ: Rutgers University Press, 1983), 25; Robert Hertz, "St. Besse: A Study of an Alpine Cult," in *Saints and Their Cults: Studies in Religious Sociology, Folklore, and History*, ed. Stephen Wilson (Cambridge: Cambridge University Press, 1983), 55–100; Jean-Claude Schmitt, *The Holy Greyhound: Guinefort, Healer of Children Since the Thirteenth Century* (Cambridge: Cambridge University Press, 1983). Peter Brown has been criticized for exaggerating the elite's control over the cult of saints. Paul Antony Hayward, "Demystifying the Role of Sanctity in Western Christendom," in *The Cult of Saints in Late Antiquity and the Early Middle Ages*, ed. James Howard-Johnston and Paul Antony Haywood (Oxford: Oxford University Press, 1999), 130.

27. Gurevich, *Medieval Popular Culture*, 59–60.

28. Roger N. Lancaster, *Thanks to God and the Revolution: Popular Religion and Class Consciousness in the New Nicaragua* (New York: Columbia University Press, 1988), 44–46.

29. Salisbury, *Iberian Popular Religion*, 232–33; Geary, *Furta Sacra*, 35–39, 152–53.

30. Rosalind Brooke and Christopher Brooke, *Popular Religion in the Middle Ages: Western Europe, 1000–1300* (London: Thames & Hudson, 1984), 195–99; Geary, *Furta Sacra*, 27–29.

31. Christian reports that in Spain saints accounted for about one-third of devotions in 1580 and less than one-tenth in 1957. Christian, *Local Religion*, 203, 206.

32. Turner and Turner, *Image and Pilgrimage*, 202–3, 206.

33. William A. Christian, *Person and God in a Spanish Valley* (New York: Seminar Press, 1972), 173.

34. Gurevich, *Medieval Popular Culture*, 43–48; Judith Devlin, *The Superstitious Mind: French Peasants and the Supernatural in the Nineteenth Century* (New Haven, CT: Yale University Press, 1987), 11–13; A. N. Galpern, *The Religions of the People in Sixteenth Century Champagne* (Cambridge, MA: Harvard University Press, 1976), 53.

35. Stephen Wilson, "Introduction," in *Saints and Their Cults: Studies in Religious Sociology, Folklore, and History*, ed. Stephen Wilson (Cambridge: Cambridge University Press, 1983), 19.

36. Gurevich, *Medieval Popular Culture*, 43–48; Devlin, *Superstitious Mind*, 15–17, 54.

37. Saints in towns were associated with occupations, but some saints were city-wide, transcending divisions of neighborhood and occupation. Christian, *Local Religion*, 57–58, 142, 149–53, 176.

38. Christian, *Person and God*, 65–68, 99–101.

39. Christian, *Local Religion*, 174–77; Christian, *Person and God*, 45–47.

40. Kselman, *Miracles and Prophecies*, 29–30; Christian, *Local Religion*, 174–75.

41. Bredero, *Christendom*, 178.

42. Gurevich, *Medieval Popular Culture*, 74; G. J. F. Bouritius, "Popular and Official Religion in Christianity: Three Cases in Nineteenth Century Europe," in *Official and Popular Religion: Analysis of a Theme for Religious Studies*, ed. Peter Hendrik Vrijhof and Jacques Waardenburg (Hague, Netherlands: Mouton, 1979), 132; Robert Muchembled, *Popular Culture and Elite Culture in France 1400–1750* (Baton Rouge: Louisiana State University Press, 1985), 103.

43. Caroline B. Brettell, "The Priest and His People: The Contractual Basis for Religious Practice in Rural Portugal," in *Religious Orthodoxy and Popular Faith in European Society*, ed. Ellen Badone (Princeton, NJ: Princeton University Press, 1990), 55–75; Ruth Behar, "The Struggle for the Church: Popular Anticlericalism and Religiosity in Post-Franco Spain," in *Religious Orthodoxy and Popular Faith in European Society*, ed. Ellen Badone (Princeton, NJ: Princeton University Press, 1990), 76–112; Joyce Riegelhaupt, "Popular Anti-Clericalism and Religiosity in Pre-1974 Portugal," in *Religion, Power, and Protest in Local Communities: The Northern Shore of the Mediterranean*, ed. Eric R. Wolf (Berlin: Mouton, 1984), 93–114.

44. Max Weber, *The Religion of India* (New York: Free Press, 1958), 166–80; David R. Kinsley, *Hinduism: A Cultural Perspective* (Englewood Cliffs, NJ: Prentice Hall, 1982), 6–8; Susan Snow Wadley, *Shakti: Power in the Conceptual Structure of Karimpur Religion* (Chicago: University of Chicago, Department of Anthropology, 1975), 108–9; Ilana Friedrich Silber, *Virtuosity, Charisma, and Social Order: A Comparative Sociological Study of Monasticism in Theravada Buddhism and Medieval Catholicism* (Cambridge: Cambridge University Press, 1995), 63–65.

45. Weber, *Economy and Society*, 288.

46. Madeline Biardeau, "The Salvation of the King in the Mahabharata," in *Way of Life: King, Householder, Renouncer*, ed. T. N. Madan (New Delhi: Vikas, 1982), 73.

47. Silber, *Virtuosity*, 105–6.

48. C. J. Fuller, *The Camphor Flame* (Princeton, NJ: Princeton University Press, 1992), 30–31, 164–77; Daniel Gold, *The Lord as Guru: Hindi Saints in North Indian Tradition* (New York: Oxford University Press, 1987), 3–8.

49. Vinay Kumar Srivastava, *Religious Renunciation of a Pastoral People* (Delhi: Oxford University Press, 1997).

50. Stanley Jeyaraja Tambiah, *Buddhism and the Spirit Cults in North-East Thailand* (Cambridge: Cambridge University Press, 1970), 124, 127, 134–36, 259–60, 278, 336; Richard Gombrich, *Theravada Buddhism: A Social History from Ancient Benares to Modern Colombo* (London: Routledge & Kegan Paul, 1988), 95–96; Richard Gombrich and Gananath Obeyesekere, *Buddhism Transformed: Religious Change in Sri Lanka* (Princeton, NJ: Princeton University Press, 1988), 56.

51. Vincent J. Cornell, *Realm of the Saint: Power and Authority in Moroccan Sufism* (Austin: University of Texas Press, 1998), 3–4, 7, 113, 116–19, 275–76.

52. Issachar Ben-Ami, *Saint Veneration Among the Jews of Morocco* (Detroit, MI: Wayne State University Press, 1998), 23, 35–39, 148–49, 151, 154.

53. Ernest Gellner, *Muslim Society* (Cambridge: Cambridge University Press, 1981), 40–53. As in Morocco, the Sufi saints in Sind, northern India, also mediated between tribes as well as between rulers and ruled and between countryside and town. Saintly families acquired considerable power in areas where state power was weak. Sarah F. D. Ansari, *Sufi Saints and State Power: The Pirs of Sind, 1843–1947* (Cambridge: Cambridge University Press, 1992), 24–29, 158–59.

54. Dale F. Eickelman, *Moroccan Islam: Tradition and Society in a Pilgrimage Center* (Austin: University of Texas Press, 1976), 162, 178–79.

55. Ben-Ami, *Saint Veneration*, 131–42. On Muslims and Jews visiting each other's shrines in medieval Syria, see Josef W. Meri, *The Cult of Saints Among Muslims and Jews in Medieval Syria* (Oxford: Oxford University Press, 2002), 107, 124, 188, 209, 281, 283.

56. Meri, *Cult of Saints*, 66–70, 94–100, 125–27, 154–55; Alex Weingrod, *The Saint of Beersheva* (Albany: State University of New York Press, 1990); Harvey E. Goldberg, "Potential Politics: Jewish Saints in the Moroccan Countryside and in Israel," in *Faith and*

Polity: Essays on Religion and Politics, ed. Mart Bax, Peter Kloos, and Adrianus Koster (Amsterdam: VU University Press, 1992), 235–50.

57. Ignaz Goldziher, *Muslim Studies* (London: Allen & Unwin, 1971), v. 2, 259, 262–64, 335–37; Vincent Crapanzano, *The Hamadsha: A Study of Moroccan Ethnopsychiatry* (Berkeley: University of California Press, 1973), 15–17; Emanuel Marx, "Communal and Individual Pilgrimage: The Region of Saints' Tombs in South Sinai," in *Regional Cults*, ed. R. P. Werbner (London: Academic Press, 1977), 29–30; Eickelman, *Moroccan Islam*, 11, 60–62; J. D. J. Waardenburg, "Official and Popular Religion as a Problem in Islamic Studies," in *Official and Popular Religion: Analysis of a Theme for Religious Studies*, ed. Pieter Hendrik Vrijhof and Jacques Waardenburg (Hague, Netherlands: Mouton, 1979), 240–42; William M. Brinner, "Prophet and Saint: The Two Exemplars of Islam," in *Saints and Virtues*, ed. John Stratton Hawley (Berkeley: University of California Press, 1987), 45, 55; Frederick M. Denny, "'God's Friends': The Sanctity of Persons in Islam," in *Sainthood: Its Manifestations in World Religions*, ed. Richard Kieckhefer and George D. Bond (Berkeley: University of California Press, 1988), 6–7; Carl W. Ernst, "Introduction," in *Manifestations of Sainthood in Islam*, ed. Race Martin Smith and Carl W. Ernst (Istanbul: Isis Press, 1993), xvi.

58. Hundert, *Jews in Poland-Lithuania*, 187; Etkes, *The Besht*, 153; Immanuel Etkes, "The Zaddik: The Interrelationship Between Religious Doctrine and Social Organization," in *Hasidism Reappraised*, ed. Ada Rapoport-Albert (London: Littman Library, 1996), 165.

59. Ahmet T. Karamushtafa, *God's Unruly Friends: Dervish Groups in the Islamic Later Middle Period, 1200–1550* (Salt Lake City: University of Utah Press, 1994), 87–89; J. Spencer Trimingham, *The Sufi Orders in Islam* (Oxford: Clarendon Press, 1971); Marshall G. S. Hodgson, *The Venture of Islam* (Chicago: University of Chicago Press, 1974), v. 2, 203–28; Ira M. Lapidus, *A History of Islamic Societies* (Cambridge: Cambridge University Press, 1988), 168–71; Michael Gilsenan, *Saint and Sufi in Modern Egypt: An Essay in the Sociology of Religion* (Oxford: Clarendon Press, 1973), 2–12, 21, 43–44; Crapanzano, *The Hamadsha*, 2–4, 17–19, 135, 170; Susan Bayly, *Saints, Goddesses, and Kings: Muslims and Christians in South Indian Society, 1700–1900* (Cambridge: Cambridge University Press, 1989), 14–16, 110–12; Christopher S. Taylor, *In the Vicinity of the Righteous: Ziyara and the Veneration of Muslim Saints in Late Medieval Egypt* (Leiden, Netherlands: Brill, 1999), 14, 63–64, 83–84, 224.

60. Sharot, *Messianism, Mysticism, and Magic*, 139–44; Ada Rapoport-Albert, "God and the Zaddik as the Two Focal Points of Hasidic Worship," *History of Religions* 18 (1979), 296–325; Gershom G. Scholem, *Major Trends in Jewish Mysticism* (New York: Schocken, 1961), 325–50.

61. Sharot, *Messianism, Mysticism, and Magic*, 154–88; Ada Rapoport-Albert, "Hasidim After 1772: Structural Continuity and Change," in *Hasidism Reappraised*, ed. Ada Rapoport-Albert (London: Littman Library, 1996), 76–140; Glenn Dynner, *Men of Silk: The Hassidic Conquest of Polish Jewish Society* (Oxford: Oxford University Press, 2006), 25–48, 118–31.

62. Moshe Idel, *Hasidism: Between Ecstasy and Magic* (Albany: State University of New York Press, 1995); Rachel Elior, "Between Yesh and Ayin: The Doctrine of the Zaddik in the Works of Jacob Isaac, the Seer of Lublin," in *Jewish History: Essays in Honor of Chimen Abramsky*, ed. Ada Rapoport-Alpert and Steven J. Zipperstein (London: Peter Halban, 1988), 393–455; Morris M. Faierstein, "Personal Redemption in Hasidism," in *Hasidism Reappraised*, ed. Ada Rapoport-Albert (London: Littman Library, 1996), 214–24; Eliot R. Wolfson, "Walking as a Sacred Duty: Theological Transformation of Social Reality in Early Hasidism," in *Hasidism Reappraised*, ed. Ada Rapoport-Albert (London: Littman Li-

brary, 1996), 180–207.

63. Dynner, *Men of Silk*, 138–40.

64. Hodgson, *Venture of Islam*, 228; Trimingham, *Sufi Orders in Islam*, 133–34; Bayly, *Saints, Goddesses, and Kings*, 95; Crapanzano, *The Hamadsha*, 15–17.

65. Sharot, *Messianism, Mysticism, and Magic*, 159–61; Dynner, *Men of Silk*, 255.

66. Trimingham, *Sufi Orders in Islam*, 104, 149, 173–74; Lapidus, *History of Islamic Societies*, 168–69; Sharot, *Messianism, Mysticism, and Magic*, 162–88.

Afterword to Part 1

1. James Mahoney and Dietrich Rueschemeyer, "Comparative Historical Analysis: Achievements and Agendas," in *Comparative Historical Analysis in the Social Sciences*, ed. James Mahoney and Dietrich Rueschemeyer (Cambridge: Cambridge University Press, 2003), 3–38; Theda Skocpol, "Doubly Engaged Social Science: The Promise of Comparative Research," in *Comparative Historical Analysis in the Social Sciences*, ed. James Mahoney and Dietrich Rueschemeyer (Cambridge: Cambridge University Press, 2003), 407–28.

2. Julia Adams, Elisabeth S. Clemens, and Ann Shola Orloff, "Introduction: Social Theory, Modernity, and the Three Waves of Historical Sociology," in *Remaking Modernity: Politics, History, and Sociology*, ed. Julia Adams, Elisabeth S. Clemens, and Ann Shola Orloff (Durham, NC: Duke University Press, 2005), 1–72.

3. Philip D. Gotdki, "The Return of the Repressed: Religion and the Political Unconscious of Historical Sociology," in *Remaking Modernity: Politics, History, and Sociology*, ed. Julia Adams, Elisabeth S. Clemens, and Ann Shola Orloff (Durham, NC: Duke University Press, 2005), 161–89.

4. Adams et al., "Introduction," 64.

5. Stephen Sharot, "Beyond Christianity: A Critique of the Rational Choice Theory of Religion from a Weberian and Comparative Religious Perspective," *Sociology of Religion* 63 (2002), 427–54.

6. John Stuart Mill, *A System of Logic* (New York: Harper & Row, 1988), 278–83; Charles C. Ragin, *The Comparative Method: Moving Beyond Qualitative and Quantitative Strategies* (Berkeley: University of California Press, 1989), 39.

7. Dietrich Rueschemeyer, "Can One or a Few Cases Yield Theoretical Gains?" in *Comparative Historical Analysis in the Social Sciences*, ed. James Mahoney and Dietrich Rueschemeyer (Cambridge: Cambridge University Press, 2003), 305–36; James Mahoney, "Strategies of Causal Assessment in Comparative Historical Analysis," in *Comparative Historical Analysis in the Social Sciences*, ed. James Mahoney and Dietrich Rueschemeyer (Cambridge: Cambridge University Press, 2003), 337–72; Peter A. Hall, "Aligning Ontology and Methodology in Comparative Research," in *Comparative Historical Analysis in the Social Sciences*, ed. James Mahoney and Dietrich Rueschemeyer (Cambridge: Cambridge University Press, 2003), 373–404.

Introduction to Part 2

1. Menachem Marc Kellner, *Maimonides on the "Decline of the Generations" and the Nature of Rabbinic Authority* (Albany: State University of New York Press, 1996), 71.

2. Joseph Sarachek, *The Doctrine of the Messiah in Medieval Jewish Literature* (New York: Hermon Press, 1968), 301–3; Gershom Scholem, *The Messianic Idea in Judaism and Others Essays in Jewish Spirituality* (New York: Schocken, 1971), 30–33; Yitzhak Baer, *A History of*

the Jews in Christian Spain, 2 vols. (Philadelphia: Jewish Publication Society, 1961), v. 1, 249.

3. Yonina Talmon, "Pursuit of the Millennium: The Relation Between Religious and Social Change," *Archives Européennes de Sociologie* 3 (1962): 125–48; Yonina Talmon, "Millenarian Movements," *Archives Européennes de Sociologie* 7 (1966): 159–200; Maria Isaura Pereira de Queiros, "Messianic Myths and Movements," *Diogenes* 90 (1975): 78–99.

4. G. W. Trompf, "Millenarism: History, Sociology, and Cross-Cultural Analysis," *Journal of Religious History* 24 (2000): 106, 110.

5. Moshe Idel, *Messianic Mystics* (New Haven, CT: Yale University Press, 1998), 7, 262–63; Moshe Idel, "Religion, Thought, and Attitudes: The Impact of the Expulsion on the Jews," in *Spain and the Jews: The Sephardi Experience, 1492 and After*, ed. Elie Kedourie (London: Thames & Hudson, 1992), 127. See also Eric Lawee, "'Israel Has No Messiah' in Late-Medieval Spain," *Journal of Jewish Thought and Philosophy* 5 (1996): 266.

6. Idel, *Messianic Mystics*, 127–28, 277.

7. Idel, *Messianic Mystics*, 266.

8. Idel, *Messianic Mystics*, 289

9. Stephen Sharot, *Messianism, Mysticism, and Magic: A Sociological Analysis of Jewish Religious Movements* (Chapel Hill: University of North Carolina Press, 1982), 13.

10. Michael Barkun, *Disaster and the Millennium* (New Haven, CT: Yale University Press, 1974).

11. Glenn Dynner, *Men of Silk: The Hassidic Conquest of Polish Jewish Society* (Oxford: Oxford University Press, 2006), 13.

12. Idel, *Messianic Mystics*, 6–7, 414–15.

Chapter 4

1. On the development of Jewish millenarianism and messianism in the ancient period, see Joseph Klausner, *The Messianic Idea in Israel* (New York: Macmillan, 1955); Sigmund Mowinckel, *He That Cometh* (Oxford: Blackwell, 1956); Norman Cohn, *Cosmos, Chaos, and the World to Come: The Ancient Roots of Apocalyptic Faith* (New Haven, CT: Yale University Press, 1993); Sheldon R. Isenberg, "Millenarism in Greco-Roman Palestine," *Religion* 4 (1974): 26–46; Ellis Rivkin, "The Meaning of Messiah in Jewish Thought," *Union Seminary Quarterly Review* 26 (1971): 383–406; *Encyclopaedia Judaica* (Jerusalem: Keter, 1972) v. 6, 860–86, and v. 11, 1497–98; John J. Collins, "From Prophecy to Apocalypticism: The Expectation of the End," in *The Encyclopedia of Apocalyptism*, v. 1, *The Origins of Apocalypticism in Judaism and Christianity*, ed. John J. Collins (New York: Continuum, 1999), 129–61; James C. Vanderkam, "Messianism and Apocalypticism," in *The Encyclopedia of Apocalyptism*, v. 1, *The Origins of Apocalypticism in Judaism and Christianity*, ed. John J. Collins (New York: Continuum, 1999), 193–228; and Jacob Neusner, William Scott Green, and Ernest S. Frerichs (eds.), *Judaisms and Their Messiahs at the Turn of the Christian Era* (Cambridge: Cambridge University Press, 1987). On the Talmudic period, see Leo Landman (ed.), *Messianism in the Talmudic Era* (New York: Ktav, 1979). Collections of texts are found in Raphael Patai, *The Messiah Texts* (Detroit, MI: Wayne State University Press, 1979); and George Wesley Buchanan, *Revelation and Redemption: Jewish Documents of Deliverance from the Fall of Jerusalem to the Death of Nahmanides* (Dillsboro: Western North Carolina Press, 1978).

2. Seth Schwartz, *Imperialism and Jewish Society: 200 B.C.E. to 640 C.E.* (Princeton, NJ: Princeton University Press, 2001), 75–76.

3. Tessah Rajak, "Jewish Millenarian Expectations," in *The First Jewish Revolt*, ed. An-

NOTES TO CHAPTER 4

drea Berlin and J. Andrew Overman (London: Routledge, 2002), 164–88.

4. Moshe Idel, "Jewish Apocalypticism," in *The Encyclopedia of Apocalypticism*, v. 2, *Apocalypticism in Western History and Culture*, ed. Bernard McGinn (New York: Continuum, 1999), 204–23; Jacob Neusner, *Messiah in Context* (Philadelphia: Fortress, 1984).

5. On the medieval period, see Joseph Sarachek, *The Doctrine of the Messiah in Medieval Jewish Literature* (New York: Hermon Press, 1968); Gershom Scholem, "Toward an Understanding of the Messianic Idea in Judaism," in his *The Messianic Idea in Judaism* (London: Allen & Unwin, 1971), 1–36; and Naham N. Glatzer, "Zion in Medieval Literature," in *Zion in Jewish Literature*, ed. Abraham S. Halkin (New York: Herzl, 1961), 83–100.

6. Sarachek, *Doctrine of the Messiah*, 301–3; Eric Lawee, "'Israel Has No Messiah' in Late-Medieval Spain," *Journal of Jewish Thought and Philosophy* 5 (1996): 256–62.

7. Shlomo Eidelberg, *The Jews and the Crusades: The Hebrew Chronicles of the First and Second Crusades* (Madison: University of Wisconsin Press, 1977), 13.

8. Eidelberg, *Jews and the Crusades*, 10.

9. H. J. Zimmels, *Ashkenazim and Sephardim: Their Relations, Differences, and Problems as Reflected in the Rabbinical Responsa* (London: Oxford University Press, 1958), 233–50; Moses A. Shulvass, *Between the Rhine and the Bosporus* (Chicago: College of Jewish Studies Press, 1964), 5–13.

10. Robert Chazan, "The Hebrew First Crusade Chronicles," *Revue des Études Juives* 133 (1974): 235–54.

11. Gershom Scholem, *Major Trends in Jewish Mysticism* (New York: Schocken, 1969), 87–90.

12. Abraham Berger, "The Messianic Self-Consciousness of Abraham Abulafia," in *Essays on Jewish Life and Thought*, ed. Joseph L. Blau (New York: Columbia University Press, 1959), 55–61; Aaron Zeev Aescoly, *Jewish Messianic Movements* (Jerusalem: Bialik Institute, 1956), 194–213 (in Hebrew); Abraham A. Neuman, *The Jews in Spain* (Philadelphia: Jewish Publication Society, 1942), v. 2, 114–15; Gershom Scholem, *Kabbalah* (Jerusalem: Keter, 1974), 53–55; Moshe Idel, *Messianic Mystics* (New Haven, CT: Yale University Press, 1998), 58–100.

13. Yitzhak Baer, *A History of the Jews in Christian Spain*, 2 vols. (Philadelphia: Jewish Publication Society, 1961), v. 1, 277–80.

14. Baer, *Jews in Christian Spain*, v. 1, 198.

15. Renee Levine Melammed, *Heretics or Daughters of Israel? The Crypto-Jewish Women of Castile* (New York: Oxford University Press, 1999), 4.

16. Baer, *Jews in Christian Spain*, v. 1, 159–62; Scholem, *Kabbalah*, 65–66; Aescoly, *Jewish Messianic Movements*, 226.

17. David B. Ruderman, "Hope Against Hope: Jewish and Christian Messianic Expectations in the Late Middle Ages," in *Essential Papers on Jewish Culture in Renaissance and Baroque Italy*, ed. David B. Ruderman (New York: New York University Press, 1992), 302–6; Joseph R. Hacker, "Links Between Spanish Jewry and Palestine, 1391–1492," in *Vision and Conflict in the Holy Land*, ed. Richard I. Cohen (Jerusalem: Yad Izhak Ben-Zvi, 1985), 111–39; Lawee, "Israel Has No Messiah," 265; E. Lawee, "The Messianism of Isaac Abarbanel, Father of the [Jewish] Messianic Movements of the Sixteenth and Seventeenth Centuries," in *Millenarianism and Messianism in Early Modern European Culture: Jewish Messianism in the Early Modern World*, ed. Matt D. Goldish and Richard H. Popkin (Dordrecht, Netherlands: Kluwer Academic, 2001), 7; Idel, "Jewish Apocalypticism," 226.

18. Idel, *Messianic Mystics*, 127–31, 277.

19. David M. Gitlitz, *Secrecy and Deceit: The Religion of the Crypto-Jews* (Philadelphia: Jew-

ish Publication Society, 1996), 74–75.

20. Baer, *Jews in Christian Spain*, v. 2, 434–49; Jacob S. Minkin, *Abarbanel and the Expulsion of the Jews from Spain* (New York: Behrman's, 1938), 143–51.

21. H. H. Ben-Sasson, "Exile and Redemption in the Eyes of the Spanish Exiles," in *Yitzhak F. Baer Jubilee Volume*, ed. S. W. Baron, B. Dinur, S. Ettinger, and I. Halpern (Jerusalem: Historical Society of Israel, 1960), 216–27 (in Hebrew); Isiah Tishby, *Messianism in the Time of the Expulsion from Spain and Portugal* (Jerusalem: Merkaz Zalman Shazar, 1985) (in Hebrew).

22. Moshe Idel, "Religion, Thought, and Attitudes: The Impact of the Expulsion on the Jews," in *Spain and the Jews: The Sephardi Experience, 1492 and After*, ed. Elie Kedourie (London: Thames & Hudson, 1992), 135–36; Lawee, "Israel Has No Messiah," 267–68; Lawee, "Messianism of Isaac Abarbanel," 21.

23. Cecil Roth, *The History of the Jews of Italy* (Philadelphia: Jewish Publication Society, 1946), 179; Moses A. Shulvass, *Rome and Jerusalem* (Jerusalem: Mosad Ha-Rav Kook, 1944), 41–67 (in Hebrew).

24. Robert Bonfil, *Jewish Life in Renaissance Italy* (Berkeley: University of California Press, 1994), 186.

25. B. Netanyahu, *Don Isaac Abravanel* (Philadelphia: Jewish Publication Society, 1953), 200–240; Isaac E. Barzilay, *Between Reason and Faith: Anti-Rationalism in Italian Jewish Thought, 1250–1650* (Hague, Netherlands: Mouton, 1967), 122–23; Yitzhak Baer, "The Messianic Movement in Spain in the Period of the Expulsion," *Zion* 5 (1933): 71–77 (in Hebrew); Lionel Kochan, *Jews, Idols, and Messiahs: The Challenge of History* (Oxford: Basil Blackwell, 1990), 170; Lawee, "Messianism of Isaac Abarbanel," 21, 27.

26. Shulvass, *Rome and Jerusalem*, 45–48; Aescoly, *Jewish Messianic Movements*, 250; Isiah Tishby, "Acute Apocalyptic Messianism," in *Essential Papers on Messianic Movements and Personalities in Jewish History*, ed. Marc Saperstein (New York: New York University Press, 1992), 267–69; Kochan, *Jews, Idols, and Messiahs*, 171; Idel, *Messianic Mystics*, 133–34.

27. Moshe Idel, "Particularism and Universalism in Kabbalah," in *Essential Papers on Jewish Culture in Renaissance and Baroque Italy*, ed. David B. Ruderman (New York: New York University Press, 1992), 343.

28. Idel, *Messianic Mystics*, 152–53.

29. Shulvass, *Rome and Jerusalem*, 44–45; Moses A. Shulvass, *The Jews in the World of the Renaissance* (Leiden, Netherlands: Brill, 1973), 9, 210; A. Marx, "Le Faux Messie Ascher Laemmlein," *Revue des Études Juives* 61 (1911): 135–38.

30. Bonfil argues that the acceptance of Jews in Italy during the Renaissance has been exaggerated and that Jewish difference and inferiority continued to be taken as a given. He writes, however, that the attribution of social inferiority did not prevent their integration into the socioeconomic fabric, and the process of acculturation, reinforced by the Jews' extreme dispersion, inevitably followed. Bonfil, *Jewish Life in Renaissance Italy*, 102–4.

31. Marjorie Reeves, *The Influence of Prophecy in the Later Middle Ages* (Oxford: Clarendon Press, 1969), 354, 358, 430–35; Donald Weinstein, *Savonarola and Florence* (Princeton, NJ: Princeton University Press, 1970), 62–63, 112–15, 166; Ruderman, "Hope Against Hope," 299–323.

32. Samuel Krauss, "Le roi de France Charles VIII et les espérances messianiques," *Revue des Études Juives* 51 (1906): 87–96.

33. Weinstein, *Savonarola and Florence*, 142–47, 167–69, 374–76.

34. Netanyahu, *Isaac Abravanel*, 247–78. Netanyahu notes the parallels between the

prophecies of Savonarola and those of Abravanel. Often the only substantial difference is that one is referring to the Florentines and Florence, whereas the other is referring to the Jews and Jerusalem. The parallels, however, are common features in millenarianism and are not sufficient to conclude that Savonarola had a direct influence on Abravanel.

35. Aescoly, *Jewish Messianic Movements*, 251–78; Aaron Zeev Aescoly, "David Reubeni in the Light of History," *Jewish Quarterly Review* 28 (1937–1938): 1–45; Shulvass, *Rome and Jerusalem*, 54–64; Cecil Roth, "A Zionist Experiment in the Sixteenth Century," *Midstream* 9 (1963): 76–81; Aziel Shohat, "Notes on the David Reubeni Affair," *Zion* 35 (1970): 96–116 (in Hebrew).

36. Aescoly, *Jewish Messianic Movements*, 266–78; Shulvass, *Rome and Jerusalem*, 61–64; Idel, *Messianic Mystics*, 144–52.

37. Shulvass, *Rome and Jerusalem*, 79–82; David Tamar, "The Messianic Expectations in Italy for the Year 1575," *Sufunot* 2 (1958): 61–88 (in Hebrew).

38. Roth, *History of the Jews of Italy*, 289–94; Salo Wittmayer Baron, *A Social and Religious History of the Jews*, 18 vols. (New York: Columbia University Press, 1952–1983), v. 14, 114–46; Bonfil, *Jewish Life in Renaissance Italy*, 72–77, 97–98. Bonfil admits that large numbers of Jews were impoverished in this period, but he argues that, following the establishment of ghettos, expulsions stopped and attacks on Jews declined.

39. Idel, *Messianic Mystics*, 159.

40. Gerson D. Cohen, "Messianic Postures of Ashkenazim and Sephardim (Prior to Sabbatai Zevi)," in *Studies of the Leo Baeck Institute*, ed. Max Kreutzberger (New York: Frederick Ungar, 1967), 117–56.

41. Elisheva Carlebach, "Between History and Hope: Jewish Messianism in Ashkenaz and Sepharad," Third Annual Lecture of the Victor J. Selmanowitz Chair of Jewish History (New York: Touro College, Graduate School of Jewish Studies, 1998).

42. Léon Poliakov, *The History of Anti-Semitism*, v. 1, *From the Time of Christ to the Court Jews* (London: Vanguard, 1975), chs. 2–7.

43. Cohen, "Messianic Postures," 144–47.

44. H. J. Zimmels, *Ashkenazim and Sephardim: Their Relations, Differences, and Problems as Reflected in the Rabbinical Responsa* (London: Oxford University Press, 1958), 12–15.

45. Ben-Sasson, "Exile and Redemption"; Tishby, *Messianism*; Tishby, "Acute Apocalyptic Messianism," 267–69; H. H. Ben-Sasson, "The Generation of the Spanish Exiles and Its Fate," *Zion* 26 (1961) 23–64 (in Hebrew).

46. Netanyahu, *Isaac Abravanel*, 87–88, 226–34.

47. Shulvass, *Jews in the World of the Renaissance*, 195–99, 207–10, 328, 333–36, 346–47, 350.

48. Idel, "Religion, Thought, and Attitudes."

49. Bonfil, *Jewish Life in Renaissance Italy*, 102–4; Kenneth Snow, *Theater of Acculturation: The Roman Ghetto in the 16th Century* (Seattle: University of Washington Press, 2001), 93–94; Stefanie B. Siegmund, *The Medici State and the Ghetto of Florence: The Construction of an Early Modern Community* (Stanford, CA: Stanford University Press, 2006), 18–21, 407–11; Robert Bonfil, "Change in the Cultural Patterns of a Jewish Society in Crisis: Italian Jewry at the Close of the Sixteenth Century," in *Essential Papers on Jewish Culture in Renaissance and Baroque Italy*, ed. David B. Ruderman (New York: New York University Press, 1992), 401–25. See also Ruderman's introduction to *Essential Papers on Jewish Culture in Renaissance and Baroque Italy*, 1–39.

Chapter 5

1. David M. Gitlitz, *Secrecy and Deceit: The Religion of the Crypto-Jews* (Philadelphia: Jewish Publication Society, 1996), 74–75.

2. Benzion Dinur, "The Emigration from Spain to Eretz Yisrael After the Disorders of 1391," *Zion* 32 (1967): 161–74 (in Hebrew); Yitzhak Baer, *A History of the Jews in Christian Spain*, 2 vols. (Philadelphia: Jewish Publication Society, 1961), v. 2, 292, 294–95.

3. Renée Levine Melammed, *Heretics or Daughters of Israel? The Crypto-Jewish Women of Castile* (New York: Oxford University Press, 1999), 32–33, 47–72; Gitlitz, *Secrecy and Deceit*, 107–9; Baer, *Jews in Christian Spain*, v. 2, 356–58; Yitzhak Baer, "The Messianic Movement in Spain in the Period of the Expulsion," *Zion* 5 (1933): 71–77 (in Hebrew); Haim Beinart, "The Converso Community in Sixteenth- and Seventeenth-Century Spain," in *The Sephardi Heritage*, ed. R. D. Barnett (London: Vallentine Mitchell, 1971), 457–78; Haim Beinart, "The Conversos of Halia and the Prophetess Ines of Herrera," *Zion* 53 (1988): 13–52 (in Hebrew).

4. Richard H. Popkin, "Jewish Christians and Christian Jews in Spain, 1492 and After," *Judaism* 41 (1992): 248–67.

5. Marjorie Reeves, *The Influence of Prophecy in the Later Middle Ages* (Oxford: Clarendon Press, 1969), 446; Américo Castro, *The Spaniards* (Berkeley: University of California Press, 1971), 78.

6. Moses A. Shulvass, *Rome and Jerusalem* (Jerusalem: Mosad Ha-Rav Kook, 1944), 66 (in Hebrew); Matt D. Goldish, "Patterns in Converso Messianism," in *Millenarianism and Messianism in Early Modern European Culture: Jewish Messianism in the Early Modern World*, ed. Matt D. Goldish and Richard H. Popkin (Dordrecht, Netherlands: Kluwer, 2001), 47, 53; Harris Lenowitz, *The Jewish Messiahs: From the Galilee to Crown Heights* (New York: Oxford University Press, 1998), 104.

7. Cecil Roth, *A History of the Marranos* (Philadelphia: Jewish Publication Society, 1932), 146–48; Goldish, "Patterns," 47.

8. Yosef Hayim Yerushalmi, *From Spanish Court to Italian Ghetto* (New York: Columbia University Press, 1971), 306–9; A. H. De Oliveria Marques, *History of Portugal* (New York: Columbia University Press, 1972), v. 1, 319; Charles E. Nowell, *A History of Portugal* (New York: Van Nostrand, 1952), 137–39; Goldish, "Patterns," 54–55.

9. Angus MacKay, "Popular Movements and Pogroms in Fifteenth-Century Castile," *Past and Present* 55 (1972): 33–67; Francisco Marguez Villanueva, "The Converso Problem: An Assessment," in *Collected Studies in Honour of Américo Castro's Eightieth Year*, ed. M. P. Hornik (Oxford: Lincombe Lodge Research Library, 1965), 317–33; Baer, *Jews in Christian Spain*, v. 2, 270–81; Henry Kamen, *The Spanish Inquisition* (London: Weidenfeld & Nicolson, 1965), 22–23, 26–32, 35–53; Stephen Haliczer, *Inquisition and Society in the Kingdom of Valencia, 1478–1834* (Berkeley: University of California Press, 1990), 210.

10. Renée Levine Melammed, *A Question of Identity: Iberian Conversos in Historical Perspectives* (Oxford: Oxford University Press, 2004), 17–26.

11. I. S. Révah, "Les Marranes," *Revue des Études Juives* 118 (1959–1960): 36–37; Roth, *Marranos*, 64–66, 69–79; Martin A. Cohen (trans.), *Samuel Usque's Consolation for the Tribulations of Israel* (Philadelphia: Jewish Publication Society, 1965), 6–8; Stephen Gilman, "The Conversos and the Fall of Fortune," in *Collected Studies in Honour of Américo Castro's Eightieth Year*, ed. M. P. Hornik (Oxford: Lincombe Lodge Research Library, 1965), 127–36.

12. Baer, *Jews in Christian Spain*, v. 2, 272–73; Beinart, "Converso Community," 464–66.

13. B. Netanyahu, *The Marranos of Spain* (New York: American Academy of Jewish Research, 1966); B. Netanyahu, *The Origins of the Inquisition in Fifteenth Century Spain* (New York: Random House, 1995), 925–49; Norman Roth, *Conversos, Inquisition, and the Expulsion of the Jews from Spain* (Madison: University of Wisconsin Press, 1995).

14. Haliczer, *Inquisition and Society*, 213–17; Melammed, *Question of Identity*, 19, 25.

15. Netanyahu, *Marranos of Spain*, 75, 190, 204–5; Roth, *Conversos*, 156.

16. Haliczer, *Inquisition and Society*, 218.

17. Yerushalmi, *From Spanish Court*, 5–9; Roth, *Marranos*, 54–63; Révah, "Marranes," 35–41; David L. Graizbord, *Souls in Dispute: Converso Identities in Iberia and the Jewish Diaspora, 1580–1700* (Philadelphia: University of Pennsylvania Press, 2004), 50–52.

18. Gitlitz, *Secrecy and Deceit*, 43–44.

19. Roth, *Marranos*, 168–94; Cecil Roth, "The Religion of the Marranos," *Jewish Quarterly Review* 22 (1931): 1–33; Beinhart, "Converso Community," 463–72; Baruch Braunstein, *The Chuetos of Majorca* (Scottdale, PA: Mennonite Publishing, 1936), 94–114, 194–202; Kenneth Moore, *Those of the Street* (Notre Dame, IN: University of Notre Dame Press, 1976), 128–30.

20. Nahum Sokolow, *Baruch Spinoza and His Time* (Paris: Imprimerie Voltaire, 1928–29), 255–59 (in Hebrew); Israel Zinberg, *A History of Jewish Literature*, trans. Bernard Martin (Cleveland, OH: Press of Case Western Reserve Library, 1975–76), v. 5, 121.

21. Goldish, "Patterns," 41–45; Gitlitz, *Secrecy and Deceit*, 106.

22. See Yerushalmi, *From Spanish Court*, 5–9; Roth, *Marranos*, 54–63; Révah, "Marranes," 35–41; Graizbord, *Souls in Dispute*, 50–52.

23. *Encyclopaedia Judaica* (Jerusalem: Keter, 1972), v. 11, 1019–25.

24. Ellis Rivkin, *The Shaping of Jewish History* (New York: Scribner, 1971), 142–49; Goldish, "Patterns," 46; Melammed, *Question of Identity*, 76, 111, 129, 173.

25. Gershom Scholem, *Sabbatai Sevi: The Mystical Messiah, 1626–1676* (Princeton, NJ: Princeton University Press, 1973).

26. Scholem, *Sabbatai Sevi*, 327–35, 383, 391–92, 435, 461–68; Jacob Barnai, *Sabbatianism: Social Aspects* (Jerusalem: Zalman Shazar Center for Jewish History, 2000), 75–83 (in Hebrew); Jacob Barnai, "The Spread of the Sabbatean Movement in the Seventeenth and Eighteenth Centuries," in *Communication in the Jewish Diaspora: The Pre-Modern World*, ed. Sophia Menache (Leiden, Netherlands: Brill, 1996), 323–31; Matt Goldish, *The Sabbatean Prophets* (Cambridge MA: Harvard University Press, 2004), 7.

27. Goldish, *Sabbatean Prophets*, 88–89, 101–10, 118, 129, 139–40. Ada Rapoport-Albert has documented the prominence of female prophets in Sabbateanism, particularly in the communities in the Ottoman Empire. Former conversos familiar with the participation of women in Christian religious trends were especially likely to accept the prophecies of women. Ada Rapoport-Albert, "On the Position of Women in Sabbatianism," in *The Sabbatian Movement and Its Aftermath: Messianism, Sabbatianism, and Frankism*, ed. Elior Rachel (Jerusalem: Institute of Jewish Studies, 2001), v. 1, 143–327 (in Hebrew).

28. Scholem, *Sabbatai Sevi*, 444–60, 535.

29. Scholem, *Sabbatai Sevi*, 7–71; Gershom Scholem, *Major Trends in Jewish Mysticism* (New York: Schocken, 1961), 244–88; Scholem, *Kabbalah*, 79 (quote).

30. Scholem, *Sabbatai Sevi*, 18–20; Scholem, *Major Trends*, 244–49.

31. Scholem, *Sabbatai Sevi*, 538, 570.

32. Jacob Katz, *Tradition and Crisis: Jewish Society at the End of the Middle Ages* (New York: Schocken, 1961), 221–24; Goldish, *Sabbatean Prophets*, 50, 69.

33. Barnai, *Sabbatianism*, 26–29, 71, 105.

34. Moshe Idel, *Messianic Mystics* (New Haven, CT: Yale University Press, 1998), 169–70, 180.

35. Moshe Idel, "Religion, Thought, and Attitudes: The Impact of the Expulsion on the Jews," in *Spain and the Jews: The Sephardi Experience, 1492 and After*, ed. Elie Kedourie (London: Thames & Hudson, 1992), 129.

36. David Biale, *Power and Powerless in Jewish History* (New York: Schocken, 1986), 157; A. P. Coudert, "Kabbalistic Messianism Versus Kabbalistic Enlightenment," in *Millenarianism and Messianism in Early Modern Culture: Jewish Messianism in the Early Modern World*, ed. Matt D. Goldish and Richard H. Popkin (Dordrecht, Netherlands: Kluwer, 2001), 112.

37. Goldish, *Sabbatean Prophets*, 50–51, 69–71, 83.

38. Scholem, *Sabbatai Sevi*, 238–67, 472–657; Bernard D. Weinryb, *The Jews of Poland: A Social and Economic History of the Jewish Community in Poland from 1100 to 1800* (Philadelphia: Jewish Publication Society, 1972), 219–20. Carlebach argues that the Ashkenazim in Germany held a belief in Sabbatai, but she admits that German Jews were inclined to a more "private expression of hope" and that they were "restrained" in their public expressions. Elisheva Carlebach, "The Sabbatian Posture of German Jewry," in *The Sabbatian Movement and Its Aftermath: Messianism, Sabbatianism, and Frankism*, ed. Elior Rachel (Jerusalem: Institute of Jewish Studies, 2001), v. 2, 1–29. From an examination of the Polish sources on the movement, Galas concludes that there was "great interest in Sabbatianism in Poland, at least similar to other countries in Western Europe." Michal Galas, "Sabbatianism in the Seventeenth-Century Polish-Lithuanian Commonwealth: A Review of the Sources," in *The Sabbatian Movement and Its Aftermath: Messianism, Sabbatianism, and Frankism*, ed. Elior Rachel (Jerusalem: Institute of Jewish Studies, 2001), 51–63. Hundert writes that the extent of the following in Poland-Lithuania in 1666 is "unresolved." Gershon David Hundert, *Jews in Poland-Lithuania in the Eighteenth Century* (Berkeley: University of California Press, 2004), 153. On the distribution and demography of the conversos and former conversos, see Rivkin, *Jewish History*, 142–49; Roth, *Marranos*, 195–235; Cecil Roth, *The History of the Jews of Italy* (Philadelphia: Jewish Publication Society, 1946), 333–35, 346–50; *Encyclopaedia Judaica*, v. 2, 895–98, v. 7, 1225–26, and v. 10, 1571; Simon Dubnov, *History of the Jews* (New York: Barnes, 1971), v. 3, 471–73, 482, 627–31; and Melammed, *Question of Identity*, 71, 111, 129.

39. Barnai, *Sabbatianism*, 42–45; Jacob Barnai, "The Sabbatean Movement in Smyrna: The Social Background," in *Jewish Sects, Religious Movements, and Political Parties*, ed. Menachem Mor (Omaha, NE: Creighton University Press, 1992), 113–22; Goldish, *Sabbatean Prophets*, 2–3.

40. Goldish, *Sabbatean Prophets*, 108, 141, 147.

41. Scholem, *Sabbatai Sevi*, 152–54.

42. B. S. Capp, *Fifth Monarchy Men* (London: Rowman & Littlefield, 1972), 26, 213; Richard H. Popkin, "Three English Tellings of the Sabbatai Zvi Story," *Jewish History* 8 (1994): 43–54.

43. Michael McKeon, "Sabbatai Sevi in England," *AJS Review* 2 (1977): 131–69. Fenton argues that Sabbatai was probably influenced by contemporary Islamic millenarianism and in particular by the Sufi mystic Muhammad An-Niyazi, who predicted that the two imams, Hasan and Husayn, would return in 1692. Paul B. Fenton, "Shabbata Sebi and His Muslim Contemporary Muhammad An-Niyazi," in *Approaches to Judaism in Medieval Times*, ed. David R. Blumenthal (Atlanta, GA: Scholars Press, 1988), v. 3, 82–88.

44. Scholem, *Sabbatai Sevi*, 333–34, 545; Capp, *Fifth Monarchy Men*, 214; Peter Toon, *Puritans, the Millennium, and the Future of Israel: Puritan Eschatology, 1600–1660* (Cambridge:

James Clarke, 1970), 137–53.

45. Scholem, *Sabbatai Sevi*, 154.

46. Andrew Branstock, "Millenarianism in the Reformation and the English Revolution," in *Christian Millenarianism: From the Early Church to Waco*, ed. Stephen Hunt (London: Hurst, 2001), 81–87; B. McGinn, "Forms of Catholic Millenarianism: A Brief Overview," in *Millenarianism and Messianism in Early Modern European Culture*, v. 2, *Catholic Millenarianism: From Savonarola to the Abbe Gregoire*, ed. Karl A. Kottman (Dordrecht, Netherlands: Kluwer Academic, 2001), 8–11; Eugene Weber, *Apocalypses: Prophecies, Cults, and Millennial Beliefs Through the Ages* (Cambridge, MA: Harvard University Press, 1999), 68–74.

47. R. H. Popkin, "Millenarianism and Nationalism: A Case Study—Isaac La Peyrere," in *Millenarianism and Messianism in Early Modern Culture: Continental Millenarianism—Protestants, Catholics, Heretics*, ed. J. C. Laursen and R. H. Popkin (Dordrecht, Netherlands: Kluwer, 2001), 77–84.

48. Popkin, "Three English Tellings," 50.

49. Goldish, *Sabbatean Prophets*, 110–18.

50. Goldish, *Sabbatean Prophets*, 34–40; Barnai, *Sabbatianism*, 33–35; Jane Hathaway, "The Grand Vizier and the False Messiah: The Sabbatai Sevi Controversy," *Journal of the American Oriental Society* 117 (1967): 665–72.

51. Cecil Roth, *A Life of Menasseh ben Israel* (Philadelphia: Jewish Publication Society, 1934). Menasseh read and was impressed by La Peyrere's work on the imminent arrival of the Jewish messiah, and he conveyed this news to Protestant millenarians in Amsterdam. Popkin, "Isaac La Peyrere," 81.

52. Barnai, *Sabbatianism*, 49; Barnai, "Spread of the Sabbatean Movement," 318.

53. Roth, *Menasseh ben Israel*.

54. Richard H. Popkin, "The Historical Significance of Sephardic Judaism in Seventeenth-Century Amsterdam," *American Sephardi* 5 (1971): 18–27; Jacob J. Petachowski, *The Theology of Haham David Nieta* (New York: Ktav, 1970), 33–36; Ellis Rivkin, *León Da Modena and the Kol Sakhal* (Cincinnati: Hebrew Union College Press, 1952), 5–6; Melammed, *Question of Identity*, 76.

55. Yosef Hayim Yerushalmi, "Conversos Returning to Judaism in the Seventeenth Century: Their Jewish Knowledge and Psychological Readiness," in *Proceedings of the Fifth World Congress of Jewish Studies*, ed. Pinchas Peli (Jerusalem: World Union of Jewish Studies, 1972), 201–9 (in Hebrew); Yerushalmi, *From Spanish Court*, 44–47.

56. Jos Nehama, *Histoire des Israelites de Salonique*, 7 vols. (Salonika, Greece: Librairie Molho, 1935), v. 5, 17–19.

57. Peter Berger, *Invitation to Sociology* (Harmondsworth, U.K.: Penguin, 1963), 51–52.

58. Nehama, *Salonique*, v. 5, 14–20.

59. Rivkin, *León Da Modena*, 7–16; Isaiah Sonne, "León Modena and the Da Costa Circle in Amsterdam," *Hebrew Union College Annual* 21 (1948): 1–28; I. S. Révah, "Spinoza et les hérétiques de la communauté judéo-portugaise d'Amsterdam," *Revue de l'Histoire des Religions* 154 (1958): 46–52; Yirmiahu Yovel, "Why Spinoza Was Excommunicated," *Commentary* 64 (November 1977): 46–52.

60. Yerushalmi, "Conversos," 202; Melammed, *Question of Identity*, 77.

61. Weinryb, *Jews of Poland*, 151, 181–205.

62. Scholem, *Sabbatai Sevi*, 1–3, 88–93, 139, 461, 591–92.

63. Barnai, *Sabbatianism*, 51–61.

64. Barnai, *Sabbatianism*, 58.

65. Weinryb, *Jews of Poland*, 171–72, 200–201, 205.

66. Trevor Aston (ed.), *Crisis in Europe, 1560–1660* (London: Routledge & Kegan Paul, 1965); Geoffrey Parker and Lesley M. Smith (eds.), *The General Crisis of the Seventeenth Century* (London: Routledge & Kegan Paul, 1978). For an account that gives greater consideration to the cultural aspects of the crisis, see Theodore K. Rabb, *The Struggle for Stability in Early Modern Europe* (New York: Oxford University Press, 1975).

67. Bernard Lewis, "Some Reflections on the Decline of the Ottoman Empire," in *The Economic Decline of Empires*, ed. Carlos M. Cipolla (London: Methuen, 1970), 215–34; D. H. Pennington, *Seventeenth-Century Europe* (London: Longman, 1970), 368–72; Robert W. Olson, "Jews in the Ottoman Empire in the Light of New Documents," *Jewish Social Studies* 41 (1977): 75–88; H. A. R. Gibb and Harold Bowen, *Islamic Society and the West* (London: Oxford University Press, 1957), pt. 2, 239–41; Nehama, *Salonique*, v. 5, 7–8, 55–98; Barnai, *Sabbatianism*, 36–39, 63.

68. Carlo M. Cipolla, "The Economic Decline of Italy," in *Economic Decline of Empires*, 196–214; Rivkin, *León Da Modena*, 18–39; Cecil Roth, *The History of the Jews of Italy* (Philadelphia: Jewish Publication Society, 1946), 333–35, 348–50.

69. J. L. Price, *Culture and Society in the Dutch Republic During the Seventeenth Century* (New York: Scribner, 1974), 42–53, 211–12; Violet Barbour, *Capitalism in Amsterdam in the Seventeenth Century* (Ann Arbor: University of Michigan Press, 1963); Immanuel Wallerstein, *The Modern World-System II: Mercantilism and the Consolidation of the European World-Economy, 1600–1750* (New York: Academic Press, 1980), 37–71.

70. Rabb, *Struggle for Stability*, 35–59, 107–15.

71. Scholem, *Sabbatai Sevi*, 651–52; Barnai, *Sabbatianism*, 35; A. Freimann and F. Kracauer, *Frankfort* (Philadelphia: Jewish Publication Society, 1929), 108, 113–17; *Encyclopaedia Judaica*, v. 13, 967–68; Max Grunwald, *Vienna* (Philadelphia: Jewish Publication Society, 1936), 91–95. In Yemen, messianism was strong during the years before 1665–66. Joseph Sadan, "A New Source on the Sabbatian Movement and Its Aftermath in the Seventeenth Century," in *The Sabbatian Movement and Its Aftermath: Messianism, Sabbatianism, and Frankism*, ed. Elior Rachel (Jerusalem: Institute of Jewish Studies, 2001), v. 1, 93–111 (in Hebrew); Yosef Tobi, "The Events of 1667 in the Yemen: Sabbatian Movement or Local Messianic Activity," in *The Sabbatian Movement and Its Aftermath: Messianism, Sabbatianism, and Frankism*, ed. Elior Rachel (Jerusalem: Institute of Jewish Studies, 2001), v. 1, 113–28.

72. Scholem, *Sabbatai Sevi*, 703–4, 710, 720–21, 800–805; Scholem, *Major Trends*, 310–12.

73. Scholem, *Major Trends*, 309.

74. Scholem, *Sabbatai Sevi*, 794–95; Scholem, *Major Trends*, 309–10.

Chapter 6

1. Gershom Scholem, "Redemption Through Sin," in his *Messianic Idea in Judaism and Other Essays on Jewish Spirituality* (New York: Schocken, 1971), 99.

2. Scholem, "Redemption Through Sin," 108–11.

3. Scholem wrote, "No matter how thoroughly fantastic and partisan the allegations of the anti-Sabbatians may seem to us, we have not the slightest justification for doubting their accuracy, inasmuch as in every case we can rely for evidence on the 'confessions' of the 'believers' themselves, as well as a number of their apologias." Scholem, "Redemption Through Sin," 114.

4. Gershom Scholem, "The Crypto-Jewish Sect of the Donmeh (Sabbatians) in Turkey," in his *Messianic Idea in Judaism and Other Essays on Jewish Spirituality* (New York:

Schocken, 1971), 142–66; Gershom Scholem, *Kabbalah* (Jerusalem: Keter, 1974), 327–32.

5. Antinomianism accompanied some of the sects of the radical Reformation, especially the offshoots of Anabaptism. For example, in 1551 in the area of Mulhausen and Langensalza, Claus Ludwig and his followers expected an imminent millennium and believed that they had achieved a state of true freedom through their religious rebirth. They believed that they were able to engage in sexual relations with any other saved person, and they proclaimed that the sexual act was the only true sacrament: The man was the bread and the woman was the wine. Claus-Peter Clasen, *Anabaptism: A Social History, 1525–1615* (Ithaca, NY: Cornell University Press, 1972), 134–39. For other cases, see pp. 122–33. Antinomianism has also emerged from millenarianism in Islam. In 1164, Hasan, the Ismaili lord of Alamut, proclaimed that he had received a message from a hidden imam that announced the millennium and freed believers from the Holy Law. Hasan and his followers began by banqueting in the middle of the fasting month of Ramadan. Bernard Lewis, *The Assassins: A Radical Sect in Islam* (New York: Basic Books, 1968), 71–75.

6. On differences between millenarianism and mysticism, see the introduction to Part 2 of this work and my *Messianism, Mysticism, and Magic: A Sociological Analysis of Jewish Religious Movements* (Chapel Hill: University of North Carolina Press, 1982), 11–16.

7. Hans Jonas, *The Gnostic Religion: The Message of the Alien God and the Beginnings of Christianity* (Boston: Beacon, 1963).

8. Dmitri Obolensky, *The Bogomils: A Study of Balkan Neo-Manichaeism* (Cambridge: Cambridge University Press, 1948); Bernard Hamilton, *Monastic Reform, Catharism, and the Crusades, 900–1300* (London: Variorum Reprints, 1979), 3–40, 115–24.

9. John Passmore, *The Perfectability of Man* (New York: Scribner's, 1970), 140–41.

10. Scholem, "Redemption Through Sin," 130.

11. Gershom Scholem, *Studies and Texts Concerning the History of Sabbatianism and Its Metamorphosis* (Jerusalem: Mosad Bialik, 1974), 47–62, 116–39 (in Hebrew); Scholem, *Kabbalah*, 228, 293–94; Scholem, "Redemption Through Sin," 126–34; Arthur Mandel, *The Militant Messiah* (Atlantic Highlands, NJ: Humanities Press, 1979), 39–42; Sharot, *Messianism, Mysticism, and Magic*, 136–38.

12. Norman Cohn, *The Pursuit of the Millennium* (New York: Harper, 1961), 177–82. See also G. Leff, *Heresy in the Later Middle Ages: The Relation of Heterodoxy to Dissent, c. 1250–c. 1450* (New York: Barnes & Noble, 1967), v. 1, 314.

13. Robert E. Lerner, *The Heresy of the Free Spirit in the Later Middle Ages* (Berkeley: University of California Press, 1972), 8–13, 71–76, 135–38, 142–44.

14. Eleanor McLaughlin, "The Heresy of the Free Spirit and Late Medieval Mysticism," *Medievalia et Humanistica*, n.s., 4 (1973): 37–54.

15. McLaughlin, "Heresy of the Free Spirit," 41–43; Lerner, *Heresy of the Free Spirit*, 200–208.

16. Lerner, *Heresy of the Free Spirit*, 3, 8, 227.

17. McLaughlin, "Heresy of the Free Spirit," 45–52.

18. Ahmet T. Karamusafa, *God's Unruly Friends: Dervish Groups in the Islamic Later Middle Period, 1200–1550* (Salt Lake City: University of Utah Press, 1994), 2–4, 13–21; J. Spencer Trimingham, *The Sufi Orders in Islam* (Oxford: Clarendon Press, 1971), 16, 28–29, 98, 267–68; Annemarie Schimmel, *Mystical Dimensions of Islam* (Chapel Hill: University of North Carolina Press, 1975), 204; Gustave E. Von Grunebaum, *Medieval Islam: A Study in Cultural Orientation* (Chicago: University of Chicago Press, 1946), 136–37.

19. Hugh B. Urban, *The Economics of Ecstasy: Tantra, Secrecy, and Power in Colonial Bengal* (Oxford: Oxford University Press, 2001), 6, 162; Hugh B. Urban, "The Cult of Ecstasy:

Tantrism, the New Age, and the Spiritual Logic of Late Capitalism," *History of Religions* 39(3) (2000): 268–304.

20. Wendy Doniger O'Flaherty, *Asceticism and Eroticism in the Mythology of Siva* (London: Oxford University Press, 1973).

21. Urban, *Economics of Ecstasy*, 7, 88–89, 143–46.

22. Mircea Eliade and Willard Ropes Trask, *Yoga: Immortality and Freedom* (London: Routledge & Kegan Paul, 1969), 204–8, 261–72, 294–305; Shashi Bhushan Dasgupta, *An Introduction to Tantric Buddhism* (Calcutta, India: Calcutta University Press, 1958), esp. 17–94; Agehananda Bharati, *The Tantric Tradition* (London: Rider, 1965), 284–95; Edward Conze, *Buddhism* (Oxford: Bruno Cassirer, 1951), 195–96, 178; D. L. Snellgrove, *The Hevajra Tantra: A Critical Study* (London: Oxford University Press, 1959), 20–24, 33–34, 43–45; Geoffrey Parringer, *Sex in the World's Religions* (London: Sheldon, 1980), 35–37, 49–50, 86, 112–13; Sidney Spencer, *Mysticism in World Religion* (Harmondsworth, U.K.: Penguin, 1963), 59, 93–96.

23. David R. Como, *Blown by the Spirit: Puritanism and the Emergence of an Antinomian Underground in Pre–Civil War England* (Stanford, CA: Stanford University Press, 2004), 111–19.

24. On the antinomian episode in New England Puritanism, see David D. Hall (ed.), *The Antinomian Controversy, 1636–1638: A Documentary History* (Middletown, CT: Wesleyan University Press, 1968); William K. B. Stoever, *"A Faire and Easie Way to Heaven": Covenant Theology and Antinomianism in Early Massachusetts* (Middletown, CT: Wesleyan University Press, 1978).

25. James Colin Davis, *Fear, Myth, and History: The Ranters and the Historians* (Cambridge: Cambridge University Press, 2002).

26. J. F. McGregor, Bernard Capp, Nigel Smith, and B. J. Gibbons, "Debate: Fear, Myth and Furore—Reappraising the 'Ranters,'" *Past and Present* 140 (1993): 155–94; J. C. Davis, "Reply," *Past and Present* 140 (1993): 94–210.

27. A. L. Morton, *The World of the Ranters: Religious Radicalism in the English Revolution* (London: Lawrence & Wishart, 1979), 71, 73–74, 77, 219–21; Christopher Hill, *The World Turned Upside Down: Radical Ideas During the English Revolution* (Harmondsworth, U.K.: Penguin, 1974), 214, 219–21.

28. Jerome Friedman, *Blasphemy, Immorality, and Anarchy: The Ranters and the English Revolution* (Athens: Ohio University Press, 1987), 19, 60, 70.

29. Hill, *World Turned Upside Down*, 215.

30. Morton, *World of the Ranters*, 78.

31. Friedman, *Blasphemy*, 102.

32. For a more extended treatment, see Sharot, *Messianism, Mysticism, and Magic*, 138–54.

33. Mendel Piekarz, *The Beginning of Hasidism: Ideological Trends in Derush and Musar Literature* (Jerusalem: Mosad Bialik, 1978), 175–215 (in Hebrew).

34. Sharot, *Messianism, Mysticism, and Magic*, 152–53, 182–83.

35. Shaul Magid, *Hasidism on the Margin: Reconciliation, Antinomianism, and Messianism in the Izbica/Radzin Hasidism* (Madison: University of Wisconsin Press, 2003).

36. Lerner, *The Heresy of the Free Spirit*, 61, 79–84; M. D. Lambert, *Medieval Heresy: Popular Movements from Bogomil to Hus* (London: Edward Arnold, 1977), 174–80.

37. Mary Douglas, *Purity and Danger* (Harmondsworth, U.K.: Penguin, 1970), 188–209.

38. The most central work here is Sigmund Freud, *Civilization and Its Discontents* (London: Cape & Smith, 1930).

39. Scholem, "Redemption Through Sin," 109.

40. Here Max Weber was in agreement with Freud. Weber wrote that "there can be no doubt that a considerable portion of the specifically anti-erotic religiosity, both mystical and ascetic, represents substitute satisfaction of sexually conditioned physiological needs." Max Weber, *Economy and Society: An Outline of Interpretive Sociology* (New York: Bedminster Press, 1968), 603.

41. For examples among Christian sects, see Werner Stark, *The Sociology of Religion* (London: Routledge & Kegan Paul, 1967), v. 2, 184–97.

42. If, as seems likely, there is less sexual repression in Western societies than in some previous centuries, both asceticism and antinomianism are less likely to appear.

43. Emile Durkheim, "The Dualism of Human Nature and Its Social Conditions," in *Essays on Sociology and Philosophy*, ed. Kurt H. Wolff (New York: Harper Torchbook, 1964), 325–40; Emile Durkheim, *The Elementary Forms of the Religious Life* (New York: Collier, 1961 [1912]), 297–308.

44. Among the antinomian movements I have discussed, the social context of the Ranters best fits this perspective. The Ranters arose, alongside many other religious sects and groups, during a period of widespread conflict when there was a breakdown of censorship and government and a disillusionment with the hopes raised by the defeat of the king's forces. Unattached migratory craftsmen, freed by the breakdown of the settlement system during the Revolution, were prepared to break with tradition and may have provided support for the Ranters (Morton, *World of the Ranters*, 90). Morton's contention that Ranterism found its major support among the urban poor (Morton, *World of the Ranters*, 17, 79, 111) has been questioned by McGregor on the basis of Quaker sources. The Quakers' rejection of conventional religious authority and the behavior of some early adherents implicated them with the Ranters, but Quaker leaders insisted on the essential difference between antinomianism and their belief that their indwelling light released them from the temptation to sin. O. F. McGregor, "Ranterism and the Development of Early Quakerism," *Journal of Religious History* 9 (1977): 349–63. Morton notes that antinomianism arose at the end of the civil war; it expressed a feeling that a new age had freed men from traditional constraints, but it also represented a reaction against the new discipline of Presbyterianism (Morton, *World of the Ranters*, 79). The Free Spirits appealed especially to marginally placed women, and Lerner suggests that a turning away from the world was a possible response of the wealthy to the economic decline, famines, plagues, and other adversities of the fourteenth century (Lerner, *Heresy of the Free Spirit*, 230–35, 243). On the social background of Sabbateanism and Hasidism, see Sharot, *Messianism, Mysticism, and Magic*, 101–14, 126–28, 131–35, 155–58.

45. Emile Durkheim, *Suicide* (New York: Free Press, 1951), 241–76. In contrast to Freud's portrayal of definite organic drives, Durkheim assumed that the human animal is born with an unformed and amoral nature. The related emphasis on the decisive influence of the social environment has been criticized as an "oversocialized conception of man," and this has been associated with a perspective that emphasizes order in society. Dennis H. Wrong, "The Oversocialized Conception of Man in Modern Sociology," *American Sociological Review* 26 (1961): 183–93. However, the individual-society dichotomy and the conflict-order dichotomy are not necessarily associated.

46. Steven Lukes, *Emile Durkheim: His Life and Work* (Harmondsworth, U.K.: Penguin, 1973), 20–26; Anthony Giddens, "The 'Individual' in the Writings of Emile Durkheim," in his *Studies in Social and Political Theory* (London: Hutchinson, 1977), 273–91. It was in terms of the second model that Durkheim analyzed individualism as a historical develop-

ment. Emile Durkheim, "Individualism and the Intellectuals," *Political Studies* 17 (1969): 14–30.

47. Norbert Elias, *What Is Sociology?* (London: Hutchinson, 1978), 107.

48. Gershom Scholem, *Major Trends in Jewish Mysticism* (New York: Schocken, 1961), 316.

49. Jonas, *Gnostic Religion*, 331–33. In expressing his disagreement with Jonas's comparison of gnostics and nihilists, Conze writes that the gnostics' beliefs and aims made life far from meaningless, and he argues that Jonas was wrong to emphasize the nontraditional character of gnosticism. Edward Conze, "Buddhism and Gnosis," in *The Origins of Gnosticism: Colloquium of Messina*, ed. Ugo Bianchi (Leiden, Netherlands: Brill, 1970), 666.

50. Johan Goudsblom, *Nihilism and Culture* (Oxford: Blackwell, 1980), 193.

51. Goudsblom, *Nihilism and Culture*, 179–81, 188.

Afterword to Part 2

1. Rodney Stark, "In Praise of 'Idealistic Humbug,'" in his *Exploring the Religious Life* (Baltimore: Johns Hopkins University Press, 2004), 23.

2. Stark, "Idealistic Humbug," 31.

3. Stark, "Idealistic Humbug," 32.

4. Peter Worsley, *The Trumpet Shall Sound: A Study of "Cargo" Cults in Melanesia* (New York: Schocken, 1968 [1957]); Weston La Barre, *The Ghost Dance: Origins of Religion* (London: Allen & Unwin, 1972). For a recent overview of explanations in terms of crisis and disruption, see Sean McCloud, *Divine Hierarchies: Class in American Religion and Religious Studies* (Chapel Hill: University of North Carolina Press, 2007).

5. Stark, "Idealistic Humbug," 39.

6. Leon Festinger, Henry Riecken, and Stanley Schachter, *When Prophecy Fails: A Social and Psychological Study of a Modern Group That Predicted the Destruction of the World* (New York: Harper Torchbooks, 1956).

7. William Shaffir, "When Prophecy Is Not Validated: Expecting the Unexpected in a Messianic Campaign," in *Expecting Armageddon: Essential Readings in Failed Prophecy*, ed. Jon R. Stone (New York: Routledge, 2000), 251–67; Simon Dein, "What Really Happens When Prophecy Fails: The Case of Lubavitch," *Sociology of Religion* 62 (2001): 383–401.

8. Michal Kravel-Tovi, "To See the Invisible Messiah: Messianic Socialization in the Wake of a Failed Prophecy in Chabad," *Religion* 39 (2009): 248–60.

Introduction to Part 3

1. Max Weber, *Economy and Society: An Outline of Interpretive Sociology* (New York: Bedminster, 1968), 389.

2. David Goodblatt, *Elements of Ancient Jewish Nationalism* (Cambridge: Cambridge University Press, 2006), 17, 22–24.

3. Shaye J. D. Cohen, *The Beginnings of Jewishness: Boundaries, Varieties, Uncertainties* (Berkeley: University of California Press, 1999), 3–7, 13–14, 69–139.

4. Philip Esler, *Conflict and Identity in Romans: The Social Setting of Paul's Letter* (Minneapolis, MN: Augsburg Fortress, 2003), 66–68.

5. Steve Mason, "Jews, Judaeans, Judaizing, Judaism: Problems of Categorization in Ancient History," *Journal for the Study of Judaism* 38 (2007): 457–512.

6. Goodblatt, *Ancient Jewish Nationalism*, 108–66.

7. Andreas Wimmer, "The Making and Unmaking of Ethnic Boundaries: A Multilevel Process Theory," *American Journal of Sociology* 113 (2008): 984–85.

8. Christine Elizabeth Hayes, *Gentile Impurities and Jewish Identities: Intermarriage and Conversion from the Bible to the Talmud* (Oxford: Oxford University Press, 2002), 161, 193–94.

9. Goodblatt, *Ancient Jewish Nationalism*, 19–25.

10. Cohen, *Beginnings of Jewishness*, 134–39.

11. Goodblatt, *Ancient Jewish Nationalism*, 29–40, 112.

12. Shaye J. D. Cohen, *From the Maccabees to the Mishnah* (Louisville, KY: Westminster John Knox Press, 1987), 215.

13. Annette Yoshiko Reed, *Fallen Angels and the History of Judaism and Christianity: The Reception of Enochic Literature* (Cambridge: Cambridge University Press, 2005), 133–34.

14. Seth Schwartz, *Imperialism and Jewish Society: 200 B.C.E. to 640 C.E.* (Princeton, NJ: Princeton University Press, 2001), 15.

15. Gary G. Porton, "Who Was a Jew?" in *Judaism in Late Antiquity: Where We Stand—Issues and Debates in Ancient Judaism*, ed. Jacob Neusner and Alan Jeffery Avery-Peck (Leiden, Netherlands: Brill, 1999), v. 2, 197–218. See also Sacha Stern, *Jewish Identity in Early Rabbinic Writings* (Leiden, Netherlands: Brill, 1994).

16. Cohen, *Beginnings of Jewishness*, 198–237.

17. Hayes, *Gentile Impurities*, 142–45, 162, 194.

18. Cohen, *Beginnings of Jewishness*, 343.

Chapter 7

1. Will Herberg, *Protestant, Catholic, Jew: An Essay in American Religious Sociology*, rev. ed. (Garden City, NY: Anchor Books, 1960); Stephen Sharot, "The Three-Generations Thesis and the American Jews," *British Journal of Sociology* 24 (1973): 151–64.

2. Nathan Glazer, *American Judaism* (Chicago: University of Chicago Press, 1957), 125.

3. Glazer, *American Judaism*, 89–91, 120–25; Benny Kraut, "American Judaism: An Appreciative Critical Appraisal," *American Jewish History* 77 (1987): 211–31.

4. Marshall Sklare, "Jewish Religion and Ethnicity at the Bicentennial," in *The Role of Religion in Modern Jewish History*, ed. Jacob Katz (Cambridge, MA: Association for Jewish Studies, 1975), 148–49.

5. Charles S. Liebman, *The Ambivalent American Jew* (Philadelphia: Jewish Publication Society, 1973), 66–69. Liebman juxtaposed folk religion, whose carrier is the community, with universal religion, which focuses on the individual rather than the existent collectivity, and elite religion, which in Judaism relates to the textual tradition (1–5, 45–49).

6. Jonathan S. Woocher, *Sacred Survival: The Civil Religion of American Jews* (Bloomington: Indiana University Press), vii.

7. Woocher, *Sacred Survival*, 67–89, 91–94, 131–46.

8. Jonathan Woocher, "'Sacred Survival' Revisited: American Jewish Civil Religion in the New Millennium," in *The Cambridge Companion to American Judaism*, ed. Dana Evan Kaplan (Cambridge: Cambridge University Press, 2005), 283–97.

9. United Jewish Communities, *National Jewish Population Survey, 2000–01* (New York: United Jewish Communities, 2003).

10. Herbert J. Gans, "Symbolic Ethnicity: The Future of Ethnic Groups and Cultures in America," *Ethnic and Racial Studies* 2 (1979): 1–20.

11. Herbert J. Gans, "Symbolic Ethnicity and Symbolic Religiosity: Towards a Comparison of Ethnic and Religious Acculturation," *Ethnic and Racial Studies* 17 (1994): 578.

12. Richard D. Alba, *Italian Americans into the Twilight of Ethnicity* (New York: Prentice Hall, 1985); Richard D. Alba, *Ethnic Identity: The Transformation of White America* (New Haven, CT: Yale University Press, 1990); Mary C. Waters, *Ethnic Options: Choosing Identities in America* (Berkeley: University of California Press, 1990).

13. Gans, "Symbolic Ethnicity and Symbolic Religiosity," 577–92.

14. Michael P. Carroll, "Stark Realities and Androcentric/Eurocentric Bias in the Sociology of Religion," *Sociology of Religion* 57 (1996): 225–39.

15. Herbert J. Gans, "American Jewry: Present and Future," *Commentary* 21 (May 1956): 422–30.

16. Gans, "Symbolic Ethnicity and Symbolic Religiosity," 578.

17. Steven M. Cohen, *American Modernity and Jewish Identity* (New York: Tavistock, 1983); Steven M. Cohen, *American Assimilation or Jewish Revival?* (Bloomington: Indiana University Press, 1988).

18. The 2000–01 National Jewish Population Survey reported a membership of 46 percent. This is probably an overestimate because the figure was based on a sample of respondents who answered the longer version of the questionnaire. The 2001 American Jewish Identity Survey reported 40 percent membership. Egon Mayer, Barry A. Kosmin, and Ariela Keysar, *American Jewish Identity Survey 2001* (New York: Center for Cultural Judaism, 2003).

19. Gans, "Symbolic Ethnicity and Symbolic Religiosity," 581–82.

20. Stephen R. Warner, "Work in Progress Toward a New Paradigm for the Sociological Study of Religion in the United States," *American Sociological Review* 98 (1993): 1044–93.

21. Gans, "Symbolic Ethnicity and Symbolic Religiosity," 577, 588.

22. Debra Renee Kaufman, "The Place of Judaism in American Jewish Identity," in *The Cambridge Companion to American Judaism*, ed. Dana Evan Kaplan (Cambridge: Cambridge University Press, 2005), 171–72.

23. Herbert J. Gans, "Comment: Ethnic Invention and Acculturation—A Bumpy-Line Approach," *Journal of American Ethnic History* 12 (1992): 43–52.

24. Gans, "Symbolic Ethnicity and Symbolic Religiosity," 584.

25. Gans, "Symbolic Ethnicity and Symbolic Religiosity," 582.

26. Jonathan D. Sarna, "The Evolution of the American Synagogue," in *The Americanization of the Jews*, ed. Robert M. Seltzer and Norman J. Cohen (New York: New York University Press, 1995); Leon A. Jick, *The Americanization of the Synagogue, 1820–1870* (Hanover, NH: Brandeis University Press, 1976); Egon Mayer, *Responses to Modernity: A History of the Reform Movement in Judaism* (New York: Oxford University Press, 1988).

27. Stephen Sharot, *Judaism: A Sociology* (New York: Holmes & Meier, 1976), 164–65.

28. Arnold Eisen, "American Judaism: Changing Patterns in Denominational Self-Definition," *Studies in Contemporary Jewry* 8 (1992): 21–49.

29. Kivisto and Nefzger and Winter interpreted their findings of positive correlations between measures of the strength of Jewish identity and measures of Jewish behavior (observances and affiliations) as nonsupportive of symbolic ethnicity. Peter Kivisto and Ben Nefzger, "Symbolic Ethnicity and American Jews: The Relationship of Ethnic Identity of Behavior and Group Affiliation," *Social Science Journal* 30 (1993): 1–12; J. Alan Winter, "Symbolic Ethnicity or Religion Among Jews in the United States: A Test of Gansian Hypotheses," *Review of Religious Research* 37 (1996): 233–47. Rebhun also argued that Gans's thesis had to be revised because the relationships between the sense of group belonging and religious behavior and affiliation strengthened over the period from 1970 to 1990. Uzi

Rebhun, "Jewish Identification in Contemporary America: Gans' Symbolic Ethnicity and Religiosity Theory Revisited," *Social Compass* 51 (2004): 349–66. However, these writers pushed the differentiation between identity and behavior further than Gans wished to take it. Gans's understanding of symbolic ethnicity as "the consumption and other use of ethnic symbols" (Gans, "Symbolic Ethnicity and Symbolic Religiosity," 578) must presumably be expressed in behavior. In fact, Winter ("Symbolic Ethnicity," 243) recognized as such when he noted that Gans specifically stated that specific ethnic practices may persist after being taken out of their original cultural context: "Most people look for easy and intermittent ways of expressing their [ethnic] identity" (Gans, "Symbolic Ethnicity," 8). Such behaviors as lighting Hanukkah candles and participation in a seder could be seen as "easy and intermittent." Their association with strength of identity, then, should not be viewed as a refutation of symbolic ethnicity.

30. Gans, "Symbolic Ethnicity and Symbolic Religiosity," 581.

31. Gans, "Symbolic Ethnicity and Symbolic Religiosity," 582.

32. Calvin Goldscheider and Alas S. Zuckerman, *The Transformation of the Jews* (Chicago: University of Chicago Press, 1984); Calvin Goldscheider, *Jewish Continuity and Change: Emerging Patterns in America* (Bloomington: Indiana University Press, 1986).

33. Goldscheider, *Jewish Continuity*, 184.

34. Calvin Goldscheider, *Studying the Jewish Future* (Seattle: University of Washington Press, 2004), 23, 28, 126–28. In comparison with American Jews, Goldscheider states that Judaism in Israel divides the Jews. He notes that Jews in Israel are not particularly religious and that the strength of Israeli Jews lies in their institutions and everyday life rather than in their Judaism (129–31). Such comments appear to assume that the secularization thesis is correct for Israeli Jews.

35. Cohen, *American Assimilation*.

36. Steven M. Cohen, "Why Intermarriage May Not Threaten Jewish Continuity," *Moment* 19 (December 1994): 54–57.

37. Steven M. Cohen, *Religious Stability and Ethnic Decline* (New York: Jewish Community Centers Association Research Center, 1998); Steven M. Cohen, *A Tale of Two Jewries: The "Inconvenient Truth" for American Jews* (New York: Jewish Life Network/Steinhardt Foundation, 2006). Another former optimist, Chaim Waxman, later argued that both Judaism and Jewishness have been waning among baby boomers. Chaim I. Waxman, *Jewish Baby Boomers: A Communal Perspective* (Albany: State University of New York Press, 2001).

38. Steven M. Cohen and Arnold M. Eisen, *The Jew Within: Self, Family, and Community in America* (Bloomington: Indiana University Press, 2000).

39. Steven M. Cohen, *Members and Motives: Who Joins American Jewish Congregations and Why*, Report 1 (New York: S3K Synagogue Studies Institute, 2006). For similar findings, see Vivian Klaff, "Defining American Jewry from Religious and Ethnic Perspectives: The Transitions to Greater Heterogeneity," *Sociology of Religion* 67 (2006): 415–38.

40. Cohen, *Members and Motives*. A comparison of the 1990 and 2000–01 national surveys of American Jewry appears to support Cohen's contention of a stable religiosity and declining ethnicity. The levels of religious observance remained largely unchanged in the "core" Jewish population: Hanukkah candle lighting dropped slightly, and small increases were seen for fasting on Yom Kippur, Passover seder attendance, and Sabbath candle lighting. However, the number of Jews who reported that most of their close friends were Jewish fell from 43 percent to 33 percent, and declines were also found for feelings of belonging to the Jewish people and attachment to Israel.

41. Charles S. Liebman, *Deceptive Images: Toward a Redefinition of American Judaism* (New

Brunswick, NJ: Transaction, 1988).

42. Goldscheider and Zuckerman, *Transformation of the Jews.*

43. Charles S. Liebman, *The Ambivalent American Jew* (Philadelphia: Jewish Publication Society, 1973).

44. Charles S. Liebman, "Ritual, Ceremony, and the Reconstruction of Judaism in the United States," *Studies in Contemporary Jewry* 6 (1990): 272–83; Charles S. Liebman and Steven M. Cohen, *Two Worlds of Judaism: The Israeli and American Experiences* (New Haven, CT: Yale University Press, 1990), 124–27.

45. Charles Liebman, "Unraveling the Ethnoreligious Package," in *Contemporary Jewries: Convergence and Divergence,* ed. Eliezer Ben-Rafael, Yosef Gorny, and Yaacov Ro'i (Leiden, Netherlands: Brill, 2003), 143–50.

46. Bethamie Horowitz, "Reframing the Study of Contemporary Jewish Identity," *Contemporary Jewry* 23 (2002): 14–34.

47. Kaufman, "Place of Judaism," 169–85.

48. Harriet Hartman and Debra Kaufman, "Decentering the Study of Jewish Identity: Opening the Dialogue with Other Religious Groups," *Sociology of Religion* 67 (2006): 365–85.

49. Charles S. Liebman, "The Essence of American Judaism," in *The Cambridge Companion to American Judaism,* ed. Dana Evan Kaplan (Cambridge: Cambridge University Press, 2005), 133–44; Bernard Susser and Charles S. Liebman, *Choosing Survival: Strategies for a Jewish Future* (New York: Oxford University Press, 1999), 78–87.

Chapter 8

1. Werner Sollors, *Beyond Ethnicity: Consent and Descent in American Culture* (New York: Oxford University Press, 1986), 5–6.

2. Wade Clark Roof and William McKinney, *American Mainline Religion: Its Changing Shape and Future* (New Brunswick, NJ: Rutgers University Press, 1987); Bruce A. Greer and Wade Clark Roof, "Desperately Seeking Sheila: Locating Religious Privatism in American Society," *Journal for the Scientific Study of Religion* 31 (1992): 346–52.

3. Jonathan D. Sarna, "Jewish Identity in the Changing World of American Religion," in *Jewish Identity in America,* ed. David M. Gordis and Yoav Ben-Horin (Los Angeles: University of Judaism, 1991), 91–103.

4. Richard D. Alba, *Ethnic Identity: The Transformation of White America* (New Haven, CT: Yale University Press, 1990); Richard Alba and Victor Nee, *Remaking the American Mainstream: Assimilation and Contemporary Immigration* (Cambridge, MA: Harvard University Press, 2003), 91.

5. Harriet Hartman and Moshe Hartman, "Jewish Attitudes Toward Intermarriage," *Journal of Contemporary Religion* 16 (2001): 45–69.

6. Alba, *Ethnic Identity*; Alba and Nee, *Remaking the American Mainstream,* 96–97.

7. Phillip E. Hammond and Kee Warner, "Religion and Ethnicity in Late-Twentieth-Century America," *Annals of the American Academy of Political and Social Science* 527 (1993): 55–66.

8. Harold J. Abramson, "Religion," in *Harvard Encyclopedia of American Ethnic Groups,* ed. S. Thernstrom, A. Orlov, and O. Handlin (Cambridge, MA: Harvard University Press, 1980). Hammond and Warner ignored Abramson's fourth pattern, in which religion is a small and insignificant part of the definition of ethnic identity, as in the case of the Romany. For a recent general review of the relationships, see Peter Kivisto, "Rethinking the

Relationship Between Ethnicity and Religion," in *The Sage Handbook of the Sociology of Religion*, ed. James A. Beckford and N. J. Demerath III (Los Angeles: Sage, 2007), 490–510.

9. Stephen Sharot, *Judaism: A Sociology* (New York: Holmes & Meier, 1976); Calvin Goldscheider and Alan S. Zuckerman, *The Transformation of the Jews* (Chicago: University of Chicago Press, 1984).

10. Nathan Glazer, *American Judaism* (Chicago: University of Chicago Press, 1957); Nathan Glazer, "American Jewry or American Judaism," in *American Pluralism and the Jewish Community*, ed. Seymour Martin Lipset (New Brunswick, NJ: Transaction, 1990), 31–41.

11. J. S. Diamond, *Homeland or Holy Land? The "Canaanite" Critique of Israel* (Bloomington: Indiana University Press, 1986); Yael Zerubavel, *Recovered Roots: Collective Memory and the Making of Israeli National Tradition* (Chicago: University of Chicago Press, 1995).

12. Stephen Sharot, *Messianism, Mysticism, and Magic: A Sociological Analysis of Jewish Religious Movements* (Chapel Hill: University of North Carolina Press, 1982), 206–24; Stephen Sharot, "Traditional, Modern, or Postmodern? Recent Religious Developments Among Jews in Israel," in *Postmodernity, Sociology, and Religion*, ed. Kieran Flanagan and Peter C. Jupp (London: Macmillan, 1996), 118–33.

13. Sharot, *Judaism*; Jack Wertheimer, *A People Divided: Judaism in Contemporary America* (New York: Basic Books, 1993).

14. Wertheimer, *A People Divided*, 30.

15. Charles Liebman and Eliezer Don-Yehiya, *Civil Religion in Israel: Traditional Judaism and Political Culture in the Jewish State* (Berkeley: University of California Press, 1983).

16. Stephen Sharot, "Judaism and the Secularization Debate," *Sociological Analysis* 52 (1991): 255–75.

17. United Jewish Communities, *National Jewish Population Survey, 2000–01* (New York: United Jewish Communities, 2003); Egon Mayer, Barry A. Kosmin, and Ariela Keysar, *American Jewish Identity Survey 2001* (New York: Center for Cultural Judaism, 2003). Nonidentification with a religion does not necessarily mean that those respondents were not religious in any way. The American Jewish Identity Survey reported that the "no religion" respondents were more likely to describe their outlook as "secular" (52 percent) than Jews-by-religion respondents were (27 percent). It should be noted, however, that the "secular" response is much higher for the Jews by religion than for Christian categories in the United States. For example, 6 percent of Catholics and 7 percent of Episcopalians said that they had a secular outlook. From the 2001 American Religious Identification Survey, Kosmin and Keysar reported that 26 percent of Jewish respondents described themselves as "secular" compared with 4 percent of "mainline Christians"; and 16 percent of Jewish respondents described themselves as "somewhat secular" compared with 5 percent of "mainline Christians." Barry A. Kosmin and Ariela Keysar, *Religion in a Free Market: Religious and Non-Religious Americans* (Ithaca, NY: PMP, 2006), 43.

18. Gary Tobin and Sid Groeneman, *Surveying the Jewish Population in the United States* (San Francisco: Institute for Jewish and Community Research, 2003).

19. Joel Perlmann, *Two National Surveys of American Jews, 2000–01: A Comparison of the NJPS and AJIS*, Working Paper 501 (Annandale-on-Hudson, NY: Levy Economics Institute of Bard College, 2007); Tobin and Groeneman, *Surveying the Jewish Population*.

20. Joel Perlmann, *The American Jewish Periphery: An Overview*, Working Paper 473 (Annandale-on-Hudson, NY: Levy Economics Institute of Bard College, 2006), 24. Perlmann asks why this category should be excluded from the "core Jewish population" when those who have not adopted another religion but say that they have no connection to things Jewish should be included. He writes that in an era of tenuous attachments the defini-

tion of the core Jewish population will be unstable because the subgroups that are both included and excluded are changing.

21. Mayer et al., *American Jewish Identity Survey*; Sidney Goldstein, "Profile of American Jewry: Insights from the 1990 National Jewish Population Survey," *American Jewish Year Book* 92 (1992): 77–173; Samuel C. Heilman, *Portrait of American Jews: The Last Half of the 20th Century* (Seattle: University of Washington Press, 1995), 111–12, 135. The numbers in the text are proportions of "born Jews," including those respondents who no longer identify with Judaism. The intermarriage rates for those who were born Jewish and identify with Judaism are smaller: 41 percent of those who married between 1980 and 1991 and 46 percent of those who married between 1991 and 2001. From a comparative religious and ethnic group perspective, the Jewish intermarriage rate of about 50 percent can be considered extremely low. The ethnic intermarriage rates of U.S.-born whites is 80 percent, and the religious intermarriage rates are 38 percent for Catholics and 65 percent for moderate Protestants, each of which would be expected to have far lower intermarriage rates than Jews, given their far greater numbers. Benjamin T. Philips and Sylvia Barack Fishman, "Ethnic Capital and Intermarriage: A Case Study of American Jews," *Sociology of Religion* 67 (2006): 487–505.

22. Davidson does not refer to her subjects as secular Jews and prefers to designate their construction of ethnic identity as a "lived religion." Lynn Davidson, "Beyond the Synagogue Walls," in *Handbook of the Sociology of Religion*, ed. Michele Dillon (Cambridge: Cambridge University Press, 2003), 261–75.

23. Heilman, *Portrait of American Jews*, 105.

24. Respondents of the 2000–01 National Jewish Population Survey who said that they were secular or ethnic in their Jewishness were only 6 percent of those who classified themselves as "just Jews." Perlmann, *American Jewish Periphery*, 16.

25. Heilman, *Portrait of American Jews*, 135.

26. Seymour Martin Lipset and Earl Raab, *Jews and the New American Scene* (Cambridge, MA: Harvard University Press, 1995), 60.

27. Goldstein, "Profile of American Jewry."

28. Steven M. Cohen, *A Tale of Two Jewries: The "Inconvenient Truth" for American Jews* (New York: Jewish Life Network/Steinhardt Foundation, 2006).

29. Wertheimer, *A People Divided*, 61.

30. Egon Mayer, *Love and Tradition: Marriage Between Jews and Christians* (New York: Plenum Press, 1985), 173–75, 232.

31. Marc Lee Raphael, *Judaism in America* (New York: Columbia University Press, 2003), 108; Sylvia Barack Fishman, *Double or Nothing? Jewish Families and Mixed Marriage* (Waltham, MA: Brandeis University Press, 2004), 127–28.

32. Wertheimer, *A People Divided*, 176.

33. Of the adults in the 2000–01 National Jewish Population Survey who reported that they were members of a synagogue or temple, 37 percent reported that they were members of Reform congregations, 33 percent were members of Conservative congregations, and 23 percent were members of Orthodox congregations. When asked to identify with a denomination, if any, 35 percent of the adults identified with Reform, 27 percent with Conservative, 10 percent with Orthodox, and 2 percent with Reconstructionism; 26 percent said they were "just Jewish." Jonathan Ament, *American Jewish Religious Denominations*, United Jewish Communities Report Series on the National Jewish Population Survey 2000–01 (New York: United Jewish Communities, 2005). An earlier survey of a number of Jewish communities in large cities found that 57 percent of conversionary

marriages were Reform compared with 30 percent Conservative and 3 percent Orthodox; the respective figures for in-marriages were 43 percent, 39 percent, and 9 percent. Peter Y. Medding, Gary A. Tobin, Sylvia Barack Fishman, and Mordechai Rimor, "Jewish Identity in Conversionary and Mixed Marriages," *American Jewish Year Book* 92 (1992): 3–76.

34. Fishman, *Double or Nothing*, 126.

35. Steven M. Cohen, *Members and Motives: Who Joins American Jewish Congregations and Why*, Report 1 (New York: S3K Synagogue Studies Institute, 2006). Of the nonaffiliated Jews, 30 percent were in-married, 8 percent were conversionary in-married, and 63 percent were intermarried.

36. Fishman, *Double or Nothing*, 128–29. Two 1998 surveys in the Mid-Atlantic region found that at least one-third of those Reform Jews who married in 1995–98 and belonged to a congregation had intermarried, and few of the marriages had resulted in a conversion to Judaism by the non-Jewish partner. Raphael, *Judaism in America*, 109–11.

37. Goldstein, "Profile of American Jewry." See also Medding et al., "Jewish Identity."

38. The survey found that 28 percent of the intermarried households were raising the children with no religion, 8 percent were raising them in another religion, and 4 percent were raising them in both Judaism and another religion. Katherine N. Gan, Patty Jacobsen, Gil Preuss, and Barry Shrage, *The Greater Boston 2005 Community Study: Intermarried Families and Their Children* (Boston: Combined Jewish Philanthropies, 2008).

39. Mayer, *Love and Tradition*, 252–66. In the 2000–01 National Jewish Population Survey, only 16 percent of respondents who were children of mixed marriages reported that Judaism was their current religion; 26 percent reported no religion or secular, and 49 percent reported that they were Christian Jews. Phillips writes that identification with Judaism was relatively rare among respondents of mixed parentage because fewer than one in five were raised as Jewish by religion. Bruce Phillips, "Assimilation, Transformation, and the Long Range Impact of Intermarriage," *Contemporary Jewry* 25 (2005): 57.

40. Mayer, *Love and Tradition*, 252–66.

41. Wertheimer, *A People Divided*, 191–92.

42. Wertheimer, *A People Divided*, 96–108; Arnold Eisen, "American Judaism: Changing Patterns in Denominational Self-Definition," *Studies in Contemporary Jewry* 8 (1992): 21–49.

43. Fishman, *Double or Nothing*, 61–69. See also Dashefsky and Heller, who found much higher figures for Jewish religious observance among the intermarried. Their sample is also quite nonrepresentative, and, in general, sampling for this topic is problematic. Arnold Dashefsky and Zachary I. Heller, *Intermarriage and Jewish Journeys in the United States* (Newton Center, MA: National Center for Jewish Policy Studies, 2008). The 2000–01 National Jewish Population Survey found that far fewer intermarried Jews observed religious practices, such as lighting Sabbath candles (5 percent compared with 39 percent of in-married) and attending a Jewish religious service monthly or more (8 percent compared with 37 percent of in-married). With respect to the major Jewish holidays, there were also substantial differences between the intermarried and the in-married, but significant proportions of the intermarried participated in the three most popular Jewish religious holidays: 41 percent held or attended a Passover seder compared with 85 percent of the in-married, 26 percent fasted on Yom Kippur compared with 66 percent of the in-married, and 53 percent lit Hanukkah candles compared with 88 percent of the in-married.

44. Nancy Ammerman, "Religious Identities in Contemporary American Life: Lessons from the NJPS," *Sociology of Religion* 67 (2006): 359–64; Wertheimer, *A People Divided*, 78–80; Charles S. Liebman, "Some Research Proposals for the Study of American Jews,"

Contemporary Jewry 22 (2001): 99–114.

45. Stephen Miller, Marlena Schmool, and Anthony Lerman, *Social and Political Attitudes of British Jews: Some Key Finds of the JPR Survey* (London: Institute for Jewish Policy Research, 1996); Sergio DellaPergola, *Jewish Demography: Fact, Outlook, Challenges* (Jerusalem: Jewish People Policy Planning Institute, 2003).

46. Stephen R. Warner, "Work in Progress Toward a New Paradigm for the Sociological Study of Religion in the United States," *American Journal of Sociology* 98 (1993): 1044–93.

47. The proportions of British and American Jews who identify as "secular" are similar (see note 17); the distribution and meanings of denominational affiliation are different. Miller et al., *Social and Political Attitudes*; Stephen H. Miller, "Religious Practice and Jewish Identity in a Sample of London Jews," in *Jewish Identities in the New Europe*, ed. Jonathan Webber (London: Littman Library of Jewish Civilization, 1994), 193–204. Schmool reports that of the British Jewish households with synagogue membership in 2001, 57 percent belonged to the mainstream ("traditional") Orthodox, 20 percent to Reform, 9 percent to Liberal, and 9 percent to the Union of Orthodox Synagogues (mainly *haredi*). Schmool notes that the consistently high proportion of British Jewry linked to a synagogue is related to the way in which Jewish burials are organized in Britain. Most synagogues have a burial society, and synagogue fees contain an element for funeral expenses, which most people pay. Marlena Schmool, "British Jewry and Its Attitudes Towards Intermarriage," in *Jewish Intermarriage Around the World*, ed. Shulamit Reinharz and Sergio DellaPergola (New Brunswick, NJ: Transaction, 2009), 63.

48. Erik H. Cohen, "Intermarriage Among Jews in France: Preliminary Remarks" (Tel Aviv: School of Education, Bar-Ilan University, 2003).

49. Fran Markowitz, "Emigration, Immigration, and Cultural Change: Towards a Transnational 'Russian' Jewish Community," in *Jews and Jewish Life in Russia and the Soviet Union*, ed. Yaacov Ro'i (Newbury Park, U.K.: Frank Cass, 1995), 403–13.

50. Caryn Aviv and David Shneer, *New Jews: The End of the Jewish Diaspora* (New York: New York University Press, 2005), 36–49.

51. Rozalina Ryvkina, "Conflicting Values Among the Jewish Population of Moscow, Kiev, and Minsk," in *Jews and Jewish Life in Russia and the Soviet Union*, ed. Yaacov Ro'i (Newbury Park, U.K.: Frank Cass, 1995), 391–402.

52. Zvi Gitelman, "The Meanings of Jewishness in Post-Soviet Russia and Ukraine," in *Contemporary Jewries: Convergence and Divergence*, ed. Eliezer Ben-Rafael, Yosef Gorny, and Yaacov Ro'i (Leiden, Netherlands: Brill, 2003), 195–213.

53. Shlomit Levy, Hanna Levinsohn, and Elihu Katz, *Beliefs, Maintaining Tradition, and Values of Jews in Israel 2000* (Jerusalem: Guttman Center, Israeli Institute for Democracy, and Avi Chai, 2002) (in Hebrew).

54. Liebman and Don-Yehiya, *Civil Religion*; Charles Liebman and Steven M. Cohen, *Two Worlds of Judaism: The Israeli and American Experience* (New Haven, CT: Yale University Press, 1990); Stephen Sharot, "Israel: Sociological Analyses of Religion in the Jewish State," *Sociological Analysis* 51 (1990): S63–S76.

55. Discussions of the 1991 survey are found in Charles Liebman and Elihu Katz, *The Jewishness of Israelis: Responses to the Guttman Report* (Albany: State University of New York Press, 1997).

56. Shlomit Levy, Hanna Levinsohn, and Elihu Katz, *Beliefs, Observances, and Social Interaction Among Israeli Jews* (Jerusalem: Louis Guttman Israel Institute of Applied Social Research, 1993), 133–36, C68.

57. Benjamin Beit-Hallahmi, *Despair and Deliverance: Private Salvation in Contemporary Israel* (Albany: State University of New York Press, 1992); Sefi Melchior and Stephen Sharot, "Landmark in Israel: Recruitment and Maintenance of Clients in a Human Potential Organization," *Nova Religio: The Journal of Alternative and Emergent Religions* 13 (2010): 61–83.

Chapter 9

1. Sammy Smooha, *Arabs and Jews in Israel*, v. 2, *Change and Continuity in Mutual Intolerance* (Boulder, CO: Westview, 1992), 83.

2. Ernest Krausz, "Eda and 'Ethnic Groups' in Israel," *Jewish Journal of Sociology* 28 (1986): 5–18.

3. Simon N. Herman, *Jewish Identity*, 2nd ed. (New Brunswick, NJ: Transaction, 1989).

4. Yair Auron, *Jewish-Israeli Identity* (Tel Aviv: Sifriat Poalim, 1993) (in Hebrew). On the decline of religiosity, see also Eliezer Ben-Rafael and Stephen Sharot, *Ethnicity, Religion, and Class in Israeli Society* (Cambridge: Cambridge University Press, 1991).

5. Auron, *Jewish-Israeli Identity*.

6. Charles S. Liebman and Eliezer Don-Yehiya, *Civil Religion in Israel: Traditional Judaism and Political Culture in the Jewish State* (Berkeley: University of California Press, 1983); James S. Diamond, *Homeland or Holy Land? The "Canaanite" Critique of Israel* (Bloomington: Indiana University Press, 1986).

7. Anthropological studies of ethnicity among Jews from North Africa and Asia include Moshe Shokeid and Shlomo Deshen, *Distant Relations: Ethnicity and Politics Among Arabs and North Africans in Israel* (New York: Prager, 1982); Shlomo Deshen and Moshe Shokeid (eds.), *Jews of the Middle East: Anthropological Perspectives on Past and Present* (Tel Aviv: Schocken, 1984) (in Hebrew); and Alex Weingrod (ed.), *Studies in Israeli Society: After the Ingathering* (New York: Gordon & Breach, 1985).

8. Shlomo Swirski, *Orientals and Ashkenazim in Israel: The Ethnic Division of Labor* (Haifa, Israel: Mahbarot Le'Mehkar U'Lebikoret, 1981) (in Hebrew).

9. Shlomo Deshen, "Ethnicity and Citizenship in the Ritual of an Israeli Synagogue," *Southwestern Journal of Anthropology* 28 (1972): 70.

10. Deshen, "Ethnicity and Citizenship," 69–82; Shlomo Deshen, "Ethnic Boundaries and Cultural Paradigms: The Case of Tunisian Immigrants in Israel," *Ethos* 4 (1976): 271–94.

11. Rina Neeman, "Invented Ethnicity as Collective and Personal Text: An Association of Rumanian Israelis," *Anthropological Quarterly* 67 (1994): 135–49.

12. Swirski, *Orientals and Ashkenazim*.

13. Eliezer Ben-Rafael, *The Emergence of Ethnicity: Cultural Groups and Social Conflict in Israel* (Westport, CT: Greenwood, 1982).

14. Ben-Rafael and Sharot, *Ethnicity, Religion, and Class*; Hannah Ayalon, Eliezer Ben-Rafael, and Stephen Sharot, "Variations in Ethnic Identification Among Israeli Jews," *Ethnic and Racial Studies* 8 (1985): 389–407; Hannah Ayalon, Eliezer Ben-Rafael, and Stephen Sharot, "The Costs and Benefits of Ethnic Identification," *British Journal of Sociology* 37 (1986): 550–68.

15. Yakov M. Rabkin, "Cultures in Transition," in *The Soviet Man in an Open Society*, ed. Tamar Horowitz (Lanham, MD: University Press of America, 1989), 251–58.

16. Zvi Gitelman, "Ethnic Identity and Ethnic Relations Among the Jews of the Non-European USSR," *Ethnic and Racial Studies* 14 (1991): 24–54.

17. Rabkin, "Cultures in Transition."

18. Vladimir Khanin, "Russian-Jewish Ethnicity: Israel and Russia Compared," in *Contemporary Jewries: Convergence and Divergence*, ed. Eliezer Ben-Rafael, Yosef Gorny, and Yaacov Ro'i (Leiden, Netherlands: Brill, 2003), 216; Eliezer Ben-Rafael, Mikhail Lyubansky, Olaf Glockner, Paul Harris, Yael Israel, Willi Jasper, and Julius Schoeps, *Building a Diaspora: Russian Jews in Israel, Germany, and the USA* (Leiden, Netherlands: Brill, 2006), 4.

19. Rozalina Ryvkina, "Conflicting Values Among the Jewish Population of Moscow, Kiev, and Minsk," in *Jews and Jewish Life in Russia and the Soviet Union*, ed. Yaacov Ro'i (Newbury Park, U.K.: Frank Cass, 1995), 391–402; Larissa Remennick, *Russian Jews on Three Continents* (New Brunswick, NJ: Transaction, 2007), 54–55; Ben-Rafael et al., *Building a Diaspora*, 24–25.

20. Ben-Rafael et al., *Building a Diaspora*, 29.

21. Ben-Rafael et al., *Building a Diaspora*, 58, 62; Remennick, *Russian Jews*, 113, 159–60; Dina Siegel, *The Great Immigration: Russian Jews in Israel* (New York: Berghahn, 1998), 66–67; Khanin, "Russia-Jewish Ethnicity," 228, 233; Marina Niznick, "The Dilemma of Russian-Born Adolescents in Israel," in *Contemporary Jewries: Convergence and Divergence*, ed. Eliezer Ben-Rafael, Yosef Gorny, and Yaacov Ro'i (Leiden, Netherlands: Brill, 2003), 237, 250.

22. Roberta Kraemer, David Zisenwine, Michal Levy Keren, and David Schers, "A Study of Jewish Adolescent Russian Immigrants to Israel: Language and Identity," *International Journal of the Sociology of Language* 116 (1995): 153–59.

23. Niznick, "Dilemma of Russian-Born Adolescents," 238, 242.

24. Eliezer Ben-Rafael, Elite Olshtain, and Idit Geijst, "Identity and Language: The Social Insertion of Soviet Jews in Israel," in *Russian Jews on Three Continents: Migration and Resettlement*, ed. Noah Lewin-Epstein, Yaacov Ro'i, and Paul Ritterband (London: Frank Cass, 1997), 367–71.

25. Ben-Rafael et al., *Building a Diaspora*, 122–30.

26. Elazar Leshem, "Being an Israeli: Immigrants from the Former Soviet Union in Israel, Fifteen Years Later," *Journal of Israeli History* 27 (2008): 29–49.

27. Fran Markowitz, "Emigration, Immigration, and Cultural Change: Towards a Transnational 'Russian' Jewish Community," in *Jews and Jewish Life in Russia and the Soviet Union*, ed. Yaacov Ro'i (Newbury Park, U.K.: Frank Cass, 1995), 403–13.

28. Ben-Rafael et al., *Building a Diaspora*, 28, 124, 330; Remennick, *Russian Jews*, 152.

29. Remennick, *Russian Jews*, 61–64. Interviews with twenty-five of the non-Jewish immigrants found that some considered their primary identity as Israeli and a few had adopted a Jewish identity. They did not consider converting to Judaism, but those who identified as Christian rarely attended church, prayed at home, or kept a cross. Ben-Rafael et al., *Building a Diaspora*, 29–30, 316–26.

30. Shlomit Levy, Hanna Levinsohn, and Elihu Katz, *Beliefs, Maintaining Tradition, and Values of Jews in Israel 2000* (Jerusalem: Guttman Center, Israeli Institute for Democracy, and Avi Chai, 2002) (in Hebrew).

Introduction to Part 4

1. Larry Shiner, "The Concept of Secularization in Empirical Research," *Journal for the Scientific Study of Religion* 6 (1967): 207–20; Karel Dobbelaere, *Secularization: A Multi-Dimensional Concept* (London: Sage, 1981).

2. José Casanova, *Public Religions in the Modern World* (Chicago: University of Chicago

Press, 1994), 19–39.

3. James A. Beckford, *Social Theory and Religion* (Cambridge: Cambridge University Press, 2003), 62–63.

4. Daniel Bell, "The Return of the Sacred: The Argument on the Future of Religion," *British Journal of Sociology* 28 (1977): 419–49; Joseph H. Fichter, "Youth in Search of the Sacred," in *The Social Impact of New Religious Movements*, ed. Bryan Wilson (New York: Rose of Sharon Press, 1983), 21–41; Jeffrey K. Hadden, "Toward Desacralizing Secularization Theory," *Social Forces* 65 (1987): 587–611.

5. Talcott Parsons, "Christianity and Modern Industrial Society," in *Sociological Theory, Values, and Sociolcultural Change*, ed. Edward Tiryakian (Glencoe, IL: Free Press 1963), 33–70; Andrew Greeley, *Religion in the Year 2000* (New York: Sheed & Ward, 1969); David Martin, *The Religious and the Secular* (London: Routledge & Kegan Paul, 1969).

6. See, for example, Bradley R. Hertel and Hart M. Nelsen, "Are We Entering a Post-Christian Era? Religious Belief and Attendance in America, 1957–1968," *Journal for the Scientific Study of Religion* 13 (1974): 409–19; Peter E. Glasner, *The Sociology of Secularization* (London: Routledge & Kegan Paul, 1977); Rodney Stark and William Sims Bainbridge, *The Future of Religion: Secularization, Revival, and Cult Formation* (Berkeley: University of California Press, 1985); and most of the contributors in Phillip E. Hammond (ed.), *The Sacred in a Secular Age: Toward Revision in the Scientific Study of Religion* (Berkeley: University of California Press, 1985).

7. Sid Groeneman and Gary Tobin, *The Decline of Religious Identity in the United States* (San Francisco: Institute for Jewish and Community Research, 2004).

8. Jeffrey K. Hadden, "Religious Broadcasting and the Mobilization of the New Christian Right," *Journal for the Scientific Study of Religion* 26 (1987): 1–24; Roger Finke and Rodney Stark, "Religious Economies and Sacred Canopies: Religious Mobilization in American Cities, 1906," *American Sociological Review* 53 (1988): 41–49.

9. Hadden, "Religious Broadcasting"; Fichter, "Youth in Search of the Sacred"; Dick Anthony, Thomas Robbins, and Paul Schwartz, "Contemporary Religious Movements and the Secularization Premise," in *New Religious Movements*, ed. John Coleman and Gregory Baum (New York: Seabory, 1983), 1–8; James T. Richardson, "Studies of Conversion: Secularization or Re-Enchantment," in *The Sacred in a Secular Age: Toward Revision in the Scientific Study of Religion*, ed. Phillip E. Hammond (Berkeley: University of California Press, 1985), 104–21.

10. Reginald W. Bibby, *Fragmented Gods: The Poverty and Potential of Religion in Canada* (Toronto: Irwin, 1987); James Davison Hunter, *Evangelicalism: The Coming Generation* (Chicago: University of Chicago Press, 1987); Roy Wallis and Steve Bruce, "A Critique of the Stark-Bainbridge Theory of Religion," in their *Sociological Theory, Religion, and Collective Action* (Belfast: Queens University, 1986), 47–80.

11. Steve Bruce, *Religion in the Modern World: From Cathedrals to Cults* (Oxford: Oxford University Press, 1996); Steve Bruce, *God Is Dead: Secularization in the West* (Oxford: Blackwell, 2002).

12. Bryan R. Wilson, *Religion in Secular Society* (London: Watts, 1966); Bruce, *Religion in the Modern World*, 131–43.

13. Egon Mayer, Barry A. Kosmin, and Ariela Keysar, *American Jewish Identity Survey 2001* (New York: Center for Jewish Studies, 2002), 38.

14. Anson Shupe and Jeffrey K. Hadden, "Is There Such a Thing as Global Fundamentalism," in *Secularization and Fundamentalism Reconsidered*, ed. Jeffrey K. Hadden and Anson Shupe (New York: Paragon, 1989), 109–22.

15. See, for example, Lionel Caplan, *Class and Culture in Urban India: Fundamentalism in a Christian Community* (Oxford: Clarendon Press, 1987); and Ian S. Lustick, *For the Land and the Lord: Jewish Fundamentalism in Israel* (New York: Council on Foreign Relations, 1988).

16. Lustick, *For the Land*; Bruce B. Lawrence, *Defenders of God: The Fundamentalist Revolt Against the Modern Age* (London: I. B. Tauris, 1990); Hava Lazarus-Yafeh, "Contemporary Fundamentalism: Judaism, Christianity, Islam," *Jerusalem Quarterly* 47 (1988): 27–39; Eric Davis, "Religion Against the State: A Political Economy of Religious Radicalism in Egypt and Israel," in *Religious Resurgence: Contemporary Cases in Islam, Christianity, and Judaism*, ed. Richard T. Antoun and Mary Elaine Hegland (Syracuse, NY: Syracuse University Press, 1987), 145–66.

17. Emmanuel Sivan, "Introduction," in *Religious Radicalism and Politics in the Middle East*, ed. Emmanuel Sivan and Menachem Friedman (Albany: State University of New York Press, 1990), 1–9.

18. Aviezer Ravitzky, "Religious Radicalism and Political Messianism in Israel," in *Religious Radicalism and Politics in the Middle East*, ed. Emmanuel Sivan and Menachem Friedman (Albany: State University of New York Press, 1990), 11–37; Gideon Aran, "Redemption as a Catastrophe: The Gospel of Gush Emunim," in *Religious Radicalism and Politics in the Middle East*, ed. Emmanuel Sivan and Menachem Friedman (Albany: State University of New York Press, 1990), 157–75. Menachem Friedman retains the label *fundamentalist* for Gush Emunim by distinguishing between its "innovative fundamentalism" and the "conservative fundamentalism" of Neturei Karta. He defines fundamentalism as "a religious outlook shared by a group of believers who base their belief on an ideal religious-political reality that has existed *or is expected to emerge in the future*" (my emphasis). Menachem Friedman, "Jewish Zealots: Conservative Versus Innovation," in *Religious Radicalism and Politics in the Middle East*, ed. Emmanuel Sivan and Menachem Friedman (Albany: State University of New York Press, 1990), 127–41. This definition encompasses too wide a range of religious movements to be useful. I believe that it is more useful to distinguish between conservative and radical fundamentalist movements than between conservative and innovative ones. Friedman's own work has shown that the ultra-Orthodox have been highly innovative in their conservatism.

19. Cf. Lynn Davidman, "Accommodation and Resistance to Modernity: A Comparison of Two Contemporary Orthodox Jewish Groups," *Sociological Analysis* 51 (1990): 35–51.

20. Stephen Sharot, *Judaism: A Sociology* (New York: Holmes & Meier, 1976).

21. Robert Liberles, *Religious Conflict in Social Context: The Resurgence of Orthodox Judaism in Frankfurt am Main, 1838–1877* (Westport, CO: Greenwood, 1985).

22. Stephen Sharot, *Messianism, Mysticism, and Magic: A Sociological Analyses of Jewish Religious Movements* (Chapel Hill: University of North Carolina Press, 1982), 206–24.

Chapter 10

1. Karel Dobbelaere, *Secularization: A Multi-Dimensional Concept* (London: Sage, 1981).

2. I take up some of the definitional issues in the secularization debate in the body of the chapter, but I favor a substantive, exclusive definition of religion rather than a functionalist or inclusive one.

3. Peter L. Berger, *The Sacred Canopy* (Garden City, NY: Doubleday, 1967).

4. Bryan Wilson, *Religion in Sociological Perspective* (Oxford: Oxford University Press, 1982).

5. David Martin, *A General Theory of Secularization* (Oxford: Basil Blackwell, 1978);

David Martin, *On Secularization: Towards a Revised General Theory* (London: Ashgate, 2005)

6. Nathan Glazer, *American Judaism* (Chicago: University of Chicago Press, 1972 [1957]), 69.

7. James Davison Hunter, *Evangelicalism: The Coming Generation* (Chicago: University of Chicago Press, 1987).

8. Hunter, *Evangelicalism*.

9. Hunter, *Evangelicalism*.

10. William B. Helmreich, *The World of the Yeshiva: An Intimate Portrait of Orthodox Jewry* (New York: Free Press, 1982); M. Herbert Danzger, *Returning to Tradition: The Contemporary Revival of Orthodox Judaism* (New Haven, CT: Yale University Press, 1989).

11. Masamich Sasakiand and Tatsuzo Suzuki, "Changes in Religious Commitment in the United States, Holland, and Japan," *American Journal of Sociology* 92 (1987): 1055–76.

12. United Jewish Communities, *National Jewish Population Survey, 2000–01* (New York: United Jewish Communities, 2003).

13. Steven M. Cohen, *Religious Stability and Ethnic Decline* (New York: Jewish Community Centers Association Research Center, 1998). A similar pattern of synagogue attendance was reported among British Jews: In 1996, 19 percent said that they attended regularly on the Sabbath, 9 percent about once a month, 31 percent on occasions, 16 percent once or twice a year, and 26 percent not at all. Marlena Schmool and Frances Cohen, *A Profile of British Jews: Patterns and Trends at the Turn of the Century* (London: Board of Deputies of British Jews, 1998), 14.

14. Jewish religiosity has often been analyzed as one aspect of Jewish identification, and in this context it has been implied that secularization is concomitant with a diminishing Jewish identification or a decline in Jewish solidarity. See, for example, Bernard Lazerwitz, "Religious Identification and Its Ethnic Correlates: A Multivariate Model," *Social Forces* 52 (1973): 204–22; and Ernest Kraus, "The Religious Factor in Jewish Identity," *International Social Science Journal* 29 (1977): 250–60. However, it has been argued that, although the process of secularization is continuing, Jewish ethnicity and solidarity are not diminished and are not likely to diminish in the foreseeable future. See Calvin Goldscheider and Alan S. Zuckerman, *The Transformation of the Jews* (Chicago: University of Chicago Press, 1984); and Calvin Goldscheider, *Jewish Continuity and Change: Emerging Patterns in America* (Bloomington: Indiana University Press, 1986).

15. United Jewish Communities, *National Jewish Population Survey*; Shlomit Levy, Hanna Levinsohn, and Elihu Katz, *Beliefs, Maintaining Tradition, and Values of Jews in Israel 2000* (Jerusalem: Guttman Center, Israeli Institute for Democracy, and Avi Chai, 2002) (in Hebrew). English Jews also reported high participation in the Passover seder, and a high proportion lit Hanukkah candles. Julius Gould, *Jewish Commitment: A Study in London* (London: Institute of Jewish Affairs, 1984). Somewhat lower percentages of lighting Hanukkah candles were recorded by earlier studies in South Africa (40 percent), Italy (41 percent), and Denmark (49 percent). Allie A. Dubb, *Jewish South Africans: A Sociological View of the Johannesburg Community* (Grahamstown, South Africa: Institute of Social and Economic Research, Rhodes University, 1977); Sergio DellaPergola, "Identificazione e osservanza ebraica in Italia," *Annuario di Studi Ebraici* (1971): 73–96; Jacques Blum, *Dansk og/eller Jøde? En Kulturdociologisk Undersøgelse af den Jødiske Minoritet i Danmark* (Copenhagen: Gyldendal, 1973).

16. Marshall Sklare, *America's Jews* (New York: Random House, 1971), 114–17.

17. Barbara Frankel, "Structures of the Seder: An Analysis of Persistence, Context, and Meaning," *American Behavioral Scientist* 23 (1980): 575–632.

18. Chaim I. Waxman, *Jewish Baby Boomers: A Communal Perspective* (Albany: State University of New York Press, 2001), 70.

19. United Jewish Communities, *National Jewish Population Survey*; Levy et al., *Beliefs, Maintaining Tradition*.

20. Levy et al., *Beliefs, Maintaining Tradition*. Similarly, in France, a survey found that, whereas 65 percent of all French Jews reported that they fasted on Yom Kippur, only 38 percent of those French Jews born in France reported that they fasted. Doris Bensimon and Sergio DellaPergola, *La population juive de France: Socio-demographie et identite* (Jerusalem: Institute of Contemporary Jewry, 1984).

21. Levy et al., *Beliefs, Maintaining Tradition*.

22. United Jewish Communities, *National Jewish Population Survey*.

23. Cohen, *Religious Stability*. Earlier surveys of American Jewish communities recorded that the lighting of Sabbath candles varied from one-fourth to two-thirds, and having separate meat and milk dishes varied from 10 percent to about one-fourth of the populations. Gary A. Tobin and Alvin Chenkin, "Recent Jewish Community Population Studies: A Roundup," *American Jewish Year Book* 85 (1985): 154–78; Jack Wertheimer, "Recent Trends in American Judaism," *American Jewish Year Book* 89 (1989): 63–162.

24. Levy et al., *Beliefs, Maintaining Tradition*.

25. For Israel, see Levy et al., *Beliefs, Maintaining Tradition*. On Jewish religious observance in England, see Schmool and Cohen, *Profile of British Jews*. From a survey of French Jews, conducted in 2002, Erik H. Cohen reported that 58 percent of the in-married kept kosher at home and 64 percent regularly lit Sabbath candles. Erik H. Cohen, *Intermarriage Among Jews in France: Preliminary Remarks* (Tel Aviv: School of Education, Bar-Ilan University, 2003).

26. Charles S. Liebman and Steven M. Cohen, *Two Worlds of Judaism: The Israeli and American Experiences* (New Haven, CT: Yale University Press, 1990), 125–27; Moshe Hartman and Harriet Hartman, *Gender Equality and American Jews* (Albany: State University of New York Press, 1996), 200–203.

27. Steven M. Cohen and Arnold M. Eisen, *The Jews Within: Self, Family, and Community in America* (Bloomington: Indiana University Press, 2000).

28. N. Kokosalakis, *Ethnic Identity and Religion: Tradition and Change in Liverpool Jewry* (Washington, DC: University Press of America, 1982), 23.

29. Cf. Shlomo Deshen, "The Varieties of Abandonment of Religious Symbols," in *The Predicament of Homecoming: Cultural and Social Life of North African Immigrants in Israel*, ed. Shlomo Deshen and Moshe Shokeid (Ithaca, NY: Cornell University Press, 1974), 33–41.

30. Marshall Sklare and Joseph Greenblum, *Jewish Identity on the Suburban Frontier* (Chicago: University of Chicago Press, 1979 [1967]); Frida Kerner Furman, *Beyond Yiddishkeit: The Struggle for Jewish Identity in a Reform Synagogue* (Albany: State University of New York Press, 1987).

31. Furman, *Beyond Yiddishkeit*, 61, 79.

32. Furman, *Beyond Yiddishkeit*, 65.

33. On the sacred-religious and profane-secular distinctions, see Melford Spiro, "Religion, Problems of Definition, and Exploration," in *Anthropological Approaches to the Study of Religion*, ed. Michael Banton (London: Tavistock, 1966), 85–126.

34. Jonathan S. Woocher, *Sacred Survival: The Civil Religion of American Jews* (Bloomington: Indiana University Press, 1986), vii.

35. Woocher, *Sacred Survival*, 172. Although the civil religion concept can be usefully applied as an analogy in an analysis of the American Jewish polity, Woocher's adoption of

the concept raises a number of problems. "Civil religion" has many definitions, but most refer to a system of shared beliefs and public rituals that symbolize and/or integrate the nation and/or state (cf. Robert N. Bellah, "Civil Religion in America," *Daedalus* 96 [1967]: 1–21; and Charles S. Liebman and Eliezer Don-Yehiya, *Civil Religion in Israel: Traditional Judaism and Political Culture in the Jewish State* [Berkeley: University of California Press, 1983]). Most American Jews are citizens of and identify with the American state, and they also identify with the Jewish nation or people, but American Jews as a collectivity are neither a nation nor a state. From the perspective of American society, American Jews constitute an ethnic group, and from the perspective of the Jewish nation they constitute one of the communities of the Diaspora. If American Jews have a civil religion, this would have to be a civil religion of an ethnic group or a civil religion of a section of the Jewish nation. American Jews are not the only ethnic group in America with common beliefs, myths, and rituals, and it is not evident that an analysis of ethnicity is deepened by adding the concept of civil religion. The usefulness of the concept can be diluted by such an application.

36. Woocher, *Sacred Survival*, 130–31.

37. Woocher, *Sacred Survival*, 93.

38. Will Herberg, *Protestant, Catholic, Jew: An Essay in American Religious Sociology* (New York: Anchor Books, 1960 [1956]).

39. Stephen Sharot, "The Three-Generations Thesis and the American Jews," *British Journal of Sociology* 24 (1973): 151–64.

40. Rodney Stark and William Sims Bainbridge, *The Future of Religion: Secularization, Revival, and Cult Formation* (Berkeley: University of California Press, 1985). Stark and Bainbridge present what might be called a partial secularization thesis: a persistence of religion but a decline of magic. For a critique of such partial theses, see Stephen Sharot, "Magic, Religion, Science, and Secularization," in *Religion, Science, and Magic in Concert and in Conflict*, ed. Jacob Neusner, Ernest S. Frerichs, and Paul Y. Flesher (New York: Oxford University Press, 1989), 261–83.

41. Stark and Bainbridge, *Future of Religion*, 402.

42. Lorne L. Dawson, *Comprehending Cults: The Sociology of New Religious Movements* (Don Mills, Canada: Oxford University Press, 2006), 88.

43. Charles Selengut, "American Jewish Converts to New Religious Movements," *Jewish Journal of Sociology* 30(2) (1988), 95–109.

44. Sklare and Greenblum, *Jewish Identity*; Sidney Goldstein and Calvin Goldscheider, *Jewish Americans: Three Generations in a Jewish Community* (Englewood Cliffs, NJ: Prentice-Hall, 1968).

45. Harold S. Himmelfarb and R. Michael Loar, "National Trends in Jewish Ethnicity: A Test of the Polarization Hypothesis," *Journal for the Scientific Study of Religion* 23 (1984): 140–54; Steven M. Cohen, *American Modernity and Jewish Identity* (New York: Tavistock, 1983); Neil C. Sandberg, *Jewish Life in Los Angeles: A Window to Tomorrow* (Lanham, MD: University Press of America, 1986); Steven M. Cohen, *American Assimilation or Jewish Revival* (Bloomington: Indiana University Press, 1988).

46. Cohen, *Religious Stability*.

47. Sidney Goldstein, "Profile of American Jewry: Insights from the 1990 National Jewish Population Survey," *American Jewish Year Book* 92 (1992): 133–38; United Jewish Communities, *National Jewish Population Survey*.

48. Gould, *Jewish Commitment*; J. Wijnberg, *De Joden in Amsterdam* (Assen, Netherlands: Van Gorcum, 1967); Doris Bensimon, "Pratique religieuse des Juifs d'Afrique du nord en

France et en Israel," *Archives de Sociologie des Religions* 26 (1968): 81–96; Doris Bensimon, *L'integration des Juifs nord-africains en France* (Paris: Mouton, 1971); Calvin Goldscheider and Dov Friedlander, "Religiosity Patterns in Israel," *American Jewish Year Book* 83 (1983): 3–39; Hannah Ayalon, Eliezer Ben-Rafael, and Stephen Sharot, "Secularization and the Diminishing Decline of Religion," *Review of Religious Research* 27 (1986): 193–207.

49. Aaron Antonovsky, "Israeli Political-Social Attitudes," *Amot* 6 (1963): 11–22 (in Hebrew); Yehuda Ben-Meir and Peri Kedem, "Index of Religiosity of the Jewish Population of Israel," *Megamot* 14 (1979): 353–62 (in Hebrew); Goldscheider and Friedlander, "Religiosity Patterns in Israel"; Peri Kedem, "Dimensions of Jewish Religiosity," in *Israeli Judaism*, ed. Shlomo Deshen, Charles S. Liebman, and Moshe Shokeid (New Brunswick, NJ: Transaction, 1995), 22–59; Shlomi Levy, Hanna Levinsohn, and Elihu Katz, *Beliefs, Observances, and Social Interaction Among Israeli Jews* (Jerusalem: Louis Guttman Israel Institute of Applied Social Research, 1993); Levy et al., *Beliefs, Maintaining Tradition*.

50. Eva Etzioni-Halevy, *The Divided People: Can Israel's Breakup Be Stopped* (Lanham, MD: Lexington Books, 2002), 92–95.

51. Ben-Meir and Kedem, "Index of Religiosity"; Levy et al., *Beliefs, Maintaining Tradition*.

52. Ephraim Ya'ar, *Science and Technology in Israeli Consciousness* (Tel Aviv: Shmuel Neeman Institute, 2006) (in Hebrew).

53. This contrasts with the pattern reported by Grace Davie for the British population: "believing without belonging." Grace Davie, *Religion in Britain Since 1945: Believing Without Belonging* (Oxford: Blackwell, 1994).

54. Shlomo Deshen, "The Passover Celebrations of Secular Israelis," *Megamot* 38(4) (1997): 528–40 (in Hebrew).

55. Elihu Katz, "Behavioral and Phenomenological Jewishness," in *The Jewishness of Israelis*, ed. Charles S. Liebman and Elihu Katz (Albany: State University of New York Press, 1997), 79–80; Etzioni-Halevy, *Divided People*, 52; Bernard Susser, "Comments on the Guttman Report," in *The Jewishness of Israelis*, ed. Charles S. Liebman and Elihu Katz (Albany: State University of New York Press, 1997), 166–71.

56. Eliezer Schweid, "Is There Really No Alienation and Polarization?" in *The Jewishness of Israelis*, ed. Charles S. Liebman and Elihu Katz (Albany: State University of New York Press, 1997), 151–58.

57. Shlomo Deshen, "The State of the Religious Rift Among Jewish Israelis: The 1993 Guttman Institute Study," in *The Jewishness of Israelis*, ed. Charles S. Liebman and Elihu Katz (Albany: State University of New York Press, 1997), 130–37.

58. A comparison of Moroccan immigrants and their sons in Israel and France demonstrates similar trends in the two countries. The least secularized Jews from Morocco tended to migrate to Israel rather than France, and this is evident in the higher level of religiosity of first-generation Moroccans in Israel. Secular trends among the second generation are evident in both France and Israel; in both cases the level of religious observance is considerably lower than that of young Jewish workers who remained in North Africa and retained a high level of observance. However, the decline in religiosity between the more religious fathers in Israel and their sons was considerably greater than that between the less religious fathers in France and their sons. As a consequence, the level of religious observance of the younger generation of North African origins became almost identical in Israel and France. Bensimon, "Pratique religieuse."

59. For earlier similar findings, see Antonovsky, "Israeli Political-Social Attitudes"; Judah

Matras, "Religious Observance and Family Formation in Israel: Some Intergenerational Changes," *American Journal of Sociology* 69 (1964): 464–75; Goldscheider and Friedlander, "Religiosity Patterns in Israel"; Simon J. Herman, *Israelis and Jews: The Continuity of an Identity* (New York: Random House, 1970); Bensimon, *L'integration des Juifs nord-africains*; and Ayalon et al., "Secularization," 193–207.

60. Shlomo Deshen, "The Religiosity of the Mizrachim: Public, Rabbis, and Beliefs," *Alpayim* 9 (1994): 44–58 (in Hebrew); Moshe Shokeid, "Cultural Ethnicity in Israel: The Case of Middle-Eastern Jews' Religiosity," *AJS Review* 9 (1985): 247–71.

61. Eliezer Ben-Rafael and Stephen Sharot, *Ethnicity, Religion, and Class in Israeli Society* (Cambridge: Cambridge University Press, 1991), 78–90.

62. Ephraim Tabory, "Residential Integration and Religious Segregation in an Israeli Neighborhood," *International Journal of Intercultural Relations* 13 (1989): 19–35.

63. Yair Sheleg, *The New Religious Jews: Recent Developments Among Observant Jews in Israel* (Jerusalem: Keter, 2001), 54–63 (in Hebrew).

64. Samuel Heilman, *Sliding to the Right: The Contest for the Future of American Jewish Orthodoxy* (Berkeley: University of California Press, 2006).

65. Kimmy Caplan, "Investigating the Haredi Society in Israel: Characteristics, Achievements, Challenges," in *Israeli Haredim: Integration Without Assimilation?* ed. Kimmy Caplan and Emmanuel Sivan (Jerusalem: Van Leer Institute and Habibbutz Hameuchad, 2003), 228 (in Hebrew).

66. Joseph Shilhav and Menachem Friedman, *Growth and Segregation: The Ultra-Orthodox Community of Jerusalem* (Jerusalem: Jerusalem Institute for Israel Studies, 1985).

67. Aviezer Ravitzky, "Religious Radicalism and Political Messianism in Israel," in *Religious Radicalism and Politics in the Middle East*, ed. Emmanuel Sivan and Menachem Friedman (Albany: State University of New York Press, 1990), 13–17.

68. Menachem Friedman, "Haredim Confront the Modern City," *Studies in Contemporary Jewry* 2 (1986): 74–96; Sheleg, *New Religious Jews*, 123–27.

69. Sheleg, *New Religious Jews*, 118, 136, 148–51.

70. Samuel C. Heilman and Menachem Friedman, "Religious Fundamentalism and Religious Jews: The Case of the Haredim," in *Fundamentalisms Observed*, ed. Martin E. Marty and R. Scott Appleby (Chicago: University of Chicago Press, 1991), 197–264; Haym Soloveitchik, "Migration, Acculturation, and the New Role of Texts in the Haredi World," in *Accounting for Fundamentalisms: The Dynamic Character of Movements*, ed. Martin E. Marty and R. Scott Appleby (Chicago: University of Chicago Press, 1994), 197–235; Stephen Sharot, "Neotraditionalism: Religious Fundamentalism in Modern Societies," in *All Souls Seminars in the Sociology of Religion*, ed. B. R. Wilson (London: Bellew, 1992), 24–45.

71. Manachem Friedman, "Life Tradition and Book Tradition in the Development of Ultraorthodox Judaism," in *Judaism Viewed from Within and from Without*, ed. Harvey E. Goldberg (Albany: State University of New York Press, 1987); Soloveitchik, "Migration," 202–6, 216–17; Heilman, *Sliding to the Right*, 129–38.

72. Nurit Stadler, "Is Profane Work an Obstacle to Salvation? The Case of Ultra Orthodox (Haredi) Jews in Contemporary Israel," *Sociology of Religion* 63(4) (2002): 455–74; Eli Berman, "Sect, Subsidy, and Sacrifice: An Economist's View of Ultra-Orthodox Jews," *Quarterly Journal of Economics* 115(3) (2000): 905–53.

73. Stadler, "Profane Work."

74. Sheleg, *New Religious Jews*, 128–30, 141–46, 157–58.

75. Michael I. Harrison and Bernard Lazerwitz, "Do Denominations Matter?" *American*

Journal of Sociology 88 (1982): 356–77.

76. Stephen Sharot, "Israel: Sociological Analyses of Religion in the Jewish State," *Sociological Analysis* 51 (1990): S63–S76.

77. Steven M. Cohen, *A Tale of Two Jewries: The "Inconvenient Truth" for American Jews* (New York: Jewish Life Network/Steinhardt Foundation, 2006). For an earlier description of a similar kind of polarization with respect to ethnic identity, see Chaim I. Waxman, *America's Jews in Transition* (Philadelphia: Temple University Press, 1983).

78. Steven M. Cohen and Arnold M. Eisen, *The Jew Within: Self, Family, and Community in America* (Bloomington: Indiana University Press, 2000), 5.

79. Orthodoxy has the greatest number of synagogues (1,501 in 2001) compared with Reform (976) and Conservative (865). The average Orthodox synagogue is considerably smaller than the average Conservative and Reform synagogues and temples. Jim Schwartz, Jeffrey Scheckner, and Laurence Kotler-Berkowiz, "Census of U.S. Synagogues, 2001," in *American Jewish Yearbook 2002*, ed. American Jewish Committee (New York: American Jewish Committee, 2002), 128–29.

80. Jonathan Ament, *American Jewish Religious Denominations*, United Jewish Communities Report Series on the National Jewish Population Survey 2000–01 (New York: United Jewish Communities, 2005). For an analysis based on the 1990 National Jewish Population Survey, see Bernard Lazerwitz, J. Alan Winter, Arnold Dashefsky, and Ephraim Tabory, *Jewish Choices: American Jewish Denominationalism* (Albany: State University of New York Press, 1998).

81. Heilman, *Sliding to the Right*, 63.

82. Jack Wertheimer, "The American Synagogue: Recent Issues and Trends," in *American Jewish Yearbook 2005*, ed. American Jewish Committee (New York: American Jewish Committee, 2005), 19.

83. Heilman, *Sliding to the Right*, 3, 41.

84. Charles S. Liebman, "Orthodox Judaism Today," *Midstream* 25 (1979): 19–26; Egon Mayer and Chaim I. Waxman, "Modern Jewish Orthodoxy in America: Toward the Year 2000," in *Dimensions of Orthodox Judaism*, ed. Reuven P. Bulka (New York: Ktaz, 1983), 391–402; Gershon Kranzler, "The Changing Orthodox Jewish Community," in *Dimensions of Orthodox Judaism*, ed. Reuven P. Bulka (New York: Ktaz, 1983), 121–30; Reuven P. Bulka, "Orthodoxy Today: An Analysis of the Achievements and the Problems," in *Dimensions of Orthodox Judaism*, ed. Reuven P. Bulka (New York: Ktaz, 1983), 7–32; Samuel C. Heilman and Steven M. Cohen, "Ritual Variation Among Modern Orthodox Jews in the United States," in *Studies in Contemporary Jewry*, ed. Peter Y. Medding (Bloomington: Indiana University Press, 1986), v. 2, 164–87.

85. Heilman, *Sliding to the Right*.

86. Sheleg, *New Religious Jews*, 91–92, 96–99; Etzioni-Halevy, *Divided People*, 56.

87. Yair Sheleg, "The Insult of Religious Zionism," *Ha'aretz*, July 25, 2005; *Ha'aretz*, May 1, 2006.

88. Shlomo Fisher and Zvi Beckerman, "Shas: Church or Sect," in *Shas: The Challenge of Israeliness*, ed. Yoav Peled (Tel Aviv: Miskal, 2001), 321–42 (in Hebrew). See also Asher Cohen, "Shas and the Secular-Religion Division," in *Shas: The Challenge of Israeliness*, ed. Yoav Peled (Tel Aviv: Miskal, 2001), 75–101 (in Hebrew); Yoav Peled, "Towards a Redefinition of Jewish Nationalism in Israel: The Enigma of Shas," *Ethnic and Racial Studies* 21 (1998): 703–27; David Lehmann and Batia Siebzehner, *Remaking Israeli Judaism: The Challenge of Shas* (London: Hurst, 2006).

Chapter 11

1. Ezra Kopelowitz and Yael Israel-Shamsian, "Why Has a Sociology of Religion Not Developed in Israel? A Look at the Influence of Socio-Political Environment on the Study of Religion: A Research Note," *Sociology of Religion* 66(1) (2005): 71–84.

2. Moshe Samet, *Religion and State in Israel* (Jerusalem: Hebrew University, 1979) (in Hebrew); Ephraim Tabory, "State and Religion: Religious Conflict Among Jews in Israel," *Church and State* 23 (1981): 275–83; Stephen Sharot, "Sociological Analyses of Religion," in *Israeli Judaism*, ed. Shlomo Deshen, Charles S. Liebman, and Moshe Shokeid (New Brunswick, NJ: Transaction, 1995), 19–32.

3. Elihu Katz, "Two Dilemmas of Religious Identity and Practice Among Israeli Jews," *Contemporary Jewry* 27 (2007): 157–69.

4. Charles S. Liebman, "Religion and Modernity: The Special Case of Israel," in *The Jewishness of Israelis*, ed. Charles S. Liebman and Elihu Katz (Albany: State University of New York Press, 1997), 85–102; Chaim I. Waxman, "Religion in the Israeli Public Square," in *Jews in Israel: Contemporary Social and Cultural Patterns*, ed. Uri Rebhun and Chaim I. Waxman (Hanover, NH: Brandeis University Press, 2004), 221–39.

5. The amendment to the Law of Return in 1970 provided that only one Jewish grandparent was required to entitle a person and her or his spouse and dependent children to the privileges provided by the law. Gershon Shafir and Yoav Peled, *Being Israeli: The Dynamics of Multiple Citizenship* (Cambridge: Cambridge University Press, 2002), 145–47.

6. Charles S. Liebman and Steven M. Cohen, *Two Worlds of Judaism: The Israeli and American Experiences* (New Haven, CT: Yale University Press, 1990), 81.

7. Elan Ezrachi, "The Quest for Spirituality Among Secular Israelis," in *Jews in Israel: Contemporary Social and Cultural Patterns*, ed. Uri Rebhun and Chaim I. Waxman (Hanover, NH: Brandeis University Press, 2004), 262.

8. Erik Cohen, "Israel as a Post-Zionist Society," in *The Shaping of Israeli Identity: Myth, Memory, and Trauma*, ed. Robert Wistrich and David Ohana (London: Frank Cass, 1995), 204–5.

9. Ezrachi, "Quest for Spirituality," 256–58; Eva Etzioni-Halevy, *The Divided People: Can Israel's Breakup Be Stopped?* (Lanham, MD: Lexington, 2002), 87.

10. David Knaani, *The Labor Second Aliyah and Its Attitude Toward Religion and Tradition* (Tel Aviv: Sifriat Po'alim, 1975) (in Hebrew); James S. Diamond, *Homeland or Holy Land? The "Canaanite" Critique of Israel* (Bloomington: Indiana University Press, 1986), 15–19; Ephaim Luz, *Parallels Meet: Religion and Nationalism in the Early Zionist Movement (1882–1904)* (Philadelphia: Jewish Publication Society, 1988), xii–xiii.

11. Baruch Kimmerling, *The Invention and Decline of Israeliness* (Berkeley: University of California Press, 2001).

12. Oz Almog, *The Sabra: The Creation of the New Jew* (Berkeley: University of California Press, 2000), 44.

13. Yoram Bilu and Eyal Ben-Ari, "Epilogue (Three Years Later)," in *Grasping Land: Space and Place in Contemporary Israeli Discourse and Experience*, ed. Eyal Ben-Ari and Yoram Bilu (Albany: State University of New York Press, 1997), 231–32.

14. Diamond, *Homeland or Holy Land*, 18–20; Luz, *Parallels Meet*, vii.

15. Almog, *Sabra*, 247.

16. Stephen L. Weinstein, "Pioneers with a Passion: A Study of Secularization and the Second Aliyah," unpublished paper (1975); Walter Laqueur, *A History of Zionism* (New York: Schocken, 1976), 282; Knaani, *Labor Second Aliyah*.

17. Almog, *Sabra*, 41–43.

18. Yael Zerubavel, *Recovered Roots: Collective Memory and the Making of Israeli National Tradition* (Chicago: University of Chicago Press, 1995), 4–23, 26; Charles S. Liebman and Eliezer Don-Yehiya, *Civil Religion in Israel: Traditional Judaism and Political Culture in the Jewish State* (Berkeley: University of California Press, 1983), 89.

19. Almog, *Sabra*, 27, 45; Anita Shapira, "The Religious Motifs of the Labor Movement," in *Zionism and Religion*, ed. Shmuel Almog, Jehuda Reinharz, and Anita Shapira (Hanover, NH: Brandeis University Press, 1998), 261–62; Kimmerling, *Invention and Decline*, 191.

20. Almog, *Sabra*, 40–51.

21. Zerubavel, *Recovered Roots*, 216–18.

22. Shalom Lilker, *Kibbutz Judaism: A New Tradition in the Making* (New York: Herzl, 1982).

23. Shapira, "Religious Motifs," 264.

24. Lilker, *Kibbutz Judaism*; Nissan Rubin, "Death Customs in a Non-Religious Kibbutz," *Journal for the Scientific Study of Religion* 25 (1986): 292–303.

25. Zerubavel, *Recovered Roots*, 33–34.

26. Menachem Friedman, *Society and Religion: The Non-Zionist Orthodox in Eretz Israel, 1918–1936* (Jerusalem: Yat Izhak Ben-Zvi, 1977) (in Hebrew); Knaani, *Labor Second Aliyah*; A. Azili, *The Attitude of HaShomer Hatzair to Religion and Tradition (1920–1948)* (Givat Haviva, Israel: Documentation and Research Center, 1984) (in Hebrew).

27. Israel Kolatt, "Religion, Society, and State During the Period of the National Home," in *Zionism and Religion*, ed. Shmuel Almog, Jehuda Reinharz, and Anita Shapira (Hanover, NH: Brandeis University Press, 1998), 277.

28. Kolatt, "Religion, Society, and State," 290, 297.

29. Ezra Kopelowitz, "Religious Politics and Israel's Ethnic Democracy," *Israel Studies* 6 (2001): 173, 177; Charles S. Liebman and Asher Cohen, "A Case of Fundamentalism in Contemporary Israel," in *Religion, Democracy, and Israeli Society*, ed. Charles S. Liebman (Amsterdam: Harwood, 1997), 59; Charles S. Liebman and Eliezer Don-Yehiya, *Religion and Politics in Israel* (Bloomington: Indiana University Press, 1984), 86.

30. Yair Sheleg, *The New Religious Jews: Recent Developments Among Observant Jews in Israel* (Jerusalem: Keter, 2001), 284–85 (in Hebrew); Boas Evron, *Jewish State or Israeli Nation?* (Bloomington: Indiana University Press), 194–95; Shafir and Peled, *Being Israeli*, 140–41.

31. Eliezer Ben-Rafael and Stephen Sharot, *Ethnicity, Religion, and Class in Israeli Society* (Cambridge: Cambridge University Press, 1991), 27.

32. Ben-Rafael and Sharot, *Ethnicity, Religion, and Class*, 27–28; Sharot, "Sociological Analyses," 21; Shlomo Deshen and Walter P. Zenner (eds.), *Jewish Societies in the Middle East* (Washington, DC: University Press of America, 1982).

33. Liebman and Don-Yehiya, *Civil Religion*, 82–83, 88–94, 109, 113.

34. Lawrence J. Silberstein, *The Postzionism Debates* (New York: Routledge, 1999), 94, 195; Uri Ram, "The State of the Nation: Contemporary Challenges to Zionism in Israel," in *Israelis in Conflict: Hegemonies, Identities, and Challenges*, ed. Adriana Kemp, David Newman, Uri Ram, and Oren Yiftachel (Brighton, U.K.: Sussex Academic, 2004), 313–16.

35. Charles S. Liebman, *Religion, Democracy, and Israeli Society* (Amsterdam: Harwood Academic, 1997), 102; Etzioni-Halevy, *Divided People*, 88–89.

36. Etzioni-Halevy, *Divided People*, 60.

37. Ephraim Tabory, "The Israel Reform and Conservative Movements and the Market

for Liberal Judaism," in *Jews in Israel: Contemporary Social and Cultural Patterns*, ed. Uri Rebhun and Chaim I. Waxman (Hanover, NH: Brandeis University Press, 2004), 285–314.

38. Asher Cohen and Bernard Susser, *Israel and the Politics of Jewish Identity: The Secular-Religious Impasse* (Baltimore: Johns Hopkins University Press, 2000), 132.

39. Katz, "Two Dilemmas," 164.

40. Tabory, "Israel Reform and Conservative Movements."

41. Benjamin Beit-Hallahmi, *Despair and Deliverance: Private Salvation in Contemporary Israel* (Albany: State University of New York Press, 1992), 11–48, 101–31; Sefi Melchior and Stephen Sharot, "Landmark in Israel: Recruitment and Maintenance of Clients in a Human Potential Organization," *Nova Religio: The Journal of Alternative and Emergent Religions* 13 (2010): 61–83.

42. Nurit Zeidman-Dvir and Stephen Sharot, "The Response of Israeli Society to New Religious Movements: ISKCON and Teshuvah," *Journal for the Scientific Study of Religion* 31 (1992): 279–95.

43. Friedman, *Society and Religion*, 92–102; Stephen Sharot, *Messianism, Mysticism, and Magic: A Sociological Analysis of Jewish Religious Movements* (Chapel Hill: University of North Carolina Press, 1982), 226–27; Cohen and Susser, *Israel and the Politics of Jewish Identity*, 17–18.

44. Gideon Aran, "The Father, the Son, and the Holy Land: The Spiritual Authorities of Jewish-Zionist Fundamentalism in Israel," in *Spokesmen for the Despised: Fundamentalist Leaders of the Middle East*, ed. R. Scott Appleby (Chicago: University of Chicago Press, 1977), 294–327.

45. Sharot, *Messianism, Mysticism, and Magic*, 233–37; Gideon Aran, "Jewish Zionist Fundamentalism: The Bloc of the Faithful in Israel (Gush Emunim)," in *Fundamentalism Observed*, ed. Martin E. Marty and R. Scott Appleby (Chicago: University of Chicago Press, 1991), 265–344. Kopelowitz, "Religious Politics," 178–79.

46. Gershon Shafir, "Institutional and Spontaneous Settlement Drives: Did Gush Emunim Made a Difference," in *The Impact of Gush Emunim: Politics and Settlement in the West Bank*, ed. David Newman (London: Croom Helm, 1985), 153–71; Aran, "Jewish Zionist Fundamentalism," 282; Ehud Sprinzak, *The Ascendance of Israel's Radical Right* (New York: Oxford University Press, 1991), 129–32; Eliezer Don-Yehiya, "The Book and the Sword: The Nationalist Yeshivot and Political Radicalism in Israel," in *Accounting for Fundamentalism*, ed. Martin E. Marty and R. Scott Appleby (Chicago: University of Chicago Press, 1994), 285–87.

47. Moshe Kohn, *Who's Afraid of Gush Emunim* (Jerusalem: Jerusalem Post, 1976), 11–20; Sharot, *Messianism, Mysticism, and Magic*, 233; Sprinzak, *Ascendance of Israel's Radical Right*, 302.

48. Liebman and Don-Yehiya, *Civil Religion*, 123–66.

49. Samuel C. Heilman, "Guides of the Faithful: Contemporary Religious Zionist Rabbis," in *Spokesmen for the Despised: Fundamentalist Leaders of the Middle East*, ed. R. Scott Appleby (Chicago: University of Chicago Press, 1977), 339.

50. Aran, "Jewish Zionist Fundamentalism," 267; Don-Yehiya, "Book and the Sword," 278–82; Liebman and Cohen, "A Case of Fundamentalism," 71.

51. Yaakov Ariel, "A Christian Fundamentalist Vision of the Middle East: Jan Willem van der Hoeven and the International Christian Embassy," in *Spokesmen for the Despised: Fundamentalist Leaders of the Middle East*, ed. R. Scott Appleby (Chicago: University of Chicago Press, 1977), 367; Gershom Gorenberg, *The End of Days: Fundamentalism and the Struggle for the Temple Mount* (New York: Free Press, 2000), 173.

52. Heilman, "Guides of the Faithful," 349, 353–54; Don-Yehiya, "Book and the Sword," 275–77.

53. Yair Sheleg, "The Insult of Religious Zionism," *Ha'aretz*, July 25, 2005; *Ha'aretz* May 1, 2006.

54. Sharot, *Messianism, Mysticism, and Magic*, 225–26; Tsvi Raanan, *Gush Emunim* (Tel Aviv: Sifriyat Hapoalim), 18–23 (in Hebrew).

55. Shafir and Peled, *Being Israeli*, 141–42; Kopelowitz, "Religious Politics," 174; Cohen and Susser, *Israel and the Politics of Jewish Identity*, 48–49.

56. Etzioni-Halevy, *Divided People*, 129.

57. Cohen and Susser, *Israel and the Politics of Jewish Identity*, 53, 57, 60–61.

58. Cohen and Susser, *Israel and the Politics of Jewish Identity*, 85–86, 93–94.

59. Cohen and Susser, *Israel and the Politics of Jewish Identity*, 64–67, 71; Etzioni-Halevy, *Divided People*, 6–22, 118–30.

Afterword to Part 4

1. Charles S. Liebman and Steven M. Cohen, *Two Worlds of Judaism: The Israeli and American Experiences* (New Haven, CT: Yale University Press, 1990), 128.

2. Liebman and Cohen, *Two Worlds of Judaism*, 168.

3. Liebman and Cohen, *Two Worlds of Judaism*, 123–38.

4. Steven M. Cohen and Arnold M. Eisen, *The Jews Within: Self, Family, and Community in America* (Bloomington: Indiana University Press, 2000).

Final Afterword

1. On the notion of world religion, see Stephen Sharot, *A Comparative Sociology of World Religions: Virtuosos, Priests, and Popular Religion* (New York: New York University Press, 2001), 5–10.

2. Fredrik Barth, "Introduction," in *Ethnic Groups and Boundaries*, ed. Fredrik Barth (Boston: Little Brown, 1969), 1–38.

3. Clifford Geertz, "The Integrative Revolution: Primordial Sentiments and Civil Politics in New States," in *Old Societies and New States: The Quest for Modernity in Asia and Africa*, ed. Clifford Geertz (New York: Free Press, 1963), 105–57.

4. Richard Alba, "Bright vs. Blurred Boundaries: Second-Generation Assimilation and Exclusion in France, Germany, and the United States," *Ethnic and Racial Studies* 28 (2005): 20–49.

5. Frank Parkin, *Marxism and Class Theory: A Bourgeois Critique* (London: Tavistock, 1979). I developed and applied this framework in Eliezer Ben-Rafael and Stephen Sharot, *Ethnicity, Religion, and Class in Israeli Society* (Cambridge: Cambridge University Press, 1991), 243–53.

Index

Abravanel, Isaac, 97, 98, 102, 280–81n34
Abulafia, Abraham, 95
Acculturation, 5–8, 24, 40; of Ashkenazim, 21; of Jews in China, 16–17, 43–46, 56; of Jews in India, 17–18; of Jews in the United States, 158–59; of Muslims in China, 49–50; and Reform Judaism, 205; of Sephardim, 21–22
Agudat Israel, 240, 249
Alba, Richard, 154, 159, 259
Aliyahs, 235, 241
Antinomianism: and Christianity, 124, 130, 287n5; and dualism, 124–29; and Free Spirits, 126–28, 133, 134, 289n44; and gnostics, 124–25, 137, 290n49; and Hasidism, 131–33; and immenentism, 130–32; in Islam, 287n5; and messianism, 124, 133; and nihilism, 137–38; and orthodoxy, 133–34; among Ranters, 120–31, 289n44; in Sabbatianism, 123, 133
Antiquity: Jews in, 12–13, 145–49
Apocalyptism, 88, 91–92
Arabic, 14; conquests, 11; empires, 11, 13, 14; language, 14, 20
Ashkenazim, 12, 19, 20–22, 30–34, 39, 40; comparisons with Sephardim, 35, 36, 37, 100–102, 103–4; in Israel, 184, 185, 186, 187, 189, 190, 192, 196, 198
Assimilation, 8; of Chinese Jews, 25–26, 51–56; of Indian Jews, 26
Auron, Yasir, 185–86

Ba'alei shem, 59
Ba'al Shem Tov, 59, 76

Ba'alei Teshuvah, 227
Babylonia, 11, 13, 16, 19, 23, 148
Barnai, Jacob, 113, 119
Ben-Israel, 12, 17–18, 23, 26
Ben-Rafael, Eliezer, 189–90
Bogomils, 125–26
Bonfil, Robert, 5
Boundaries: ethnic, 257–62; religious, 10, 14, 26, 28, 30, 31, 38, 43, 257–62; social, 26, 30, 35
Britain: Jewish religious identification and practice in, 179–80
Buddhism: in China, 43, 50, 51, 54–55; and saints, 63, 68–72; Tantrism in, 128–30

Canaanites, 185, 196
Canonization, 148
Carlebach, Elisheva, 100
Casanova, José, 201
Castes, 69, 260; among Jews in India, 17, 26, 39
Cathars, 125–26
Ceremony: and ritual, 212
Chabad, 141
China: Jews in, 12, 16–17, 22–23, 24–26, 37, 39, 42–43, 260; Muslims in, 25; religion in, 24, 25, 43, 47–48, 260; social structure of, 25–26, 53. *See also* Kaifeng
Christianity: boundaries of, 30, 31; Jews under, 19–22, 30–32; and Sabbatian movement, 114–16
Christians: comparisons with Jews, 6, 21, 22; in China, 50–51; interactions with Jews, 7, 19, 21, 31, 35, 36; under Islam, 27, 28

INDEX

Church: policy toward Jews, 30–32
Citizenship: in Israel, 233–34
Civil Religion, 304–5n35; of American Jews, 152–53, 214–16; of Israeli Jews, 241, 242, 247
Cochin Jews, 12, 17, 23
Cohen, Gerson D., 100
Cohen, Shaye, 146, 147, 148, 150
Cohen, Steven, 155, 160, 161–63, 164, 165, 176, 210, 212, 217, 225–26, 253–54, 255
Cohn, Robert L., 60–61
Comparative perspective, 3–4, 7–9, 40–41, 80–82, 139, 165, 207
Confucianism, 24, 43, 44, 258; and Judaism in Kaifeng, 44–46, 47–48, 56
Conservative Jews, 162, 163, 171, 175, 176, 179, 226, 227
Conservative Judaism, 213, 214, 226; in Israel, 205, 242–43, 253–54
Conversion, 56, 168, 259, 260, 261, 262; to Christianity, 22, 37, 105; to Islam, 11; to Judaism, 11, 149–50, 170, 175, 176
Conversos: influence of Catholicism on, 109; and the Inquisition, 107, 108; and Jewish practice, 108–9; millenarianism among, 105–10, 140, 261; numbers, 105; occupations of, 107, 108
Crusades, 31, 39, 94, 101, 139
Cults: in Israel, 182, 243–44; in the United States, 216

Datiim (religious), 221, 229, 230, 253. *See also* Orthodox Jews
Davidson, Lynn, 174
Denominations 202, 253; Jewish, 214, 226–27, 251
Deshen, Shlomo, 40, 187
Dhimmis, 28, 40
Diaspora, 4, 10–12
Discrimination, 28, 35–36
Douglas, Mary, 134
Dualism: and antinomianism, 124–29
Durkheim, Emile, 124, 136–37, 152, 289n45, 289n46

Eber, Irene, 53–54
Eda (pl. Edot), 183–85, 186, 187, 188, 189, 190, 191, 196, 198, 258
Edot Ashkenaz, 184. *See also* Ashkenazim in Israel
Edot ha'Mizrach, 183, 185, 186, 187, 188, 189, 190, 191, 192, 196, 198

Eisen, Arnold, 162–63, 164, 165, 212, 255
Elukin, Jonathan, 39
Endelman, Todd, 3–4
England: Jews in, 33
Ethnic: culture, 152; group, 145, 147, 184; groups in the United States, 159–60, 169; identities, 168, 170, 172–78, 183; religion, 257–58; social ties, 152
Ethnicity: as basis of religiosity, 151, 152, 166; and boundaries, 257–62; from descent to consent, 168; and intermarriage, 177; symbolic, 154–57, 159, 164, 165, 292–93n29
Excommunication, 34–35
Expulsions, 12, 33, 39; from Spain, 23, 37, 96–97, 102–3

Feudal society, 33, 38
Folk religion, 58
Former Conversos: migration, 110; and Sabbatean movement, 113–14, 117–19, 120
France: Jews in, 11–12, 33, 145; religious identities in, 180
Frank, Jacob, 126, 137
Frankist movement, 126
Freud, Sigmund, 124, 135–36
Fundamentalism, 203, 208, 302n18. *See also* Neotraditionalism
Furman, Frida Kerner, 213–14

Gans, Herbert, 154–60
Geonim, 14
Germany: Jews in, 11–12, 21, 33, 37
Ghardaia Jews, 16, 29, 30
Ghetto, 6, 7, 29, 30, 31–32, 33, 37
Glazer, Nathan, 151
Gnostics, 124–25, 137
Goldberg, Harvey E., 5
Goldish, Matt, 111, 113
Goldscheider, Calvain, 160–61, 163
Goodblatt, David, 146, 147, 148, 149
Gush Emunim, 203, 204, 246–47

Haredim, 172, 186, 196, 205, 218, 221–25, 229, 244, 249–50, 254
Haredization, 228, 229, 230, 254
Hasidei Ashkenaz, 19
Hasidism, 59, 88, 223; and antinomians, 131–33; and messianism, 141; saints in, 75–78
Heilman, Samuel, 175, 227

INDEX

Herberg, Will, 151, 215
Herman, Simon, 185, 186
Hierocratic organizations, 62, 63, 64, 68, 69, 73, 78
Hinduism, 18, 26, 258, 260; and saints, 68–71; Tandrism in, 128–29

Idel, Moshe, 87–88, 89, 97, 113
Identities: of American Jews, 152, 172–78, 295n17; of French Jews, 180; Helene, 147–48; Israelite, 146, 147; of Israeli Jews, 181–96; Jewish, 147, 149, 169–72, 183, 185, 207–8, 215–16, 262; religious and ethnic, 168, 182, 207–8, 215–16, 261; of Russian Jews, 180; secularist, 170–71
Immanentism, 130–32
India: ethnic and religious division in, 258; Jews in, 12, 17–18, 23, 37, 39; social structure of, 26
Inquisition, 106, 107, 108, 109, 117, 140
Intermarriage: of American Jews, 151, 153, 157, 160, 162, 168, 172–73, 174, 175; of British Jews, 179; children of, 177, 297nn38, 39; of French Jews, 179; of Israeli Jews, 181; and Reform Judaism, 175–76, 297n36; and religious practice, 176–77, 178, 226, 297n43
Ioudaios. *See* Judean
Iraqis (Jews/Israelis), 190, 191
Islam, 26–27; boundaries, 14, 26; in China, 55; Jewish communities under, 13, 14–16, 23–24, 27–30, 40; saints in, 72–76
Israel: and American Jews, 153, 155, 161, 162, 163, 164; ancient kingdoms of, 10–11, 146–47; public religion in, 232–43, 251, 255. *See also* Zionism
Israeli Identity, 183, 185, 300n29; relationship with Jewish identity, 185, 186, 189, 192, 193, 194, 195, 251
Israeli, Raphael, 55
Israelite religion, 148
Italy: Jews in, 5–6, 33, 34, 280n30, 282n38; millenarianism in, 97–100, 102, 103

Jesuits: in China, 50–51
Jonas, Hans, 125, 137
Judah, 146, 147
Judea, 11, 12
Judean, 11, 146, 147, 148, 150

Kabbalah, 22; and messianism, 88, 95, 96; and Sabbatean movement, 112–13, 121
Kaifeng, 12, 23; acculturation of Jews in, 43–46, 56; assimilation of Jews in, 51–56; Jewish occupations in, 25, 42, 51–52; Jewish population of, 22, 42; Jewish settlement in, 16, 42; stone inscriptions of, 44–46. *See also* China: Jews in
Kant, Immanuel: on Chinese Jews, 50
Kaufman, Debra, 156, 164–65
Kibbutzim, 238, 239, 242
Kook, Rabbi Abraham Issac, 244–45, 248
Kook, Rabbi Zvi Yehuda, 245, 248
Krausz, Ernest, 184
Kurdish Jews, 16, 29–30

Lerner, Robert, 127
Leslie, Donald Daniel, 45, 46, 47, 52
Liebman, Charles, 152, 153, 163–64, 165, 253–54, 291n5
Likud, 246–47, 251
Literati: and Christians in China, 50–51; and Kaifeng Jews, 43, 44, 45, 46, 47, 48, 51, 53, 56

Mafdal (National Religious Party), 240, 245, 250
Magic, 15, 21, 58–59; and messianism, 88
Maimonides, 45, 86, 94
Marcus, Ivan G., 6–7, 40
Martin, David, 207
Martyrdom, 22, 40
Massacres: of Jews, 22, 31, 36, 37, 38, 39, 40, 119
Matrilineal principle, 149–50
McLaughlin, Eleanor, 127
Menasseh ben Israel, 116–17
Menachem Mendel Schneerson, 141
Mesoriti (traditional), 218, 219, 220, 229–30, 243, 251
Messiah: Jewish, 60, 86, 87, 89, 92–94, 95, 96, 98, 107, 109, 141. *See also* Sabbatai Zvi
Messianism, 87–88, 89, 93, 94, 95, 96, 100, 102, 104, 109–10; and religious Zionism, 244–49, 252; and secular Zionism, 236, 237, 247. *See also* Millenarianism, Millenarian movements
Millenarianism, 87, 139; and ancient Judaism, 91–93; and antinomianism, 124, 133; Christian, 116; comparisons of Sephardim and Ashkenazim, 94–95, 100–2, 103–4; among conversos, 105–

INDEX

Millenarianism (*continued*)
10; and Crusades, 94; and expulsion from Spain, 96–97, 102–3; and former conversos, 110, 113–19; in Italy, 97–100, 102–3; and kabbalism, 95; and mysticism, 88; in Portugal, 106–7; in Spain, 95–96, 105–6. *See also* Messianism

Millenarian movements, 87, 139; of Ascher Lemlein, 97; and crises, 88–89, 103–4, 120–21, 139–40; and disconfirmation of prophecy, 141. *See also* Sabbatean movement; Gush Emunim

Mimuna, 15, 192

Mixed marriage. *See* Intermarriage

Mizrachi, 240, 241, 244, 245

Mizrachim. *See* Edot ha'Mizrach

Molcho, Solomon, 98, 99, 107

Moroccans (Jews/Israelis), 189, 191, 306n58

Morocco, 15, 16, 23, 27, 28, 29, 40; saints in, 73, 74

Muslims: in China, 48–50, 54, 55; under Christianity, 30, 35; comparisons with Jews, 5; interaction of Jews with, 15, 29, 30. *See also* Islam

Nathan Ashkenazi, 110–11, 113, 121

Neeman, Rina, 188, 192

Neotraditionalism, 203, 204, 221–25, 229, 231

Neturei Karta, 185, 240

New Age, 128, 168

New religious movements, 216. *See also* Cults

Nietzsche, 137

Occupations of Jews, 32–33; in antiquity, 12; in China, 16, 42, 51–52; in Eastern Europe, 34; in Middle East and North Africa, 15, 28; in Spain, 35, 37; in United States, 163

Oppenheimer, Aharon, 46

Orthodox Jews, 161, 163, 175, 176, 179, 189, 205, 208, 226, 227, 228, 229

Orthodox Judaism, 205, 226; establishment in Israel, 220, 232, 242, 243, 253–54, 255; modern, 205, 227–28, 229. *See also* Orthopraxy

Orthopraxy, 208, 209, 213, 216, 222, 225, 243, 244. *See also* Orthodox Jews

Ottoman Empire: former conversos in, 114; Jews in, 24, 27, 28, 29

Out-marriage. *See* Intermarriage

Passmore, John, 126

Persecution of Jews, 3; of Ashkenazim, 39–40; under Christianity, 31; in Middle East and North Africa, 27, 40; in Spain, 35

Pilgrimages, 74–75

Plaks, Andrew, 45, 47

Pluralism, 43, 151, 152, 167–68

Poland: Jews in, 24, 31, 33–34, 119

Polarization: between religious and secular Jews, 151–52, 218, 225–31, 254

Poles (Jews/Israelis), 191

Pollak, Michael, 45, 52

Porete, Marguerite, 127

Porton, Gary, 149

Portugal: Jews in, 23

Postmodernism, 167

Postmodern Jews, 162

Post-Zionism, 242

Privatization: of religion, 162–63, 167–68, 201, 212, 232, 252, 255; of secular Zionism, 242

Rabbinic Judaism, 148, 149–50; and Second Temple Judaism, 148

Rabbis, 13, 20, 21, 34, 36; attitude to magic, 21; and Jewish identity, 148

Ranters, 130–32, 289n44

Rashi, 6

Reform Jews, 162–63, 175, 176, 177, 178, 213, 214, 226, 227

Reform Judaism, 156, 158–59, 171–72, 175, 177, 178, 179, 197, 205, 213, 214; in Europe, 205; in Israel, 205, 242–43, 253–54

Religiosity: diminishing decline of, 216–17; among Israeli Jews, 186, 217–21; symbolic, 154–57, 159, 164

Religious beliefs, 201, 208, 209, 213, 214, 215, 218, 231

Religious observance: of American Jews, 151, 152, 160, 161–62, 163, 164, 165, 210, 211, 217, 253, 293n40, 304n23; of British Jews, 303n15; of French Jews, 304nn20, 25; of Israeli Jews, 181, 210, 211, 217–20, 253; of Russian Jews in Israel, 196, 220; and secularization, 209–10

Reubeni, David, 98–99, 106–7

Rites of passage, 218

Rumanians (Jews/Israelis), 188, 189, 191

Russian Jews: in Israel, 192–96; in Russia, 34, 180

INDEX

Sabbatai Zvi, 110, 114, 121, 122, 123, 140, 281

Sabbatean movement, 110; antinomianism in, 123, 141, 261, 286n3; and Christianity, 114–16, 117; and former conversos, 113–14, 117–19, 121–22, 283n27; and Islam, 116, 284n43; and Lurianic kabbalah, 112–13, 121; and massacres of Jews in Poland, 119; prophecies in, 111, 283n27; spread of, 111, 284n38

Saints 15, 51, 63; in Buddhism, 63, 68–72, 78, 79; in Catholicism, 61, 64–68, 78, 273–74n25, 274nn31, 37; in Hasidism, 59–60, 75–78; in Hinduism, 68–71, 78, 79; in Judaism, 60–61; and Max Weber, 61–63, 69; among North African Jews, 60, 51, 73–75, 79; in Sufism, 75–76, 77, 79, 275n53

Salvation, 85–86; in Buddhism and Hinduism, 68–70

Scholem, Gershom, 112–13, 114–15, 119, 121, 123, 126, 135, 137, 140, 141

Schwartz, Seth, 148–49

Sects: in China, 53–54, 55

Secularism: in Eastern Europe, 170, 234; in Israel, 171, 172, 195, 219; in the United States, 151, 171; in Zionism, 234–39

Secularization, 154, 161, 169, 170, 197, 201–21, 251; dimensions of, 201; of immigrants in Israel, 189, 192; in Israel, 233, 293n34; and secularism, 172; thesis, 201–2, 206, 212–16, 230–31, 305n40

Sephardim, 21–22, 35–37; comparison with Ashkenazim, 35, 36, 37

SHAS (Sephardic Religious Party), 230, 250

Sklare, Marshall, 152, 153, 210

Snow, Kenneth, 6

Spain: Jews in, 11, 21–22, 23, 35–37

Stark, Rodney, 139, 140, 216

State: and religion in Israel, 232, 233, 240–41; and religion in the United States, 255; symbols of, 234

Sufism, 15; saints in, 75–76, 77, 79, 275n53

Survival: of Jews in Kaifeng, 52–53, 55, 56

Swirski, Shlomo, 188, 191

Synagogue: attendance in Britain, 303n13; attendance in Europe, 170; attendance in Russia, 180; attendance in the United States, 155, 161, 210, 216; and ethnicity, 151, 153, 157, 166; membership in Britain, 179–80, 298n47; membership in the United States, 151, 155–57, 158, 159, 160, 163, 175, 176, 177, 226, 292n18, 296n33

Syncretism, 4–5, 8, 10, 14, 16, 18, 22, 24, 26, 54, 178; in China, 40, 44, 47, 50, 51, 54

Talmud, 13; Babylonian, 13, 14, 15

Tantrism, 128–30

Temple, 11, 12, 93

Thaumaturgy, 58, 60, 85. *See also* Magic

Trompf, G. W., 87

Tunisians (Jews/Israelis), 187

Ulema, 72, 73

Ultra-Orthodoxy, 203, 204, 205, 221, 225, 227, 228, 239, 240, 241, 244; *See also* Haredim

Ultra-Orthoprax. *See* Ultra-Orthodoxy

United States: ethnic identities of Jews in, 172–78; ethnicity in, 156, 157, 159, 168–69; ethnicity of Jews in, 151–66; Jewish population in, 173, 295–96n20; religion in, 151, 156, 203; religiosity of Jews in, 151–66, 210, 212, 217; religious identities of Jews in, 172–78, 203

Weber, Max, 24–25, 44, 61–63, 80, 85, 145, 147, 259, 289n40

Wexler, Paul, 11

Wilson, Bryan, 206–7

Woocher, Jonathan S., 152–53, 214–16

World religions, 257–58

Xu Xin, 42, 47, 48, 52, 53

Yemen: Jews in, 27, 28, 29

Yiddish, 20, 172; culture, 172; culturalism, 152, 171

Yishuv, 236, 239, 244, 249

Zaddikim, 59–60, 76–78

Zionism, 170, 189, 192, 193; and immigrants, 241; privatization of, 242; religious, 221, 229, 240, 244–49, 252, 254; sacralization of, 204; as secular religion, 234–39; socialist, 152, 234–39, 245; and ultra-Orthodox (hardeim), 222, 239–40, 252

317

www.ingramcontent.com/pod-product-compliance
Lightning Source LLC
Chambersburg PA
CBHW080612230426
43664CB00019B/2863